Christian Slavery

EARLY AMERICAN STUDIES

Series Editors
Daniel K. Richter, Kathleen M. Brown, Max Cavitch, and David Waldstreicher

Exploring neglected aspects of our colonial, revolutionary, and early national history and culture, Early American Studies reinterprets familiar themes and events in fresh ways. Interdisciplinary in character, and with a special emphasis on the period from about 1600 to 1850, the series is published in partnership with the McNeil Center for Early American Studies.

A complete list of books in the series is available from the publisher.

Christian Slavery

Conversion and Race in the Protestant Atlantic World

Katharine Gerbner

PENN

UNIVERSITY OF PENNSYLVANIA PRESS

PHILADELPHIA

Published by
University of Pennsylvania Press
Philadelphia, Pennsylvania 19104-4112
www.upenn.edu/pennpress

Printed in the United States of America
on acid-free paper

10 9 8 7 6 5 4 3 2 1

Library of Congress Cataloging-in-Publication Data

Names: Gerbner, Katharine, author.
Title: Christian slavery: conversion and race in the protestant Atlantic world / Katharine Gerbner.
Other titles: Early American studies.
Description: 1st edition. | Philadelphia: University of Pennsylvania Press, [2018] | Series: Early American studies | Includes bibliographical references and index.
Identifiers: LCCN 2017046031 | ISBN 9780812250015 (hardcover: alk. paper)
Subjects: LCSH: Slavery and the church—Atlantic Ocean Region—History. | Slaves—Religious life—Atlantic Ocean Region—History. | Christian converts—Atlantic Ocean Region—History. | Atlantic Ocean Region—Race relations—History.
Classification: LCC HT913 .G47 2018 | DDC 270.086/25—dc23
LC record available at https://lccn.loc.gov/2017046031

For Sean

Contents

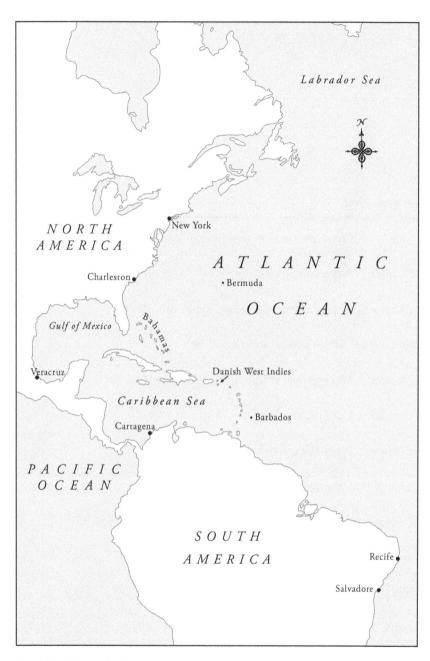

Map 1. The Atlantic World

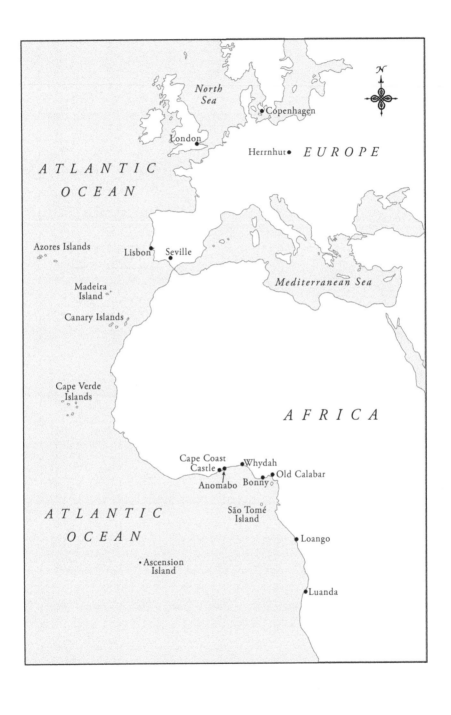

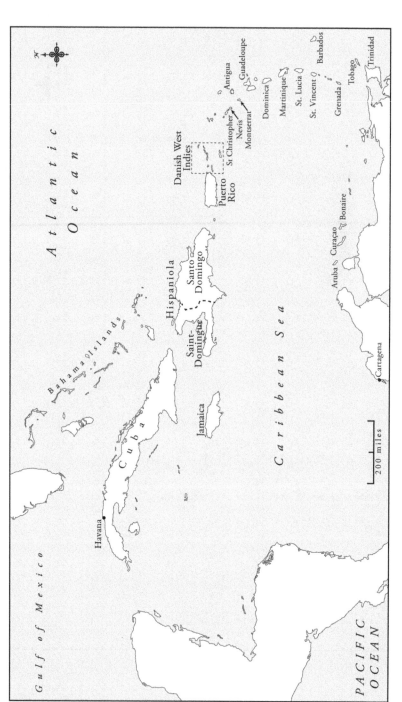

Map 2. The Caribbean

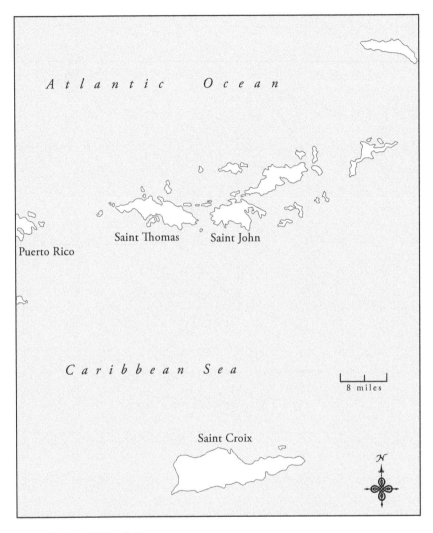

Map 3. The Danish West Indies

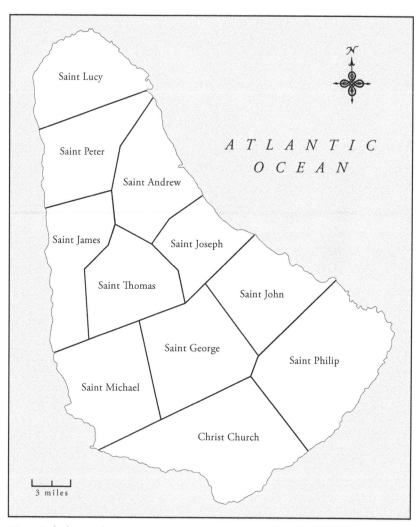

Map 4. Barbados Parishes

Introduction

On November 16, 1651, a man named Lazarus entered the Anglican church in Christ Church parish, Barbados. As he walked toward the church doors, he passed the "strong pair of Stocks" where public punishments took place. The church itself was a wooden structure and one of the oldest buildings on the island. Constructed in 1629 just two years after the first English settlers arrived, the church would meet a tempestuous end: it was destroyed by flood in 1669 and washed out to sea. The second and third iterations of the church were destroyed by hurricane. But before the first church structure met its watery demise, it served as the site of Lazarus's baptism. Lazarus, who was described only as "a negro" in the church register, was the first Afro-Caribbean to receive baptism in the Anglican Church on Barbados. Neither his age nor place of birth were given, nor any indication of godparents or kin.[1]

Lazarus's baptism challenged the emerging culture of slavery in the Protestant Atlantic world. The Anglican Church in Barbados was exclusive, the domain of slave owners and government officials. While most historians have downplayed the relevance of Christianity in the seventeenth-century Protestant Caribbean, viewing the sugar colonies as islands of depravity, the Anglican Church was central to the maintenance of planter power in Barbados and elsewhere.[2] The planter elite believed that their status as Protestants was inseparable from their identity as free Englishmen. Like their counterparts in England, they purchased pews, memorialized themselves within church walls, and used the church as a place for both punishment and politics. Aside from the stocks that sat outside its doors, the church was the site of island elections and served as a community bulletin board where white inhabitants could post news about stolen goods or runaway slaves.

Unlike the parish churches in England, however, the Anglican Church in Barbados was restricted. It separated masters from their enslaved "heathen" laborers and marked Anglo-Barbadians as both English and free. The association between Protestantism and freedom was so strong that most slave owners came to dismiss the idea that their slaves were eligible for conversion. In 1661, when the English Parliament instructed Lord Willoughby, the reinstated governor of Barbados, to "[win] such as are purchased . . . as slaves to the Christian faith and [make] them capable of being baptized thereinto," the Assembly and Council refused to pass Willoughby's 1663 bill "recommending the christening of Negro children, and the instruction of all adult Negroes, to the several ministers of this place."[3] By 1680, the Barbadian planters' stance against slave conversion had become even more pronounced. When William Blathwayt, on behalf of the Lords of Trade and Plantations in London, wrote to the merchants of Barbados to inquire as to "the unhappy state of the negroes and other slaves in Barbadoes by their not being admitted to the Christian religion," the self-titled "gentlemen of Barbados" explained that "the conversion of their slaves to Christianity would not only destroy their property but endanger the island, inasmuch as converted negroes grow more perverse and intractable than others."[4]

Anticonversion sentiment was one of the defining features of Protestant slave societies in the seventeenth and early eighteenth centuries. While enslaved Africans in Spanish, French, and Portuguese colonial societies were regularly introduced to Catholicism and baptized, whether willingly or not, Protestant slave owners in the English, Dutch, and Danish colonies tended to view conversion as inconsistent or incompatible with slavery. Their anticonversion sentiment was indicative of the changing meaning of Protestantism in the American colonies: over the course of the seventeenth century, Protestant planters claimed Christian identity for themselves, creating an exclusive ideal of religion based on ethnicity—a construct that I call "Protestant Supremacy."

Protestant Supremacy was the predecessor of White Supremacy, an ideology that emerged after the codification of racial slavery. I refer to "Protestant" Supremacy, rather than "Anglican" or "Christian" Supremacy, because this ideology was present throughout the Protestant American colonies, from the Danish West Indies to Virginia and beyond. It was most likely to develop in places with an enslaved population that was larger than the free population, such as Barbados, Jamaica, or South Carolina. In these colonies, Anglican, Dutch Reformed, and Lutheran slave owners conceived of their Protestant identities as fundamental to their status as masters. They constructed a caste system based on Christian status, in which "heathenish" slaves were afforded no rights or privileges while Catholics, Jews, and non-conforming Protestants were viewed with suspicion and distrust, but granted more protections.

When Protestant missionaries arrived in the plantation colonies intending to convert enslaved Africans to Christianity in the 1670s, they encountered slave societies that had already developed churches founded on exclusion. Planters regularly attacked missionaries, both verbally and physically, and blamed the evangelizing newcomers for slave rebellions, regardless of evidence to the contrary. Missionaries responded to this hostile environment by articulating and promoting a vision of "Christian Slavery" that reconciled Protestantism with bondage.

"Christian Slavery" was a polysemic concept. At the most basic level, it was an attempt to Christianize and reform slavery. Protestant theologians and missionaries drew on biblical descriptions of slavery as well as the ideal of the godly household to encourage slave owners to assume responsibility for the spiritual lives of their enslaved laborers. They also noted that Christian slavery had a long and well-established history in Europe and the Catholic American colonies. As missionaries faced opposition from slave owners, however, the meaning of "Christian Slavery" shifted. Missionaries increasingly emphasized the beneficial aspects of slave conversion, arguing that Christian slaves would be more docile and harder working than their "heathen" counterparts. They also sought to pass legislation that confirmed the legality of owning enslaved Christians. Over time, they integrated race into their arguments for Christian slavery. Since the ideology of Protestant Supremacy used religion to differentiate between slavery and freedom, missionaries suggested that race, rather than religion, was the defining feature of bondage.

Protestant missions to enslaved people have traditionally been examined within the context of antislavery thought, and have often been evaluated on humanitarian terms. During the seventeenth and early eighteenth centuries, however, it is more accurate to understand the conflict between missionaries and slave owners as a clash between Protestant Supremacy, which excluded enslaved people from Christianity, and Christian Slavery, which sought to include slaves within the Protestant community. In this period before the abolitionist and proslavery movements of the eighteenth and nineteenth centuries, it is possible to see the early Protestant debates about Christianity and slavery in a new light. In contrast to historians who have studied the origins of antislavery, I emphasize the ways that Quaker, Anglican, and Moravian missionaries fought hard to accommodate slavery to their Christian principles and argue that their efforts bore fruit in legislation affirming that Protestant status was compatible with perpetual bondage.[5] As a result, their advocacy should be understood within the long history of pro-slavery thought as well as an antecedent of antislavery and abolition.

The tendency to read abolition into the early Protestant missions is especially pronounced in the Quaker historiography. Very little has been written on Quaker slaveholding practices in their own right, rather than as a prelude for abolition.[6] Quaker founder George Fox's feelings on slavery, for example, are usually considered within the context of antislavery thought.[7] A transatlantic, interdenominational understanding of seven-teenth-century Quaker ideas about slavery reveals something different. With a large community of slave-owning Friends in Barbados, Quakers were among the first Protestants to think seriously about how slavehold-ing would affect Christian practice. Their ideas, publications, and pro-conversion stance affected not only the Society of Friends, but also members of other Protestant denominations. Furthermore, their publica-tions did not lead solely to antislavery thought; their influence can be found in the developing rhetoric of paternalism and Christian slavery as well.

Unlike the Quakers, Anglicans and Moravians were not leaders in the eighteenth-century abolitionist movement. Regardless, many scholars have read a humanitarian impulse into their early missionary ventures.[8] Re-cently, this approach has come under critique.[9] Most notably, historians have shown that missionary Anglicanism was responsible for a series of laws and opinions that strengthened slavery in order to encourage slave conversion.[10] I support and expand this critique by incorporating Quakers, Anglicans, and Moravians into an interdenominational study. The first Anglican publications on slavery were spurred, in part, by Quaker polemics, and both imperial and denominational rivalry played a major role in deter-mining the objectives of the Anglican Society for the Propagation of the Gospel (SPG). Similarly, the Moravians were in close contact with Anglican churchmen in the 1730s, and had a complicated relationship with members of the SPG and the Society for the Propagation of Christian Knowledge (SPCK).[11] Far from anticipating an antislavery position, these Protestant missionaries articulated and circulated a vision for Christian slavery that laid the groundwork for the proslavery apologists of the eighteenth and nineteenth centuries.

Interdenominational rivalry and communication networks played an important role in this story. Quakers were the first Protestant group to advocate for slave conversion and as they increased their missionary efforts, they attacked the Anglican Church for its failure to act. As Anglicans and Quakers became involved in a print war over the relationship between Protestantism and slavery, Anglicans moved to establish their own evangelizing presence in the New World. While Anglican progress was slow, the growing international network of missionaries made it easier for the Moravians, who were in contact with members of the SPG in England, to join the evangelizing effort in the 1730s.

The Protestant Caribbean was a geographical center of these debates. Both Quaker and Moravian missions began in the West Indies, while the SPG was active in early eighteenth-century Barbados. Missionaries who began their work in the Caribbean traveled throughout the colonies and published polemical pamphlets on both sides of the Atlantic. Missionaries communicated with imperial officials in London and Copenhagen and with their own church headquarters. Quakers initially addressed all correspondence to Swarthmore Hall, the home of Margaret Fell Fox, while they later made the London Yearly Meeting their central administrative body. Anglican missionaries communicated with the Secretary of the SPG and the Bishop of London, while the Moravians exchanged letters and diaries with the church leadership in Herrnhut, Germany, and Bethlehem, Pennsylvania.

The transatlantic network of Protestant missionaries crossed both imperial and confessional lines. Some missionaries, particularly within the Moravian Church, traveled between the Danish colonies in the West Indies and the British colonies of North America. Others, such as the French Huguenots who became Anglican missionaries, had intimate knowledge of Catholic practice regarding slavery. In the Caribbean, some islands like St. Christopher were split into French Catholic and English Protestant sections, making interimperial and interconfessional comparisons especially poignant. These imperial and confessional borderlands show that Protestant ideas about slavery often emerged in relation to Catholic practice. Protestant missionaries were simultaneously envious and dismissive of the large numbers of enslaved and free blacks baptized in the Catholic Church. They denigrated Catholic baptism as meaningless and criticized Catholic missionaries and priests for failing to truly educate enslaved people in Christian doctrine.

Protestant missionaries and black Christians created an extensive, multilingual archive about slavery and Christianity in the Protestant American colonies. The Moravian sources, which are written primarily in German, Dutch, and Dutch Creole, are a particularly rich resource for understanding daily life in the Caribbean and North America. The Moravian records promise to redefine scholarly understanding of black Christian practice but they have been underutilized by both Anglophone and German-speaking scholars because they are written in *Sütterlin*, an archaic form of German script.[12] In addition to the diaries, letters, and church registers kept by missionaries, the Moravian archives include a small number of letters written by enslaved and free Afro-Caribbean converts—some of the only such documents available for the period. These documents give scholars the extremely rare opportunity to analyze the texts written by, rather than about, Afro-Caribbean men and women in the eighteenth century. I use these sources to better understand when and why enslaved and free Africans chose to engage in Christian rituals in the Protestant Caribbean.[13] I also compare diaries written by different missionaries in order to paint a multi-perspectival picture of mission culture and everyday life.

The Quaker and Anglican sources do not match the Moravian sources in the detail or volume of their observations about Afro-Protestant practice. As a result, I have turned to social historical methods, in addition to other strategies, to get a sense of broad, demographic patterns relating to the participation of enslaved and free Africans in Quaker and Anglican rituals. Besides reading letters written by missionaries, I have analyzed the baptismal and marital registers for Anglican churches, Quaker meeting minutes, and governmental and official records, including wills, censuses, and official correspondence. Still, the chapters on Quaker and Anglican missions focus more heavily on transatlantic debates *about* slave conversion, rather than an analysis *of* slave conversion itself. Yet these two topics—the transatlantic debate and the actual decisions of enslaved and free Africans to participate in Christian rituals—are inextricably connected. Only by examining everyday life in the Protestant plantation colonies *and* the broader debate regarding slave conversion is it possible to gain a full understanding of the Atlantic dimensions of Protestant missions and slave conversion in the early modern world.

At the heart of this inquiry is the concept of "conversion," a term that must be used with caution.[14] There are two central criticisms of the term. First, some scholars have suggested that it falsely implies that converts abandoned one belief system for another. As anthropologists Jean and John Comaroff have written, "the very use of 'conversion' as a noun leads, unwittingly, to the reification of religious 'belief.'" As they explain, "this abstraction makes spiritual commitment into a choice among competing faiths, and 'belief systems' into doctrines torn free of all cultural embeddedness."[15] Second, some historians have argued that using the word "conversion" reflects missionary intentions, rather than the experiences of non-Europeans. Within the context of imperial expansion and Atlantic slavery, these contentions are particularly significant, because many "conversions" took place within highly unequal colonial encounters.

As a result, many historians have studiously avoided the term. As Anthony Grafton and Kenneth Mills have written, scholars prefer to "quietly avoid religious conversion or else append it to a brace of more fathomable (and historiographically fashionable) alternatives."[16] Alternatives to the term include words like "appropriation" and "affiliation," which emphasize the choices of non-Europeans, or "syncretism" and "hybridity," which focus on the blending of cosmologies. While these terms have their advantages, I believe that historians must wrestle with the problematic connotations of conversion in order to better understand the experiences of both European and non-European Christians. Rather than allowing Christian missionaries to decide who is a true convert, historians should recognize the ongoing tension within the word "conversion" and use a variety of methodological techniques to examine how non-Europeans perceived and narrated their engagement in Christian rituals.

The concept of conversion has never been stable. Conversion has a contentious history within Christianity in general and Protestantism in particular. Etymologically, conversion derives from the word "turning," a movement from one thing to another. Within a Christian context, this "turning" has been qualified and defined in a number of ways. While early Christian conversion efforts targeted "pagans," in medieval Europe, the term *conversio* often referred to the transition of an individual from a secular to a monastic life.[17] In the splintered churches of sixteenth-century Europe, conversion became a declaration of spiritual and political allegiance to a true Church, whether that church was Roman Catholic, Lutheran, Dutch Reformed, or the newly formed and internally contentious Church of England.[18]

Some early modern Protestants distinguished not only between Christians and heathens, but also between saved and unsaved Christians. By making such distinctions, these reformers introduced new complexity into the meaning of conversion. Deconstructing conversion became a major theme for Puritan and Pietist theologians in the seventeenth and eighteenth centuries. Puritans stressed that conversion was the transformation of an individual by grace and they developed a "morphology of conversion" that codified each step in that process. Some Puritan churches went so far as to require all of their applicants to verify their status as "visible saints" with a conversion narrative. While individual narratives differed, there were recognizable patterns in these early modern "conversions": an awareness of sin led to humiliation, repentance, and the hope for God's grace. Experience of God's saving grace was followed by period of doubt and reassurance.[19]

Quaker ideas about conversion, which they termed "convincement," emerged from Puritan theology.[20] Like Puritans, Friends saw conversion as an experience that occurred within the lifespan of an individual and they narrated their own convincements in journals, letters, and other publications.[21] Yet they differed from Puritans in their emphasis on "inward light" and their belief that "the Holy Spirit was in every man."[22] As a result of their perfectionist tendencies, Quakers rejected both baptism and a formal ministry, since the indwelling seed of God could be found in any person.[23] These theological differences had a major effect on Quaker missions, as Friends offered little in the way of ritualized events that could mark new converts as members of their community.

While Quakers were radical in their rejection of baptism and a ministerial class, both Puritan and Anglican members of the Church of England maintained the significance of baptism as the central rite in Christian conversion.[24] Unlike radical Puritans, however, most Anglicans did not privilege an experience of saving grace as the most important element of conversion. Instead, their conception of Christianity was based on cultural practice, education, and knowledge. These priorities were clearly demonstrated in the Anglican missionary ventures. Thomas Bray, the founder of the SPCK and the SPG, made the publication and circulation of catechisms, alongside the creation of libraries and schools, the primary means of evangelization.[25] The SPG trained Anglican missionaries to demand both Christian knowledge and "civilized" behavior from non-European baptismal candidates.[26]

The debates about baptism and conversion in early modern England were part of a broader conversation about the meaning of true Christianity throughout Protestant Europe and the American colonies.[27] In Germany, the Pietist movement took inspiration from English Puritanism in its effort to revitalize the Lutheran Church.[28] August Hermann Francke (1663–1727), one of the leading Pietist figures, corresponded frequently with Puritans throughout the Atlantic world and wrote about his own conversion as an inner struggle (*Busskampf*) followed by a sudden breakthrough (*Durchbruch*).[29] The Moravians, whose roots lay in both Pietism and the Hussite tradition in what is now the Czech Republic, developed their own version of evangelical conversion that replaced despair about one's own sinfulness with the "ideal of self-abandonment and childlike trust in the love of the bleeding Saviour."[30] The Moravian leader Count Ludwig von Zinzendorf criticized the Pietist emphasis on struggle in the conversion process, inciting a feud between Moravians and the Halle Pietists that traversed the Atlantic.[31]

As this brief survey illustrates, there was no consensus among early modern Protestants about what constituted conversion. While some denominations retained the same ritualized events, such as baptism, even the details of these rites were highly contested: should all infants be baptized? Did adults require an experience of "saving grace" to participate in the Lord's Supper? And what role should education and literacy play in the conversion process? These questions and debates took on new meanings as Quaker, Anglican, and Moravian missionaries crossed the Atlantic on missions to bring the gospel to enslaved Africans. Within the context of Caribbean slavery, Protestants sometimes maintained and sometimes altered their conception of conversion to fit their new environment. As they did so, they redefined Protestant practice in the Atlantic world.

As early modern Protestants debated the meaning of true conversion, what did conversion mean to the enslaved and free blacks who were the object of the Protestant missions? While the cultural and religious diversity of the African and Creole populations in the Americas make this question difficult to answer, some general conclusions can be made. First of all, it is important to acknowledge that many enslaved and free Africans living in the Protestant colonies would have been exposed to Christianity in Africa or Latin America. For example, the Kingdom of Kongo had embraced Christianity as early as the fifteenth century, and many men and women were familiar with Catholicism before they were enslaved. Kongo Christianity was deeply inflected by African cosmology and Christianity could form the foundation for new communities in the New World.[32] Some blacks were also Muslims.[33] Indeed, the Moravian missionary

C. G. A. Oldendorp translated the word "God" as *Allah* for the enslaved Fula men and women he met in St. Thomas and St. Croix.[34] Most enslaved and free blacks, however, would have engaged in non-Abrahamic religious practices.

Regardless of their religious backgrounds, enslaved and free black men and women did not interpret the rites that marked Protestant conversion in the same way as Protestant missionaries. This disjuncture presents a problem for historians. If conversion meant something quite different to non-European converts than it did for missionaries, how is this interaction best described? Scholars have come up with a variety of answers to this question.[35] While earlier research viewed non-European conversion as a form of acculturation, an agent of colonial expansion, or a method of slave control, more recent scholarship has emphasized the appropriation of Christianity by Africans and African Americans. African "survivals," syncretism, and hybridity have all been proposed as models to describe the process of conversion.[36] Yet disagreement remains about whether conversion represented a form of creolization or an "Africanization" of Christianity.[37] While proponents of creolization emphasize the creation of new religious traditions in the Americas, advocates of the Africanization thesis insist that African religious practices remained largely intact within African American Christianity.[38] While the division between these approaches has become somewhat blurred, scholars have increasingly emphasized the Africanness of black Christianity.

Aside from highlighting the Africanness of black Christianity, recent scholarship on black Christian practice in North America has continued to view conversion to Christianity through the lens of "accommodation" or "resistance" to slavery. While older scholarship tended to view Christianity as an ameliorating force on slave plantations—a method of slave control—more recent studies have moved in the opposite direction. Some historians have argued that Christianity provided an important theological impetus for rebellions on both sides of the Atlantic, while others have argued that spiritual practices among slaves were "persistently resistant."[39]

While the emphasis on resistance has illuminated important aspects of Afro-Protestant practice, it has obscured the significant role that enslaved and free blacks played in transforming the culture of Atlantic Protestantism for both blacks and whites. The black embrace of Protestantism forced whites to reconsider the relationship between religion, freedom, and slavery. By joining churches and participating in Protestant rituals, enslaved and free black Christians implicitly undermined the ideology of mastery and religious exclusivity that formed the cornerstone of Protestant Supremacy. Enslaved and free Christians also read and interpreted scripture in new ways that challenged white Christian culture. Their eagerness to learn how to read and write were particularly troublesome for both planters and missionaries, who realized that literacy gave black Christians a powerful tool to advocate for themselves and their communities.

Research on Afro-Protestantism generally begins with the Great Awakening of the 1740s. Scholars have argued that Anglicans and Reformed Protestants failed to appeal to enslaved and free blacks, but that evangelical religion spread among blacks because it fostered egalitarianism, was more accessible to illiterate individuals, and relied less on education than former missionary ventures. While most blacks did not join institutional churches, evangelical Christianity became integrated as the "folk religion" of slaves and ex-slaves as an "invisible institution."[40]

I revise this narrative by emphasizing the significance of Afro-Protestant conversion *before* the evangelical revivals of the mid- and late eighteenth centuries. I argue that historians have overstated the significance of emotive worship for the appeal of Christianity. While this was certainly an important feature of evangelical Protestantism, it downplays the powerful draw of literacy that was associated with Protestant conversion both before and after the Great Awakening. Furthermore, historians have paid too little attention to the strong anticonversion sentiment that existed throughout the Protestant regions of North America and the Caribbean in the seventeenth and eighteenth centuries. Planters' desire to prevent their slaves from accessing Christian knowledge affected the perception of Christianity among the enslaved population. By guarding the pages of their Bibles and keeping their most intimate rituals behind closed doors, Protestant slave owners made Christianity a sign of mastery and power.

In spite of planter resistance, a small but significant number of Africans and Afro-Caribbeans won access to Christian rites such as baptism and the Lord's Supper. As they did so, slave owners adapted. They created the concept of "whiteness" and revised their prerequisites for voting to exclude nonwhite Christians from enfranchisement. By the end of the seventeenth century, the term "white" had begun to replace "Christian" as an indicator of freedom and mastery.

While a number of historians have examined this shift from religious to racial terminology, my research emphasizes the significance of mission work and slave conversion in the creation of new racial and religious categories.[41] I argue that the baptism of enslaved and free Africans implicitly challenged the religious justifications for slavery in the seventeenth century Protestant Atlantic world. As a small but significant number of Africans and African Americans chose to participate in Christian rites such as baptism, they forced Protestants to redefine their definition of race and their concept of freedom. Faced with a growing population of black men who were both free and Christian, Protestant slave owners changed their laws to incorporate race and exclude Africans and their descendants from enfranchisement.

Ideas about religious difference remained central to racial terminology well into the eighteenth and nineteenth centuries. Terms such as "white" grew out of religious categories like "Christian." As a result, scholars examining the origins of White Supremacy must look to the ideology of Protestant Supremacy that emerged in the seventeenth century. While this religious heritage can be easily forgotten, whiteness continued to be mobilized in ways that suggested the continued significance of religion. In the Protestant Atlantic world, whiteness could be used to justify religious exclusion, much as the term "Christian" had before it. Thus whiteness retained religious undertones, explaining why many slave owners continued to resist slave conversion well into the eighteenth century.

Chapter 1

Christian Slaves in the Atlantic World

In 1657, the English traveler Richard Ligon published an account of his visit to Barbados during the late 1640s. In one anecdote, Ligon described an encounter with an enslaved man who told him that he wanted to become a Christian. Ligon promised his companion to "do [his] best endeavor" and when he returned, he "spoke to the Master of the Plantation." To his surprise, Ligon was told that "the people of that Iland were governed by the Lawes of England, and by those Lawes, we could not make a Christian a Slave." Realizing that the slave owner had misunderstood his intentions, Ligon pointed out that his "request was far different from that," and that he "desired him to make a Slave a Christian," not to make a Christian a slave. The master, at last comprehending the issue at hand, responded that "being once a Christian, he could no more account him a Slave, and so lose the hold they had of them as Slaves, by making them Christians; and by that means should open such a gap, as all the Planters in the Iland would curse him."[1]

Despite the planter's protestations, Christian slaves were easy to find in the Atlantic world. From Algiers to Mexico City, enslaved Christians labored on plantations, in workshops and in households, in cities and on rural plantations.[2] In the Americas, Christian slaves were of African or Native American descent, while in North Africa, Europeans were regularly captured and enslaved on the Barbary Coast, where they encountered strong pressures to embrace Islam.[3] Christianity—and specifically, Protestantism—would eventually come to play a central role in the lives of enslaved men and women in North America and the Caribbean. In the antebellum United States, Protestantism was a core feature of proslavery ideology and Southern planters claimed that their plantations were modeled on the slave-owning households of the Old Testament. But even in the seventeenth century, evangelization was touted as a central justification for slavery. Both Protestants and Catholics argued that enslavement benefited Africans because it saved them from their "heathen" past. Given the overwhelming evidence for Christian slavery, why did this seventeenth-century English planter object when Richard Ligon asked him to introduce one enslaved man to Christianity?

While Christians had been enslaving their coreligionists for over a millennium, there was also a long history of discomfort with owning fellow Christians. The enslavement of Christians was uncontroversial during Roman times, but the decline of slavery in northwestern Europe, combined with the threat of Islam in Iberia and the Mediterranean, gradually led to a consensus within Christendom that Christians should not enslave other Christians. The medieval conventions for enslavement, however, were challenged in the fifteenth and sixteenth centuries as the *Reconquista* fueled Portuguese and Spanish expansion into the Atlantic world. As Europeans encountered new religious "others," they needed new justifications for enslavement. In Latin America, the Iberian monarchs encouraged slave conversion in order to legitimize slavery, control slave behavior, and check the power of their colonists. While some Catholic slave owners resisted evangelizing to their slaves, slave baptism eventually became pro forma.

When Protestant nations expanded across the Atlantic a century later, they adopted Iberian practices of enslavement but redefined the relationship between slavery and Protestantism. Dutch, Danish, and English laws were unclear about the effect of Protestant baptism on slave status and Protestant theologians disagreed about if and when baptized slaves should be manumitted. Without missionary orders or strong centralized churches, Protestant nations also lacked the infrastructure to implement evangelization policies. Thus while imperial authorities frequently exhorted Protestant planters to convert their slaves, most refused to do so. Instead, Protestant colonists created religious institutions that restricted the religious opportunities for enslaved and free Africans in the Dutch, English, and Danish colonies. With a small number of notable exceptions, they refused to recognize their slaves as potential Christians.[4] Understanding the long and complicated relationship between Christianity and slavery—as well as the diversity of legal and theological beliefs about slave baptism in the Atlantic world—helps to explain why most Protestant planters resisted slave conversion in the mid-seventeenth century.

Slavery and Early Christianity

The early Church not only accepted slavery, but also preached that enslavement could be spiritually advantageous.[5] Believers described themselves as "slaves of Christ" and while masters were urged to treat their slaves humanely, there was no ban on enslaving other Christians. The Roman Church itself owned numerous Christian slaves, particularly on monastery lands, and early Christian theologians consistently reconciled slavery and Christianity.[6] St. Augustine used slavery as a metaphor for sin and described true freedom as spiritual, rather than material. For Augustine, slavery was both a consequence of and a remedy for origin sin. Similar connections between sin and slavery could be found in the writings of Saint Ambrose, Ambrosiaster, Saint Isidore of Seville, and Philo of Alexandria.[7]

Freeing one's slaves was considered a pious act, but it was neither expected nor common. Still, by viewing manumission as a religious performance, the Roman Church connected the ideas of freedom and Christianity. Constantine, who legalized Christianity in the Roman Empire, allowed priests to manumit slaves in churches, suggesting that some slave owners viewed manumission as a spiritual act.[8] But while manumission was associated with Christian charity, there was no question that slavery itself was compatible with Christian life and that Christians could own their coreligionists.[9]

During the early medieval period, it remained possible for Christians to own other Christians, but it was generally prohibited to sell a Christian to a non-Christian.[10] In Justinian's *Code*, compiled in the sixth century, Jews, pagans, or heretics who were found in possession of a Christian would be fined and their slave would be freed.[11] While Justinian's *Code* was intended to be universal, several local councils sought to clarify the relationship between Christianity and slavery. A Church Council at Clichy in 626/7 decreed that Christians who sold their slaves to Jews or pagans would be excommunicated.[12] In 743, the Church Council at Estinnes denounced the sale of Christians to pagans and in the late eighth century, the Church Council at Meaux suggested that Christians should be sold to other Christians instead.[13] The repeated attempts to prohibit the trade in Christian slaves suggest that the practice continued throughout the early medieval period. With traders offering good prices for Christian slaves, neither the Church nor the Christian kingdoms of Europe were able to fully abolish the trade.[14]

While the Church sought to prohibit the sale of Christians to non-Christians, Christians continued to own their coreligionists.[15] Over time, however, two developments challenged the accepted notion that Christians could keep other Christians as slaves. First, the rise of the manorial system in northwestern Europe led to a decline in chattel slavery and a concurrent shift in the ethic of slaveholding. While various forms of unfreeness persisted, chattel slavery and the enslavement of Christians largely disappeared from northwestern Europe.[16] Second, the rise of Islam in Iberia and the subsequent Reconquest led to a gradual ban on the enslavement of Christians in southern Europe, where chattel slavery persisted.[17]

Enslaving non-Christians, whether Muslims or pagans, was intended to expand and defend Christendom.[18] Yet questions remained about the relationship between conversion and manumission. If Christians could not be enslaved, then what was the status of formerly non-Christian slaves who embraced Christianity? In the thirteenth century, King Alfonso X of Castile issued the famous law code, *Las Siete Partidas*, which sought to alleviate conditions for the enslaved and provide routes for manumission for slaves who led Christian lives. Baptism did not lead to freedom, but it was an important step on the path to manumission.

Las Siete Partidas aimed to Christianize slaveholding. In practice, however, some slave owners prevented Muslim slaves from accepting baptism and refused to allow their converted slaves to attend Christian services. Pope Innocent III had acknowledged this reticence in 1206 and blamed it on the fear that baptism would result in a loss of profit. By the late medieval period, then, the enslavement of Christians was taboo and military conquest on the frontiers of Christendom, which provided new sources for slaves, was intimately tied to the ideal of conversion. Yet the actual conversion and integration of religious others into Christendom remained a subject of controversy. Some slave owners prevented the conversion of their non-Christian slaves, while others viewed the conversion of their household as an important Christian duty. In Iberia, converted Muslims, known as *moriscos*, were viewed with suspicion and eventually expelled in the early seventeenth century. Their expulsion, along with the expulsion of the *conversos* (converted Jews) demonstrated the difficulty of defining and policing Christian orthodoxy within Christendom.[19]

Iberian Expansion and African Slavery

The relationship between Christianity and slavery continued to evolve as Iberian nations expanded into the Atlantic and encountered new religions.

In the mid-fifteenth century, Europeans looked west to establish trade routes for new sources of spices and slaves. The Portuguese settled the Atlantic islands of Madeira (1419), the Azores (1427), and the Cape Verde Islands (1450), and established trading posts along the African coast.[20] Portuguese merchants were most interested in gold, but they found African slaves easier to acquire, due to a well-established trans-Saharan slave trade.[21] In the 1440s and 1450s, the Portuguese sought approval from the Pope for their slave trading. Beginning in 1442, Portuguese activities in Africa were deemed a crusade and, in 1452, Pope Nicholas V issued the Brief *Dum Diversas*, which granted King Alfonso V of Portugal "full and free permission to invade, search out, capture and subjugate the Saracens and pagans and any other unbelievers and enemies of Christ wherever they may be . . . and to reduce their persons into perpetual slavery."[22] *Dum Diversas* regarded the enslavement of Africans to be part of the Holy War of Reconquest.[23] It also granted the Portuguese Crown the authority to act as the head of the Church in Africa and, later, in Brazil, a right known as the *padroado real*.[24] In 1454, Nicholas V reconfirmed his support for Portuguese expansion in the brief *Romanus Pontifex*. Later Popes reiterated the grants in 1456, 1481, and 1514.[25]

As trade on the African coast became more established, Portuguese monarchs sought to maintain their religious claims in Africa. In 1490, King João II sent priests, along with European goods, to the Kingdom of Kongo, where several nobles accepted Christian baptism. In the early sixteenth century, the King of Kongo, Afonso I, declared Christianity the official religion of the realm. Elites were sent to Portugal for education and in 1518, Afonso I's son Henrique was consecrated as a bishop. Elsewhere, Portuguese attempts to create joint religious/commercial partnerships were less successful. And even in Kongo, tensions developed between African Christian rulers and Portuguese traders who enslaved indiscriminately. As Afonso I wrote to João III in 1526, the Portuguese merchants "bring ruin to the country" and enslave "nobles and even royal kinsmen."[26]

While Christianity expanded in the Kingdom of Kongo and elsewhere, questions remained about how slave trading could be deemed a legitimate Christian enterprise. While such matters were less troubling to individual merchants and traders, royal and ecclesiastical officials took an active interest in the religious implications of the growing African slave trade. In 1513, Manuel I was granted papal permission to erect a font in Lisbon for the baptism of slaves and between 1514 and 1521, he developed a set of

Ordenações to regulate both slaves and the slave trade. Slaves were to be baptized in the Atlantic islands and the *feitorias* on the African coast, though the absence of religious instruction was acknowledged as a problem.[27]

Baptism was intended to integrate enslaved Africans into Christendom and legitimize claims that Portuguese activities were, indeed, part of a Holy War. Questions persisted, however, about when and how these enslaved Africans would be converted to Christianity. While the Africans who were transported to Iberia were regularly baptized and often participated in Catholic rituals, those who arrived on the Atlantic island of São Tomé were sometimes baptized, but rarely instructed in the Christian religion.[28] Still, the veil of religious hegemony was important to maintain for both the Portuguese and the Spanish, who insisted—at least in principle—that African slaves belonged in the Christian community.

Slavery and Catholicism in Latin America

Slavery in the Americas required new justifications and legal codes. In 1493, Alexander VI issued two Bulls extending the rights that had been granted to Portugal in West Africa to Spain in the "Indies." In these and later bulls, the Pope also conferred upon the Spanish monarchs the *patronato real* which, like the Portuguese *padroado real*, granted the Crown the right to establish and govern the Catholic Church in the Americas. The *padroado real* and the *patronato real* authorized the Iberian monarchs to erect all ecclesiastical structures, choose their own clerics, define ecclesiastical jurisdictions, and collect revenues. These privileges gave the Crown unprecedented control over the church in the colonies, a bureaucratic arrangement that would have a major impact on policies toward slavery and evangelization in the Americas.[29] The Church became a source of royal power as the Crown sought to control and govern its own colonists.[30]

The Iberian monarchs decreed that Africans should be baptized before they arrived in the Americas, but it was unclear exactly when and how they should be introduced to Christianity. Charles V commanded that Africans should be baptized before they left the African coast, but even when priests did perform baptisms (which was only occasionally), there was rarely any instruction in Christian doctrine. In 1545, the Spanish Crown issued a new set of ordinances for the governance of Africans in the New World that emphasized both Christianization and Spanish language acquisition. All slave owners were commanded to baptize newly arrived slaves, provide chapels on their estates, and allow their slaves to hear Mass.[31]

While both Church and Crown advocated for slave conversion, Catholic slave owners, like their Protestant counterparts in the seventeenth century, often resisted evangelizing to their enslaved workers, especially on large plantations. As in the Protestant colonies, some planters argued that allowing slaves time to go to church on Sundays would reduce their productivity. This was particularly true in the sugar-producing regions of Brazil. When enslaved people were given Sundays off, they were often expected to cultivate their own plots of land to provide food for themselves. Jesuit missionaries in Brazil criticized this method of organizing labor and argued that masters should provide their slaves' food and clothing so that Sundays could be left for worship.[32]

Some slaveholders were brought to court on the charge that they prohibited their slaves from attending Mass. In 1617, Bartolomé Sánchez, a resident of Peru, was accused of forcing his slaves to work on Sundays and feast days, and of punishing those who did attend Mass. Two enslaved people gave testimony against their master and while Sánchez's behavior was admonished, it is unclear whether Sánchez was actually punished.[33] The Jesuit missionary Alonso de Sandoval believed the greatest impediment to Christianizing blacks was the perception that Christian slaves were less valuable than newly arrived *bozales* from Africa. His assertion is supported by Frederick Bowser's analysis of the Peruvian slave trade. Comparing the relative prices of *ladinos* and *bozales*, Bowser concluded that Spanish slave purchasers preferred *bozales* because "ladinos (and particularly *criollos*) were considered too knowing of Iberian ways to be easily disciplined." Furthermore, some slave owners "regarded the Christian faith as subversive of obedience."[34]

The Spanish Crown responded to slave-owner resistance as early as 1544, when a royal decree "deplored the fact that many slaveholders forced their blacks to work on Sundays and on the feast days of the Church."[35] They declared that slaves were to hear Mass on these days alongside the rest of the population. The following year, the Crown again emphasized the importance of Christianizing African slaves. Planters were instructed to build chapels on their estate where slaves could pray every morning. On Sundays and holy days, blacks were to have religious instruction. Furthermore, newly arrived slaves were to be baptized and instructed in the Spanish language within six months.[36]

The Iberian monarchs and colonial officials viewed the conversion of slaves as a method of control and security. Integrating slaves into the Christian community would check the power of colonists while simultaneously disciplining the enslaved population. As Francisco de Toledo, the Viceroy of Peru (1569–1581), wrote, "one of the restraints that can be put on [the slaves] for the security of the said kingdom . . . would be that the blacks become Christians, understanding the teachings that they receive."[37] Church and Crown also encouraged slave marriage. They hoped that marriage, which was a sacrament of the Church, would pacify the slave population and prevent interracial and intercaste unions.[38]

Many enslaved and free Africans seized the opportunity to participate in, redefine, and utilize the institutions and rituals of the Church on their own terms. The presence of chapels on rural plantations and the ritual of baptism were significant for at least some enslaved Africans. Historian James Sweet has described how the African healer Domingos Alvarez vividly recalled the details of his baptism, which he integrated into the framework of vodun.[39] Enslaved men and women also sought out the sacrament of marriage. As in Iberia, slaves in Latin America were allowed to marry, though marriage was more common in urban areas.[40] Since marriage was a sacrament of the Church, it presumed that the enslaved were members of the Christian community.[41] While Church and Crown hoped that marriage would regulate slave behavior, the recognition of slave marriage also provided a legal and religious opportunity for enslaved and free blacks to construct new identities, limit the power of masters, and demand a small number of rights. Ecclesiastical judges could intervene if a master attempted to sell an enslaved person away from his or her spouse. In some cases, slave masters were threatened with fines and excommunication for seeking to separate a married couple.[42]

One of the most important Catholic institutions for enslaved and free blacks in Latin America were confraternities, or religious brotherhoods, which were locally governed lay organizations.[43] Like other Catholic institutions in the Americas, the African confraternities in the Americas were modeled on Iberian precedents. The first African *cofradía* was founded in Seville in the fourteenth century, well before the transatlantic slave trade and the colonization of the Americas. This religious brotherhood, located in the San Bernardo parish, was a "legally constituted and recognized corporation" that operated its own hospital and organized social and religious events for its members, including funerals, poor relief, and religious festivals.[44] The earliest black confraternities in Portugal, meanwhile, were founded in the fifteenth century. By 1530, there were numerous black brotherhoods in both Portugal and São Tomé.[45] In Brazil, Jesuit missionaries in Pernambuco established the first confraternity, dedicated to Our Lady of the Rosary, for enslaved Africans in 1552.[46]

Both the Church and the Crown supported the establishment and growth of black confraternities. In 1576, the Portuguese king ordered that tithes collected from baptized slaves should be used for black churches, lay brotherhoods, and other spiritual affairs.[47] In the late sixteenth century, Pope Gregory XIII declared that black brotherhoods could help to indoctrinate newly converted slaves.[48] Unlike their medieval predecessors, which were normally organized by profession or trade, confraternities in the Spanish and Portuguese colonies were divided by race and social class. Black confraternities were often divided along ethnic and linguistic lines, and they provided a space where Africans, both enslaved and free, could "congregate freely, exchange information, pool resources, define corporate interests, and promote corporate goals."[49] Some confraternities, like Our Lady of the Rosary in Bahia, admitted individuals from a particular region.[50] They elected their own leaders, defined their own constitutions, and monitored their members' behavior. Spanish and Portuguese officials usually viewed confraternities as organizations that promoted social order, so they were able to operate with relative independence. Several scholars have demonstrated how members incorporated both African and Catholic rituals into their practice, and some have argued that confraternities, while ostensibly Catholic, served to strengthen African religious and cultural traditions in the Americas.[51]

Regardless of how "African" or "Catholic" the confraternities were, the institutions were of utmost importance to enslaved and free blacks. With the aid of their confraternities, slaves could work to purchase their freedom, seek protection against cruel masters, or gain legal assistance.[52] Black confraternities also submitted petitions to church and government officials arguing for spiritual equality for black Christians. Partly as a result of the confraternities, opportunities for manumission, inherited from Iberian law, were also reasonably attainable in some regions. *Coartación*, which referred to a slave's ability to purchase his or her own freedom for a just price, led to a robust free black population in Latin America, particularly in cities.

"Free Air," Baptism, and Protestant Slavery

Protestants, like Catholics, accepted slavery as part of the natural order. While slavery was not technically legal in much of Western Europe, Protestants were well acquainted with slavery through travel, stories, and experience—both as slave owners and slaves. Protestant travelers encountered slavery in Russia, Ireland, Southern Europe, and Africa, as well as the Americas. In the sixteenth century, English and Dutch privateers captured Spanish and Portuguese ships and confiscated both bullion and slaves. In some cases, they allied with former slaves against the Spanish. As Protestants increased their maritime activity, they too were subjected to slavery at the hands of North Africans and Turks. In fact, while Protestants often encountered African slaves, they wrote and talked more often about their own enslavement. In English slave narratives, religion played a central role as enslaved Protestants sought to reconcile their "freeborn" condition with their new status as slaves.[53]

Following natural law tradition, Protestant theorists generally agreed that the enslavement of non-Christians was justifiable through capture in a just war. In England, the jurist Alberico Gentili (1552–1608) wrote that slavery "belongs to the law of nations" and that while Christians should not enslave other Christians, they could capture and enslave non-Christians.[54] The Dutch humanist Hugo Grotius took a similar position. The "law of nations" justified enslavement, particularly for "barbarians and savages."[55] Writers like Gentili and Grotius "dominated mainstream European thinking about slavery" and helped to justify the enslavement of Africans and Native Americans.[56]

While most Protestants believed that slavery was natural, they tended to view their own lands as uniquely free. The concept of "free air" held that slaves would be freed upon arrival in a specific region. In the twelfth century, the city of Bremen "became a sanctuary for escaped serfs or slaves, who were deemed free after residing for one year and a day within the city's walls."[57] In thirteenth-century Toulouse, municipal authorities made a similar assertion, as did some English chartered towns.[58] As municipalities grew into "free" nations, however, they conflicted with the institution of slavery.[59]

"Free air" was not confined to Protestant nations—it had a long tradition in Catholic France while Iberian monarchs occasionally issued free soil legislation for specific regions.[60] But Protestants frequently invoked the concept, particularly as the slave trade expanded into northern Europe. In the sixteenth century, an English court declared in *Cartwright's Case* (ca. 1569) that "England was too pure an Air for Slaves to breath in," thereby suggesting that English law did not recognize slavery.[61] In 1596, a Dutch trader arrived in Middelburg with 130 enslaved Africans. The city decreed that slaves could not be sold within the city limits and that all the Africans on board were to be emancipated. These proclamations of freedom, however, were not as significant as they may appear. George van Cleve has argued that Cartwright's Case was interpreted at the time as an attempt to limit the punishment of slaves—not as a call for emancipation.[62] Similarly, in Middelburg, the enslaved Africans were not freed. Instead, the States General allowed them to be shipped—and sold—in the West Indies.[63]

Religious difference was central to developing Protestant beliefs about slavery. In 1677, two trover cases used religion to define the nature of slavery in England. In *Butts v. Penny* (1677), the court held that slavery was permissible in England but that "baptism would enfranchise slaves." Similarly, *Lowe v. Elton* (1677) viewed slavery as dependent upon non-Christian status. In 1696, Chief Justice Holt ruled in *Chamberlaine v. Harvey* that "a negro cannot be demanded as a chattel" under English law, but would more accurately be called a "slavish servant." These rulings added to the uncertain legal climate regarding slavery and religious conversion—particularly in Protestant colonies.[64] Would enslaved people who converted to Protestantism remain slaves? And did Protestant baptism signify legal manumission?

Protestant theologians attempted to answer these questions by reconciling slavery with Protestantism. At the Synod of Dort, a gathering of Reformed Church leaders held in 1618, attendees responded to questions raised about slavery. They asked whether slaves born in Reformed households should be baptized and, if so, whether baptism would set them free. Participants noted that if baptism led directly to manumission, slave owners were likely to discourage it. The synod took no formal position on the matter, leaving the question up to individual heads of households. The published proceedings did, however, reinforce the general prohibition on selling Christian slaves to non-Christians. They also suggested that baptized slaves "should enjoy equal rights of liberty with other Christians," though this liberty did not include a right to manumission.[65]

While the Synod of Dort failed to make an official pronouncement about the relationship between baptism and slavery, Protestant theologians agreed that slaves should be educated and encouraged to convert to Protestantism. In 1638, the Dutch Reformed minister Godfried Udemans published the influential *On the Spiritual Rudder of the Merchant Ship*, which justified bondage for "heathens" but "urged that they be well treated and educated in true Christian principles, with freedom possible after seven years of service."[66] The English theologians William Perkins and Richard Baxter believed that slavery was divinely sanctioned as long as slaves were introduced to Christian practice and treated with firm Christian benevolence. Like servants, slaves could be part of "a stable Christian household ruled by the Bible and right reason."[67]

Despite a general consensus that slaves should be introduced to Christianity, Protestants disagreed about what constituted proper preparation for baptism. In the splintered churches of sixteenth- and seventeenth-century Europe, baptism had become increasingly politicized and Protestants disagreed about the nature of conversion and the bounds of the Christian community. While Catholics debated whether baptism should occur before or after religious instruction, Protestants disagreed about whether infants should be baptized; whether an individual should be "dipped" or "sprinkled" with water; and whether conversion had to be preceded by education or an experience of saving grace. Many Protestants also expected non-Europeans to become "civilized" before they could be Christianized. This meant adopting European dress, behavior, and marital customs. The disputes about the meaning of conversion meant that Protestants often delayed or refused to baptize even willing converts.

Protestant theologians were similarly unclear about the consequences of Protestant conversion for slave status. While some Protestant authorities insisted that slaves should be manumitted upon baptism or after serving a limited number of years, others argued that baptism had no effect on property rights. The English Puritan William Perkins accepted the institution of slavery but argued that a master could not separate families or hold bondsmen in "perpetuall slaverie."[68] The Lutheran theologian Johann Buddeus had similar scruples about the inheritability of slavery. Richard Baxter supported legislation that made baptism "equivalent to emancipation," in the hopes that this would encourage Christianization.[69]

Ministers who traveled to the colonies were more likely to support the view that Protestant baptism did not affect slave status. Morgan Godwyn, an Anglican minister who traveled to Virginia and Barbados, argued that Christian slaves would make better workers and that there were no grounds to believe that baptism necessitated manumission.[70] The New England Puritan Cotton Mather agreed that slavery was compatible with Protestant conversion.[71] Their arguments would come to dominate the Protestant missionary enterprise, which found itself at the mercy of slave owners.

Complicating the issue further was the absence of any imperial law governing the relationship between slavery and baptism. As we have seen, Spain and Portugal had a long legal and ecclesiastical tradition governing the relationship between Catholicism and slavery. In the French empire, the *Code Noir* (1685) clarified that slaves should be catechized and baptized but would retain their status as chattel after their conversion.[72] Dutch, Danish, and English law, by contrast, remained silent on the issue throughout the seventeenth century.[73] Instead, colonists developed a patchwork of colonial legislation that only occasionally addressed the legal consequences of slave baptism. As a result, Protestant slave owners remained uncertain about whether religious conversion would weaken their property rights.

As Protestant nations expanded overseas, the theological and legal uncertainty about slave baptism would have significant consequences. While Protestants often used religion to justify colonization and enslavement, slave owners controlled enslaved peoples' access to Protestant baptism. Even after colonial legislatures began to pass laws verifying the legitimacy of owning Christian slaves, slave owners were largely distrustful of slave conversion and they resisted the efforts of missionaries to evangelize to their slaves.

Slavery and Religious Toleration in the Dutch Atlantic

The Dutch were the first Protestant power to develop an empire in the Atlantic world. When the Dutch West India Company (WIC) conquered Pernambuco in 1630, they hoped to convert Catholic churches in the colony into "truly Christian" Protestant churches and bring the enslaved population into the Reformed community, believing that it would cultivate loyalty.[74] Without missionary orders or a strong national church, however, the Dutch instead developed a policy of religious toleration that broke with Catholic precedent.[75] Not only did the Dutch allow Jews to live openly as Jews, but they also neglected to baptize or catechize slaves.[76] In Dutch Brazil, the WIC found itself at the mercy of Portuguese planters, leading Johan Maurits, the governor-general from 1637 to 1644, to promise freedom of conscience to the Catholic population. Thus instead of proselytizing the enslaved population, Dutch plantation owners allowed Catholic chapels to be built on their lands. The WIC also faced a persistent shortage of Protestant ministers.[77]

The few Reformed ministers who served in Dutch Brazil were defensive about the lack of African members in their churches. They argued that enslaved Africans had no interest in the church, practiced polygamy, and worked on the Sabbath. Still, despite these barriers, some Africans did receive religious instruction and join the church, particularly in urban areas. This was largely due to the efforts of individual ministers such as Vincent Soler, a former Augustinian friar who had converted to Calvinism. Soler baptized the children of Catholic Africans and advocated for the creation of a school to educate baptized slave children. By 1654, some 600 Africans had been baptized in the Dutch Reformed Church of Recife.[78]

The Dutch developed similar policies of religious toleration in other American colonies. In Curaçao, which was captured by the Dutch in 1634, the majority of the population was Catholic, a legacy of Spanish colonization. Officially, open practice of Roman Catholicism was banned, but in reality, the Dutch allowed the enslaved and mixed-race populations to practice Catholicism. After the loss of Dutch Brazil in 1654, the WIC adapted its slave policy to permit greater freedom of worship for Catholics and they allowed Catholic priests to visit the island to baptize slaves.[79] More than fifty Catholic priests visited Curaçao between 1680 and 1707. By the end of the seventeenth century, nearly all people of African descent were Catholic.[80]

In New Netherland, where there was no previously established Catholic church, some blacks, particularly those with previous Catholic experience, joined the Dutch Reformed Church. According to one estimate, by 1660, more than half of New Netherland's black population had been baptized in the Dutch Reformed Church.[81] Over time, however, the majority of white settlers became resistant to slave conversion—particularly after the English invasion. In 1649, some settlers argued that if slaves truly wanted to become Christian, then "Christian love requires that they be discharged from the yoke of human slavery."[82] The increasing resistance to slave conversion was also a consequence of the rising social status of black Christians. By the 1660s, ministers "suspected that the Africans were more interested in freedom than in Reformed Protestantism."[83]

The Dutch policies on religious toleration and baptism had both theological and bureaucratic roots. In the Spanish and Portuguese colonies, the *patronato real* and *padroado real* gave the Iberian monarchs full control over the colonial church. Including enslaved Africans within the Christian community was in the best interest of the Iberian monarchs, who aimed to check the power of their colonists through ecclesiastical and administrative bureaucracies. The Dutch West India Company did not have the means or the incentive to sponsor large-scale ecclesiastical development. The WIC was under pressure to produce revenues for subscribers and the investors of the WIC were religiously diverse, including some Jews as well as Protestants.

Over the course of the seventeenth century, the Dutch Reformed Church also raised their standards for baptism, thereby making it more difficult for non-Europeans to be accepted into Protestant congregations. In the mid-seventeenth century, the Reformed Church began requiring baptismal candidates to make a confession of faith—a more difficult hurdle for conversion than the earlier precondition of reasonable instruction. At the same time, the Reformed Church reclassified all Catholics—including Africans baptized by Catholic priests—as pagans. Before this declaration, children of Catholic slaves had been eligible for Protestant baptism as infants. Afterward, they had to undergo Christian education in preparation for a confession of faith.[84]

The preferences of enslaved and free blacks were another crucial factor in determining the role of the Dutch Reformed Church in the American colonies. By the seventeenth century, Catholicism had become an important component of Luso-African culture. Catholic brotherhoods had been established as central institutions within enslaved and free black communities across the Atlantic world. The Dutch had neither the means nor the will to present an appealing alternative to the practice of Catholicism in their colonies, particularly in the Caribbean basin. Instead, they allowed Afro-Catholic practice to flourish within their colonial borders.

Rather than extending the Protestant Church, then, colonization and slave trading constricted the Dutch Reformed Christian community. By offering religious toleration to Catholics, Africans, and Jews, the WIC redefined the Reformed Church as an institution that was, in effect, limited to the Dutch merchant class. The failure of the Dutch to develop an effective strategy for converting African slaves set a new precedent for Protestant slavery. Occasionally, Reformed ministers would make a concerted effort to reach the enslaved population and some enslaved and free blacks sought out the Reformed Church on their own. But the Dutch precedent was one of sporadic evangelization and minimal results. Most importantly, the Dutch broke with Catholic practice by excluding most Africans from the Christian community.

Law, Slavery, and Baptism in the English Atlantic World

The English, like the Dutch, touted evangelization as a major justification for expansion. The conversion of non-English people—especially Indians—would not only prove the universality of the English church; it would aid the colonization process by introducing "heathens" to "superior" English civilization. John Foxe's *Acts and Monuments*, which went through four editions between 1563 and 1583, decried the Spanish empire as the Antichrist and called upon the English to defeat their Catholic enemy. Richard Hakluyt, whose "A Discourse Concerning Western Planting" articulated an ideological vision for English colonization, argued that Native Americans needed to be rescued from Catholic idolatry and that New World plantations would solve England's economic problems. Both he and Walter Raleigh urged the English monarchs to endorse and support a nationally funded colonization scheme.[85]

Despite the efforts of Haykluyt, Raleigh, and others, neither Elizabeth I nor James I fully embraced the imperial vision. Instead, England followed the Dutch model. The Crown endorsed private trading companies that were entrusted to spread the state church to the colonies. The Virginia Company, founded in 1606, touted evangelization as a central aspect of its mission and the Company was responsible for recruiting and supporting ministers in the colony. In the first decade after settlement, the Virginia Company sent seven ministers to Jamestown and in 1619, the General Assembly of Virginia formally established the Church of England. Yet there was no resident bishop assigned to the colonies. In England, bishops were responsible for recruiting clergy and making sure that ministers were properly maintained. The episcopal hierarchy provided support and authority to ministers that relieved them from full dependence on their parishioners.[86]

The lack of a resident episcopal hierarchy in the English colonies meant that the national church was never fully transplanted.[87] The churches that did develop were lay-controlled. This was true both in royalist colonies like

Virginia and Barbados, where the Church of England was established, and in the Puritan colonies of Massachusetts and Connecticut. This institutional structure had important consequences for the relationship between slavery and Protestantism, particularly in the English plantation colonies. In Barbados, slave-owning planters controlled both the church and the colonial government. The vestries and churchwardens, elected by freeholders, solidified their control over ministers while the governor exerted authority over both the vestries and ministers and acted as the chief arbiter of disputes. Lacking strong links to the bishop of London or any other episcopal representative, ministers were unable to challenge the plantocracy on any substantial issue. In these colonies, the church became, in Arthur Dayfoot's words, a "planters' church."[88]

The English colonies also lacked missionary orders that could be entrusted with the propagation of the English church. In the Portuguese and Spanish colonies, the Jesuits, Franciscans, Dominicans, and other orders organized and funded missionary efforts to both Native Americans and Africans. The Church of England had no parallel organizations during the seventeenth century.[89] After the English Civil War (1642–1651), the Commonwealth government disestablished the Church of England, causing a crisis of authority throughout the English empire. Without missionary orders or a national church, the conversion and baptism of non-Europeans in the colonies varied widely. In Puritan colonies, such as Massachusetts and Bermuda, Indians and Africans were at least initially considered to be potential members of the Church, though Puritans disagreed about how or when these non-Europeans should be included into the Christian community.[90]

While some Protestants included non-Europeans within their Christian communities, most Protestant slave owners—particularly in the burgeoning plantation colonies—displayed resistance toward slave conversion. In Virginia, some enslaved Africans were initially able to use Christian baptism as a way to advocate for freedom but over time, Virginia planters developed and articulated what one historian has described as an ideology of "hereditary heathenism" that excluded Africans and Indians from the Christian community.[91] Similarly, the planter elite in Barbados formulated an ideology of Protestant Supremacy that separated "Christians" from "Negroes" and rejected the possibility for conversion.

European travelers recognized the changing views on Protestantism and slavery in the American colonies. Richard Ligon, who departed for the

Caribbean in 1647, was traveling with a group of loyalist exiles and arrived in Barbados in the midst of the sugar revolution that was transforming the colony.[92] He made his observations just as colonists were in the process of establishing their religious and political institutions to support the sugar plantation complex. As Ligon observed, Protestant planters, like their Catholic counterparts, sometimes sought to restrict their slaves' access to Christianity. The Barbadian planters, however, wielded greater control over the Church than their Latin American counterparts, and were more able to exercise an exclusive vision of Christianity.

Over the course of the seventeenth century, Protestant slave owners would use religion to define mastery and police their enslaved population. They developed an ideology of Protestant Supremacy that linked Christian status to mastery and whiteness. The contest over the role of Protestantism within Atlantic slavery, however, had only just begun. The exclusive vision of Christianity touted by Protestant planters would be challenged by missionaries, by imperial officials, and by enslaved men and women who advocated for their right to become Christians.

Chapter 2

Protestant Supremacy

On September 27, 1661, the Assembly of Barbados passed two acts relating to the island's labor force: *An Act for the better ordering and governing of Negroes* and *An Act for the good governing of Servants*. Ministers were instructed to read the acts to their parishioners twice a year so that "no Person may pretend any Ignorance in this Act or Statute, or any Branch, or Clause thereof."[1] While historians have written about the passage of these acts, analyzing their method of labor control and showing that they set a precedent for other slave codes, they have overlooked the role of the clergy in reciting and reinforcing these laws.[2] This is an important omission, for it was through the mouths of ministers that the brutal labor laws in Barbados were enunciated, year after year.

Just as Barbadian laws set a legal precedent for Protestant slavery, Barbadian planters set a new religious precedent by creating and articulating an ideology of Protestant Supremacy that undergirded and supported a brutal regime of slavery. Protestant Supremacy emerged out of the uncertain theological and legal climate surrounding Protestant baptism in the Atlantic world. It defined mastery through religious belonging and excluded most enslaved people from the established Protestant churches. In Barbados and elsewhere, nonconforming Protestants, Jews, and Catholics were treated with suspicion but offered more rights and privileges than "heathen" slaves.

The *Act for the better ordering of Negroes* was first read in church in early February 1662. The reading probably occurred either before or directly after church services. The transition from sermon to ceremonial recitation likely seemed incongruous, as the Slave Code contained little reference to Christian charity. The act referred to enslaved men and women as a "heathenish, brutish and an uncertain dangerous kind of people" and sought to control every aspect of slave life. Slaves were prohibited from traveling outside their plantation without a ticket and the punishment for committing "any Violence to any Christian" was severe: whipping on the first offense, slitting the nose, branding and whipping on the second and "such greater corporal punishment as [slave owners] shall think . . . to inflict" on the third. Year after year, island inhabitants would have heard that their "Negroes" committed "many heinous and grievous crimes, murders, burglaries & robbing in the highway," and that these "brutish slaves" did not deserve "legal trial of twelve men of their peers . . . as the subjects of England [did]."[3]

As these recitations demonstrate, the parish church functioned not only as a place of worship, but also as a communal space for making announcements, posting notices, sharing news, and verbally reinforcing labor laws. Christianity—in this case, Anglicanism—played a central role in maintaining and enforcing plantation slavery. Slaves, who were consistently referred to as "negros," were juxtaposed with the "Christian" population, suggesting that only "heathens" were eligible for enslavement and that "negros" could never be "Christian."[4] Anglican churches played an important role in maintaining and displaying the established hierarchy on the island through seating arrangements, burial locations, architecture, and sermons. Ministers were expected to support the slave system by reciting labor laws and posting notices about runaways or stolen items.

Critics, both then and now, have accused West Indian planters of being irreligious. One historian has suggested that the planters were "scarcely noted for their religious zeal" while others have been more critical, suggesting that English colonists "sank into a hopeless moral torpor, eating, drinking, and fornicating themselves into an early grave."[5] While Protestant colonists in the seventeenth-century Caribbean certainly deserve criticism, they were not irreligious. Religion played a fundamental role in shaping Protestant planter culture. Like their counterparts in Barbados, slave owners in the Dutch, Danish, and other English colonies saw themselves as Protestant and used their religious identity to justify oppression. Protestant rituals, such as marriage, baptism, and funerals, became integrated into a broader culture of exclusion that helped to define and maintain the brutal labor system in the plantation colonies.[6]

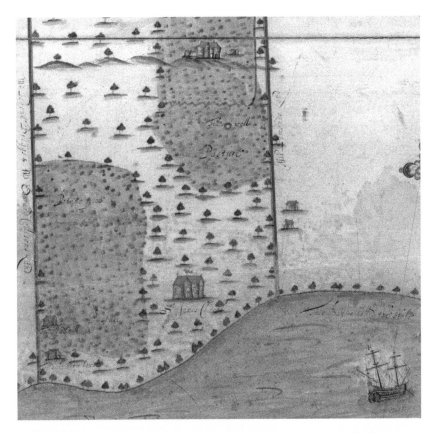

Figure 1. Detail of Fort Plantation in Barbados drawn by John Hapcott, [1646]. The image includes the earliest known depiction of a church in Barbados. St. James Church was built in 1628, just one year after the English colonists settled on the island. Courtesy of the John Carter Brown Library, Brown University.

The Planters' Church

Barbados was settled in 1627 by a group funded by London merchant William Courteen. Just two years later, the island had been divided into parishes, based on the English system.[7] In 1637, the Reverend Thomas Lane notified Archbishop Laud of Canterbury that six churches and some chapels had been constructed. Over the next decade, five new parishes were added to accommodate the growing population.[8] The parish formed the basis of both ecclesiastical and civil administrations in Barbados and other

English West Indian islands. Each parish was governed by a vestry made up of members elected by the freeholders of property. In this lay-based institutional structure, the vestry was responsible for the maintenance of the church and for providing a salary for the minister.[9] Taxes supporting the colonial government were collected by parish (see Map 4).

As in England, the organization of church space embodied both theological dogma and social authority. Pews faced the preaching box and the communion table, while the floors were often made of gravestones and inscribed with pious phrases.[10] Pews could be purchased and the most elite members of a congregation reaffirmed their status through the ritual of attending church. Governors usually held the most impressive seats. In 1676, the local vestry paid four hundred pounds of sugar to refurbish Governor Atkins's pew, while other pews were reserved for vestrymen and churchwardens. Seating was important and the vestry made efforts to keep church attendants in their proper places.[11]

The location of a pew conferred both social and religious significance. In 1698, four Bridgetown residents received permission "to erect a pew at the south side of the Church by the great door for themselves and families near unto the place where some of their relations are enterred."[12] Four other churchgoers preferred to sit on the pew "on the right hand where Geo. Peers Esq. and several others sit," while the pew "at the Great door, on the south side of the Church," was "fitted up and is appointed for the use of Captains of Ships or Strangers."[13] By 1717, the demand for pews was so great that the vestry enlarged the gallery to make room for several more families.[14] Seats in the back of the church and in the galleries were left open for nonelite parishioners, including poorer whites and free people of color.[15]

Parishioners financed improvements to the church structures through taxes, donations, and bequests. In 1660, the vestry of St. John established a committee "for the building of a Church of stone."[16] In St. Michael's parish church, located in Bridgetown, the improvements were more elaborate. The windows on the north side of the church were glazed in 1676, while the vestry paid Mr. Benjamin Crocker for "carrying the steeple five feet higher . . . and for making the Cornishes" in 1715.[17] That same year, "the Committee for superintending the steeple" agreed to "erect a spire on the steeple of thirty five feet high." The church was also "painted and whitewashed," and several "decays in the Church walls" were repaired.[18] In 1716, the vestry ordered "bells [to] be forthwith h[u]ng in wheels to ring," and a "wooden winding stairs" was built "from the Belfry floor of the sd. tower, to the floor on which the sd. bells are to be placed."[19] The improvements meant that St. Michael's church became an arresting physical and aural presence in Bridgetown, as the imposing steeple projected the sounds of church bells on a regular basis.

The church regularly received bequests or gifts from parishioners. Mrs. Elizabeth Paynter left "two small silver cups" to St. Michael's parish church in 1676, while Mr. John Mills bequeathed "the sum of three hundred and fifty pounds sterling for the buying and purchasing of a good and convenient Organ."[20] Mr. Mills's gift prompted the building of "a good and convenient Gallery" for the organ on the west end of the church. "Twenty-six feet long" and adorned with "twisted or waved [wood] work," the gallery faced the communion table and boasted "ten pillars."[21] The new gallery and organ gave St. Michael's church in Bridgetown an air of prominence.

Many of the church's most dedicated supporters sought burial inside, making the church interior simultaneously a place of worship and a memorial to the Barbadian elite. In St. Michael's parish church, both the walls and floors were decorated with inscriptions. In 1676, the Vestry granted John Davis, Esq. a deed for "a parcel of ground on the Southside of the Chancel" for "him and his heirs and relations" in return for a "purple velvet pulpit cloth and cushion with gold fringe."[22] Near the center of the porch, Col. Edward Chamberlaine was interred in 1673, "aged 50 years." His burial place was decorated with his crest—an "animal's head over wreath and arms." Ten years later, the Honorable William Sharp, a judge on the island, was buried "under the Communion table" with a crest over family arms. Sharp may have received this prestigious location because he "gave the land on which the church stands."[23] Other churches had fewer monumental inscriptions. In St. George parish, Thomas Meell's burial place, marked in blue marble on the floor of the church, was one of just a handful constructed in the seventeenth century.[24] In St. James parish church, Edward Littleton, the Barbadian judge and author of the pro-planter tract *The Groans of the Plantation*, was put to rest under a Latin inscription.[25] The north porch floor of All Saints Chapel in St. Peter held the remains of Giles Hall, a man whose domestic slave, Anna, was awarded her freedom for warning her master about an impending slave rebellion in 1675.[26] These monumental inscriptions were a testament to the social and political power of the planter elite who saw the church as central to their personal and public lives.

While the church played an important role in displaying and maintaining elite planter culture, most English colonists opted to conduct marital and baptismal services in their homes. By favoring private domestic space over the more public and communal space of the church, elite whites excluded blacks and poor whites from their most intimate rituals. Residents recognized that the preference for domestic rituals was unique: just as "most Countrys have some particular Customs," here marriages were "always solemnized in their houses (never in the Churches)."[27] Within the privacy of their own homes, members of the elite class could say their vows, celebrate with friends, and feast for a day or more. Only then would the couple "ma[k]e their appearance in due form" at church. The preference for domestic marriage over church rites was so great that many were willing to pay more than triple the price to conduct the service in their homes.[28] Most also chose to purchase an expensive marriage license from the governor rather than have the marriage banns announced in church three weeks in a row. The preference for domestic marriages and licenses allowed couples the greatest amount of privacy possible and shielded them from the gossip and publicity induced by banns.[29]

Baptisms were similarly exclusive. Within the Church of England, baptism was a basic rite that included naming, initiation into a Christian community and the creation of an extended kin network through godparents. Like marriages, baptisms in Barbados were often performed at home. As Thomas Walduck wrote, baptism was done "with Deliberation and provision, and always in their houses, never in the Churches."[30] Godparents were chosen from among friends and relatives. Due to the high mortality rate on the island, parents sometimes chose as many as three or four godparents. They might also ask proxies to stand in for godparents who lived in England. By taking these steps, parents could provide their children with strong transatlantic networks. Other parents, finding the tradition of godparenthood too "popish" for their tastes, preferred a simpler ceremony.

Regardless of the theological particulars, baptism was a time for celebration as a child was welcomed into the church covenant and an earthly community. When a parish minister died, it sometimes took years for a replacement to arrive, leaving parishioners "destitute of a Minister, to baptize our Children or bury our dead."[31] In such cases, parishioners sometimes turned to nonconforming ministers or they waited to baptize several children at once. After the baptismal ceremony, parents provided elaborate feasts for friends and family. In the English West Indies, baptismal celebrations were so important that some parents waited to have their children baptized until they could afford to throw a proper feast. The significance placed on feasting and socializing at these religious rites underlines their importance within elite white culture. Waiting until "the good time comes, and the hog is fat," the parents of a baptized child could present themselves to their community in the best possible light.[32]

As elite whites solidified and strengthened their communities by marrying, baptizing, and celebrating in their homes, marriage banns and church rites became associated with people of lower status. Poor whites were often unable to pay for a domestic service or a license when they chose to marry under the auspices of the established church and were rarely able to convince a minister to come to their home to baptize their child. Adult baptisms also tended to take place in the church, since they were not accompanied by a parental feast. Free people of color were sometimes married and baptized within the church, although their access to these rites was not guaranteed.[33]

Aside from displaying plantocratic influence, the parish church functioned as a center of communication and public punishment. In the 1640s, the Barbados Assembly instructed the churchwardens of every Parish to "provide a strong pair of Stocks to be placed . . . near the Church or Chapel." Every Sunday, the constables, churchwardens, and sidesmen were to "walk and search Taverns, Ale-houses, Victualling-houses, or other Houses, where they do suspect laws and debauched Company to frequent." If they found anyone "drinking, swearing, gaming, or otherwise misdemeaning themselves," they brought them to the stocks "to be . . . imprisoned [for] the Space of Four Hours." In 1668, the assembly passed another law "preventing the selling of Brandy and Rum, in Tipling-houses near the Broad-paths and High-ways." The act targeted "Servants and Negroes" and complained that "on Sabbath-days, many lewd, loose, and idle persons, do usually resort to such Tipling-houses, who, by their drunkenness, swearing, and other miscarriages, do in a very high nature blaspheme the name of God, profane the Sabbath, and bring a great scandal upon true Christian Religion."[34] The presence of stocks close to the church tied church attendance to the theater of public punishment.

Election days reinforced the centrality of the parish church to the island's political system. In 1656, Governor Daniel Searle signed an act instructing "all the Freeholders of every Parish within this Island" to return to "their respective Parish-churches, every year" in order to choose their sixteen-man vestry. A 1721 law further specified the details of the day: "all Elections" were to begin "immediately following the day of the third publication of the Writs in the Churches or Chapels of the several Parishes, between the hours of eight and nine in the morning." Voting would "continue without interruption till the Poll shall be finished and shut up, which shall not be before the hour of four in the afternoon, unless by the consent of all the persons who stand as Candidates in each respective Parish."[35] Election days at church were rowdy and tumultuous. In 1699, the assembly passed an act bemoaning that "many undue and illegal Practices have been used by Menaces and Threats to awe and force Men to vote contrary to their Inclinations and Consciences, to the manifest violation of the freedom of Elections of Assembly-Men and Vestry-Men."[36] Not only freeholders but also servants and perhaps some slaves would have been present on such days, crowding around and inside the parish church.

Finally, the parish church served as the community bulletin board, providing information and news to colonists. When the bishop of London wrote a "Memorandum" concerning marital practices in Barbados in 1680, he requested "a table of marriages, according to the institution, to be hung up in every church."[37] In 1711, the assembly passed an act requiring the "Rector of each Parish-church in this Island" to publish all enacted laws. The most important acts passed by the Barbados Assembly were read aloud by the minister biannually, while less important acts may have just been read once, probably for the benefit of the illiterate.

Beyond official pronouncements, white colonists also posted notices for lost or missing items. The 1688 *Act for the governing of Negroes*, like the 1661 act, mandated that "every Overseer of a Family" search "all his Negro-Houses" every fortnight. If they found anything that they "suspect[ed] or kn[e]w to be stolen Goods," they were to provide "a full and ample Description of the Particulars . . . to the Clerk of the Parish" who was to "set upon the Posts of the Church-Door a short Brief that such lost Goods are found, whereby any Person that hath lost his Goods may the better come to the Knowledge where they are."[38] As this law shows, the clerk served as the point person for the parish community, while the "posts of the church door" functioned as a space for announcements regarding anything from local news to labor control.

The Anglican Church was a meaningful institution in the Protestant Caribbean. Elites reinforced their standing by buying pews and memorializing their families in the stone foundations of the church; they employed the church as a site of island elections; and they used the pulpit to proclaim their labor laws. In all of these instances, the Church stood together with the colonial government as an instrument of planter power.

The Church of England in Imperial Context

Despite the importance of the Anglican Church for the planter elite, Anglican ministers had very little influence on the island government. The Church of England was disestablished during the mid-seventeenth century, meaning that local vestries were able to consolidate control over the church in Barbados. Recognizing this imperial context is critical for understanding how and why Protestantism came to play such an important role in defining and maintaining the slave system that developed on the island. With little oversight from London, planters were able to articulate and implement a new ideology of Protestant Supremacy to support their burgeoning slave society.

As early as 1637, the minister Thomas Lane wrote to the archbishop of Canterbury, William Laud, to complain that the vestries had too much control over the church. He hoped that Laud, as "a principal of the learned Commissioners appointed by the King to examine and rectify all complaints from the plantations," would intercede on his behalf.[39] While he may have intended to help, Laud was imprisoned soon thereafter and executed in 1645. As England descended into Civil War, colonial churches received virtually no oversight or support, though they were advised to maintain "Liberty of Conscience in Matters of Religion."[40]

In the 1650s, the Commonwealth government sought to claim more control over the colonies. In 1651, Sir George Ayscue was instructed to "reduce" the rebel colony of Barbados and by January 1652, the colony had surrendered. Once Ayscue took control in Barbados, he passed an act for liberty of conscience and disestablished the Church of England. The Book of Common Prayer was suppressed, but informally reinstituted soon afterward. Some colonists in Barbados took up "swords, canes and cudgels" to defend their church and at least one minister refused to send his copy of the Book of Common Prayer to be confiscated. Instituting a policy of religious toleration proved easier because the island hosted not only a wide variety of Protestants, but also a number of Sephardic Jews and some Catholics.[41]

While the Commonwealth government hoped to exert more control over the colonies, it faced a massive shortage of ministers. Moreover, the disestablishment of the national church meant that a large number of ministers were "ejected" while only a small number were brought into service. As a result, there was no way to meet the colonial demand for ministers. It was in this environment that Quakers and other religious sectarians landed on Barbados and successfully "convinced" a number of residents. The island became a "nursery of truth" for the young Society of Friends.[42]

Aside from claiming more authority over the English colonies, the Commonwealth government launched an offensive against the Spanish Empire, intended to finance their imperial ambitions and spread Protestantism. The Western Design, a centralized and state-controlled vision of imperialism, was met with a tepid and unwelcome response in Barbados, where colonists were forced to host a large expeditionary fleet for several months. While Cromwell's force was able to capture Jamaica from the Spanish, the expedition was deemed a failure at the time. Barbadian colonists resented the intrusive relationship and they used the language of English liberties to argue for their rights as equals, rather than subjects, of the imperial government in London.[43]

In 1660, Charles II was invited back to England, ushering in a new era of monarchy. In Barbados, the governor denounced the "rash follies" and "rebellious errors" of the Interregnum, replaced the state's arms with the arms of the king, and required the entire assembly to say the Oath of Allegiance. Yet while the Restoration marked a decisive break with the revolutionary period of the mid-seventeenth century, the new imperial government followed many of the trends set in place by the Commonwealth. Charles II kept Jamaica and worked to expand the trade networks, commercial policies and the imperial vision of the commonwealth. Instead of restoring the rights of proprietors, he subsumed colonies under royal control.[44]

After the Restoration, the reestablished Church of England gradually began to assert more authority in the colonies. Charles II instructed his Council for Foreign Plantations to take "effectuall care of the propagat[i]on of the Gospell in the severall forrainn Plantacons" by providing more orthodox ministers for the colonies and considering how "servants or slaves may be best invited to the Christian Faith and be made capable of being baptized thereunto." He added that it was "to the honor of our Crowne and of the Protestant Religion that all Persons in any of our Dominions should be taught the knowledge of God and be made acquainted with the Misteries of salvation."[45]

Henry Compton, who became bishop of London in 1675, attempted to gain jurisdiction over the Anglican churches in the American colonies by convincing governors that all colonies were "within [his] diocese." He began to correspond with Jonathan Atkins, the governor of Barbados (1674–1680), soon after he was appointed.[46] While Compton claimed wide jurisdiction as early as 1675, however, it was not until the 1680s that the Lords of Trade granted him any official authority.[47] Even then, his only real power was the ability to authorize new clergy heading to posts in the colonies.[48]

English colonists frequently resisted the bishop of London's instructions. As the eighteenth-century Jamaican planter-historian Bryan Edwards wrote, "The bishop of London is said to claim this island as part of his diocese, but his jurisdiction is renounced and barred by the laws of the country; and the governor or commander in chief, as supreme head of the provincial church, not only inducts into the several rectories . . . but he is likewise vested with the power of suspending a clergyman of lewd and disorderly life *ab officio*, upon application from his parishioners."[49] In other words, the planter elite controlled the colonial church by implementing or ignoring the suggestions of the bishop of London at will and dismissing colonial ministers who proved unsatisfactory.[50]

The subordination of the ecclesiastical administration to the civil government had significant repercussions in the Protestant colonies. Upon their arrival in the Caribbean, Anglican ministers found themselves to be dependent on the governor and vestries for their maintenance and support. Without a strong connection to the episcopacy in England, colonial clergymen were at the mercy of their parishioners and the bishop of London was unable to execute his own agenda in the colonies.

The planters' authority over the colonial church was particularly consequential with regard to slave conversion. Responding to reports that slave owners were generally averse to converting their slaves to Christianity, Henry Compton included a passage on the subject in his "Memorandum Concerning the Church" of 1680. Compton reassured colonists that the "apprehensions of planters that the conversion of slaves may deprive the owners of their present power and disposal of them" were to be "dispelled as groundless."[51] Forty years after Compton's *Memorandum*, however, little attention had been paid to the bishop of London's recommendations. When Edmund Gibson, Compton's successor, wrote to the colonial clergy in 1723 to inquire, among other things, about the status of "any Infidels, bond or free, within your parish," only three of the twenty-eight ministers in the West Indies reported that anything had been done for the conversion of enslaved or free blacks. Edward Briery, minister of St. Lucy's, explained that "their conversion must be the work of authority," suggesting that he would need the support of the civil government in order to proceed.[52] Alexander Deuchar, minister of St. Thomas's parish, gave a similar answer: "I know not neither do I use any Mean towards their Conversion," he wrote. "Nor do I see any practicable without the Authority & Concurrence of the civil power."[53]

"Christians" and "Negroes"

While Anglican ministers wielded little power in Barbados, Christianity was central to defining both slavery and servitude. An examination of the acts passed in Barbados during the seventeenth century shows that while laws from the 1640s imagined Christianity as a doctrine or belief, those passed in the 1660s used the term "Christian" as shorthand for "nonslave." This shift in taxonomy was due, in part, to the "sugar revolution" that transformed the labor system of the island. As Barbados became a society with a majority slave population, Christianity increasingly became used as an ethnic indicator, juxtaposed with the word "negro." The changing representation of Christianity is also evident in travel narratives from the same period.[54] Both reflect a larger shift occurring within Protestant planter culture. The taxonomy provided an implicit justification for slavery by suggesting that "negroes" were "heathen" and thus could be legitimately enslaved.

In the 1640s, the Barbados Assembly passed a series of laws intended to promote Christianity and the cultivation of "godly households." These laws reflected English social thought of the period by emphasizing moral behavior and household piety. *An Act concerning Morning and Evening Prayer in Families*, which was passed sometime between 1642 and 1650, instructed families to hold household prayers twice a day and mandated church attendance for everyone living within two miles of a church; otherwise, inhabitants were expected to attend twice a month. The law also threatened punishment to any servant who was absent from church. A master who prevented his servant's attendance would be held responsible. Immoral behavior, such as swearing, was to be punished.[55] While this law was probably not strictly enforced, its passage suggests that church attendance was considered significant, as were education and moral policing. It also suggests that elite planters were trying to encourage the cultivation of "godly households" on the island. This ideal, which was widespread and influential in England, was based on the belief that a good society was dependent on the existence and cultivation of godliness within families. Governed by the master of the house, all members of the extended family—including women, children, servants, and slaves—were intended to join in regular prayer and develop a firm Christian bond that united the "little commonwealth" in godly devotion.

The Barbadian laws from the 1640s defined Christianity as a set of practices and beliefs. Lawmakers were concerned that children and servants had not learned the "Fundamentals of the Christian Religion" or the "Points of the Christian Faith." In these passages, religion was something that could be taught and learned. These characteristics implied evangelical potential: "Parents or Masters of Families" were expected to take initiative to teach and instruct subordinates in the "Christian Religion and the Articles of the Christian Faith."[56]

Between 1640 and 1661, the sugar revolution fundamentally altered the meaning of Christianity. Small landholdings were converted into large land units growing sugar on a commercial basis. Demand for arable land led to widespread deforestation as eager immigrants sought to make a profit from the booming sugar economy.[57] These changes transformed Barbados even as elite planters aimed to "transplant" English institutions and maintain their identities as pure Englishmen.[58] In Barbados and, later, Jamaica, the supply of European servants could not meet planter demand. English merchants imported thousands of enslaved Africans while Puritan colonists in New England forcibly transported Indians to the English Caribbean.[59] By the early 1660s, enslaved laborers had replaced European indentured servants as the island's primary work force.[60]

Even as the population of slaves expanded rapidly, indentured servants and bound European laborers continued to be transported to the islands. Poor people, political prisoners, captured soldiers and Irish Catholics volunteered or were sentenced to labor in the colonies. The majority of indentured servants were Irish Catholics who were viewed with disdain by English Protestants. Elite Anglo-Barbadians privileged Protestant Christianity as the "arbiter of freedom" and elevated Englishness over other ethnicities. The Irish, with their "barbaric" customs and Catholic beliefs, were viewed as standing apart from English civilization.[61]

Some indentured servants used their status as English Protestants to protest their bondage. In the 1650s, two "free-born" Englishmen named Marcellus Rivers and Oxenbridge Foley wrote a series of letters and petitions to Parliament, claiming their rights as free men based on their status as English Protestants. These documents were published together in 1659 under the title *Englands Slavery, or, Barbados Merchandize*. The authors, sold into slavery after the Salisbury Rising in 1654, denied ever taking up arms and claimed that they were "sold . . . to most inhumane and barbarous persons, for 1550 pound weight of Sugar apiece . . . as the goods and chattels of Martin Noel, and Major Thomas Alderne of London, and Captain Henry Hatfell of Plymouth." Rivers insisted that his enslavement was "a breach made upon the free People of England" while another petitioner argued that his imprisonment was illegal because he "was never in any Military Action since . . . 1644." He asked how the English could "expect freedom" and be preserved from "being sold for Slaves."[62]

In the pamphlet, Rivers and Oxenbridge emphasized their identity as Protestants and argued that their treatment was "beyond expression of Christian imagination."[63] Their pamphlet was discussed in Parliament, where English officials used it to debate whether English men could be enslaved. Yet neither Oxenbridge nor Rivers protested the legitimacy of African or Native American slavery. Instead, they constructed their argument around religious difference and national rights. Implicit in their argument was the consensus that non-English and non-Christian peoples were legitimate slaves.

The centrality of Christianity to the slave system was also evident in the travel narratives written about the island. Richard Ligon, who published his *History of Barbadoes* in 1657 about his visit to the island in the late 1640s, consistently juxtaposed "Negroes" with "Christians." In his description of island defenses, he wrote that "Lines, Bulwarks and Bastions" had been built to defend inhabitants from "any uproar or commotion in the Island, either by Christian servants, or the *Negro* slaves." In another passage, he noted that it was "a strange thing, that the Negroes, being more than double the numbers of the Christians . . . should not commit some horrid massacre upon the Christians, thereby to enfranchise themselves, and become Master of the Iland."[64] In these two passages, Ligon posited two separate usages of the word "Christian." In the first, servants were distinguished from "Negro slaves" by their Christian status, even though *both* servants and slaves were a threat to the island's inhabitants. In the second passage, the population of "Negro slaves" was contrasted with the "Christians" on the island and it was considered "strange" that the "Negros" had not committed some "horrid massacre upon the Christians." Here, "Negroes" were imagined to be a singular threat to all of the "Christian" inhabitants, which presumably included both servants and masters. While the type of threat differed in these two passages, Ligon's consistent use of the term "Christian" to refer to all non-slaves on the island reinforced the idea that "negroes" would always be "slaves" and would never be "Christian."

As the island embraced sugar production, planters struggled to maintain control over their laborers—both enslaved and indentured. The effect of these demographic changes on the meaning of Christianity was evident by 1661, when the Barbados Assembly passed a series of laws designed to reorganize the entire labor force of the island. Unlike the laws from the 1640s, these acts invoked Christianity as an indicator of ethnic identity. *An Act for the good governing of Servants* sought to protect "Christian" servants from excess brutality and death. Masters were forbidden from burying "any Christian Servant . . . until the Body of such Servant hath been viewed by the next Justice of the Peace, or a Constable and Two of the Neighbours of the Parish."[65]

The importance of "Christianity" in distinguishing servants from slaves can be seen most clearly in the *Act for the better ordering and governing of Negroes*. The act used the word "Christian" seven times—more than in all previous acts combined. In each case, Christianity was used as an ethnic category that was placed in opposition to the categories of "Negro" and "slave." When the law stated that "Negroes" were to be punished if they committed "any violence to any Christian," the implication was that a "Negro" could not, by definition, be a Christian. Similarly, the Barbados Assembly was concerned about the island's increasing number of slaves: "Unless we have a considerable number of Christians to balance and equal their strength," they wrote, the safety of the island was at risk. Their solution was to increase the population of "Christian servants" by calling on "every freeholder [to] provide himself with one Christian servant for every twenty acres of land."[66]

The decision to place "Christian servants" and "negro" slaves in separate categories was strategic: it aimed to undermine cooperation between the laboring classes. Before 1660, Barbadian laws usually treated servants and slaves in a similar manner. As the population of enslaved Africans grew to a majority, however, Protestant planters sought to elevate the status of

European servants. The Slave Code of 1661 called Africans "brutish," a word that was associated with beasts, and did not provide any positive rights to enslaved people.[67] By contrast, the 1661 Servant Act provided more rights for "Christian servants" than had previously been afforded.[68] The use of the term "Christian," rather than "Protestant," suggests that Irish Catholic servants were to be included in the "Christian" category and granted marginally more protections than "negro" slaves. Indeed, by the end of the seventeenth century, some Irish Catholic servants had become slave-owning landholders in their own right.[69] The rising status of Irish Catholics and other European servants signaled the development of a caste system based on Christianity.

When a new slave code was developed in 1688, it affirmed much of the 1661 act, but diverged in important ways. It prohibited slaves from beating drums, blowing horns, or using "any other loud instruments."[70] Calling the slaves of the island "barbarous, wild and savage," the 1688 code revealed an intensification of the ideology of Protestant Supremacy and an escalating fear about slave rebellion. Both slave codes sought to distinguish "Negroes," who were assumed to be slaves, from "Christians." The fact that the Barbadian legislators continued to use the word "Christian"—rather than English, white or European—to differentiate freeholders and servants on the island from "Negroes"—shows the extent to which rights and privileges became dependent upon a Christian identity. Seeking to establish and maintain a rigid hierarchical system, elite planters used religion to relegate enslaved people to underclass status and suggest that they were "outside the boundaries of English law."[71]

Protestant Supremacy in the Atlantic World

The shifting meaning of Protestantism in Barbados paralleled changes in other plantation colonies. In Antigua, a 1644 law "Against Carnall Coppullation between Christian and Heathen," used religious difference to police sex between Europeans and non-Europeans. Jenny Shaw has suggested that "the language of the act . . . effectively created a universe in which only 'white' people could be Christian, leaving the category 'heathen' for 'negroes' and 'Indians.' "[72] A 1675 Nevis law, entitled "White Men Not to Keep Company with Negroes," also attempted to "fix the identities of Africans and English once and for all by reserving the category of Christian for 'white' people alone."[73] Similarly, in Virginia, planters came to embrace a belief that non-Europeans were "hereditary heathens" who were ineligible for Christianity. Morgan Godwyn, who visited Virginia and Barbados in the 1660s, observed, "These two words, *Negro* and *Slave*, being by custom grown Homogeneous and Convertible; even as *Negro* and *Christian*, *Englishman* and *Heathen*, are by the like corrupt and Partiality made *Opposites*; thereby as it were implying, that the one could not be *Christians*, nor the other *Infidels*."[74]

Generally, the ideology of Protestant Supremacy was strongest in the plantation colonies, and it became more pronounced as the slave population grew to a majority. In the Danish West Indies, where sugar cultivation was not adopted until the late seventeenth century, early laws encouraged slave owners to promote Christianity within their households. Once the slave population surpassed the free population, however, access to Christianity became more restricted and slave owners violently resisted the efforts of missionaries to convert their slaves.[75]

In some colonies, particularly those with fewer enslaved people, access to Christianity was less restricted. One historian has suggested that Puritans in New England and Bermuda "still considered Indians and Africans to be potential members of the body of Christ," though they disagreed about how or when these non-Europeans should be included into the Christian community.[76] In some Puritan colonies, indentures for people of color regularly included a clause specifying instruction in Christianity. In Bermuda, "*Christian* could overlap with *Indian* or *Negroe* as well as with *English* or *white*," while in New England, these categories were less flexible after King Philip's War.[77]

Throughout the Protestant Atlantic world, local conditions and circumstances shaped perceptions about who belonged within the Christian community. In New England, the turmoil of King Philip's War resulted in natives being viewed as "hereditary heathens." In Bermuda, a 1676 law exiled free people of color unless they agreed to re-enslave themselves, meaning that ideas about race were calcifying even as the category of "Christianity" remained comparatively open. In the Protestant Caribbean and Virginia, by contrast, enslaved people were increasingly viewed as "heathens" who could never become Christian. English, Dutch, and Danish colonists formulated an ideology of Protestant Supremacy that excluded most slaves from the Christian community. This ideology was on display in the Barbados Slave Codes of 1661 and 1688, as well as other laws that afforded enslaved people no rights and juxtaposed "negroes" with "Christians."

Even as the ideology of Protestant Supremacy spread, it came under attack. The Quaker leader George Fox, who visited Barbados in 1671, criticized Protestant planters and Anglican ministers for failing to encourage slave conversion. His reproach was reiterated by the Anglican minister Morgan Godwyn, who cited Fox's publications. Reports like Fox's and Godwyn's spurred metropolitan authorities to increase pressure on colonial governors and ministers. At the same time, a small minority of enslaved and free blacks won access to Christian baptism in the Protestant plantation colonies. Their conversion implicitly undermined Protestant Supremacy, forcing planters to reconsider their language of mastery. Eventually, the language of race would replace religious terminology in the Protestant Atlantic world. Even as it did, however, the legacy of Protestant Supremacy persisted.

Chapter 3

Quaker Slavery and Slave Rebellion

When George Fox, widely regarded as the founder of Quakerism, arrived on Barbados at the beginning of October 1671, he was deeply troubled by the effect of slave owning on his followers. He expressed his concerns in a sermon to Barbadian Quakers that was later published under the title *Gospel Family-Order, Being a Short Discourse Concerning the Ordering of Families, both of Whites, Blacks and Indians.* The tract provides great insight into Fox's thoughts on slavery, freedom and the proper order of the world. Fox described how his "Spirit [was] troubled . . . to see that Families were not brought into Order." Responding to what he considered to be slave promiscuity, he reminded his followers, "God made . . . Male and Female, not one Man and many Women, but a Man and a Woman." Fox believed that the "polygamous" behavior of enslaved men and women was corrupting the sacred Quaker household. In order to combat corruption, he encouraged Friends to "preach the everlasting Covenant, Christ Jesus, to the *Ethyopians,* the *Blacks* and the *Tawny-Moors* . . . in your families." Introducing slaves to Christianity would allow them to "be free Men indeed."[1]

Fox's concern for family order—and his tacit acceptance of slavery—has traditionally been interpreted within the context of Quaker antislavery thought. While some scholars have argued that Fox's comments reveal protoabolitionist sentiment, pointing to Fox's suggestion that Friends limit the terms of their slaves' service, others have seen Fox's position as a disappointing anomaly for an otherwise egalitarian radical.[2] Few have considered Fox's comments within the context of the seventeenth-century Atlantic world, where debates about slavery and Christianity were becoming increasingly important and tense in both colony and metropole.[3]

Fox's statements should be interpreted within a transatlantic and multi-denominational context. His stance on slavery was radical, but not because of antislavery undertones. Instead, Fox's efforts to reconcile slavery with Christian practice defied and undermined the ideology of Protestant Supremacy.

While eighteenth-century Quakers played a central role in the abolitionist crusade, seventeenth-century Quakers like Fox were at the forefront of the attempt to adapt slavery to Christianity. Fox's tracts were read not only by other Quakers, but also by Anglicans on either side of the Atlantic. In England and the Americas, Fox's pro-conversion stance sparked controversy by forcing Protestants—both Quaker and Anglican—to consider how slavery could be reconciled with Christian living. While Anglicans in England were generally receptive to pro-conversion arguments, ministers and planters in Barbados moved in the opposite direction. When a slave rebellion was discovered on the island four years after Fox's visit, the plantocracy legislated against Quaker evangelization, further entrenching the ideology of Protestant Supremacy. In 1676, they passed *An Act to prevent the people called Quakers, from bringing Negroes to their Meeting*, which claimed that Quakers were at fault for the attempted rebellion because they brought enslaved men and women "into their Meetings" and taught them the gospel. As a result, they wrote, "the safety of this Island [was] hazared."[4] By highlighting Quaker proselytizing efforts rather than their refusal to bear arms and join the militia, which had been the focus of attacks in the past, the Council of Barbados linked slave rebellion to religious conversion. In the year following the attempted rebellion, Quakers were persecuted for allowing their slaves to meet for worship. These arrests marked the first time any Protestant group in the British West Indies had been persecuted for missionary activity.

The connection between proselytizing and slave rebellion had major implications for the perception of missionary work in the Protestant Atlantic world. As slave owners in the plantation colonies grew anxious about how to control their growing numbers of slaves, they took precautions to shield their human property from potentially disruptive social and religious forces. Once missionaries were associated with rebellion, it became increasingly difficult for proselytizing Christians to convince fearful slave owners that converted slaves would not, as the governor of Barbados put it in 1675, "rebel and cut their Throats."[5]

Quakers and Slavery

Quakers did not intend to become central to Atlantic debates about slavery. But the missionary impulse of the early Quakers, combined with the political structure of the English Atlantic in the mid-seventeenth century, meant that the largest community of Quakers outside the British Isles was in the slave and sugar-rich island of Barbados. It was in Barbados—not in the northern American colonies—that the first "publishers of Truth" found success. When Ann Austin and Mary Fisher, the first Quaker missionaries to arrive in the West Indies, landed on the island in 1655, their first converts included slave-owning planters, merchants, indentured servants, and craftsmen.[6]

Upon their arrival, the Quaker movement was less than a decade old. Quakerism was one of a handful of radical religious groups that responded to the disruptions of the English Civil War (1642–1651) and the collapse of the monarchy by awaiting the imminent return of Christ.[7] Early Friends followed the lead of George Fox, a young man from the English midlands who claimed to know "nothing but pureness, and innocency."[8] Fox rejected the "hireling ministers" of the established Church and preached that "tender" people could claim spiritual authority by giving themselves over to the seed of the indwelling Christ. He rejected social conventions that validated earthly hierarchies and urged his followers to stop doffing their hats to superiors and to replace the honorific term "you" with the more informal "thou."

Quakerism was born in itinerancy and a number of early Friends left England to spread their message across the seas. These first "publishers of truth" included both men and women and they traveled not only to Barbados, but also to Europe, Turkey, North Africa, and the Puritan stronghold of New England, among other places.[9] Indeed, Mary Fisher and Ann Austin were en route to New England when they arrived in Barbados. For while their fervor drew them to the Puritan colony, their reliance on English shipping networks meant that the Caribbean would be a site of central importance to the traveling Quakers who were intent on carrying Truth to North America.

In 1655, when Fisher and Austin arrived on the island, Barbados was in the midst of the sugar revolution that was transforming the demography and economy of the small island. Mary Fisher and Ann Austin encountered a colony in transition, with a labor force that included both enslaved people and indentured servants. Many Friends were, themselves, indentured servants or political exiles.[10] Lewis Morris, an early convert to Quakerism in Barbados, began his career as an indentured servant for the Puritan Providence Island Company. Morris had amassed wealth and political power by the time he was "convinced" by traveling Quaker missionaries in Barbados. Other Friends were less fortunate.[11] By 1680, however, at least eighty percent of Quaker converts in Barbados owned at least one slave.[12]

Barbados was, like much of the English Atlantic, embroiled in religious dissent. As a result, Quakers found fertile ground on the island. While early Friends had difficulty gaining a foothold in New England, Barbados was more lenient on religious radicals like Quakers. In fact, Henry Fell, a Quaker missionary who arrived on the island in 1656, wrote that the "Governour is a moderate man where by [Quaker] persecution (as to Imprisoning) is restrained." In the same letter, he described how Mary Fisher and Ann Austin had been "very cruelly used and searched for Witches" in New England before they were forced to sail back to Barbados.[13] Quakers were not the only dissenters to find success on the island. Henry Fell noted that "Joseph Salman (who was a ringleader of the Ranters in England) is gotten here to speake," and that "heare are others as Baptists some are convinced of the truth."[14]

Quaker missionaries attracted planters, merchants, and craftsmen on Barbados. Within a year of Fisher and Austin's arrival, Henry Fell wrote that "pretty many people [are] convinced of the truth," and that Friends "meet together in silence in 3 severall places." While the names and backgrounds of many of these early converts is unknown, the most dedicated new Friends included Thomas Rous and Lewis Morris, two wealthy sugar planters who had lived on the island since 1638.[15] With the patronage and protection of these powerful planters, Quaker missionaries were somewhat shielded from abuse by non-Quaker colonists.[16]

Despite the growing number of Quaker slave owners, there is no evidence that Barbadian Friends considered slavery to be at odds with their convictions. Nor did traveling Friends who visited Barbados remark on the existence of slaves laboring on Quaker plantations. The first person to comment on the topic in writing was George Fox, who wrote an epistle in 1657 "To Friends beyond the Sea, that have Blacks and Indian Slaves." Despite the fact that Fox had never seen the colonies in person, he was "moved to write" to Friends in "all the plantations" that "God is no respector of persons," and that "he hath made *all nations of one blood*." The Epistle reminded Friends to attend to the spiritual lives of their subordinates. While Fox did not give explicit instructions—his only direct order was to "be merciful"—he had a clear vision of the universal gospel: "the gospel is preached to every creature under heaven; which is the power that giveth liberty and freedom, and is glad tidings to every captivated creature under the whole heaven."[17]

The 1657 Epistle reflected Fox's conviction that the spirit was universal, but he did not question the social hierarchy that allowed Friends to have "Blacks and Indian Slaves." Slavery was acceptable as long as Friends embraced spiritual equality. This important distinction can also be seen in Fox's approach to language. In his book on grammar, entitled *A Battle-door for Teachers & Professors to Learn Singular & Plural*, Fox elaborated upon his belief that Friends should change their speech to embrace the informal pronoun "thou" while disregarding the more formal "you." The pronoun "you" was originally the second personal plural in English, but over time, it became a way to demonstrate respect when addressing an individual. Fox argued that the use of "you" to address individuals was a "popish" invention and that true Christians should purge it from their speech. Fox argued that the distinction between "thou" and "you" was in conflict with the Quaker belief that "God is no respecter of persons." Using the pronoun "you" was too deferential and it paid homage to worldly political and social distinctions: "And now you that say *thou* to your servants of mean account (as you call it) and *you* to your servants of the better rank, and *your worship* to all others . . . Ye who through your ambition speak contrary to your own Grammars, Teaching and Bible; and so are fallen into respect of persons, saying to your Negers and Slaves *thou*, but to your better servants *ye* or *you*, and to one another *your worship;* Is not this the Antichrist, who is exalted above all that is called God?"[18] Fox's critique of English pronouns provides insight into his ideas about slavery and spiritual equality. While he appeared to support an egalitarian view of society, disregarding social distinctions by promoting the use of the informal pronoun "thou," upon closer examination, his theology accepted some established hierarchies. Fox did not urge Friends to manumit their "Negers and Slaves." Instead, he reminded them that even the lowliest slave was equal to his or her master in the eyes of God.

The only other Quaker to write about slavery during the mid-seventeenth century was Richard Pinder, who published *A Loving Invitation*

(To Repentance and Amendment of life) Unto all the Inhabitants of the Island of Barbadoes in 1660. Following Fox's 1657 *Epistle*, Pinder warned "Masters, and Owners of the severall Plantations" who have "Slaves, and Bond-Men" that "they are of the same Blood, and Mould, you are of," and that they should not be allowed to "perish, or suffer." Pinder also advised masters to prevent their overseers from "rul[ing] in such Tyranny over your Negroes." "If you do," he continued, "you will bring blood upon you, and the cry of their blood shall enter into the eares of the Lord of the Sabbath . . . and it shall cause his wrath to break forth upon you." By criticizing the brutality of the labor system in Barbados, Pinder sought to reform slavery, not to end it. He, like Fox, aimed to make slave owning—and indentured servitude—compatible with Christian discipline and he believed that excessive violence undermined the order of society and threatened the stability of Christian households.[19]

Aside from Fox's texts and Pinder's *Loving Invitations*, Quakers wrote little about slavery until Fox's visit to the Barbados in 1671. Yet Friends were not silent about their own sufferings. After Cromwell's death and the beginning of Restoration in England, colonial governments began to pass laws against Quakers and other dissenters. In Barbados, the first anti-Quaker law was passed in 1660, just as the Restoration was beginning in England. The Barbados Council announced not only that the "patents from Oliver or Richard Cromwell [were] declared . . . to be void," but also named "Reasons against the being and sect of the Quakers within Barbadoes" and "[imposed] fines . . . upon all willfully refusing to serve in military affairs."[20] Aside from their refusal to bear arms, which was the primary reason for their persecution, Quakers drew scorn on two other counts: their refusal to take oaths, and their refusal to pay church dues. Quakers also interrupted Anglican services and sowed resentment among the Anglican clergymen living on the island.[21] Joseph Besse, a Quaker hagiographer who recorded his people's sufferings around the world, documented 237 cases of Quaker persecution in Barbados between 1658 and 1695.[22]

Friends were either fined or sent to prison for their disobedience. Most of the Quaker "sufferers" were men, although there are some cases of female persecution, like that of Elizabeth Piersehouse, a widow who was fined 1500 lbs. of sugar "for not sending Men to serve in the Militia."[23] Fines were paid in sugar, slaves, or both. Though sugar was the most common fine, Richard Gay was forced to give up "one of his best Negro Men and one Horse, appraised at 7500 lb. of Sugar . . . for not sending his People to help build

Figure 2. A New Map of the Island of Barbadoes, by Richard Ford[e], [London, 1675–1676]. Ford, who was a Quaker, refused to include any island fortifications and did not use the word "church." Barbados Governor Jonathan Atkins included Ford's map in his 1680 correspondence to the Lords of Trade and Plantations in London. Atkins was critical of the map and wrote that he "cannot commend it much. . . . [The creator] is a Quaker, as your Lordships may perceive by his not mentioning the churches nor expressing the fortifications, of both which they make great scruple." CO 1/44, no. 63. Courtesy of the Harvard Map Collection.

Forts, and for what they called Church-dues." The fate of the seized slaves is unclear, though the individuals who collected the fines probably kept them. In the Gay case, Besse reported that "John Steart and Nathanael Maverich, Commissioners," ordered the seizure while "Joseph Hobbs, Constable," made the collection. "The whole [fine]," Besse continued, was "by them kept."[24]

In Besse's *Collection of Sufferings*, which were compiled in the eighteenth century but based on correspondence from the seventeenth, one sees the uncontroversial nature of slaveholding among Quakers in Barbados. Slaves are, like other commodities, taken from the possession of Friends in retribution for their refusal to pay tithes or support the militia. But Besse's *Collection* is also evidence of an important institutional development within Quakerism: the effort to record and catalogue the sufferings of Friends, which culminated in 1675 with the establishment of the London-based "Meeting for Sufferings" that lobbied the king and Parliament on behalf of Friends in the British Isles and abroad. By focusing on the sufferings inflicted upon their own kind, Quakers strengthened their identity as a religious group.

The effort to catalogue sufferings was part of a broader attempt to solidify an institutional structure of Monthly, Quarterly, and Yearly Meetings for Friends. In the late 1660s, George Fox and other Quaker leaders wrote to all Friends and urged them to establish regular meetings and inform the London Yearly Meeting of their questions, concerns, and activities. As Frederick Tolles has written, these meetings "provided the real foundation for the structure of Quaker church government whose apex was the Yearly Meeting at London."[25] When George Fox traveled to Barbados in 1671, his primary intention was to solidify this institutional structure by "[bringing] the transatlantic Quaker communities into line with the Society at home, both in practice and Church government."[26]

Fox's trip to Barbados had far-reaching consequences. It was the first time that the Quaker leader had visited the Caribbean, and it had a profound effect on his ideas about slavery. While Fox had reminded Friends in 1657 that "all nations" were of "one blood," he did not provide instructions on how to act on this conviction. In *Gospel Family-Order*, the publication that emerged from Fox's experiences on Barbados, the Quaker leader updated his reaction to slavery. While Fox was concerned about the brutality of slavery, he was most troubled that "Families were not brought into Order." Like later Protestant missionaries, he criticized familial structures among the enslaved—particularly polygyny, the practice of taking more than one wife, which was common in much of West and West Central Africa.[27]

Fox's focus on family order should be interpreted as part of a larger effort to define the Society of Friends as a "spiritual family." In 1652, George Fox met Margaret Fell, the wife of Thomas Fell, who would marry Fox after the death of her husband. After Margaret Fell was convinced of the Truth, her home, Swarthmore Hall, became the vital center for a dispersed network of itinerant Quaker preachers. It was to Swarthmore Hall that Quaker missionaries addressed their letters, and it was from Swarth-more Hall that they received advice and assurance. In their communica-tions, Margaret Fell and George Fox took on the roles of the Mother and Father for the children of Truth.

The earliest letters from Friends in Barbados display this developing familial network within the transatlantic Quaker community. In the mid-1650s, Mary Fisher wrote to George Fox as her "deare father" and identified herself as "thy child begotten into the truth."[28] Henry Fell, another early missionary to Barbados, wrote, "we are of one houshould, & have one Father whose care is over all & provides for all, and soe are all his children like unto him."[29] When Fox sought to organize the fledging sect into an ordered denomination, the ideal of the household took on increased sig-nificance.[30] By rooting Quaker piety in the household, Fox and Fell placed a high standard of religious engagement on each member of the family, from master to slave.[31]

Fox's response to enslaved men and women must be seen within this longer history of the Quaker family. Since Fox envisioned the true Christian life to be one that included a godly household, slave "polygamy" was not only immoral—it was a threat to the most fundamental Quaker institution. The only solution was to reform the household from the inside out, and this meant the conversion and reformation of every individual. Thus Fox's command to "preach the everlasting Covenant, Christ Jesus, to the *Ethyopi-ans,* the *Blacks* and the *Tawny-Moors* . . . in your families" was an urgent one because the fate of the master depended on the piety of his subordi-nates. Introducing slaves to Christianity would not only allow enslaved Africans to "be free Men indeed"—it would also allow slave-owning Quaker families to mimic the piety of Swarthmore Hall, the ideal Quaker household.[32]

Due to Fox's influence, at least some Friends took steps to carry the gospel to their slaves. In December of 1671, while Fox was still on the island, John Stubbs wrote to Margaret Fell Fox, "The truth is frely preached both to white people and black people Solomon and I have had severall meetings among the Negroes in the plantations. . . . But thy husband . . . hath had more then any of us we feel the lords presence and power in that service as well as [when] we speake among the white people &c." He added, "thy husband had the first meeting with them. And then after a while it fell upon me and Sollomon and it was a great crosse at the first but now its made more easy."[33] As Stubbs acknowledged, it was Fox who "had the first meeting with [blacks]." This suggests that prior to Fox's visit, Friends had made no active effort to convert their slaves to Christianity. Stubbs also confirmed that Friends continued to meet with blacks after Fox's departure, although this had been "a great cross at . . . first." The difficulty that Stubbs encountered is not surprising, given the disparities in culture, language, and social position that divided Friends from their slaves. As a result, it is difficult to know how effective their meetings may have been, though Stubbs insists that they had been "made more easy" with time.

Later missionaries also mentioned slave meetings in their travel narratives. Joan Vokins included the following description in her published account, *God's Mighty Power Magnified: As Manifested and Revealed in his Faithful Handmaid*, based on her visit in 1681:

> And when I arrived, I met with many Friends in Bridg-Town . . .
> most Days I had two or three Meetings of a Day, both among the
> Blacks, and also among the White People: And the Power of the
> Lord Jesus was mightily manifested, so that my Soul was often
> melted therewith, even in the Meetings of the Negro's or Blacks, as
> well as among Friends. And when I had gone through the Island,
> and was clear, having been well refreshed with Friends, in the feeling
> of the Heavenly Power; and in the strength of the same I came
> aboard the Ship for my Native Land again.[34]

From these sources, it is clear that Friends on Barbados made a concerted effort to organize meetings for their slaves, though it is less clear how enslaved men and women responded to these efforts. Indeed, there is a persistent lack of information about the actual functioning of the slave-owning Quaker household. No meeting records have survived from the West Indies, but there are dozens of surviving epistles and letters. These documents, however, tend to rely on conventional expressions of love and tenderness and never venture into pointed observations of Barbadian slavery or slave culture.

While there is little evidence from the West Indies about how slave-owning Quaker families functioned, a small number of records have survived from Quaker settlements elsewhere in the Atlantic world. Friends in North America used their connections to Barbados to import enslaved Africans into Maryland, Virginia, Carolina, East and West Jersey, and Pennsylvania.[35] Like Barbadian Quakers, they struggled to bring slavery in line with their religious discipline. In Maryland, Quakers congregated in Annapolis, Somerset, and what is now known as Talbot County. Many of the Friends who settled on the Eastern Shore had worked the favorite Quaker circuits of the day. Wenlock Christison, one of the most influential leaders of Maryland Friends, had spent time in Barbados and had been sentenced to hang in Boston before he settled in Maryland. Given his past, it is not surprising that Christison used his connections to send "some negroes . . . out of Barbadoes."[36]

Like Friends elsewhere, North American Quakers sought to balance their antiwar testimony with the increasingly brutal norms associated with slave control and punishment. These tensions came to the fore in 1699 when Nathan Newbie, a member of the Chuckatuck meeting in Lower Virginia, was accused of beating his slave to death. In a letter addressed to the mens' and womens' meetings at Chuckatuck, Newbie wrote: "I never intended his death neither did I give him any Blow which I thought might Take his life but this I must Confese that not many days before hee died I did Correct him sharply hee gieving mee great occation for the same."[37] Newbie claimed to be sorry for what he had done, though he seemed most concerned that his name had been dirtied: "Sorrow did Arise in mee," he wrote, "which was not easly Removed. . . . the black Clouds of infamous Reports . . . hanged over mee."[38] It was the "infamous Reports" of his actions that bothered Newbie more than the death of his "negroe." Still, it is clear that he had been too brutal in his treatment of his slave, and the members of his meeting presumably disciplined him (the Minutes do not include systematic information on discipline). Yet despite his transgressions, Newbie remained a Friend. In 1707, eight years after writing his letter of defense, Newbie became a traveling minister. Even then, he had problems with his reputation. Though the minutes do not say why, they do record that "some friends [were] Disattisfied as concerns Nathan Newby's testimony."[39] Eventually, Newbie was approved for the ministry, but other Friends continued to have doubts about him.

The Newbie episode sheds light on the difficulties that Quakers had when they accepted slavery. How, for example, should a Quaker slaveholder treat his or her slave? How should enslaved people be disciplined? And how could the Quaker community maintain its peace testimony in a slave society? It seems that Friends tolerated a certain amount of violence within households but that Newbie crossed the line: the death of his slave, just days after he had been "corrected," meant that he had gone too far.

While Friends struggled to balance the tension between their religious convictions and the physically and sexually violent practices associated with Atlantic slavery, how did enslaved men and women respond to becoming "members" of Quaker households? Historians must build on a variety of historical sources, from literature on West African cultural and religious practices to hints about a particular enslaved person's background based on small pieces of information, to gain insight into the experiences of enslaved people in Quaker families. Scholars must use their imaginations carefully but aggressively to consider the variety of responses enslaved Africans may have had to Quaker proselytizing. If Quakers had, as George Fox prescribed, taught their slaves about Quaker doctrine, for example, what would theological terms such as the "indwelling Christ" have meant to Africans and creoles in the West Indies?

In her innovative study of Quakers and slavery on Barbados, Kristen Block used a careful elaboration of sources to imagine how two enslaved Africans, Nell and Yaff, might have responded to the Quaker faith. Nell and Yaff were both enslaved to Lewis Morris, the wealthy and prominent Quaker living on Barbados in the late seventeenth century. Nell and Yaff are mentioned only once in the written record when they are both described as "faithful" servants in Morris's will. Nell was to be manumitted after the death of Morris's wife, while Yaff was bequeathed to William Penn. Building on research done on African ethnicities and Quaker practice, Block imagined the lives and experiences of Yaff and Nell within Morris's Quaker household. She suggested that Nell and Yaff may have been attracted to points of overlap between West African and Quaker religiosity, and that these similarities may have helped them forge religious bonds with their master. The centrality of dreams and portents, the Quaker denunciation of the plantation culture of "Pride, Drunkennesses, Covetousness, Oppression and deceitful-dealings" and the society's rules of deference that leveled social distinctions may all have contributed to Nell and Yaff's interest in Quakerism.[40] Block's research suggests that enslaved men and women could take an interest in Quaker practice for both religious and social reasons, and that there were a handful of common characteristics between Quaker and Afro-Caribbean practices.

While some domestic slaves may have participated in Quaker meetings and family-based worship sessions, Friends never succeeded in spreading their faith to the enslaved population at large. Their failure can be attributed, in part, to their preoccupation with behavioral and cultural practices such as marriage, which led Friends to spend more time disciplining behavior than participating in communal worship with the enslaved. The Quaker rejection of sacramental practices such as baptism may also have weakened the attraction of their faith. Later Protestant missionaries like the Moravians found that baptismal ceremonies were often in high demand among the enslaved population. Without such rituals, Quakerism may have appeared to be ineffectual and unattractive. Similarly, there is no evidence that Quakers taught enslaved people to read or write as some Anglican and Moravian missionaries did. Finally, Quaker evangelists did not provide enslaved men and women with leadership roles within their religious communities. By emphasizing the patriarchal family and the role of the master in cultivating a godly household, Friends weakened their appeal to the enslaved.

Atlantic Repercussions: Anglican Discourses on Slavery

Although it is difficult to say how enslaved men and women interpreted Quaker proselytizing, there is a wealth of information about the responses of other whites. When George Fox called for the conversion of slaves in Barbados, he helped to spark a debate on both sides of the Atlantic about the relationship between Protestantism and slavery. Fox's stance on slavery and evangelism crystallized upon his return to England, when he published a pamphlet in response to his experience in Barbados, an eighty-page diatribe addressed *To the Ministers, Teachers and Priests (So called and so Stileing your Selves) in Barbadoes.* In addition to berating the non-Quaker spiritual leaders for immoral behavior and the disorderly nature of non-Quaker English households, Fox attacked the Anglican ministry for refusing to convert Africans and Indians. "If you be Ministers of Christ, are you not Teachers of Blacks and Taunies (to wit, Indians) as well as of the Whites?" he asked. "For, is not the Gospel to be preached to all Creatures?" By making evangelization the lynchpin of his attack on the Anglican Church in Barbados, Fox inserted himself into a dialogue about the relationship between Protestantism and slavery.[41] The publication of *Gospel Family-Order* in 1676 further emphasized Fox's argument about the necessity for conversion.

Fox's remarks produced different reactions on either side of the Atlantic. Morgan Godwyn, an Anglican clergyman who traveled to Virginia and

Barbados in the 1670s, published *The Negro's and Indians Advocate* in 1680, in which he argued that blacks and Indians should be converted to Christianity. *The Negro's and Indians Advocate* was a direct response not only to the plantation life Godwyn had observed in the Americas, but also to George Fox's invective against the ministers and preachers of Barbados. Godwyn joined Fox in his sharp criticism of clergy who refused to baptize slaves or teach them the gospel. Blacks, he wrote, were allowed only in "the most distant part of the [Christian] meeting place" and they were not taught "the necessity and benefit" of baptism.[42] Also like Fox, Godwyn insisted that Christian slaves would be more obedient.

In order to develop his argument, Godwyn recounted his discovery of Fox's pamphlet *To the Ministers*. The anecdote, which is described in the introduction to Godwyn's 174-page text, explains how "a petty Reformado Pamphlet was put into my hand by an officious FRIEND, or Quaker of this Island." Godwyn then quoted Fox's pamphlet for a full two pages, admitting that the "Quakers Harangue," as he called it, made him "question with my self, If the gospel be *good Tidings*, why should it be concealed, or hid?" With this chastening introduction, Godwyn then went on to make his argument that "the Negro's (both slaves and others) have an *equal Right* with other men to the Exercise and Privileges of Religion; of which 'tis most unjust in any part to deprive them."[43]

Godwyn's decision to begin *The Negro's and Indians Advocate* with a lengthy quotation from Fox's *To the Ministers* demonstrates how the Quaker name could be invoked to motivate an Anglican audience in England. It also shows how Quakers were being identified with the position to convert slaves to Christianity. Quakers were generally regarded as a disorderly and disruptive force in society, so Godwyn's use of Fox's pamphlet was bold. It was intended to shame the Anglican clergy into recognizing their own failures by highlighting the virtues of their enemies.

Morgan Godwyn wrote *The Negro's and Indians Advocate* sometime between 1672, when Fox's pamphlet was published, and 1675. His timing coincided with the introduction of a series of bills in Parliament that encouraged the conversion of slaves.[44] These documents, which were recently discovered among the papers of Robert Boyle, are not attributed to a particular author, but it is possible that Godwyn penned the documents himself. Among other potential authors are Sir Robert Southwell, who discussed the issues of slavery and Christianity with Godwyn, and Robert Boyle.[45] Either way, the arguments used to support slave conversion in the bills are reminiscent of *The Negro's and Indians Advocate*. The presence of the draft bills in the Boyle Papers shows that ideas like those that Godwyn articulated in *The Negro's and Indians Advocate* were circulating in England.

The parliamentary bills, which were drafted in the last quarter of the seventeenth century and the beginning of the eighteenth, show how Anglicans responded to the troubling descriptions of colonial Christianity described by Fox and Godwyn. Instead of attacking colonial ministers, as Fox and Godwyn had, the authors of these documents responded to anti-conversion sentiment by confirming the legality of Christian slavery. The draft of one bill, entitled "An Act on Barbados," noted that "few or none of [the slaves in Barbados] are or are like to be converted to the Christian Religion because if they are soe converted they become free." The bill concluded that in order to "encourag[e slaves] to turn to and receive the Christian Religion," owners must be assured that they would "not loose their property." The most expedient solution to promote slave conversion would be for Parliament to confirm that "all and every Negroe and Negroes . . . who shall turne to the Christian faith and be baptized" would remain the property of their owners "as if they had never turned to the Christian faith or been baptized."[46]

A later draft was more aggressive in its attempt to convince slave owners to convert their slaves. "An Act to remove certain discouragments & Hinderances of the Conversion of the Infidels" echoed Fox's appeal to the "Masters of Families" by calling on their sense of "Duty" to "take care of their Families and Servants." The document warned that it was not only a "great Reproach to the Church of England" to keep slaves ignorant of Christianity, but it could also "provoke some severe judgment of God."[47] A third document, which compiled a series of "Proposals for the propagating of the Christian Religion and converting the Slaves, whether Negroes or Indians, in the English plantations," addressed more specific issues that were raised by both Fox and Godwyn. Regarding the question of marriage, the authors concluded that if Christian slaves were "marry'd," they should "not be sold separately, nor dispos'd of or transported, but so as they may live together, or so near to one another, as that they may live a Christian & conjugal life." The document also proposed some checks to a master's cruel treatment, and stated that all masters must "not only allow their slaves to be instructed, but be oblig'd to take some suitable care to cause or instruct & catechise their Slaves in the Principles of the Christian Religion."[48]

While these latter two documents sought to protect slaves and reform slaveholding practices by limiting the power of masters, a final bill returned to an apologist stance by emphasizing a master's right to his enslaved property even after baptism. This bill, drafted sometime between 1702 and 1714, declared that "no Negro or other Servant who shall hereafter be baptiz'd, shall be thereby Enfranchis'd."[49] This last document, which was found among the papers of Thomas Tenison, the archbishop of Canterbury at the time, suggests that by the turn of the century, the concerns about slave conversion articulated by travelers like Fox and Godwyn had instigated a broad attempt to confirm the legality of Christian slavery in the English Parliament. While the bills were unsuccessful, their presence illustrates the existence of an extensive and far-reaching debate about the role of Protestantism and slavery in the English Atlantic that reached the upper echelons of the ecclesiastical and political hierarchy of the English government.

While these early bills did not specifically mention George Fox's *To the Ministers*, later documents reinforced the significance of the Quaker specter in Anglican debates about Christianity and slavery. In 1708, Francis Brokesby published a pamphlet entitled *Some Proposals Towards propagating of the Gospel in our American Plantations*, with a preface by Morgan Godwyn that once again referenced Fox's pamphlet.[50] Then, in 1710, *The Observer*, a Whig newspaper, published an imaginary conversation between "A Gentleman" and *The Observer* in which the Gentleman asked the *Observer* whether the issue of slavery and Christianity had ever been raised before. *The Observer* answered:

> We had a Book printed many Years since, call'd, *The Negroes and Indians Advocate*; and a Supplement to it afterwards, by M.G. a Presbyter of the Church of England. . . . And our Ministers in Barbadoes, were upbraided by the Quakers there, whom they would not allow to be Christians, and ask'd by them, Who made you Ministers of the Gospel to the white People only, and not to the Tawneys and Blacks also? So that in short, by this more than heathenish Practice, we not only become a Reproach to all that bear the Christian Name, but even to the Pagans themselves, who by this, and our barbarous Usage of them, are strengthen'd in their Aversion to our holy Religion.[51]

As these documents suggest, George Fox's endorsement of slave conversion and his attack on the Anglican clergy for their failure to convert slaves aided the development of a pro-conversion, proslavery discourse in England. Morgan Godwyn's discovery of Fox's pamphlet incited the minister into action. Godwyn, in turn, used the Quakers rhetorically to motivate his readers. Although the efforts of Godwyn and other concerned Anglicans did not lead to a successful bill in Parliament, the debate had long-term implications for the role of Christianity in the English empire. Specifically, it linked the argument for slave conversion, propagated by Fox and Godwyn, with an adamantly proslavery and pro-conversion position that sought to reaffirm the rights of slave owners by divorcing Protestantism from freedom and clarifying that Christian slaves were still the legal property of their masters.[52]

Attempted Rebellion and the Quaker Negro Act

While Fox's message, articulated through Morgan Godwyn, had a generally positive reception in England, Anglican ministers in Barbados reacted with outrage and indignation. Following Fox's visit in 1671, six ministers sent a "Humble Petition and Address of the Clergy of Barbados" requesting the suppression of the Quakers who continued to interrupt church services and attack the Church of England for being "both in doctrine and discipline false, erroneous and anti-Christian."[53] Despite the ministers' outrage, the Barbados Council took no action against Quaker proselytizing. Its inaction suggests that as late as 1672, the Council did not share the same concerns as the Anglican ministers. They were more interested in preventing a slave rebellion than preventing Quakers from proselytizing to their slaves.

While the Barbados Council seemed unconcerned with Quaker proselytizing in 1672, their position changed three years later in the wake of an attempted slave rebellion that rocked the small island. In May of 1675, a group of enslaved African men planned to take over the island and crown "an ancient Gold-coast Negro" named Cuffy as the king of the island.[54] The revolt was to begin on June 12, 1675, and the enslaved rebels planned to kill their English masters and take control of the island. The rebellion would be coordinated by "trumpets . . . of elephants teeth and gourdes [which were] to be sounded on several hills."[55] After successfully taking control of the island, Cuffy was to be crowned "in a chair of state." Jerome Handler has suggested that Cuffy "may have been an *obeah* man, a prominent figure among Barbados's plantation slaves" and that the chair or stool of state "was of fundamental significance to the Ashanti and other Akan peoples as a symbol of political authority and group permanence and identity."[56] The symbolic meaning of the chair of state suggests that the rebellion, which excluded both women and creoles, was organized by newly arrived enslaved men who gained inspiration from their experiences prior to European enslavement.

To the relief of Barbadian planters, the plot was discovered by a house slave named Anna/Fortuna two weeks before it was to take place.[57] Anna was enslaved to Gyles Hall, one of the first settlers of South Carolina, who had been in absentia for much of the 1670s.[58] One of Hall's other slaves, a young man of about eighteen from the Gold Coast, had been involved in planning the rebellion but would "[not] consent to the killing of his master" and had, as a result, returned home. According to the narratives of the rebellion, Anna/Fortuna overheard this man "discoursing with another Coromantee Negroe working with him. . . . *He would have no hand in killing the* Baccararoes *or White Folks*."[59] Sometime afterward, she informed her master or mistress. Word of the impending rebellion spread quickly among the planter class, who acted quickly and violently: 107 slaves were accused of involvement; forty-two were found guilty and executed publicly. Five others "hanged themselves, because they would not stand trial."[60] Anna, meanwhile, was granted her freedom "in recompense of her eminent service in discovering the intended rebellion of the negroes."[61]

Within a year, the Council of Barbados had passed a series of laws designed to secure the island against any future insurrections. In April of 1676, it passed a supplement to the 1661 *Act for the better ordering and governing of Negroes*, adding new features and specifying consequences for rebellious behavior. The daily policing of slaves was increased and freedom of movement was limited. The Council aimed to prevent enslaved people from meeting without supervision and they revamped the "ticket system" by requiring "slaves leaving their estates . . . to carry a ticket signed by their owners." Disobedience was treated severely. A first offense carried a punishment of severe whipping, while a fourth offense led to execution.[62]

The extreme punishments were typical of a tyrannical slave regime. But the Council of Barbados also made a third more unexpected move: a month before passing the renewed *Act for the better ordering and governing of Negroes*, the Council passed *An Act to prevent the People called Quakers, from bringing Negroes to their Meeting*.[63] This act asserted that "many Negroes have been suffered to remain at the Meeting of Quakers as hearers of their Doctrine, and taught in their Principles, whereby the safety of this Island may be hazared." If, the act continued, "any Negro or Negroes be found with the said People called Quakers, at any time of their Meeting, and as hearers of their Preaching that such Negroe or Negroes shall be forfeited." The "seizing party" would receive "one-half" of the slaves seized. Within a year, Ralph Fretwell was "prosecuted for eighty Negroes being present at a Meeting in his House" and Richard Sutton was taken to court "for thirty Negroes being present at a Meeting."[64]

Quakers defended themselves against Anglican attacks by arguing that conversion taught slaves to be peaceful. When William Edmundson, a Quaker minister who visited the island in 1675, was berated by an Anglican minister named Ramsey and subsequently by Governor Atkins for "making the Negroes Christians, and [making] them rebel and cut their Throats," Edmundson replied that "it was a good Work to bring them to the Knowledge of God and Christ Jesus, and to believe in him that died for them, and for all Men, and that would keep them from rebelling or cutting any Man's Throat." According to Edmundson's journal, Governor Atkins was convinced by his argument and the minister Ramsey "ask'd them Forgiveness."[65] Though this seems unlikely, given that Jonathan Atkins would, just months later, pass the Quaker Negro Act, it demonstrates the tactics Quakers used to defend themselves against attacks: they argued that knowledge of the gospel would prevent rebellious behavior, not incite it.

Despite their argument that Christian slaves would be obedient and docile, Quakers failed to convince slave owners that they should convert their slaves and by 1680, a strong anticonversion opinion had been established in Barbados. Meanwhile, sentiment in England had been moving in the opposite direction and the Lords of Trade were convinced that the role of religion in the West Indies needed to be improved. So when the "gentlemen of Barbados" responded to a letter from the Lords of Trade and Plantation in 1680, which had asked them to consider the "means whereby the Negroes might bee admitted to Christianity without prejudice to ye Planters," the planters rejected the idea firmly. They informed the Lords that "the conversion of their slaves to Christianity will not only destroy their property but endanger the saf[e]ty of the Island, inasmuch as such Negros as are converted usualy grow more perverse and intractable than others." They further explained that since there was "a great disproportion of Blacks to Whites," there was "noe greater security than the diversity of their Languages as they are brought from several Countries." Since conversion would require instruction in the English language, it would "giv[e] them an opportunity and facility of combining together against their Masters and of destroying them."[66] They also added that conversion would make slaves less saleable and adversely affect the profits of the Royal African Company. The Lords of Trade and Plantation concluded that while conversion was still an important goal, it would be necessary to proceed "with due caution and regard to the property of the Inhabitants and safety of the Island."[67]

The Barbadian Quaker Diaspora and Antislavery Thought

While Quakers led the campaign to convert slaves to Christianity in the 1670s, their influence on the island faded in the 1680s and 1690s, as did their commentary about slave conversion. Although Joan Vokins mentioned that she attended meetings "among the Blacks" in 1681, the Barbados Council ceased persecuting Friends for bringing slaves to their meetings in the 1680s, focusing instead on the refusal of Friends to support the militia, pay tithes and swear. There are a number of possible explanations for this shift. Friends may have lost their fervor for conversion, though they certainly did not cease their efforts completely, as Vokins' comments reveal. Another possibility is that the Council lost interest in the Quaker Negro Act, though this is doubtful since it was renewed in 1678 and 1681.[68] A third interpretation is that Friends changed their methods. While the Quaker Negro Act prevented Friends from "bringing Negroes to their Meetings," Vokins' observations suggest that meetings were segregated, making it more difficult to prove that Friends were breaking the act. What is clear, however, is that the Quaker community began a long period of decline during the last two decades of the seventeenth century. In the early 1680s, the Quaker community was torn apart by internal disagreements. John Rous, one of the leading Friends on the island, revealed to George Fox that a group of "Separates" were spreading false papers around Barbados. While this was not the first time disunity had spread to Quakers in Barbados, Friends on the island claimed that the discord in the early 1680s "had done more hurt than either James Naylour or John Perrot," the two previous causes of dissention.[69] This period of disunity was followed, in the late 1680s and early 1690s, by devastating bouts of smallpox. In 1694, Richard

Hoskins wrote that it had "pleased ye Lord to Remove from amongst us so many of our antient and honourable Brethren" and that a "pestalential Distemper" had "Raged several years."[70]

By 1706, the Quaker community on Barbados had declined so significantly that the Quarterly Meeting informed the London Yearly Meeting, "We are a Remnant left as a few after ye shaking of a Tree in an orchard some of us childless, some fatherless, some widows, some orphans, and a poor afflicted people here hath been."[71] As the Quaker population decreased, persecution also declined. After 1688, Friends benefited from the more tolerant government of William and Mary and they reported fewer sufferings to the London Yearly Meeting. In their 1706 Epistle they wrote, "Our Publick sufferings have been Eased under ye Queens authority in ye latest Governments."[72] Quakers remained a presence on Barbados for several decades, but as they gained acceptance, they ceased to play a central role in conversations about slavery and Protestantism in the Caribbean.

Despite their declining influence on Barbados, Quakers helped to develop and spread the ideology of Christian slavery. George Fox and William Edmundson both articulated arguments for Christian slavery that emphasized the importance of Christian living and conversion. When William Penn founded Pennsylvania in 1682, a number of Barbados Quakers immigrated to the new Quaker haven.[73] They arrived in Pennsylvania with enslaved Africans and a commitment to the ideology of Christian Slavery based on Fox's *Gospel Family-Order*. Wealthy slave-owning Quakers like Lewis Morris, who relocated from Barbados to the Middle colonies, worked to silence the doubts that other Quakers had about slavery.[74]

When some Quakers in Pennsylvania began questioning slavery in the 1680s, Barbadian Quakers rejected their antislavery arguments. In 1688, a group of Quakers who settled in Germantown, Pennsylvania authored the first antislavery protest in North America. The Germantown Quakers hailed from the borderlands between modern-day Holland and Germany and most had been Mennonites before their conversion.[75] In Pennsylvania, the Germantown Quakers built on their experiences as a persecuted religious minority in Europe to develop their antislavery arguments. They compared the oppression of blacks in Pennsylvania to the oppression of Quakers and Mennonites in Europe, noting, "there are many oppressed for Conscience sacke" in Europe, while "here there are those oppressed, wch are of a black colour." Since the oppression of Quakers and Mennonites was not only religious, but also political and social, this suggests that the Germantowners believed that blacks, like Quakers in Europe, should be granted political and religious rights.[76]

The Germantowners used the specter of Turkish and North African slavery to support their claims. They began their Protest with a reminder that Christians—including Quakers—were often enslaved by Turks "and sold for slaves into Turkey." Appealing to the fear of piracy and captivity, they reminded their readers that Europeans are often "fearful and faint-hearted . . . [at] sea, when they see a strange vessel—being afraid it should be a Turk, and they should be taken." The reminder of Islamic slavery was apt, as many Quakers had been taken captive in North Africa and Quaker epistles regularly updated Friends on the status of their enslaved brethren.[77] For the Germantown Quakers, it was hypocritical for Christians to do "as Turks doe," and they chided their coreligionists, concluding that slavehold-ing was "worse for them, which say they are Christians."[78]

In their protest, the Germantowners emphasized the conflict between the Quaker peace testimony and the violent nature of slaveholding. What would happen, they asked, if these "stubbern men should joint themselves, fight for their freedom and handel their masters & mastrisses, as they did handel them before"? Would Friends "tacke the sword at hand & warr against these poor slaves"? The inherent violence of slaveholding was prob-lematic for Friends, and the Germantown Friends utilized this discomfort to their advantage, suggesting that enslaved men and women had "as much right to fight for their freedom, as you have to keep them as slaves."[79]

Finally, the Germantowners referred to Friends' desire to attract new immigrants to the Quaker colony. At three separate points, the authors noted that their families and acquaintances were hesitant to immigrate to a land with slaves. The "marketable" aspects of Pennsylvania were its inex-pensive land, its unobtrusive government, and its religious liberty. The institution of slavery—with its potential for slave rebellion—worked against this image. For the Germantowners, who were desperate to attract more settlers from their own homelands, this was a major concern. But their primary concern, and the core of their argument, remained humani-tarian. The Germantown Quakers thoroughly rejected the "traffik of men-body" and called for "liberty of ye body" to accompany "liberty of con-science." By doing so, they made a rights-based argument against slavery that insisted that all individuals should have liberty of both "body" and "conscience."[80]

The Germantowners presented their protest to the Monthly Meeting at Dublin, where it was deemed too "weighty" an issue and referred to the Philadelphia Quarterly Meeting. The members of the Quarterly Meeting again deferred judgment and sent the Germantown Protest to the Yearly Meeting, the reigning meeting in Pennsylvania. The scribe for the Yearly Meeting was careful to note the ethnicity of the petitioners, commenting that "some German fr[ien]ds" had presented a paper "Concerning the Law-fullness and unlawfullness of Buying and keeping of Negroes." After some discussion, the motion was rejected for having "so General a Relation to many other Prts."[81]

While the Germantown Protest was rejected, it helped to spark a debate about the relationship between Quakerism and slavery in Philadelphia. In 1693, during the midst of the "Keithian schism" that divided the Pennsylvania Quaker community, some Germantown Quakers sided with the Quaker schismatic George Keith and helped to write the first printed protest against slavery, *An Exhortation and Caution to Friends Concerning Buying or Keeping of Negroes*. The *Exhortation* reiterated many of the arguments developed in the Germantown Protest. It condemned slavery and called on all Christians to recognize that "Negroes, Blacks, and Taunies are a real part of Mankind, for whom Christ hath shed his precious Blood, and are capable of Salvation, as well as White Men." Unlike the Germantown Protest, however, the *Exhortation* was never formally considered by the Philadelphia Yearly Meeting because it was associated with George Keith. Keith, who would later convert to Anglicanism and become the first missionary for the Society for the Propagation of the Gospel, never again promoted the antislavery agenda of the *Exhortation*. It is likely that he supported the *Exhortation* in order to attack the Quaker leaders of the Philadelphia Yearly Meeting who supported slavery.[82]

In the years following the Germantown Protest and the *Exhortation*, several Pennsylvania Friends submitted petitions to the Yearly Meeting related to slaveholding.[83] While some argued that Friends should reject slaveholding, one of them, written by the recent Barbadian immigrant George Gray, demonstrates the persistent influence of George Fox's vision of Christian Slavery. Instead of excluding blacks from the Quaker household, as some antislavery Quakers had proposed, Gray proclaimed that it was "the Duty of every Master & Mistress" to keep "Nigro[s] as Servants untill they are in Some Measure brought into a Christian Life." Like Fox in *Gospel Family-Order*, Gray was ambiguous about when or if Christianized slaves should be freed, but unambiguous in his conviction that Christianization was the duty of masters. He developed his argument with a lengthy biblical defense. Gray believed that blacks were "Heathen by Nature," and pleaded with masters to "bring [their blacks] unto Christianity or a Christian Life that [they] may be free m[e]n Indeed & in Truth." His ideas about Christian practice emphasized behavior over belief. Masters needed to encourage blacks to keep "family Meetings" and to discourage them from "rude[ness,]" "danc[ing], drink[ing] & hav[ing] Merry Meetings [that] are bad examples to all people." He accused blacks of disrupting First Days and "provokeing one another to doe Wickedly" and he urged Quaker masters to keep their slaves busy during the week so they did not have "Liberty to flock & go abroad in Company," which allowed for the opportunity to "do Mischeif & plott & Contrive."[84]

Gray was aware that his ethic of Christian slavery was nearly identical to the stance of George Fox, and he invoked the Quaker founder directly: "It Could be Well to take the advice of that ancient and faithfull Servant of the Lord G F [George Fox] to have & keep Meetings with them [i.e. the blacks], and it is not only his advice but the advice of many faithfull Servants of the Lord More, as William Edmundson and William Dewsbury." Gray also knew that he had the strength of precedence on his side. For decades, Quakers in Barbados had integrated slavery into their religious practice by advocating for conversion and family meetings. The Quaker conversion ethic placed pressure on the "Rulers of familyes" to take responsibility for their entire household and to teach blacks, who were "heathen by Nature," about "the Kingdome of God & their everlasting happiness."[85]

George Gray was one of many Quakers who emigrated from Barbados to the Middle Colonies in the late seventeenth century. While some Friends developed antislavery beliefs, these slave-owning Quakers continued to voice their support for evangelization and slavery.[86] One historian has argued that the influence of Gray and other Quaker slave owners resulted in the Yearly Meeting's decision to reprint George Fox's *Gospel Family-Order* in 1701.[87] By emphasizing Fox's pro-conversion statements, these Friends aimed to make benevolent slave owning the orthodox Quaker position in colonial Pennsylvania. They succeeded in delaying the official Quaker rejection of slaveholding for nearly a century.

Quakers like George Gray and George Fox helped to develop and spread the ideology of Christian Slavery. Even as they criticized the form of slavery developing in the Americas, these Quakers argued that Christian influence would promote proper marriage and social order. They also insisted that Christian slaves were more docile than others, that they were less likely to rebel, and that they would be more productive. They put these ideas in print and circulated them as they traveled throughout the Atlantic world.

The ideas that emerged from the Quaker community in Barbados were not only central to the developing discourse about slavery in the Quaker diaspora; they also helped to polarize the transatlantic Anglican community. While ministers in England accepted the idea of Christian slavery, most colonial ministers and slave owners resisted the calls for conversion. Instead, they embraced the ideology of Protestant Supremacy and insisted that mission work would endanger the safety of their fragile society. Yet even as they rejected the missionary message, Protestant planters occasionally allowed or encouraged favored slaves to receive baptism. Over time, the small but influential population of Christian slaves and free black Christians ushered in new challenges to Protestant Supremacy.

Chapter 4

From Christian to White

In 1697, the Barbados Assembly passed an *Act to keep inviolate, and preserve the Freedom of Elections*. The act offered a definition of freeholders for the first time in the island's history, stating that "every *white Man* professing the Christian Religion, the free and natural born Subject of the Kind of *England*, or naturalized, who hath attained to the full Age of One and Twenty Year, and hath Ten Acres of Freehold . . . shall be deemed a Freeholder."[1] The clause decisively excluded all nonwhite Christians from enfranchisement. The 1697 act was part of a broader shift in the Protestant American colonies to codify race and slavery.

Toward the end of the seventeenth century, Protestant slave owners gradually replaced the term "Christian" with the word "white" in their law books and in their vernacular speech. Scholars have long recognized that whiteness emerged from the protoethnic term "Christian."[2] Yet the intimate relationship between slave conversion and whiteness has not been fully appreciated. By pairing baptismal records with legal documents, it becomes clear that the development of "whiteness" on Barbados was a direct response to the small but growing population of free black Christians.

The Barbados parish registers indicate that at least 320 individuals identified as "negros" or "mullattoes" were baptized between 1650 and 1725. The total was likely much higher since only four of eleven church registers have survived for this period. The growing population of free and enslaved Christians had a subtle but substantial effect on the racial taxonomy of Barbados. Over the course of the seventeenth century, the meaning of whiteness expanded to include a wide range of ethnic and political attributes that far exceeded its former meaning as a physical descriptor. By

1700, whiteness had replaced Christianity as the primary indicator of freedom and mastery. Yet while the taxonomy evolved, Protestantism remained bound to whiteness in important ways: planters remained resistant to widespread slave conversion, and the church continued to play a central role in the maintenance of planter power.

Intimacy played an important role in this history. As Ann Stoler has written, "intimate domains—sex, sentiment, domestic arrangement, and child rearing—figure in the making of racial categories and in the management of imperial rule."[3] It was in the "intimate domain" of the plantation and urban household that ideas about race and religion were negotiated on a daily basis. Even as planters rejected external pressure from the metropole or missionaries to convert their slaves, hundreds of slave owners encouraged or allowed a small number of enslaved people to be educated in Christian doctrine and baptized. Over the course of the seventeenth century, these intimate relationships influenced the construction of race, religion, and mastery on the island. As Christian slaves and freed Christians became a regular presence in church, new categories developed to exclude them from full participation in the culture of freedom.

Slave Conversion in the Planters' Church

The first enslaved person baptized in the Anglican Church was named Lazarus. Nothing is known about him apart from his designation as a "negro" and his participation in the baptismal ceremony at Christ Church, Barbados in 1651. More baptisms followed, and ministers diligently entered details about each rite. Between 1651 and 1669, Reverend Richard Gray and his successor, William Johnson, recorded the baptisms of twenty-six Afro-Caribbean men, women and children, all of whom were probably enslaved.[4] This number far outpaced the rate of slave baptisms in other parishes. In St. Michael's Church in Bridgetown, only four nonwhite baptisms were recorded in the same period. In St. Philip's, there was just one. After 1670, Christ Church was surpassed by the urban center of Bridgetown, where the higher concentration of both free people of color and domestic slaves meant easier access to Christian rituals.

The emergence of slave baptism seems to contradict ideology of Protestant Supremacy that prevailed on the island. Why did planters strongly resist slave conversion in principle while simultaneously allowing hundreds of their own enslaved laborers to embrace Christianity? The answer to this question is twofold. First, it is important to note that the actual number of baptized slaves was always a tiny fraction of the total slave population. In 1680, for example, only forty-three nonwhite people were baptized in Christ Church parish, compared to a total population of 4,723 enslaved Africans. In other words, less than 1 percent of the Afro-Caribbean population had been baptized by 1680.

The second answer relates to family culture and gender politics. Charles Irvine, the minister of St. Philip parish, hinted at this connection in 1724. Writing in response to the bishop of London's query regarding the state of the "Infidels, bond or free," within his parish, and "what means are us'd for their Conversion," Irvine replied that "The Negroes in general are Infidels, of whom there are about 10,000 in this Parish & no means us'd for their Instruction." Irvine's answer thus far resembled the answers of most of the other ministers on the island, who also claimed that "no means" were used to convert the Negro "Infidels." Yet Irvine then went on to add—almost as an afterthought—that "in most Families some chief slaves are instructed & baptized." He also mentioned that he had "baptised some hundreds [him]self."[5] By simultaneously claiming that "no means" were used for the conversion of slaves and that he himself had baptized "hundreds," Irvine dissociated the "masses" of enslaved people on the island from the individuals, the "chief slaves," who he knew and personally baptized. Irvine's comments show that Anglican religious culture in Barbados was both intimate and personal. It reflected and reinforced family networks, friendships, gender order, and power dynamics between masters and slaves. The decision about when, or if, a particular enslaved person was to be instructed in Christian doctrine and offered Christian baptism was a personal one, dependent on the relationships between members of a household.

Between 1650, the year of Lazarus's baptism, and 1725, eighty-seven enslaved men were baptized, at least twenty-seven of whom were adults.[6] While the minister did not record occupations, most of them would have been "chief" slaves—men who worked as drivers, head boilers, personal servants or other elite positions.[7] This argument is supported by the fact that only a small number of enslaved men were baptized on each estate—usually no more than one or two individuals. These men would have interacted more frequently with whites than field slaves, and they were often granted special privileges and opportunities. Their increased authority and responsibility, however, came at a price. The politics of mastery were complicated, particularly between masters and slaves who had close interpersonal relationships. As Rhys Isaac's analysis of Virginia planter Landon Carter's diary has shown, Carter's relationship with his attendant, Nassew, was both intimate and fraught. Carter considered Nassew both a skilled medical practitioner and a bold knave or trickster, and fluctuated in his trust for his closest slave. Carter also wrote in detail about Nassew's drunkenness and spent significant periods of time contemplating how to combat this behavior. Overall, he sought to dominate Nassew not only through physical attacks, but using psychological and religious tactics as well. As Isaac concluded, "The master's straining past the slave's body to claim his soul, and the guilt that this approach was intended to induce . . . surely took its toll."[8] Lazarus, like other elite male slaves, may have had a similar relationship with his master.

Lazarus's baptism was followed the next year by that of Peter, an enslaved mixed-race child. Peter's father, Jacob Heming, was a white man who probably initiated the ritual and was likely present at the baptismal font. Peter's mother was not named but was likely enslaved to Jacob. The minister recorded only that Peter was "begotten of a negro." While Peter was the only child baptized in 1652, he was certainly not the only "mulatto" child born that year. Sexual relationships between white men and black women were common on Barbados. As other historians have argued, the inhabitants of the British West Indies were comparatively open about their interracial relationships. This was in marked contrast to the Chesapeake, where sex between masters and slaves certainly existed, but was not readily acknowledged.[9]

"Mulatto" children were far more likely to be baptized than "negro" children. Even though the majority of enslaved children on the island were identified as "negro," more than half of baptized children were, like Peter, "mulattoes." Of the forty-five enslaved children baptized before 1725, only nineteen were identified as "negro," compared to twenty-two who were described as "mulatto" or who had clear interracial parentage. Four were not given a racial descriptor. As these data show, enslaved mixed-race children were more likely to be baptized than "negro" children. Men like Jacob Heming may have wanted to acknowledge their children through baptism, or they may have felt strongly that providing them with baptism would protect their offspring.

While Jacob Heming probably initiated Peter's baptism, what role did Peter's mother play? And what type of relationship did she have with Jacob

Heming? In all likelihood, Peter's mother was enslaved to Peter's father. As an enslaved woman, she had a limited set of options. Within households and on plantations, a patriarch used his mastery over a woman's labor to create opportunities for sex that gave his dependents little choice or say.[10] Through manipulative tactics, "servants and slaves could not only be forced *to* consent, but this force was also refigured *as* consent."[11] Dependent women, whether they were servants or slaves, could make choices within this framework of mastery to improve their own condition, but their options were always confined. So while it is impossible to know how Peter's mother viewed Jacob Heming, she certainly had a very narrow set of options placed before her. Once her son was born, what did she think when Heming brought him to the baptismal font? She may have been resentful that he was inducting her son in a foreign ritual or she could have seen Christian baptism as another cloak of spiritual protection that could aid her child as he came of age in a brutal slave society.

Though Peter's mother probably played no part in her son's baptism, other enslaved women were identified and acknowledged by the island's ministers. In 1667, a "negro woman called Sillian" brought her son Richard to the baptismal font in Christ Church. Richard, a "mulatto," was the first of three children that Sillian brought to church. Her son Thomas, also a "mulatto," was baptized on January 1, 1669, while her daughter Mary was brought into the church covenant nearly two years later, on December 31, 1670. There is no record that Sillian herself was ever baptized. So why did she bring her children to church? She may have believed that Christian baptism was more meaningful and efficacious than any other religious ritual or she could have paired baptism with Afro-Caribbean religious rites.

Some enslaved women chose to be baptized alongside their children. Hannah, a twenty-one-year-old woman in the home of Justice Hall, was baptized on July 18, 1704, the same day as her four-month-old son John. George Marshal, Edward Nusum, Mrs. Cotterel, and Mary Gay served as witnesses. The rites, which took place in St. Michael church in Bridgetown, were characteristic of an urban baptism. Hannah was, like most enslaved women in Bridgetown, probably a domestic slave who served in close quarters with her master and mistress. As a domestic, she may have been the personal servant to Mrs. Hall or worked as a cook or house cleaner. If she was Mrs. Hall's attendant, she may have cultivated a close personal relationship with her mistress. Perhaps Mrs. Hall took a personal interest in Hannah's spiritual life, encouraging her interest in Christianity. As island elites, the Halls may have prided themselves on proselytizing to their house slaves. Alternatively, Hannah may have been introduced to Christian doctrine by other whites in Bridgetown. She certainly had a special relationship with her godparents—it may have been their influence that incited Hannah's interest in baptism.

There is no indication that interracial sex played a part in Hannah's baptism, but it was an important factor for other enslaved women. Just under 20 percent of the enslaved women baptized were identified as the sexual partners of white men, though this is likely a low estimate since interracial sex was not always acknowledged in the baptismal register.[12] In one case, the slave owner and merchant John Peers brought three enslaved women, along with at least fourteen children, to be baptized between 1670 and 1683. Hester, Susanna and Elizabeth were baptized together on June 8, 1670. The pastor listed the women as "negro women slaves to John Peers."[13] Thirteen years later, John Peers returned to church to baptize nine of his children. Three were "begotten of a mul[atto] woman named Susanna," another three were "begotten of a mul[atto] woman named Elizabeth," while the final third were "begotten of Dorothy Spendlove," who was probably a white woman.[14] John Peers, then, was actively involved in bringing both his sexual partners and his mixed-race children to the baptismal font. When he died in 1688, he gave the bulk of his estate to the children from his first and second marriages, but gave "Elizabeth Ashcroft," "Susannah Mingo a black," and "Dorothy Spendlove" as well as their children use of his "house & grounds."[15]

The case of John Peers and his many children reflects the interconnection between sexual and religious cultures in seventeenth-century Barbados. As the baptisms of Elizabeth, Susanna, Dorothy, and their children show, religious culture cannot be understood without examining intimate relationships and power dynamics. Yet while interracial sex was certainly an important factor in the creation of a baptized nonwhite population, its influence should not be overstated, particularly for adults. The majority of adults baptized do not appear to have been in sexual relationships with white men. Most enslaved baptized adults were men, not women, and only a minority of the women were identified as sexual partners. This evidence suggests that the most important factor leading to baptism for adults was maintaining a close relationship with a master or mistress. The importance of a master's consent can be seen in the baptismal records. Ministers recorded that some masters served as witnesses in the baptism of their slaves, thereby displaying not only their consent, but their approval and support. Other times, such as for the baptism of a woman named Elizabeth, the pastor noted that Elizabeth had "her master's free consent."[16]

Overall, intimacy, either sexual or social, was the greatest factor contributing to the growth of an enslaved Christian population. Most slave owners opposed slave conversion in principle, but they made exceptions for individuals in their households with whom they felt close. Many decided to baptize their interracial children, with or without the consent of enslaved mothers. Some "privileged" their most trusted male and female slaves with access to baptism. As these trends show, family politics and personal networks were central to the growth of an enslaved Christian population on Barbados. Over time, these daily practices would have a major effect on the history of race and the development of new taxonomies. As enslaved Christians began to make their presence known in Anglican churches, white Christians reconsidered the relationship between Protestantism and freedom.

Free Black Christians and the Challenge to Protestant Supremacy

While some slave owners were content to baptize their favored slaves, a small number of slave owners went a step further by manumitting enslaved people who had been especially "loyal" and trustworthy. The free black population on Barbados was never large. Still, its influence was greater than its size. This was particularly true of the "free negroes" who chose to be baptized in the Anglican Church. These Afro-Caribbean Christians implicitly challenged the ideology of Protestant Supremacy in Barbados, where the term "Christian" was used as a protoracial category that separated "negro" slaves from "free" Euro-Caribbean men and women.

On September 9, 1677, Charles Cuffee was baptized in St. Michael parish. His baptism probably took place inside the church, since Cuffee likely lacked the funds and status to pay for a home visit. As the minister noted in his church register, Cuffee had recently been "freed by his master," making him the first free black to be baptized on the island.[17] The fact that Cuffee's baptism followed his manumission suggests that there remained a ceremonial connection between Christianity and freedom. Cuffee's decision to be baptized in the Anglican Church gave him new standing within Barbadian society: while he could already work for himself and accumulate property and capital as a freeman, Christianity offered social and spiritual benefits. By partaking in baptism, Cuffee received spiritual protection from an established religious practitioner and entered into a new and exclusive community. By joining the Anglican Church, Cuffee was making a claim for himself: as a free Christian man, he had acquired most of the markings of a freeholder. According to Barbadian law at the time, he would be eligible to vote in elections and, at least hypothetically, run for office if he could acquire enough property.

Cuffee may or may not have attended church regularly, participated in worship services, or taken an active role in his church community. What is known is that in 1689, twelve years after his baptism, he brought two children to the baptismal font: Thomas, aged ten, and Mary, aged five. The minister noted that they were the "son & dau of Charles Cuffee free Christian negro." The added reference to Cuffee's Christian status in the minister's entry suggests that Cuffee was known and recognized as both a freeman and a Christian. Additionally, the minister recorded the children's godparents: Andrew Miller and Thomas Alford acted as Godfathers, while Hannah Lamply and Ellen Hall served as Godmothers to the children. Cuffee's relationship with these four individuals, all white, suggests that Cuffee and his family had created a network of support for themselves among the island's white Anglican population.

Charles Cuffee continued to bolster his Christian status in 1694 when he and Mary Jones, another free black, were married on June 25. Mary was baptized the same day. Unlike Cuffee's baptism, however, their marriage was not the first of its kind: by 1694, the minister of St. Michael's parish had already consecrated at least six marriages involving free blacks.[18] The first of these took place on January 25, 1684 with the marriage of John Corsoe and Anne Williams. The trend picked up in the 1690s, with three weddings recorded in 1694 alone, including that of Charles Cuffee and Mary Jones. Charles and Mary strengthened their ties to the church as their family grew. In 1697, their son Charles was baptized in St. Michael parish church. Other free black Christians also brought their children into the church covenant. John Corsoe brought his daughters Rachell, aged eight, and Bridget, aged four, to the baptismal font the year after his marriage to Anne Williams. Thomas and Mary Ravell had already baptized their daughters Diana, Katha[rine] and Mary by the time of their marriage in 1688. Charles Hector and Hannah Davis, who were married on July 21, 1706, displayed a different pattern by baptizing their children in their infancy.

Hannah and her daughter Joan, nine months, were baptized on the day of Hannah's marriage. Hannah must have been pregnant at the time, because her daughter Mary, aged three months, was baptized the following December. As the timing of these births and marriages show, free Afro-Caribbeans decided for themselves when church sacraments should be bestowed. Many of their children were baptized before their parents' marriages, and parents sometimes waited years before deciding to baptize a child. They may have postponed baptism for a number of reasons. Some parents waited until they could afford to host a feast in celebration, while others may have had personal or spiritual grounds for delay. Either way, free Afro-Caribbean families followed patterns similar to those of Euro-Caribbean families on Barbados, who also tended to wait years to baptize children, and often chose to baptize several children at once.

These marriages and baptisms reveal the appearance of a small but significant population of free black Christians on Barbados. By the end of the seventeenth century, free Afro-Caribbeans were making church an integral part of their family life, marking both marriages and baptisms with Anglican rituals. These trends continued in the early eighteenth century.[19] In the 1680s, the number of baptized free blacks jumped from two to fifteen. It nearly doubled ten years later, with twenty-seven baptisms in the 1690s. The rate of baptisms then evened out over the next several decades, ranging from twenty-three to twenty-six. Most of the baptisms occurred in the parish of St. Michael, which contained the urban center of Bridgetown. Christ Church and St. Philip also showed a sizable number of freed Christians, while St. James had fewer free black baptisms.

By 1725, at least 107 free people of color had been baptized in Barbados. While this was a small percentage of the nonwhite population, it was a sizable percentage of the free black population. Comparing these numbers to data collected by Jerome Handler and John Pohlmann, it is reasonable to assume that at least a quarter and probably a majority of free blacks chose to be baptized in the Anglican Church.[20]

As the number of free nonwhite people grew, so did their presence in churches. While free blacks made up only a fraction of the Christian population, their attendance at church services and their participation in church sacraments did not go unnoticed. This would have been particularly true in Bridgetown, where the majority of free nonwhite Christians resided. While it is unlikely that all 107 free black Christian attended church regularly, it is probable that at least a handful of free blacks were present at

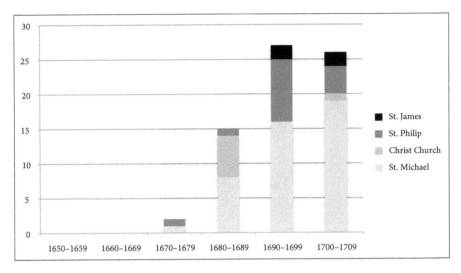

Figure 3. Free people of color baptized on Barbados, 1650–1710.

most church functions. During the 1690s, their presence would have been increasingly noticeable, as a dozen free people of color were married and sixteen baptized in St. Michael's parish church alone.

The Creation of Whiteness on Barbados

The increasing presence and rising status of free black Christians created an implicit challenge to the ideology of Protestant Supremacy on Barbados.[21] By the late seventeenth century, dozens of free people of color had been baptized, and many were baptizing their children. As a result, a small but growing class of free Christians of African or mixed African and European ancestry could have been eligible as freeholders. In 1694, when Charles Cuffee and Mary Jones were married, the most recent legislation regarding voting had been passed during the Interregnum and there was no firm definition of a "freeholder." In 1656, Governor Daniel Searle approved *An Act concerning Vestries,* which required "all the Freeholders" to "repair to their respective Parish-churches" in order to elect vestrymen by their own "free voices." The act did not, however, specifically define freeholders. Instead, the definition would have been the same as in English common

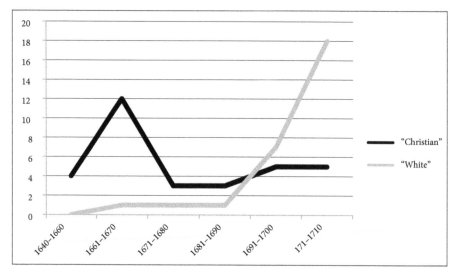

Figure 4. Terminology used in the *Acts of the Barbados Assembly.*

law. In England, freeholders were adult, Christian, propertied, and male. Since free black Christians could attain all of those markers, they were technically eligible for freeholder status.[22]

As the number of free black Christians grew, the Barbadian lexicon shifted to exclude the new potential voters from enfranchisement. While Christianity still functioned as an indicator of ethnic difference, it was gradually replaced by the phenotypic term "white." An analysis of all the laws passed in Barbados between 1650 and 1725 shows that the term "white" was used just three times in laws passed between 1660 and 1690. In the last decade of the century, however, usage increased dramatically, peaking in the first decade of the eighteenth century. References to Christianity or Christians, meanwhile, showed an inverse trend, peaking in the 1660s and then dropping to just six usages in the first three decades of the eighteenth century combined.

While some of the variation can be attributed to the types of acts that were being passed, the overall trend in undeniable: by the eighteenth century, whiteness had replaced Christianity as the primary indicator of nonslave status.[23]

The category of whiteness came into being within the Barbadian law books as a method of slave control. The first reference to the term was in the 1661 *Act for the better ordering and governing of Negroes.* If a "negro" was sentenced to death, the law entitled three freeholders to "cause execution to be done" either by the "common executioner" or "by what other executioner can be got either white man or negro." In this passage, the word "white" was used as a physical descriptor in opposition to the term "negro." The close proximity of "white man" and "negro" in this sentence suggests that whiteness was dependent on the literal and rhetorical existence of "negroes" for its conceptual development.[24] The second reference to whiteness came fifteen years later after the attempted slave rebellion in 1675. The Barbados Assembly passed *A supplemental Act to a former Act for the better ordering and governing of Negroes,* in which it warned that "any Negro or Negroes that shall be found out of the plantation . . . not having a white man with them," would be punished.[25] The same clause was repeated in 1688 in the newly revamped *Act for the governing of Negroes.* Again, the adjective "white" was used only within the context of "Negroes," not as a standalone term. Furthermore, in both cases, whiteness was defined within the context of slave control and punishment.[26]

Beginning in the 1690s, whiteness took on new meanings and connotations. While it remained an instrument of slave control, it also began to indicate ethnic identity, replacing the adjective "Christian" in the acts regarding servants. The 1696 *Act for the speedy supply of Arms, Ammunition, Stores and white Servants* used the word "white" rather than "Christian" to modify "servant," as did a series of acts "for the Encouragement of White Servants" passed in 1697, 1699, 1701 and 1703. It was in these acts that the shift from "Christian" to "white" is made most obvious. Up until 1696, the Barbados Assembly had periodically passed an act to encourage Barbadians to hire more servants to perform labor. These acts, the first of which was passed in 1677, were always given a variation on the title *An Act to encourage the bringing in of Christian Servants to this Island.* In 1697, just a year after the last of these acts was passed, a new version of the act was written. This act, however, had a new title: *An Act for the Encouragement of White Servants, and to ascertain their Allowance of Provisions and Clothes.* The sudden shift in the terminology referring to servants provides clear example of a more gradual change that was taking place in the Barbadian taxonomy.[27]

It was not until 1697, when the population of free black Christians had grown to at least thirty individuals, that the Assembly and Council clarified the definition of freeholder. The *Act to keep inviolate and preserve the freedom of Elections* acknowledged that "it hath not been hitherto fully and plainly ascertained how the Inhabitants of this Island shall be qualified to render them capable to Elect or be Elected Members of the Assembly or Vestry-Men, or to try real Actions." As a result, "manifold Disputes and Controversies have arisen." While the act did not explain what the "disputes and controversies" were, the existence of free nonwhite Christians likely provoked "disputes." It was after this preamble that the act specified that freeholders must be *"white M[e]n* professing the Christian Religion, the free and natural born Subject of the Kind of *England*, or naturalized, who hath attained to the full Age of One and Twenty Year, and hath Ten Acres of Freehold."[28]

While the 1697 act defined a freeholder as "white," a revised version of this act, passed twelve years later in 1709, went a step further. The second version of the *Act to keep inviolate, and preserve the Freedom of Elections* added a clause that narrowed the possible interpretation of "white": "And be it further enacted by the Authority aforesaid, That no Person whatsoever shall be admitted as a Freeholder, or an Evidence in any Case whatsoever, whose original Extract shall be proved to have been from a Negro, except only on the Tryal of Negroes and other Slaves."[29] This clause excluded not only slaves, but all freedmen who had any African ancestry, from enfranchisement. Significantly, it also rejected the testimony of nonwhite individuals from court "except . . . on the Tryal of Negroes and other Slaves."

The 1709 act is the first evidence of the "one drop rule" in Barbadian law. Instead of using "white" as physical descriptor or even a general ethnic category, it restricted enfranchisement to individuals with only European ancestry. It condemned free Christians, whether mixed-race or black, to underclass status, regardless of their religious affiliation or cultural practice.

Whiteness in the Protestant Atlantic

By the early eighteenth century the concept of whiteness had been transformed. While the term "white" had been used sparingly in the 1660s, 1670s, and 1680s, it was primarily a physical descriptor: "negros" had to be escorted by a "white man" if they wanted to leave their plantation without a ticket, for example. Christianity, rather than whiteness, was the defining feature of nonslave status on the island in the mid-seventeenth century. Servants were distinguished from slaves because they were "Christian" and slaves were forbidden to commit "any violence to any Christian." Over time, however, this taxonomy proved to be insufficient—or at least increasingly ambiguous. As a small number of slave owners chose to manumit favored slaves, many of these newly freed men and women recognized the political, social, and spiritual significance of Christianity, and sought out baptism for themselves. Once free and baptized, their presence created an implicit challenge to the standard taxonomy on the island: could all free, Christian and propertied men be accepted as freeholders? Or should those "English" liberties be reserved for Englishmen alone? The acts passed in the late 1690s answered those questions. They redefined the term "freeholder" to include whiteness as a prerequisite for enfranchisement, thereby excluding all free nonwhite Christians. In 1709, the revised *Act to keep inviolate, and preserve the Freedom of Elections* cleared up any doubt about the definition of whiteness by adding the clause that "no Person whatsoever shall be admitted as a Freeholder . . . whose original Extract shall be proved to have been from a Negro."[30] By the early eighteenth century, then, whiteness had been reified into a potent social and political category on Barbados, replacing Christianity as the most salient axis of difference.

The emergence of whiteness in Barbados paralleled developments in other Protestant colonies. In each case, the language of race was intimately connected to debates about slave conversion. Between 1660 and 1700, several colonies passed laws that sought to sever the relationship between Protestant baptism and freedom and to define slavery through race rather than religion. In 1664, the General Assembly in Maryland passed a law affirming that all blacks and other slaves "shall serve Durante Vita." While the act itself did not mention baptism, it was originally proposed because members of the assembly thought it "very necessary for the prevencion of the damage Masters of such Slaves may susteyne by such Slaves pretending to be Christned And soe please the lawe of England."[31] Such deliberation suggests that enslaved men and women recognized the close alignment of Protestant baptism and freedom and used it to their advantage.[32]

Another Maryland act, passed in 1671, took a more active stance on the issue. It asserted that slave owners had neglected to "instruct [their slaves] in the Christian faith" or allow them to "receive the holy Sacrament of Baptisme" because they believed that it would make their slaves free. The act reassured planters that an enslaved person could receive the sacrament of baptism after his or her arrival in the colony and still remain enslaved. Moreover, the children of baptized slaves would also serve for life.[33] Similarly, the 1665 "Duke's Laws" of New York assured colonists that the law would "not extend to sett at Liberty Any Negroe or Indian Servant who shall turne Christian after he shall have been bought by Any Person."[34] Virginia legislators were the next to address the issue of baptismal freedom when they, in 1667, answered questions about the legal status of enslaved children who, "by [the] Charity and piety of their owners," were made "p[ar]takers of the blessed Sacrament of Baptisme." The law affirmed that "the Conferring of Baptisme doth not allow the Condition of the slave as to his Bondage or freedome," and the lawmakers hoped that this affirmation would "Endeavore the propagation of Christianity by permitting Children though slaves, or those of greater growth if capable to be admitted to that sacrament."[35]

As in Barbados, the Virginia law was likely prompted by the rising status of enslaved and freed Christians. Rebecca Goetz has shown that in the decades leading up to the 1667 act, several enslaved people used baptism in order to bolster their arguments for freedom. While there is no evidence that an enslaved person was freed on the basis of baptism alone, baptism was "one of a number of factors [used] to negotiate . . . freedom."[36] In 1654, for example, the mixed-race woman Elizabeth Key sued for her freedom, using her status as a baptized Protestant to support her claim. She won her case on the grounds that "shee hath bin long since Christened Col. Higginson being her God father and that by report shee is able to give a very good account of her fayth."[37] In Key's case, her intimate relationships with whites, her Protestant baptism, and her knowledge of Christianity were the crucial factors leading to her manumission.

Even as a handful of colonies moved to separate the sacrament of baptism from the rights and freedoms of English people, it took time for the language of race to replace religion. Thus the inclusion of enslaved people within the Christian community remained an exception rather than the rule, and English colonists continued to use Christianity to distinguish Europeans from enslaved Africans and Indians. A 1670 statute in Virginia, for example, declared "all servants not being Christians imported into this country by shipping shalbe slaves for their lives," suggesting that slavery was defined by heathen status and method of arrival, rather than race.[38] In South Carolina, which was established in 1663 as a proprietorship, the 1669 Constitution made clear that conversion would not change the "civil dominion" of a master over a slave.[39] Despite this assurance, most slave owners in South Carolina—many of whom hailed from Barbados—resisted slave conversion.

As this conflicting evidence suggests, the last three decades of the seventeenth century were a period of transition, as Protestantism was gradually divorced from freedom in a piecemeal fashion, colony by colony. This shift was accompanied by the codification of racial slavery, as "white" replaced "Christian" in the colonial taxonomy. Edward Rugemer has shown that the Jamaica Slave Act of 1684, which was based on the 1661 Barbadian *Act for Better Ordering*, made one key change in the text of the act: they exchanged the word "Christian" for "white." The law also clarified that "if a slave were to become a Christian, conversion would in no way alter his or her status as a slave." Rugemer suggests that the Jamaican Assembly was responding directly to the criticism of Quakers like George Fox, as well as increased pressure from the bishop of London to promote slave conversion.[40] They may also have been responding to the presence of enslaved and free black Christians on the island.

In all of these cases, three interconnected influences spurred the creation of whiteness: the arguments of Protestant missionaries, the conversion of free and enslaved people of color, and the escalating pressure of imperial authorities who wanted Protestant slavery to be Christianized. Of those three factors, the actions of enslaved and freed Christians were likely the most important. As blacks recognized the significance of Protestant baptism and sought to secure more rights, slave owners responded by protecting their property and redefining mastery to emphasize race rather than religion. This strategic move was intended to weaken the status of free blacks and solidify their control over enslaved laborers.

The shift from "Christian" to "white" was halting and incomplete. Even as Protestant slave owners redefined mastery in racial terms, they continued to exclude the majority of enslaved men and women from Christian rites. The sustained resistance to slave conversion demonstrates the persistent connection between Protestantism and whiteness. The fledgling ideology of White Supremacy emerged from the foundation of Protestant Supremacy and it would take decades before slave owners felt secure enough in their whiteness to accept widespread slave conversion.[41] It would require strong proslavery arguments from missionaries and other concerned Protestants to convince planters that allowing their slaves to convert to Christianity would not threaten the stability of their societies.

Thus even as the language of whiteness emerged, missionaries and imperial authorities sought to reassure slave owners that Protestantism could coexist with enslavement. The enduring resistance to slave conversion is evident in the life of one Barbadian slave owner, Christopher Codrington, who struggled to reconcile slavery with his religious practice. Codrington, who was appointed governor-general of the Leeward Islands in 1699, tried to convince his fellow planters that conversion would not endanger their livelihoods. Yet he also recognized the political and inter-imperial dimensions of slave baptism. A focus on Codrington's life demonstrates the complicated and multi-faceted aspects of slave conversion as an imperial, political, and moral problem.

Chapter 5

The Imperial Politics of Slave Conversion

In 1698, Christopher Codrington, a third-generation Anglo-Barbadian, was appointed governor-general of the Leeward Islands. In his official instructions, Codrington was told to "see that Divine Service" was kept "according to the Church of England," to make sure that churches were "built and kept orderly" and "to encourage the conversion of negroes."[1] The imperial order regarding slave conversion was pro forma by the late seventeenth century, but Codrington's response was not. "The instruction I am most inclined [to follow]," he wrote, "I shall be least able to observe." Speaking specifically about the instruction to encourage slave conversion, he wrote, "I shall be certainly opposed by all the Planters . . . much more if I should promote the baptising of all our slaves."[2]

Christopher Codrington understood both colonial and metropolitan positions regarding slave conversion. Raised in Barbados as heir to one of the wealthiest sugar planters in the English empire, he was intimately acquainted with the ideology of Protestant Supremacy that kept enslaved men and women outside of Protestant churches. Yet unlike most white Creole planters at the time, Codrington was educated in England and spent much of his life in Europe. In London and Oxford, he encountered the pro-conversion stance that was common among elite Anglicans at the time. These connections gave Codrington unique insight into the entrenched challenges to slave conversion in the colonies as well as the insufficient and misguided metropolitan plans to promote Christianity among slaves.

Focusing on Codrington's life helps to illuminate the complicated struggle to reconcile Protestantism and slavery within an imperial context, even as race emerged as the primary justification for enslavement. Since Codrington was himself a major slaveowner, examining his world helps to create a more nuanced picture of Protestant planters. While Codrington was in favor of conversion in principle, like other Protestant slave owners, he agreed that "the christening of our negroes without the instructing of them would be useless to themselves and pernicious to their masters."[3]

A study of Codrington's life also reveals the influence of Catholic empires on Protestant ideas about slave conversion. Codrington spent many years both fighting and befriending the French. He participated in the Nine Years War in continental Europe as well as several expeditions against the French in the West Indies. During the brief period of peace between the Treaty of Ryswick and the War of Spanish Succession, he traveled between Paris and London, enjoying both English and French society. When he was appointed governor-general of the Leeward Islands, he lived on St. Christopher, a tiny island that was split into French and English sections. These experiences profoundly influenced Codrington's vision for a Christianized slave system. In the French example, Codrington saw an answer to the problem of slavery in the English colonies. Rather than relying on solitary ministers and missionaries, he concluded that Christianizing the Protestant colonies would require considerable institutional support.

When Codrington died, he bequeathed two of his Barbados plantations, part of the island of Barbuda, and several hundred slaves to a newly formed Anglican missionary organization, which he incorrectly named "the Society for propagation of the Christian Religion in Forreighn parts."[4] He wrote in his will that his plantations should serve as a college to train "Professors and Scholars" who were under "vows of Poverty Chastity and obedience." The reference to vows of poverty, chastity and obedience were identical to those taken by Jesuits and exposed the depth of Codrington's admiration for French Catholic practices.

Codrington's vision had far-reaching, though unexpected, consequences. When he died in 1710, his will transformed the newly created Anglican missionary society, the Society for the Propagation of the Gospel in Foreign Parts (SPG), into a slave-owning organization, a topic explored in the following chapter. This chapter focuses on Codrington's life and emphasizes the importance of viewing slave conversion as both a religious and an imperial issue. As governor-general, Codrington saw how slave baptism influenced imperial politics. It could be used to mobilize support for a regime or to justify an attack on an enemy island. Religious opportunity also affected the decisions of enslaved men and women who were aware that the Catholic Church offered benefits that were not available in Protestant colonies. These political aspects of slave conversion are a reminder that Protestants constructed and enacted their policies on slavery and Christianity in the shadow of Catholic empires. As I showed in Chapter 1, Protestants simultaneously derided and envied Catholic custom, grudgingly acknowledging that Catholics had converted far more enslaved people than Protestants. Acknowledging the significance of interimperial exchange on Protestant ideas about slavery shows how debates about slave conversion in the Atlantic world were constantly evolving in a dynamic, multi-imperial, and multireligious context.

Slavery, Baptism, and Freedom Among the French and English

The French, like the English and Dutch, had a long and cherished tradition of "free soil" that equated the boundaries of France with freedom.[5] In the seventeenth century, when France began to colonize parts of the Americas and French merchants eagerly engaged in the slave trade, French theologians and legal scholars, like their Protestant counterparts, debated how "free soil" and Catholic baptism could be reconciled with slavery. The French philosopher Jean Bodin criticized the Portuguese and Spaniards who, "having brought the Negroes into the Christian religion, keep them nevertheless and all their posterities for slaves."[6] In 1607, the French legal scholar Antoine Loisel wrote that "all persons are free in this Kingdom, and as soon as a slave reaches its borders and is baptized, he is manumitted."[7] These concerns were strikingly similar to those of English and Dutch Protestants and they show that debates about slavery and baptism were not confined to the Protestant Atlantic world.

Over the course of the seventeenth century, the French practice of enslavement diverged from English, Dutch, and Danish custom. In 1625, a Norman sailor named Belain d'Esnambuc settled the island of Saint-Christophe. After obtaining a royal charter for the Compagnie de Saint-Christophe et îles adjacentes, French settlers eagerly engaged in the slave trade. Ten years later, the Company had expanded into the nearly islands of Martinique, Guadeloupe and Dominica. The rapidly growing number of slaves within the French imperial domain renewed debates about Catholicism, "free soil," and slavery. As in the Protestant Atlantic, concerns were raised about whether baptism would result in manumission. The Capuchins, in particular, were vociferous and unrelenting in their attack of French colonial slaveholding. They argued that baptized slaves should not be sold and they questioned the legitimacy of enslavement.[8]

French authorities responded to these concerns as early as 1646, when Commandeur Blondel de Longvilliers de Poincy confirmed that "the Christian 'Negroes' and their descendants were to be maintained in perpetual bondage."[9] The Capuchins were expelled from Saint-Christophe and replaced with missionaries of the Dominican and Jesuit orders who were eager to demonstrate the compatibility of Catholicism and slavery.[10] Unlike the Capuchins, Dominican and Jesuit missionaries argued that enslavement was necessary for Africans' salvation and that slaves generally preferred captivity to freedom in a heathen land. The Dominican missionary Jean-Baptiste Du Tertre insisted that slavery originated in Africa and that "fifteen thousand slaves, who would never have had any knowledge of God in their country," had been baptized in the French islands. Slavery was "the principle of their happiness," and "their disgrace is the cause of their salvation, because the faith they embrace in the islands prepares them to know God, and to love and serve him."[11]

The Jesuit and Dominican presence was integral to the spread of Catholicism among the enslaved population. In 1655, the Jesuit missionary Pierre Pelleprat described how he met with both Indians and Africans on holy days, and that they had "translated the Lord's Prayer, the Hail Mary, and the Apostle's Creed, the Ten Commandments, etc., into their languages."[12] Jean Mongin, a Jesuit missionary who lived on Saint-Christophe in the 1680s, wrote that enslaved people were generally receptive to baptism. He catechized newly arrived slaves in order to prepare them for baptism and presented those who progressed with a gift, such as "an image, a medallion, or a rosary."[13] French slave owners, unlike their Protestant counterparts, were generally unperturbed by the conversion of enslaved people. Jean Mongin wrote that most were eager to have their slaves baptized. Some, however, prevented their slaves from marrying in the church because it made selling them more difficult. Mongin "took some masters to court" to fight for enslaved couples' right to marry. He also advocated for enslaved people who were mistreated by their owners.[14]

In the second half of the seventeenth century, the French expanded their Caribbean holdings and in 1664, they placed all French islands under the authority of the Compagnie des Indes Occidentales. This administrative shift was part of a larger effort to standardize colonial policies regarding slavery.[15] In the same year, governor-general de Tracy's *Reglement*, the "Police des Isles," defined "Negroes" as "movable property" and urged masters to baptize their slaves.[16] Twenty years later, King Louis XIV went a step further when he issued the *Code Noir* (1685), a wide-ranging edict on the regulation of slavery and Catholicism in the French Caribbean.

The *Code Noir* sought to alleviate concerns that slavery was un-Christian.[17] It ordered masters to instruct and baptize their slaves and prohibited work on Sundays and holy days. Masters could still beat their slaves, but "torturing, mutilating, and killing . . . remained in the exclusive domain of royal judges."[18] Catholicism was proclaimed the sole religion of the French empire and the public exercise of any other religion was explicitly banned. The *Code Noir* also required all overseers and managers of plantations to be Catholic. Overall, the *Code Noir* paired royal absolutism with Catholic hegemony.[19]

Over time, demographic and political shifts would undermine the missionary effort in the French Caribbean. In Saint-Domingue, slaves outnumbered free people by a ratio of 9:1 by 1754. This transformation, coupled with the rise of anticlericalism, led to a suppression of mission work. The expulsion of the Jesuit order in the 1750s and 1760s compounded the decline of the Catholic mission to slaves in the French Caribbean.[20] But at the end of the seventeenth century, the majority of enslaved people in the French Antilles were baptized Catholics. The spread of Catholicism was aided by the choices of enslaved men and women, a lack of resistance among Catholic slave owners, and the efforts of the Catholic missionaries, particularly the Dominicans and Jesuits.

While the French fortified their Catholic identity, purging Protestants from their midst and clarifying the relationship between slavery and Catholicism, England moved in a different direction. In 1688, the Catholic-leaning James II fled to France. William of Orange and his wife Mary, the daughter of Charles II, captured the crown in the so-called Glorious Revolution. The new rulers moved quickly to affirm the Protestant culture of the country and they offered freedom of worship to nonconforming Protestant denominations in the Toleration Act of 1689.[21] The Toleration Act secured the Church of England's privileged place as the national church, but by officially tolerating dissent, it weakened the coercive power of the church and led to fears that moral and social turmoil would follow. In this new environment, Anglican churchmen took it upon themselves to promote their church's role in English life by founding their own voluntary societies.[22]

In the decades after the Glorious Revolution, Anglicans and nonconformists alike showed a heightened concern for manners and moral reform and they founded voluntary societies to combat perceived vices. The early 1690s saw the establishment of the Society for the Reformation of Manners (SRM), the first of many such organizations that aimed to reduce heterodox thinking and sinful behavior by prosecuting offenses like drunkenness, prostitution, and swearing. The SRMs melded religious and secular aims by focusing on public order—a strategy characteristic of the period. By 1694, there were sixteen similar societies with nearly three hundred members (almost all male) operating in London and Westminster.[23]

The most important Anglican visionary was Thomas Bray, an English clergyman who feared the influence of Quakers and other nonconformists on the national English character. In the wake of the Toleration Act, he wrote: "The Enemy has . . . enter'd through our Breaches into the very heart of our City (as St. Austin calls the Church of God). . . . All the Grand and Fundamental Articles, both of Natural and Revealed Religion, are now either most furiously storm'd by Atheists, Deists, and Socinians on the one hand, or secretly and dangerously undermined by Enthusiasts and Antimoniams on the other."[24] Bray hoped to strengthen the Anglican Church by founding lending libraries and creating a central missionary body to promote the Church of England.

In accordance with this vision, Bray joined together with other concerned churchmen in 1699 to form the Society for the Propagation of Christian Knowledge (SPCK), the forerunner of the SPG, which was founded two years later. The SPCK counted among its ranks both high and low churchmen; Tories and Whigs. As a result of this complex political makeup, the SPCK focused on broad, consensus-oriented goals that would strengthen the role of the clergy within English society. They promoted catechisms, literacy, and moral teaching in order to reinvigorate the Anglican Church.

Christopher Codrington and Slave Conversion

It is likely that Christopher Codrington knew of the SPCK when it was founded in 1699. While he was not a member of the organization, his

Oxford tutor, George Smalbridge, would later become an influential member of SPG, the SPCK's sister organization. Several of his relatives in Gloucestershire also had ties to the SPCK and the Bristol SRM.[25] Either way, he was certainly influenced by the prevailing culture of religious voluntarism and the concern for moral reform that pervaded elite English society. Like other reformers, he was worried about the religious state of the English colonies. But unlike Bray, who focused his efforts on converting English people at home and abroad, Codrington was more interested in the prospect of slave conversion.

Codrington brought a new perspective to the debates about slavery and Protestantism based on his upbringing in Barbados, his education in England, and his experience fighting the French. His grandfather, Christopher Codrington I, had been one of the pioneer colonists of Barbados. He arrived in 1628, just after the first settlement of the island, and married the sister of Sir James Drax, a prominent settler of Barbados who helped to introduce sugar cultivation on the island. Codrington I followed his brother-in-law's lead by becoming one of the first sugar planters in the English Caribbean. Christopher Codrington II, who was born on Barbados in 1640, took advantage of his father's early connections and land to amass a huge amount of wealth as a planter, soldier, and politician. He became a member of the Barbados Council at twenty-six and was appointed deputy governor in 1669 at twenty-nine. He also extended his reach beyond Barbados, purchasing large tracts of land in Antigua and Barbuda with his brother John.[26]

Codrington III, who was born in 1668, spent the first years of his life at his family's estate in St. John parish, one of the less populated regions of Barbados. At age twelve, Codrington was sent to England for education, where he was influenced by the social thought of the day. The opportunity to attend school in England set Christopher III apart from his father and grandfather. The elder Codringtons had focused their efforts on building the family fortune in the West Indies. When Christopher III was born in 1668, the social standards of the Barbadian elite had begun to evolve. As big planters consolidated their power, they sought new ways to assert their prestige through both wealth and cultural practice. Central to their sense of identity was the concept of "Englishness."[27] The Barbadian elite cultivated their English identity by sending their sons back to England to be educated in the elite institutions of the mother country. Thus like other successful West Indian planters, Christopher Codrington II decided to send

Figure 5. Christopher Codrington, by R. Clamp, after Sir James Thornhill. Stipple engraving, published 1796. Courtesy of the National Portrait Gallery, London.

his young son to school in England to renew and reassert his family's English identity.

Christopher Codrington III would have been one of the first Anglo–Caribbeans to participate in this ritual of reconnection. He arrived in England in 1680 and was educated first at Dr. Wedale's school in Enfield before continuing on to Oxford in 1685. At Oxford, Codrington developed a love for books, theater, and other literary engagements. He also met a number of influential individuals who remained lifelong friends. Among these were his tutor, George Smalridge; Robert Boyle's great nephew Charles Boyle; the politician and writer Joseph Addison; and the classical scholar Thomas Creech. Charles Boyle would later defend Codrington against attacks, while George Smalridge's brother John became the manager of Codrington's Barbados plantations.[28]

In 1692, Codrington was granted a leave from Oxford to volunteer for military service in the Antilles, where King William hoped to expel the French from the area. He arrived in Barbados on February 28, where he reunited with his father. The elder Codrington had increased both his wealth and his prominence during his son's absence. Now, as governor-general of the Leeward Islands, he contributed troops and ammunition to the military expedition. The mission succeeded in raiding French sugar mills and settlements in Martinique, but it was eventually abandoned after illness, military failures, and waning supplies weakened the troops. In late April, Governor Codrington sailed back to the Leewards with his son so the two men could examine the military resources on Antigua, Nevis, and St. Christopher—an experience that would prove valuable when the younger Codrington replaced his father as governor-general.[29]

After a month of travel, Codrington III departed for North America and then England with his regiment. The expedition itself had been a failure, but Codrington returned to Oxford with important experience and a captaincy title. He graduated from Oxford the following January with a Master of Arts, thereby bringing his formal education to a close. In the spring of 1694, Codrington continued his military engagement as a private captain in King William's effort to expel the French from Flanders. Once peace was declared in 1697, the twenty-nine-year-old Codrington traveled between Paris and London, where he spent time with his friends Charles Boyle, Spencer Compton, and Matthew Prior.[30] His days were largely spent writing poetry, collecting books, and socializing. Aside from literary and theatrical pursuits, Codrington became acquainted with John Locke and continued to deepen his love for philosophy that he had cultivated at Oxford.[31]

Codrington voiced his concerns about slave conversion as early as 1699, the same year that Bray formed the SPCK. In 1698, Codrington received the news that his father had died suddenly in Antigua and in February 1699, he was rewarded for his military service with his late father's post as governor-general of the Leeward Islands. It was then that he proposed to William Popple that the English islands were in need of a "regular clergy . . . under vows of poverty and obedience." Codrington suggested that Popple "humbly propose" his idea to "the Archbishop and Bishop of London." If they were able to find "a number of apostolical men who are willing to take much pains for little reward," Codrington would promise both "protection and countenance." The degree of Codrington's commitment is evident in his concluding statement: "I am very sincere in this matter. . . . [N]oe consideration of interest shall hinder me from promoting boldly and impartially a design that may be pleasing to God and truely beneficial to my fellow-creatures."[32]

By the end of the seventeenth century, then, Christopher Codrington had already identified slave conversion as a key element of concern. Unlike many of his compatriots in London, however, he was sympathetic to the concerns of Protestant planters and recognized the difficulties involved in converting enslaved men and women to Christianity. With his Barbadian upbringing and English education, he brought a new perspective to the debate on Protestantism and slavery.

Slave Conversion and Imperial Politics

Slave conversion was not only a moral concern. It was also an important factor in imperial politics. In 1699, Codrington began conducting affairs as the governor-general of the Leewards. Of chief interest during this time was the island of St. Christopher. With a total area of just sixty-five square miles, St. Christopher had long been split between the French and English. The result was a fraught coexistence in which both English and French inhabitants were at the mercy of imperial politics and wars beyond their control. In 1666, the French had conquered the entire island, but the Peace of Breda reversed their victory and restored English claim to half the island. In 1690, the English repaid the favor and drove the French from the island. The Treaty of Ryswick, however, returned the island to its prewar status, meaning that the English were forced to return part of the island to French control. It was during this moment of transition that the younger Christopher Codrington was appointed governor-general.[33]

The process of transference was complicated by a number of factors. First was the French accusation that the English had intentionally burned

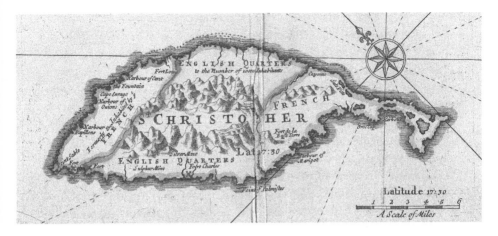

Figure 6. Detail of the island of Saint Christopher from *The principall islands in America belonging to the English Empire* (London, [1696]). The English-controlled portion of the island was flanked on either side by French-controlled areas. Courtesy of the John Carter Brown Library, Brown University.

their plantations after the Treaty was signed, thereby depriving the French of their livelihood. In a letter from two French officials to the Council of Trade and Plantations in London, the officials complained that when the French returned to the island, "they found all the houses and shops ruined and demolished, wells spoiled and filled, reservoirs burst, sugar canes eaten by cattle or burnt, all within six or seven months." They demanded that "instructions should be given to M. de Codrington to compel the individuals who have done this shameful damage or who have made a profit out of it to indemnify the French proprietors or at least to replace at their own expense the materials they have removed."[34] The Council of St. Christopher disputed these accusations and wrote that much of the destruction had occurred before peace was declared and in accordance with the instructions of the elder Codrington. Anything afterwards was done "without any authority and not known, and might be as well by negroes as white men."[35]

The second complication involved runaway slaves. During their conquest of the island, the English had captured a number of enslaved men and women belonging to the French. When the French returned to the island, they demanded that their slaves be returned to them. The English responded that the slaves were legitimate war spoils, though a number of the captured slaves ran back to their French masters of their own accord.

Apparently, some of the runaway slaves included several from the Codrington estate. In 1699, the President and Council of Nevis reported that "21 negroes belonging to Col. Codrington and Col. John Hamilton of Antigua" had run away to the French "since the conclusion of the peace." The report went on to note that the English feared that their slaves, many of whom were taken from the French during the war, would continue to run away.[36]

Codrington was unwavering in his support for English imperial interests, which aligned nicely with his own. In a letter to the Council of Trade and Plantations dated July 10, 1699, Codrington insisted, "the negroes became the property of the conquerors, were fairly divided between the fleet and army and sold off." He maintained that the English position was "founded on the Law of Nations" and added, "the negroes are as much our property as our cattle." The most intriguing element of Codrington's response, however, related to religion. At some point, the French referred to the fact that many of their slaves had been baptized as Catholics. They likely argued that Catholic slaves should remain under Catholic—and French—imperial control, rather than English. To this, Codrington answered, "The pretence of religion is idle. Christianity does not alter the condition of men nor destroy the right of tenure by which slaves are held. This is incontestable in the Civil Law and the French practise in consequence of it." These sentences indicate that Codrington knew about the debate regarding the role of Protestantism in the English slave colonies and that he believed that the issue had been resolved in law. Codrington also criticized French practice, noting that while they "baptise all their slaves," he "dare[d] not say they make them Christians." He, like most other Protestants, was skeptical of Catholic baptismal practices. Baptized slaves in the French colonies, he suggested, could not be considered true Christians because they were not sufficiently educated and prepared.[37]

Codrington's comments demonstrate the political ramifications of the debate about slave baptism. Conversion could be used to mobilize support for an imperial regime or to justify an attack on an enemy island. Codrington was particularly critical of the French argument that it was religious "conscience" that led them to "keep our negroes." As he elaborated in a letter to the Lords of Trade and Plantations, "Suppose, My Lords, five hundred or a thousand or ten thousand negroes should get off Barbados to Martineque and applying themselves to the Monks would undoubtedly admit them to baptism, and the negroes would of course be good Roman Catholicks, the French might then say, though they could not keep our negroes as slaves, yet they were obliged to protect them as men and Christians desiring to live as good Roman Catholicks, and who, if restored to the English would not be allowed the practice of that religion."[38] Codrington feared that Catholic baptism could be used to lure enslaved men and women away from the English and into French hands. The French could then use the slaves' Catholic status to retain them on the grounds that if they were "restored to the English," they "would not be allowed the practice of [Catholicism]."[39]

Codrington also knew that enslaved people made strategic decisions regarding baptism and that they sought out the protections of the Catholic Church when possible. As Codrington explained in a letter to the Council of Trade and Plantations: "a great number of negroes will certainly get off in sloops and boats, both from a natural desire of changing their masters upon the least severe usage, and upon the encouragement of these many holydays the French allow their slaves."[40] Apart from a greater number of holy days, enslaved people likely knew that it was sometimes possible to appeal to priests in order to gain protection from violent masters or to resist being sold away from their families—opportunities that were not available in English islands.[41]

Franco-English Exchange in the Caribbean

In 1700, Codrington met Francis Le Jau, a French Protestant from Angers, France. Le Jau was one of thousands of Huguenots who fled France after the revocation of the Edict of Nantes in 1685. The Edict of Nantes, which was issued in 1598 by Henry IV, had ended the Wars of Religion and granted French Protestants religious, economic, and political rights. Less than a century later, however, Louis XIV revoked the edict in an effort to make Catholicism the sole religion of the empire. The revocation was issued the same year as the *Code Noir* and both sought to solidify the Catholic identity of France and its colonies. The revocation banned the practice of Protestantism and forced Huguenots to convert, resist, or clandestinely flee, since emigration was prohibited. While most converted, thousands of Huguenots fled France and emigrated to Protestant lands throughout the Atlantic world.[42]

Le Jau left France in 1685 when he was twenty years old. He first immigrated to England, where he converted to Anglicanism. Soon thereafter, he attended Trinity College, Dublin, where he earned an MA (1693), BD (1696), and DD (1700).[43] Le Jau would later become known as one of the most successful missionaries for the SPG. Before then, however, he served as a parish minister in the Leeward Islands. He arrived in Montserrat in March 1700, just months before Codrington. It is unclear when the two men met, but Le Jau reported later that the governor was his "great friend" and that Codrington "did what he could to relieve him" of the miseries of his post. As Le Jau explained, the parish system in the Leeward Islands was in great disrepair. In Montserrat, he found only one minister serving four parishes. In St. Christopher, Le Jau himself was responsible for three parishes and, like other colonial ministers, he was dependent on the inhabitants for his maintenance. While they provided him with a "house built with wild Canes & Thatcht," the structure was "never finish'd," and he did not receive the £60 sterling per year that he had been promised.[44]

In their meetings together, Le Jau and Codrington discussed the state of Christianity in the islands. Like Le Jau, Codrington felt that ministers should be provided with a salary from London so that their position was not so "precarious." When churchmen were "at the Mercy of the People," they were unable to "do their duty without fear." The tension between ministers and lay people was particularly acute with regard to slave treatment and baptism. While Le Jau found "the Negroes [to be] generally sensible & well disposed to learn," he felt it was "the Barbarity of their Masters which makes 'em stubborn." Lacking food or clothing, slaves were forced to steal to survive. The only time they were able to work for themselves was on Sunday, meaning that any minister who "proposed the Negroes should be Instructed in the Christian faith" would be met with resistance. Furthermore, Le Jau had "2000 Negroes in his parishes," which was clearly "too much for one Minister to instruct."[45]

In contrast to the English, "the French papists" on St. Christopher had "5 or 6 Ministers [for the same] Number of Negroes." Enslaved and free blacks could be "baptiz'd & married in their Churches," they "kept Sundays and holy days" free, and "had officers to hear & redress their Grievances." This was due, in part, to the fact that the French clergymen "had their Maintenance ascertain'd." The existence of baptized slaves in the French and Spanish colonies, he continued, was well known to English planters. So while many planters claimed that baptism would "make [their] Negroes free," this was purely deceitful. The real source of anticonversion sentiment,

Le Jau believed, was that "the Planters would be obliged to look upon [their slaves] as Christian Brethren, & use 'em with humanity."[46]

Le Jau's report provides insight into Codrington's own experiences and opinions during his tenure as governor. Codrington's letters from 1699—before he departed for his post—show that he was already concerned about the "souls" of slaves. It is no surprise, then, that he became "great friend[s]" with Le Jau, a minister who shared his concerns. While the actual content of their conversations is a matter of conjecture, the two men certainly influenced each other's thoughts and convictions on the subject. The fact that Le Jau would go on to become one of the few missionaries to pursue an agenda of slave conversion in North America while Codrington would bequeath an unprecedented fortune to the SPG is hardly a coincidence. The two men took seriously the role of Christianity in a slave society, and both sought to improve the Protestant example by building on Catholic precedent.

Le Jau's comments point to the significance of interimperial exchange for English ideas about slave conversion. While English and French people intermingled throughout the Atlantic world, St. Christopher fostered a unique level of fraught intimacy. With the French settled on either end of the island and the English in the middle, colonists were compelled to coexist with an unusual level of closeness. Interactions between French and English settlers were common, particularly during peacetime, and cultural differences in slaveholding practices were on full display. The high level of familiarity between English and French colonists was evident in Le Jau's comments. He reported extensively not only on the French practice of baptizing slaves and funding colonial priests, but also gave a detailed description of the French part of the island. Like the English, the French had split their colony into six parishes. But while the English churches were made of "wild canes & thatch'd," the French had "2 stately stone churches."[47]

The French were also well aware of English precedent. One particularly astute observer was the French priest Jean-Baptiste Labat, a Dominican monk who served in the French Antilles from 1694 to 1705. Initially appointed as a parish priest in Martinique, Labat went on to become the *Procureur Synic* of the Martinique mission and, in 1702, the Superior of the Guadeloupe Mission. He later published an account of his life in the West Indies entitled *Nouveau voyage aux isles de l'Amerique*.[48] During his decade in the West Indies, Labat traveled extensively, visiting Dominica, St. Vincent, St. Lucia, San Domingo, and St. Christopher, among others.[49] In 1700, he traveled to Barbados, where he observed that the English clergy "do not instruct [the slaves] and do not baptise them." In his opinion, the English regarded their enslaved laborers "as beasts to whom every licence is allowed." They permitted their slaves to "have several wives and to leave them as they please." Punishments were severe, leading many slaves to rebel against the "ruthless tyrants" and forcing the English to "resort to arms" to suppress revolt.[50] While Labat's text was intended to valorize the French colonial venture at the expense of the English, it is significant that many of his observations correspond with those made by Le Jau and Codrington, as well as other English observers. Both French and English authors agreed that the English provided very little support for colonial ministers and that English planters generally refused to baptize their slaves.

Labat's thoughts about English slave culture are of particular interest because Labat met Codrington in late 1701, about a year before Codrington wrote his will. En route between Guadeloupe and Santo Domingo, Labat stopped at St. Christopher, where he dined at the home of an English officer. By coincidence, Codrington called on the officer the same evening and Labat reported it was "a piece of pure good fortune" because he had "long wished to meet" the governor-general.[51] Labat's description of the evening provides another perspective on Codrington's comportment and behavior as the governor of the Leeward Islands. Before his arrival, "trumpets were heard," a common practice to announce the governor's presence. Aside from the two trumpeters who "rode in front," Codrington was accompanied by eight servants and "nine or ten negroes" who "ran in front of the trumpeters." At dinner, Labat introduced himself to Codrington as "an engineer" and he was amused to hear that Codrington's companion, who was clearly a "chaplain," also introduced himself as an engineer. Labat's thinly veiled disguise—and his ability to recognize other disguises—is suggestive of the broader culture of interaction between French and English. By turning a blind eye to religious identity, imperial representatives could interact more easily with their "enemies."[52]

At the dinner table, Labat was impressed and flattered by Codrington's willingness to speak French, but found him and the other Englishmen "vain." He was particularly appalled by the way the governor spoke about the Irish. Codrington, for his part, asked the priest a "hundred questions about [his] voyage." He spoke "so quickly" that Labat could not keep up. "He asked two or three questions before I had time to answer," the priest wrote afterwards. Labat also noted that Codrington "was far more sober than are most of his nation as a rule." Labat's comments give an impression of a man who was serious, curious, and self-important. Codrington was legitimately interested to hear about Labat's experiences and travels, but he spoke with arrogance about other nations, and thought highly of himself.[53]

Labat did not mention whether he discussed religion with Codrington, though it is possible that he did. Regardless, it is clear that Codrington's thoughts on slave missions were greatly influenced not only by French precedent, but also by his personal relationships with French Catholics on St. Christopher. These day-to-day interactions between English and French settlers had consequences—not only for imperial politics, but also for the culture of Protestant slavery.

Last Will and Testament

On May 4, 1702, the newly crowned Queen Anne formally declared war against Louis XIV, thereby joining the War of Spanish Succession. When Codrington heard the news, he moved quickly to expel the French from St. Christopher and Nevis. After succeeding in this initial endeavor, he hoped to move on to Martinique and Guadeloupe. Yet months passed before reinforcements from England arrived. Codrington urged his home government to move quickly, emphasizing the importance of swift action. While he waited, he raised troops of his own on St. Christopher's, though his efforts were frustrated by deep-seated resentments and divisions within the colonial population. So when a sickly and inadequate force of English troops finally arrived in Antigua in February of 1703, Codrington was deeply disappointed. The delays had given the French time to prepare for their attack and Codrington's opportunity to attach his name to a great military victory was receding quickly.[54]

It was at this moment that Christopher Codrington decided to write a will. On February 22, 1703, Codrington sat down to compose a "Last Will and Testament" in which he disposed of his "worldly Estate."[55] He dispersed a number of his plantations to his "nearest Kinsman," the Lieutenant Col. William Codrington, providing smaller amounts to other friends and family members. To his alma mater All Souls College, Oxford, Codrington gave his book collection along with £10,000 to be used for the construction of a new library. And to the "Society for propagation of the Christian Religion in Forreighn parts," he gave his Barbados plantations and part of the island of Barbuda. His "desier" was:

> To have the Plantations Continued Intire and three hundred negros at Least Kept always thereon, and A Convenient number of Professors and Scholars Maintained there, all of them to be under the vows of Poverty Chastity and obedience, who shall be oblidged to Studdy and Practice Physick and Chyrurgery as well as divinity, that by the apparent usefulness of the former to all mankind, they may Both indear themselves to the People and have the better oppertunitys of doeing good To mens Souls whilst they are Takeing Care of their Bodys. But the Particulars of the Constitution I Leave to the Society Compos'd of good and wise men.[56]

This short paragraph, tucked in the middle of Codrington's will, would later force the SPG to redefine itself as a slaveholding organization. Yet the text itself puzzled many early readers—particularly its reference to "vows of Poverty Chastity and obedience," which seemed oddly Catholic. In order to decipher this passage, it is important to recognize how Codrington's experiences in England, France, and the Caribbean influenced his thoughts and hopes for the English empire and its colonial citizens. In bringing a "number of Professors and Scholars" to his Barbados plantation, Codrington aimed to transport some small part of Oxford to the West Indies and to cultivate Barbados as a center for learning and education. The obligation "to Studdy and Practice Physick and Chyrurgery as well as divinity" was a recognition of the physical challenges presented by life in the Caribbean. Sickness and death were a matter of daily life and Codrington himself had battled a number of serious illnesses. Furthermore, with "three hundred negros" on the plantation, Codrington hoped that medicine and religion would work together by "doeing good To mens Souls whilst . . . Takeing Care of their Bodys."

Finally, Codrington revealed the enduring influence of his French Catholic acquaintances when he insisted that all scholars should be under "vows of Poverty Chastity and obedience." As the Rev. William Gordon would later explain to the SPG, Codrington hoped his estate would be filled with "monks and missionaries" who would be "employed in the Conversion of Negroes and Indians." He developed this idea, Gordon wrote, "from his Conversation with a Learned Jesuit of St. Christophers," with whom he exchanged "several letters about ye Antiquity, Usefulness, and Excellency of a Monastic Life." Whether the learned Jesuit was Labat or another priest, the influence of the Catholic orders and their role in New World slave societies was powerful.[57]

On April 7, 1710, Christopher Codrington died in his childhood home at the age of forty-two. He was buried the following day in St. Michael's Church, Barbados, where the Rev. William Gordon gave his funeral sermon. Gordon heaped praise on Codrington for knowing the "True Value of Learning and Piety," characterizing him as "an Accomplish'd Well-bred Gentleman" and a "Universal Scholar" who had an "Affection for a Monastic Life." After learning of Codrington's bequest to the SPG, Gordon added an introductory letter to his sermon and dedicated it to the members of the Society. In his introduction, Gordon wrote that Codrington's will would "set a Noble PATTERN to all those, whom Providence hath Blessed with Plentiful Fortunes, arising from their Commerce with the *yet Dark and Unbelieving Parts of the World*." He hoped that others would "Consecrat[e] some Part of their Great *Estates*, to the Conversion and Instruction of those *Infidels*, to whose Labour, under Providence, they owe their Wealth and Affluence."[58]

Codrington, who died unexpectedly of fever, may have intended to compose a longer and more explicit will. As the attorneys of the estate wrote the following year, his was "a Soldier's Will" written while Codrington was "in his boots" preparing for the expedition to Guadaloupe.[59] William Gordon felt that if Codrington had been "more Apprehensive of his Death," he would have "done yet Greater Things for the advancement of Learning and Piety."[60] As it was, it was left to the living to interpret and execute Codrington's last wishes. Unfortunately for the SPG, the unusual language of his bequest—particularly the reference to "vows of poverty chastity and obedience"—provided grounds for dispute. Soon after his will was made public, Lieutenant William Codrington, Codrington's closest kinsman, presented a litany of arguments against the legality of Codrington's bequest. He argued that the Society was not legally qualified to take the estates; that Codrington's bequest was "popish & consequently . . . void"; and that seventy of the slaves on his estate had been purchased after his death and thus belonged to his heir at law.[61]

As controversy brewed, William Gordon wrote to the SPG, informing them of the situation and providing critical information about Codrington's intentions. It is from Gordon, rather than the text of Codrington's will, that slave conversion is listed as a principal concern and Codrington's French Catholic influences are explained. As Gordon wrote, "the design of the bequest was the maintenance of Monks and Missionaries" who were to be "employed in the Conversion of Negroes and Indians." Codrington's ideas were taken "from his Conversation with a Learned Jesuit of St. Christophers" with whom he had exchanged "several letters about ye Antiquity, Usefulness, and Excellency of a Monastic Life." Gordon also noted that he had sent his funeral sermon to London to be printed and that Dr. George Smalridge, Codrington's Oxford tutor, would "present it to them, on [his] behalf."[62] On November 17, 1710, the secretary of the SPG reported that he had received "several copies of a Sermon preach'ed by the Reverend Mr. William Gordon at the funeral of General Codrington (which sermon was dedicated to the Society)" by Dr. Smalridge. Smalridge wanted the secretary to distribute the sermon to "every Member."[63]

Upon receipt of Codrington's will in 1710, the Society made a critical change to the document. As noted previously, Codrington's reference to "vows of poverty Chastity and obedience" raised eyebrows among many and became fodder for one of William Codrington's many arguments against the document's legitimacy. Several members of the Society also questioned the meaning of the phrase. As Codrington's friend, Bishop Tanner, wrote in a letter, the reference seemed "very monastic," a subtle but damning comment.[64] Archbishop Tenison addressed the issue as well. While he did not claim outright that the phrase was too Catholic, he did tactfully reject Codrington's wishes, citing a lack of "stock": "As to the proposal of breeding up poor Boys in order to their being Missionaries, it was spoken of at the beginning of the Society, but the stock was too slender to Admit of it. Now we have another expedient of that kind, Col. Codrington's College. . . . The cutting of any other Channels, will (I fear) drain our Stock too much."[65] As this passage shows, Archbishop Tenison reinterpreted Codrington's vision of scholars who were under "vows of poverty, chastity, and obedience" as a call to "breed . . . up poor Boys." Recruiting and training poor boys for work in the mission field was a more palatable option for Anglicans and, as Tenison mentioned, the Society had considered such an option at the beginning of the century. Yet neither option was feasible: As Tenison noted, such a plan would "drain our Stock too much." In the end, the reference to "vows of Poverty Chastity and obedience" was quietly deleted from Codrington's will.

This alteration, while seemingly minor, signaled an underlying problem in the Protestant missionary enterprise: lack of infrastructure and funding.

Not only did Codrington's plan sound too Catholic, it also required too much investment. The SPG did not have the ability to support the education, training, and deployment of the number of missionaries that could enact Codrington's plan. While financing could not ensure success, the lack of institutional support and the insufficient missionary supply plagued the SPG in Barbados and elsewhere. It was this dual problem—of financing and philosophy—that doomed the Society's program of slave conversion in the Caribbean. Instead of creating a robust missionary institution on Codrington's estates, the Society sent only one catechist to combat the entrenched opposition of colonial planters. Their master-centered missionary approach further weakened their appeal to slaves.

Christopher Codrington was a man of many worlds: as a slave owner and governor-general of the Leeward Islands, he was intimately aware of the anticonversion sentiment of his Protestant planter peers. With his elite English education, he was familiar with the ideology of Christian Slavery heralded by Quakers and Anglican elites. His experience fighting and befriending the French, both in Europe and in the Caribbean, gave Codrington further insight into the relationship between slavery and Christianity.

In his struggle to bridge the ideologies of Christian slavery and Protestant Supremacy, Codrington looked to the French Catholic example in order to create a new vision for slavery based on missionary monasticism. While the SPG sought to downplay the Catholic influence on Codrington's will, it was undeniably significant. Codrington's dream of a monastic college was just one example of the persistent and dynamic influence of Catholicism on Protestant ideas about slave conversion. It was a vision that had consequences: Codrington's bequest transformed the Society for the Propagation of the Gospel into a slave-owning missionary body, a development that had profound effects on Anglican views on slave conversion. As slave owners, leaders of the SPG adapted their perspective on slavery and Protestantism as they faced obstacles to converting their own slaves.

Chapter 6

The SPG and Slavery

When Christopher Codrington composed his will in 1703, the Society for the Propagation of the Gospel in Foreign Parts was not yet two years old. Yet Codrington's vision of a monastic college in the West Indies clashed with the SPG's strategy at the time. His bequest, which included hundreds of enslaved men and women and two plantations in Barbados, would transform the young Society into a slave-owning organization. But in 1703, the Society had shown very little interest in either enslaved Africans or the West Indies. Instead, the SPG was focused primarily on the northern American colonies, and it targeted Quakers and other "unchurched" Protestants rather than slaves. The conversion of non-Europeans was also an objective for the SPG, but it was secondary to the needs of English men and women. In one of the SPG's first annual sermons, given in 1704, Gilbert Burnet outlined these priorities concisely: "Our Designs upon Aliens and Infidels," he wrote, "must begin in the Instructing and Reforming our own People, in opening Schools every where, in sending over Books of good Instruction, and above all things, in encouraging and preparing many Labourers to go into that Harvest."[1] For Burnet, as for other members of the SPG, the English, who were in great need of books, schools, and orthodox ministers, were the first priority. The second priority was Indians, whose conversion had long been coveted by Protestants. Enslaved Africans, if they were mentioned at all, were an afterthought.

Between 1701, the year that the SPG was founded, and 1710, when Codrington's bequest was revealed, two individuals encouraged the Society to make slave conversion a more central part of its mission: Elias Neau, a New York merchant, and Francis Le Jau, Christopher Codrington's "great friend" who relocated to Goose Creek, South Carolina in

Figure 7. Seal of the Society for the Propagation of the Gospel in Foreign Parts, [London, 1706]. An Anglican minister, holding an open bible, is greeted by Native Americans exclaiming *Transiens adiuva nos* (come over and help us). Courtesy of the John Carter Brown Library, Brown University.

1706. The similarities between the two men are striking. Both were born in France to Protestant families and both emigrated in their early adulthood due to religious persecution; both spent time living and working in the West Indies, where they would have seen the differences between English, French, and Spanish slaveholding practices; and both responded to the Society's directions with a new and fervent vision, urging the SPG to make enslaved Africans a higher priority for evangelization. While the two men never met—Neau was stationed in New York while Le Jau was in South Carolina—both encountered the ideology of Protestant Supremacy from slave owners and they reported their difficulties to the SPG. Neau helped to turn the Society's attention to legal advocacy to support slave baptism while Le Jau introduced a new pledge to the baptismal ceremony that clarified that conversion did not result in manumission. Despite their efforts, however, anticonversion sentiment persisted and in 1712, a slave rebellion in New York was blamed on Elias Neau and Christian slaves, demonstrating the persistence of Protestant Supremacy in the early eighteenth century.

Neau and Le Jau's correspondence made slave conversion an increasingly important aspect of the SPG's mission. So when Codrington's bequest was revealed in 1710, the SPG viewed it as a godsend—an opportunity to prove to the world that Christianity and slavery could be profitably united. The Society had high hopes for the plantation: without interference from other slave owners, the SPG could demonstrate the benefits of a truly Christianized slave system. Yet the realities of plantation management overshadowed the Society's proselytizing mission and undermined the Society's appeal to the enslaved. The management of the Codrington estate meant that key members of the Society, including the bishop of London and the archbishop of York, regularly made decisions about buying, selling, controlling, and disciplining enslaved people. By 1730, the Society's reliance on slave labor and their increasing ties to the West Indian planter class meant that they became ever more entrenched in the system of Atlantic slavery.

Elias Neau and the First Anglican Mission to Slaves

The first individual to target enslaved Africans for the Anglican Church was neither an Anglican nor an Englishman. Elias Neau was raised in Moëze, France to a family of Huguenot sailors. In 1679, when he was eighteen years old, he left France "upon account of [his] Religion" and proceeded to Santo Domingo.[2] When the edict of Nantes was revoked in 1685, he relocated to Boston, where he married Suzanne Paré, another Huguenot refugee. Five years later, he moved to New York where he worked as a merchant.[3] Neau's ties with the West Indies remained strong and in 1692, he sailed from New York to Jamaica. While en route, French privateers captured his ship and Neau, who refused to denounce his religious beliefs, spent the next five years as a galley slave and prisoner. When he was finally released in 1697, he published an account of his experiences, entitled *An Account of the Sufferings of the French Protestants, Slaves on board the French Kings Galleys*.[4] His publication circulated among Protestants throughout Europe, including several members of the SPG.[5] Impressed with Neau's fervent commitment to Protestantism, the Secretary of the Society wrote to Neau to recruit him as a lay catechist to the Iroquois.[6]

Neau responded to the Society's request with a suggestion: he was eager to reach out to the "great Number of Slaves which we call Negroes of both Sexes & of all ages, who are without God in the World and of whom there is no manner of Care taken."[7] In another letter, he emphasized the importance of converting slaves rather than Indians because "there are not nigh so many Indians in these Countries, as there are Negro slaves."[8] Neau's lobbying marked an important turning point for the fledgling Society. While the conversion of the Indians had long been a heralded cause for Protestant missions, the conversion of slaves—particularly enslaved Africans—had received far less attention. The Society's initial plan for Neau, to catechize the Iroquois, was consistent with a more general concern for Indian conversion projects. By arguing for the significance of slave conversion, Elias Neau helped to bring the Society's attention to enslaved Africans.

In the following years, Neau worked to convert the enslaved population in New York, providing them with catechisms and other texts. Most of his students were African, though some were Native American slaves living in the city. Initially, he visited his catechumens, or students, in the homes of their masters, but as their numbers grew, he converted part of his own home into a school.[9] In 1705, Neau counted forty-six catechumens and by 1707, there were over one hundred.[10] During meetings, Neau led his students in a call-and-response catechism that he developed specifically for enslaved adults, since there was no official SPG catechism for such a purpose. The catechism included information on where God existed (everywhere), on whom He depends (Himself), how He made himself known (By his words), and how He teaches (through the Holy Spirit). Neau included the catechism in one of his letters, adding that he hoped that the Society would develop one of their own.

Over time, Neau adapted the structure of his meetings to better suit his students' interests and background. Two of his adjustments were particularly significant. First, he translated the Lord's Prayer into three languages—one Native, and two African.[11] Second, he began to teach "prayers & Singing of Psalms," an alteration that drew an "abundance of people to see and hear them."[12] Neau used materials from the Society, such as Psalm books, to "teach [his] Catechumens to sing as well as pray."[13] He believed that by "praying and singing these divine Praises," his catechumens "obey[ed God's] Commands."[14] Neau's choice to include prayers and singing helped to increase his popularity among the enslaved: while he had noted some drop-off among his catechumens in 1705 and 1706, he soon reported that his numbers were increasing again.[15] He was also delighted that "some of them appear affected with the truths of our Religion."[16] Neau's modifications suggest that he was flexible and accommodating in his approach to evangelization.

Neau's evangelism contrasted with the efforts of other local ministers. While Neau began his meetings with the Lord's Prayer in English, Thoroughgood Moor, the SPG missionary assigned to the Iroquois, believed that the "infinite Being ought not to be Invoked by a people who know it not." As his statement suggests, Moor did not believe that enslaved Africans could understand the Christian God and should not be taught to invoke him.[17] Neau also encountered resistance from Rev. William Vesey, the rector of Trinity Church, who believed that Neau's English was insufficient for the task of evangelization. Vesey would have preferred for Neau's salary to be used to hire his own assistant.[18] Neau himself acknowledged some of these shortcomings in his letters, and promised to "proceed but slowly" with evangelization because "Mr Vesey is not pleased." He was well aware of the difficulties inherent in his mission, writing that he was "frighten[ed]" of the obstacles.[19]

While some of Neau's strategies caused consternation among the Anglican clergy, much of his approach was quite orthodox. He relied heavily on published texts sent to him from the Society and encouraged his students to read and memorize Anglican catechisms, letters, and books. In 1705, Neau wrote that he had given each of his catechumens at least one piece of reading material, either a book, a letter, or a catechism.[20] From the perspective of the Society, this was wonderful news, evidence of increased interest in Christianity and progress in Neau's mission.

For enslaved men and women, books became an incentive to attend the school. In March 1706, Neau wrote that several catechumens attended just 2 or 3 classes, but "ke[pt] the Books notwithstanding."[21] As the numbers of his catechumens grew, Neau wrote frequently to the Society, requesting more reading material. In 1707, he asked for "200 Catechisms of ye smallest sort" and in 1710, he reported that he had "dispersed a great many of the little Tracts . . . to several apprentices and young Boys and Girls." Neau believed that the books increased attendance at his classes, but he continued to wonder whether some of his students came "only come for the Books."[22]

Neau's concern that his catechumens came "only . . . for the Books" suggests that both he and his students were aware of the significance of literacy in New York society. Reading and literacy were closely linked not only to Christian conversion, but also to ideas of freedom. And unsurprisingly, it was because of these connections that Neau, like Godwyn before him, met with resistance from slave owners who feared that conversion would make their slaves free. As Neau wrote to John Hodges, "Several believe that if the Negros were Baptised, they could be no longer [be] kept as Slaves after they are admitted into the Christian Church." As a result, baptism would "Rui[n] the Plantations [t]hat subsist only by the Labor of those Slaves."[23] Neau was skeptical of this rationale, calling it "Covetousness" in one letter, and "Preten[s]e" in another.[24] In 1704, he wrote that he could "not Conceive" of the reason for this reticence, "seeing that neither the Law nor the Gospel authorizes their Opinions."[25]

Neau responded to Protestant Supremacy by seeking to reform laws to ensure the legality of owning Christian slaves. This approach focused on accommodating and appeasing the concerns of slave owners. Neau hoped that a law supporting slave baptism would ease the fears of slave owners and prevent slaves from "pretend[ing] to a Temporal Liberty."[26] Neau's strategy was twofold. First, he joined together with local ministers, including William Vesey, the minister of Trinity Church in New York, to lobby the Assembly of New York to pass a law encouraging slave conversion. He requested that the Society write to Lord Cornbury, the governor of New York, to "desire him to pass an Act of Assembly whereby it should be enacted that all the Inhabitants should be obliged to p[er]mit all their Slaves to be instructed & that their Religion should make no Alteration in their Condition."[27]

Second, he urged the Society to promote a similar law to Parliament. As he wrote to John Hodges in 1704, "in Order to facilitate [their] Conversion, It would be necessary that our Parliament should by a Positive Law press the Necessity that all the Inhabitants [have] their Negroes & Indians baptiz[e]d & Instructed in the [Christia]n Religion."[28] Neau's inspiration for this law came from his knowledge of Catholic slavery in the Atlantic world. Just as "the Fr[ench] & the Span[ish] . . . baptize all their slaves w[i]thout giving them Temporall Liberty," he wrote, so should the "Slaves of the English . . . be baptiz'd w[he]n they have been Instructed & should Continue Slaves."[29]

Neau's efforts were rewarded in 1706 with a New York law entitled "An Act to encourage the Baptizing of Negro, Indian and Mulatto Slaves."[30] Neau, who wrote that he had "made a great stir here to procure an act of Assembly in Favor of the Propagation of the Faith," was delighted. The first clause of the act countered the "groundless Opinion that hath spread itself in this Colony, that by the baptizing of such *Negro, Indian* or *Mulatto* Slaves, they would become Free, and ought to be set at Liberty." Neau enclosed a copy of the act and reported that he now had "hope for better success" with his conversion project. And indeed, Neau did see almost immediate effects, particularly after Mr. Vesey urged his congregants to send their slaves to Neau's catechism classes. In July 1707, Neau wrote that the act of assembly had given him "some encouragement in [his] Instruction of Slaves," and his number of catechumens rose to 75.[31]

The 1706 act, however, did more than confirm the legality of baptizing slaves without freeing them. The second and third clauses racialized the definition of slavery and restricted the rights of enslaved men and women. Following in the tradition of Virginia's 1662 law, the second clause declared that "all and every *Negro, Indian, Mulatto* or *Mestee,* shall follow the State and Condition of the Mother." The final clause of the act stated that "no Slave whatsoever in this Colony, shall at any Time be admitted as a Witness for or against any Freeman, in any Case, Matter of Cause, Civil or Criminal, whatsoever."[32]

The full text of the 1706 act demonstrated the close connection between Christian Slavery and the consolidation of race-based slavery. While Neau was probably not responsible for the additional clauses restricting the rights of enslaved men and women, he was willing to accept—and even support—the amendments because they provided slave owners with greater security. By redefining slavery as heritable through the mother and prohibiting enslaved men and women from testifying against freemen in court, slave owners in New York succeeded in creating a more restrictive and race-based system of slavery.[33]

Neau also succeeded in motivating the members of the Society in London to develop their own legislative efforts to "Draught . . . a Bill to be offer'd to Parliament for the conversion of the Negroes in the Plantations to the Christian Faith."[34] In October 1703, the Society read one of Neau's first letters, urging the creation of "a law w[hi]ch permitted the Inhabitants to cause their Negroes to be Instructed and Baptized." At the same meeting, the Society agreed to delegate John Hooke, a "senior figure in the English bar," to draft such a bill for Parliament.[35] At the following meeting, the Society approved Mr. Hooke's bill and sent it to the Lord Archbishops of Canterbury and York and the Lord Bishop of London, who were notified of "the Desire of the Society that it may be brought into Parliament."[36]

The bill demonstrated Neau's influence on the Society. A draft of the bill annotated by Lord Thomas Tenison, the archbishop of Canterbury, referred to the ideology of Protestant Supremacy described by Neau as well as the "mistaken Opinion that the Interest of the Master in his Negro or Servant, is taken away or Lessen'd by the Negro or Servant becoming a Christian." To "prevent such Neglect," the act declared, "no Negro or other Servant" who was baptized would be "thereby Enfranchis'd."[37] While the bill was not enacted, two years later, letters from Neau and William Vesey again prompted the Society to take action on the issue of slave baptism. In March 1706, several influential members of the Society discussed the possibility of creating an empire-wide law regarding slave conversion, rather than tackling the issue piecemeal, colony by colony. They were led by Francis Nicholson, a colonial administrator and influential member of the SPG, whose experience as governor of Virginia and Maryland had brought him into contact with the common refrain that baptism would lead to freedom. In a series of meetings, Nicholson acquainted members of the Society with colonial laws from Virginia, Maryland, and Jamaica that severed the link between baptism and freedom. The Society agreed that a "Declarative Law" would be needed to clarify the situation throughout the entire imperial realm.[38]

The Society continued to lobby for pro-conversion legislation through the 1710s and 1720s. In 1715, they discussed a "Clause to be offer'd in Parliament" obliging "all Masters of Owners of such *Negro Slaves,* To cause their Children to be Baptiz'd within *Three* Months after their Birth; and to permit them when come to Years of discretion, to be instructed in the Christian Religion on the *Lord's Day.*" Despite their baptism and education, the "respective Owners or Proprietors" would have the "same Right, Title, and Property to them as they had before." Again, the Society used Catholic practice to support their aims, noting that the practice of enslaving "is practised all the World over, even in Countries of the *Romish* Communion."[39] As the SPG's legal advocacy demonstrates, concerned Protestants often reacted to anticonversion sentiment by seeking to strengthen and solidify a system of slavery that embraced Christianization and perpetual bondage.

Despite the Society's efforts to convince white colonists that conversion did not pose a threat to slavery, New Yorkers remained distrustful of Christian slaves. Their distrust, while normally muted, became manifest in the wake of a slave insurrection that rocked New York in spring 1712. In the early hours of April 7, 1712, between twenty and thirty enslaved people set fire to a house in New York City. According to the Rev. John Sharpe, many of the rebels were from the Gold Coast—"of ye Nations of Carmantee & Pappa"—and they had "plotted to destroy all the whites in order to obtain their freedom."[40] Sharpe believed that the leader of the rebels was "a free negroe who pretends sorcery"—likely an important political and spiritual leader. The free black leader bound the rebels to secrecy and "gave them a powder to rub on their Cloths" so they felt "confident." On the night of the insurrection, the rebels "stood in the streets & shot down and stabbed" townspeople as they emerged from their homes to respond to the fire.[41] One of the rebels, Robin, allegedly stabbed his master, Adrian Hoghlandt, while another named Tom was accused of shooting Adrian Beekman with a handgun.[42] Overall, nine whites were killed and several more were wounded. Soon thereafter, the militia was called and the rebels retreated "into the woods" where they were able to hide "by the favour of the night."[43] After an intense search, about seventy enslaved people were accused of conspiring and twenty-one were executed. Six others killed themselves before the militia could capture them, with one man killing his wife before shooting himself.[44]

Retribution for the insurrection was violent and gruesome. After brief trials that began on April 11, some were "burnt others hanged, one broke on the wheele, and one hung a live in chains in the town." Governor Hunter wrote to the Lords of Trade in London that the rebels were given "the most exemplary punishment . . . that could be possibly thought of." He compared the reaction to the British Caribbean "where their laws against their slaves are most severe." While in the West Indies, "a few only are executed for an example," in New York, "21 [were] executed."[45]

Blame for the rebellion was not limited to the convicted. In the following weeks, white New Yorkers found fault with black Christians and Elias Neau. John Sharpe wrote that the conspiracy "open'd the mouths of many ag[ainst] negroes being made Christians" and that Neau's school was "blaimed as ye main occation of [the rebellion]."[46] Neau confirmed that the rebellion raised the "Scruples in the Minds of our Inhabitants against my School" by suggesting that instruction in Christianity led their slaves to rebel.[47] Neau defended himself by insisting that the Christian religion commanded "Obedience to all Inferiors."[48] In fact, he had long argued that "the Christian religion inspires slaves to love and obey their masters and mistresses."[49] He convinced the governor that his students "had no share in the Conspiracy of the Negroes," but still struggled to gain support among the general populace.[50]

While condemnation of Neau's school was widespread, only two of Neau's students were among the accused, one of whom was probably innocent. Sharpe wrote that this man "was condemned on Slander Evidence in ye heat of ye Peoples resentment," and that he "declare[d] his inocency wth his dying breath." It was only after his execution that "he was pitied and proclaimed innocent by ye Generality of ye People."[51] The other of Neau's students was Robin, the enslaved man who was accused of murdering his master, Adrian Hoghlandt.[52] While it is unclear whether Robin played a central role in the rebellion, he was almost certainly involved. When John Sharpe questioned him, he admitted to knowledge of the rebellion but insisted that he was "not guilty of any bloodshed." After the revolt, Robin was "hanged in chains for the murder of his Master," and later executed.[53]

Robin's interest in Christianity may have been a motivating factor in his decision to rebel. For at least two years before the rebellion, Robin attended Neau's catechism classes. During that time, he petitioned his master, Adrian Hoghlandt, for permission to be baptized, but was consistently refused. Robin's conflict with Hoghlandt over baptism suggests that while the accusations of white New Yorkers were certainly overblown, Christianity cannot be completely discounted as a contributing factor to rebellion. While Neau and his supporters insisted that conversion would make slaves more docile and obedient, the fact that the majority of slave owners, like Hoghlandt, prohibited slave baptism, likely contributed to its allure. Indeed, Neau sometimes taught his students to read without the knowledge of their masters—a decision that clearly undermined the authority of slave owners.

Suspicion of non-European Christians was not limited to enslaved blacks. According to John Sharpe, the first two suspects of the rebellion were Spanish Catholic Indians who were thought to have "most under-standing to carry on a plot" because they were "Christians."[54] Sharpe's comments suggest that Christianity was associated with education, knowledge, and privilege. Because the Spanish Indians were Christian, white New Yorkers presumed that they would have the intelligence, capacity, and desire to free themselves from bondage. These reactions suggest that most Europeans continued to treat Christianity as an exclusive privilege reserved for free people, not slaves, and they were distrustful of all non-Europeans who claimed to be Christian.

The persistence of Protestant Supremacy—even as slavery was becoming increasingly race-based—can be seen in the continued usage of the noun "Christian" to indicate "European." In Governor Hunter's letter about the revolt, for example, he wrote, "nine Christians were killed," thereby implying that whiteness and Christianity remained overlapping categories. The persistent slippage between religion and race is indicative of how strongly Christianity was associated with mastery, knowledge, education, and power.

In the wake of the rebellion, the New York Assembly moved to tighten its slave laws. In December 1712, it passed "An Act for Preventing, Suppressing, and Punishing the Conspiracy and Insurrection of Negroes, and other Slaves," and in February 1713, they added a "Law for Regulating Negro and Indian Slaves in the Night Time."[55] Neau believed that the latter law was a direct attack on his school. In September 1713, he wrote to the Society, "it is well known that [my students] do not come . . . to be catechized till after Sun Sett (and oftentimes without their Masters knowledge)," and that they do not have access to "Lantherns or Candles."[56] As a result, the restriction on mobility was a "Snare for [his] school."[57]

The 1713 law drew attention to the fact that Neau operated his school at a physical distance from the English church. Neau held his catechism classes at night on the second floor of his own home. When the Society requested that Neau hold classes at church, he explained that many of his catechumens would not attend if they had to enter the church.[58] Neau stated that his students were too "bashfull" to go to church, though it is likely that the Anglican space was unappealing for other reasons. As Neau wrote, they were "not so willing to spend the only rest day they have in godly works," and they preferred to congregate in the evenings at candlelight. The resistance to black and Indian attendance at Trinity Church seems to have come from both sides. Neau wrote that there was "no room in our Church" for nonwhites, and that even some white families could not fit. Furthermore, Rev. Vesey did not make enslaved people a priority, and had "no leisure to catechise them poor Slaves."[59]

These factors suggest that despite his claims to the contrary, Neau's school *was* a subversive force in the city. In the restrictive slave society of New York, where lawmakers and slave owners aimed to control the movements and knowledge of enslaved people, Neau taught enslaved men and women to read, gave them books, and encouraged them to disobey their masters by walking through the streets at night. Neau and other advocates of Christian Slavery minimized the radical elements of their mission in their correspondence with the Society. After the rebellion, they were particularly careful to distance themselves from any rebellious activity. Thus despite Robin's involvement in the rebellion, John Sharpe wrote that the rebels "were found to be such as never frequented Mr. Neaus School."[60] He also insisted that "the Persons whose Negros have been found guilty are such as are declared opposers of Christianizing Negroes," thereby suggesting that a truly stable slave society would be a thoroughly Christian one.

The Society followed Sharpe's example in its response to the 1712 rebellion. In the Abstract of the Proceedings for their Annual Meeting for 1713, which was published and distributed throughout the Protestant Atlantic world, they ignored evidence of Robin's involvement in the rebellion and stated that "there was not a *Catechumen* in the Fact, or suffer'd for it, but *one*, who too late was pitied, and proclaimed innocent by the Generality of the People." They also quoted Sharpe's conclusion that "the Persons, whose *Negroes* have been found guilty, are such as are declared Opposers of *christianizing* Negroes."[61] By rejecting any connection between rebellion and slave conversion, the Society sought to strengthen the argument that Christianization would help to sustain and support the system of slavery.

Francis Le Jau and South Carolina

Like Elias Neau, Francis Le Jau was influential in turning the SPG's attention to slave conversion. After spending three years as a parish minister in the Leeward Islands, where he met frequently with Christopher Codrington, Le Jau returned briefly to England. On November 12, 1705, just as Neau was lobbying to pass legislation on slave baptism, Le Jau "presented a paper concerning religion in the Caribbee Islands." In it, he commented on the miserable state of the established Church in the Leeward Islands, the ill treatment of slaves, and the inability of ministers to even "propose" the education and baptism of slaves. While the enslaved men and women he met were, for the most part, "sensible & well disposed to learn," Le Jau blamed the "barbarous" behavior of their masters for making them "stubborn." They were forced to steal food in order to live and were not given enough clothing or rest. If a minister proposed to instruct slaves "in the Christian faith," planters would be "angry" because it would "consume their profit" by cutting in on their work time.[62]

Le Jau drew on the French and Spanish example in his paper and suggested that English planters were well aware that slavery was compatible with Christianity. While slave owners claimed that "baptism [would] make negroes free," they knew that the "negroes now in their possession . . . came from the French or Spaniards & consequently [were] baptized." Le Jau suggested, instead, that the planters refused to accept slaves as "Christian Brethren" because it would force them to "use 'em with humanity."[63] Le Jau's presentation coincided with the Elias Neau's efforts to pass parliamentary legislation on slave conversion and his comments surely reinforced the need for action.[64]

Soon after his presentation, Le Jau accepted a position as an SPG missionary in Goose Creek, South Carolina.[65] For the next eleven years, he updated the Society with regular accounts of his struggles to convert blacks, whites, and Indians in the low country. Initially, Le Jau reported that the situation looked promising. "Masters and parents," he wrote, "are well satisfyed that their Children and slaves may be taught how to become Christians," and several enslaved people attended church.[66] Soon thereafter, Le Jau sought to reserve "a day in the week for the Instruction of poor Indians and Negroes," and noted that the enslaved were treated "better than in the Islands."[67] By November 1708, about a year and a half after his arrival, he wrote that "several negroes have asked me for the holy baptism," but he saw "no necessity to be too hasty." Le Jau wanted to wait for "proof of their good life by the testimony of their Masters."[68] Four months later, he reported that there were "pretty many" slaves baptized, in addition to two "Negroes Communants."[69]

Le Jau's approach to slave conversion was cautious and accommodating. He took care not to antagonize slave owners and he made sure to gain permission for instruction and baptism. Yet despite his precaution and his early successes, Le Jau's outlook soon shifted. In March 1709, he complained that "many Masters can't be perswaded that Negroes and Indians are otherwise than Beasts." While he exhorted his enslaved congregants "to perseverance and patience," he was frustrated by the "unjust, profane & inhumane practices" among slave owners.[70] Like Neau, Le Jau found that several masters denied their slaves access to baptism, claiming that they would be thereby manumitted.

Eventually, Le Jau confronted the problem of Protestant Supremacy by forcing all adult slaves to make the following declaration before their baptism: "You declare in the presence of God and before this Congregation that you do not ask for the holy baptism out of any design to free yourself from the duty and Obedience you owe to your Master while you live but meerly for the good of your Soul and to partake of the Graces and Blessings promised to the Members of the Church of Jesus Christ."[71] By making this declaration of loyalty to one's master a part of the baptismal ceremony, Le Jau adapted and altered Anglican ritual to better fit the demands of slave owners.

While Le Jau primarily blamed planters for his difficulties, his letters also hinted at a more complicated story. Some enslaved men and women had embraced Christian practice in a way that challenged the ideology of Christian slavery promoted by Le Jau. Specifically, Le Jau was concerned with the authority of literate slaves. Early into his tenure as SPG missionary at Goose Creek, Le Jau complained bitterly about some of the most educated blacks. At one point, he wrote, "the Negroes are generally very bad men, chiefly those that are Scholars."[72] Over time, Le Jau became increasingly skeptical about the consequences of teaching reading and writing. In 1710, Le Jau recounted an event with an enslaved man who he described as "the best Scholar of all the Negroes" and a "very sober and honest Liver." Apparently, this man had prophesied that the "moon wou'd be turned to Blood," a prediction he "read . . . in a Book."[73] Le Jau was alarmed that this man had put "his own Construction upon some Words of the Holy Prophet's."[74] Le Jau did not want his enslaved congregants to develop their own interpretations of the Bible and he concluded, "those men have not judgment enough to make a good use of their Learning."[75] The incident revealed Le Jau's discomfort with black authority and his growing reticence to promote literacy. He urged the Society to reserve such skills only for the "fittest persons."[76]

While Le Jau's approach to evangelization differed from Neau's legislative efforts, both men offered the SPG a window into the intensity and persistence of Protestant Supremacy in the American colonies. Their letters also hinted at more complex interactions between planters, slaves, and missionaries. In particular, they suggested that black Christians were interpreting scripture in new, important, and sometimes subversive ways. These subtleties, however, were excluded from the SPG's larger narrative about slavery and Christianity. Instead, the Society focused on the general problem of anticonversion sentiment displayed by the planters as their central obstacle.

The influence of Neau and Le Jau is evident not only in the Society's minutes and legislative efforts, but also in its annual sermons, which were published and distributed in Europe and America. Until 1706, the sermons made no mention of slaves, focusing instead on the plight of Protestantism among the English at home and abroad.[77] In 1706, however, the conversion of slaves took on a more public role with John Williams' sermon. Williams acknowledged that slaves were "too often discouraged, and refused to be made Christians," and he made a biblical case for slavery, emphasizing that Christianity did not give a slave "Authority to claim his Liberty from the believing Master."[78] William Beveridge's sermon the following year went even further in encouraging slave conversion, claiming that the reason that "multitudes of Heathens are brought out of *Africa* every Year, and made Slaves to Christians in *America*" was so that they could be "taught the Principles of the Christian Religion." He also hoped that some would eventually "be fit to be sent back again into their own Country, with full Instructions to preach the Gospel to those Nations."[79]

These sermons suggest that slave conversion became an increasingly important component of the SPG's mission after Le Jau and Neau began communicating with members of the Society. The fact that two French-born Protestants, both with Caribbean connections, were responsible for turning the SPG's attentions to slave conversion is a reminder of the importance of cross-cultural exchange, French influence, and pan-European Protestantism on English ideas about slavery and Christianity. Yet Le Jau and Neau were not the only sources of influence. In December 1706, the same year that William Beveridge gave his sermon encouraging slave conversion, the SPG minutes included a reference to the Anglican minister Morgan Godwyn's *Negro's and Indians Advocate* (1680). The phrasing of the minute suggests that Godwyn's book was unknown to most Society members and had only recently been rediscovered by Mr. Kennett. It was "Agreed to lay the sd Book before the Society & move them for their

Directions therein."[80] The rediscovery of Godwyn's book at this crucial time shows the enduring influence of Godwyn's ideas, even as his texts were periodically forgotten and then rediscovered. It also shows the malleability of the SPG as individual members or colonial missionaries brought attention to new concerns and questions.

Frustrated by the ideology of Protestant Supremacy described by Le Jau and Neau and reminded of Godwyn's thoughts on the subject from decades before, the SPG in these years aimed to both reform and reinforce the institution of slavery. The sermons given by Williams and Beveridge illustrate this dual objective. While neither man questioned the legitimacy of slavery, both criticized the culture of slavery that had developed in the Americas and implied that only moral Christian masters had a right to own slaves. This perspective is evident in Beveridge's comment that Christian slaves had no "Authority to claim his Liberty from the believing Master." The addition of the adjective "believing" implied that an unchristian master had no such right. Similarly, Beveridge suggested that the entire justification for African slavery lay in Christianization, implying that God "would never have suffered" such an institution if slaves were to remain "heathens."[81]

The Codrington Bequest and Transition to Slave Ownership

By 1710, slave conversion had become a topic of increasing importance within the Society. While European colonists remained the focus of the SPG's foreign missions, Elias Neau and Francis Le Jau helped to call attention to enslaved men and women. They convinced key members of the Society that slave conversion was a matter of significance, even though it was fraught with difficulties—primarily due to the obstructionism of slave owners. So when the Society learned of Christopher Codrington's death and his bequest of two plantations and several hundred slaves, they were delighted. While Neau and Le Jau's efforts had been stymied by the unchristian behavior of slave owners, the Society now had the opportunity to become masters in their own right and display to the world the potential of a truly Christianized slave system.

Codrington's bequest flooded the members of the Society with optimism. This optimism is evident in William Fleetwood's sermon from 1711. Fleetwood articulated a radical vision of Christian slavery that went further than previous SPG sermons in its condemnation of Protestant slaveholding culture. Pivoting between bold criticisms of slavery and a profoundly pragmatic approach to the demands of trade and national progress, he dismantled three "excuses" that slave owners had given to defend their anticonversion sentiment. To the claim that baptism would make slaves free, Fleetwood answered that the "Liberty of Christianity is entirely Spiritual." To the argument that Christian slaves would have to be treated with "less Rigour," Fleetwood replied that it was a "great Mistake" to treat even a "*Savage*" or an "*Infidel*" with "Inhumanity." And to the pretense that it would be unlawful to sell a Christian slave, Fleetwood insisted that the "growth of *Christianity*" was all that mattered: "let the Christians," he continued, "be Sold, and Bound, and Scourged, condemn'd to Bonds and Imprisonment, to endure all Hardships and Disgrace, *and to enter into Heaven, Blind, and Halt, and Maimed*, rather than having two Eyes, and Hands and Feet entire, to perish Miserable. That is the Sum of all I have been saying." Fleetwood's comments united tropes of martyrdom with a fervent passion for Christian expansion.[82]

Fleetwood's vision for a Christianized slavery culminated with a description of Codrington's bequest and the possibilities it offered to both the SPG and the British Empire. "We are now, by the Munificence of a truly *Honourable Gentleman*," he revealed to his audience, "our selves become the *Patrons* of at least *Three Hundred Slaves*." Fleetwood believed that the bequest was an act of providence. "I see," he continued "and cannot but adore, the gracious Hand of God." It was at Codrington's plantations that the SPG could implement its vision: "We must instruct [the slaves] in the Faith of Christ," Fleetwood stressed, "bring them to Baptism, and put them in the way that leads to everlasting life." In so doing, they would set a precedent for the rest of the world: "This will be preaching *by Example*, the most effectual way of recommending Doctrines, to a hard and unbelieving World, blinded by Interest, and other Prepossessions." Even if "all the Slaves throughout *America*, and every *Island* in those Seas, were to continue Infidels for ever," he concluded, "yet *ours alone must needs be Christians*."[83]

Fleetwood's sermon was indicative of the reforming zeal that dominated the Society at the time of Codrington's bequest. After the 1712 slave revolt and its repercussions on Neau's mission, the Society was particularly eager to prove that Christianization was in no way a threat to slavery. The Codrington plantation, where the Society acted as both master and missionary, provided the perfect opportunity to make such a point. And indeed, soon after news of the revolt reached London, the Society dispatched Joseph Holt, a Cambridge-educated minister and physician, to serve as both missionary and medical practitioner on the Society's lands. Leaders of the Society hoped that Holt, who had experience in the colonies and was well recommended, would care for both the bodies and the souls of the enslaved men and women on Codrington's estates. In the Society's Annual Proceedings of 1713, they announced Holt's mission just after their description of the New York slave revolt. They hoped that Holt's tenure would provide a "good Beginning" and they reminded readers of Fleetwood's pronouncement two years before that even if "all the Slaves in *America* . . . were to continue Infidels . . . yet ours alone must needs be Christians."[84]

Despite best intentions and a good salary, however, Holt's mission survived only one year. The Society had chosen Holt because he was trained in "Physick and Surgery" as well as ministry—a Qualification specified in Codrington's will. Yet in his letters, Holt seemed more interested in the bodily illnesses of the enslaved than their spiritual lives and worship practices. In his first letter after his arrival in Barbados, Holt wrote that he found "abundance of the Negro's infirm and diseased, some blind, Sundry dimsighted, others have the Yaws, Ulcers, Tumors, Lameness, besides common Sicknesses which are ye daily infirmities."[85] A month later, he elaborated further upon the spread of a "General Indisposition . . . thro' ye whole Island," one of the worst in years.[86] The only enslaved individuals he mentioned were those who had died upon his watch—a "young negro woman that was distempered," an "old negro woman that dyed of Gout in her Stomach" and a "Negro man" who died in a "Convulsive delirium."[87]

Holt's detailed discussion of disease contrasted with his bland description of religion and mission work, which focused almost exclusively on the need for a chapel on the estate. He deemed a chapel an "Absolute necessity . . . both for ye regular daily ministration & for the decency of every Solemnity."[88] Holt's insistence on formality was not well suited to his position, and it likely encumbered his missionary venture.[89] Another impediment to Holt's mission work was the rigid work schedule on the estate. While the Society had instructed the estate's manager, Mr. Smalridge, to provide the slaves with free time on Saturday afternoon so they could attend services on Sunday, Mr. Smalridge refused. According to Smalridge, the demands of the harvest were too great to permit the enslaved to have Saturday afternoons free.[90] While Smalridge eventually heeded some of the Society's demands, the pressures of the workweek continued to create tension, pitting religious instruction against profitability.[91]

Due to these conflicts, Holt had little time or space to proselytize to the slaves on his own terms. When a vacancy opened up at a nearby parish, Holt wrote to the Society requesting to be considered as the replacement.[92] Soon thereafter, he left his post to conduct business in North America. When the Society heard of Holt's departure, they dismissed him from service and wrote to Mr. Smalridge and Mr. Ramsay, the SPG's manager and attorney in Barbados, to make sure that Holt did not receive any more funds.[93] Holt, who had returned to the estate by June 1714, explained that he had not abandoned his post, but his pleas failed to persuade the Society.[94]

After Holt's dismissal, the Society's next two missionaries died soon after their arrival, and the position was left vacant for nearly a decade. During this time, the SPG turned its attention to building Codrington College. The building of a College was expensive and ambitious, and it dragged on for decades and did not open until 1745.[95] The Society also became increasingly embroiled in the heated politics of Barbados, where several powerful individuals—including the local minister, Rev. Charles Cunningham, and the governor Robert Lowther—claimed that the Society was "misappropriating Christopher Codrington's bequest." It was not until Lowther was called back to London and Cunningham died that the Society finally decided to send another missionary to Barbados.[96]

Even in the late 1720s and 1730s, however, when Thomas Wilkie, the SPG's new catechist, and Arthur Holt, Joseph Holt's son, made a concerted effort to convert slaves, the entangled goals of profit and proselytizing undermined the Society's mission to slaves.[97] Thomas Wilkie, who was appointed in 1726, reported that while younger slaves were "very docile & capable to learn any thing," as soon as they were old enough to work, they had "very little time to learn in and they [were] very unwilling to come near me."[98] Wilkie's report suggests that the work routine directly conflicted with his ability to catechize the enslaved population on the estate. Once they were forced to work six days of backbreaking labor, the enslaved viewed catechism classes as an intrusion into their scarce free time.

While most enslaved people avoided catechism classes, Wilkie reported that three adults had shown interest in them and that two of them "go to Church every Sunday." He hoped to have them prepared for baptism by Easter. Notably, one of these three individuals was not owned by the

Society, but belonged "to a Gentleman whose Estate adjoins" Codrington plantation. Wilkie's description of his catechism process provides insight into the appeal Christianity may have had for these individuals, even as the majority of enslaved people rejected the Society's mission. Wilkie's approach to conversion rested, like Neau's, on providing basic lessons in reading and teaching his students how to "repeat ye Creed & Lord's prayer." He wrote that he had taught three adults how to read and that they spent "every Sunday afternoon with [him]." He also noted that his three adult catechumens "seem much concern'd what will become of their immortal Souls, after their natural death."[99]

Like Neau and Le Jau, Wilkie found that the white inhabitants of the Island were averse to slave conversion, though their sentiments did not greatly affect his mission since the enslaved people at Codrington were owned by the Society. Still, his description of Protestant Supremacy suggests that teaching literacy, which was closely tied to Protestant conversion, was a great concern for planters. Wilkie wrote that with the exception of the clergy, the whites on the island were "against the conversion of ye Negroes" because they believed it to be "of ill consequence to teach them letters." The ability to read and write, they believed, would make the enslaved more prone to "run away from their Masters into the woods for months together."[100]

With interest in his mission low, Wilkie suggested to the Society that Mr. Smalridge "command . . . [the] younger [children]" to come to his classes, noting that "they dread [Smalridge's] displeasure." Wilkie was sure that if the enslaved children came to him "every day for an hour," he could "bring many of them to read and understand ye principles of ye Christian religion in a few years." The Society heeded Wilkie's suggestion and wrote to Mr. Smalridge, requesting that he "give all proper Encouragement to Mr. Wilkie in teaching the Negroes," and "oblige them to come to church on Sunday."[101] By doing so, the Society used their power as slave owners to coerce their enslaved workers to attend Christian services. This approach redefined Christianity as an obligation, rather than a choice, and it meant that resistance to Christian instruction could result in discipline from Mr. Smalridge.

Once Mr. Smalridge was instructed to "oblige" the enslaved to attend catechism classes, the number of Wilkie's catechumens rose. By the end of 1730, the Society noted that with "due Encouragement," thirty-seven individuals had been baptized: twenty-two adults and fifteen children.[102] It is not clear from the Society's notes or Mr. Smalridge's letters what the consequences were of resisting catechism classes or Christian baptism. Yet there are several signs that the Society's dual role as master and missionary compromised their appeal to the enslaved.[103] Perhaps the most egregious example of this was the decision to brand "SOCIETY" onto the chests of newly arrived slaves. This practice, which began in 1724 when Mr. Smalridge purchased "a Silver mark to mark ye Negros Society," continued until 1732, when Arthur Holt complained to the Society that it was "a Cruelty which I believe ye Society will think proper to Discourage."[104] Even after branding was forbidden, however, the Barbados Committee approved of other coercive and violent measures, such as the threat of sale and the use of "moderate correction," to control the enslaved population.[105]

The Society's ownership of the Codrington estates had a profound impact on the SPG's stance on slavery and race, as well as their approach to evangelization. In order to run Codrington, members of the Society adapted the strategies of absentee planters. The Society established a Barbados Committee made up of lay members and clergy who had an interest in the West Indies. The Barbados Committee, which included Archbishop Thomas Tenison and Codrington's Oxford tutor George Smalridge (the brother of Codrington's estate manager), met regularly and oversaw the Society's manager and attorneys.[106] Through the demands of management, these key members of the Society were regularly confronted with decisions about buying, selling, and disciplining enslaved people as well as other issues related to running a large sugar plantation. The minutes of the Barbados Committee are primarily concerned with these business-related issues and only occasionally mention the Society's missionary efforts. They indicate that while slave conversion remained a goal, the Society operated the Codrington estates primarily as a sugar plantation and they prioritized profits over mission work.

Gradually, the SPG distanced itself publicly from the Codrington bequest. While the bequest had played a central role in Fleetwood's 1711 Annual Sermon, David Humphreys intentionally omitted it from his 1730 *Historical Account of the Incorporated Society for the Propagation of the Gospel in Foreign Parts*. In the preface, Humphreys wrote that the "Estate is not applicable to the general Uses of the Society, such as the supporting of Missionaries, Catechists, and Schoolmasters" and that the SPG "act only as Trustees."[107]

Despite the difficulties the Society faced at Codrington and elsewhere in the colonies, members of the SPG remained committed to slave conversion. One of the most significant figures during this period was Edmund Gibson, a longtime member of the Society who was appointed Lord Bishop of London in 1720. In 1723, Gibson sent questionnaires to all Anglican clergy in the American colonies inquiring, among other things, about the "Infidels, bond or free, within your Parish; and what means are us'd for their Conversion."[108] Gibson was clearly concerned by the responses he received. In 1727, he published two letters: one addressed "To the Masters and Mistresses of Families in the English Plantations Abroad" and the second "To the Missionaries there." In the first, Gibson wrote that he had been "not a little troubled" to hear "how small a Progress has been made" toward converting slaves to Christianity. Furthermore, he lamented the fact that "all *Attempts*" to convert slaves "have been by too many industriously discouraged and hinder'd." He was dismayed by the persistence of "mistaken Suggestions" that "*Baptism* would make in the Condition of the *Negroes*."

Gibson's letter highlighted the arguments that had become the cornerstones of the SPG's stance on slave conversion: (1) that the ideology of Protestant Supremacy, with its anticonversion sentiment, was the greatest obstacle to the spread of Christianity; (2) that baptizing slaves was perfectly legal; and (3) that Christian slaves were more obedient and docile than their non-Christian counterparts. The SPG paid for Gibson's letter to masters to be printed ten thousand times and distributed throughout the colonies. A second edition was published in 1729 and the letter was also translated into French.[109]

While a few missionaries wrote that Gibson's letter had helped to convince some masters to baptize their slaves, at least one slave-owning clergyman was outraged by Gibson's assumptions about colonial slavery.[110] In 1730, three years after Gibson's letter was circulated, the Rev. Robert Robertson, a clergyman in Nevis who was not associated with the SPG, published an anonymous response entitled *A Letter To the Right Reverend the Lord Bishop of London from An Inhabitant of his Majesty's Leeward-Caribee Islands.* Robertson, who later wrote that he feared the bishop's misinformation would be "propagated over *Europe*," wrote a blistering critique of Gibson and his letters.[111]

According to Robertson, Gibson was completely ignorant of the true obstacles for slave conversion in the colonies. While Gibson believed that the greatest impediment to slave conversion was the incorrect assumption that baptism would lead to freedom, Robertson insisted that "there is not a *Sugar* or *Guinea*-Trader of any Note in *London, Bristol,* or *Liverpole,* but could have told your Lordship that it is impossible *Baptism,* or any the like Privilege, should *destroy the Property the Masters have in their* Negro-*Slaves,* or the Right of selling them again at Pleasure."[112] Instead, Robertson argued that education and baptism provided slaves with dangerous tools that they could use to navigate the legal system to their own benefit. In other words, allowing enslaved men and women to be educated and baptized *was,* in fact, a threat to slavery, but not for the reasons that Gibson had assumed.

Furthermore, the Anglican Church did not have the institutional capacity to serve English colonists, let alone undertake a massive evangelical mission to the enslaved. As Robertson explained, "Churches were not begun to be built in the *Leward-Islands*" until "after the Restoration," and with the exception of William Stapleton and Christopher Codrington, its governors had done little to support the Church of England.[113] The clergy stationed in the West Indies were badly compensated and there were not enough ministers to perform the work necessary. Robertson estimated that "the Number of Parochial Ministers (and there are no others) in *Barbadoes,* the *Leward-Islands,* and *Jamaica,* is seldom above, and sometimes under, *Forty*; and the Negro-Slaves in the same Islands are, I think, computed at about *Two Hundred Thousand* Men, Women and Children."[114] Above all, Robertson was resentful that colonial planters—and West Indian planters in particular—had been depicted as greedy, immoral, and cruel masters. Robertson pointed specifically to the publications of the Society as guilty of spreading this image. He quoted a passage from the 1716 *Abstract of the Proceedings of the Society for the Propagation of the Gospel in Foreign Parts,* which stated: "It has been often represented from the Press, and in Conversation almost every where, that the great Obstruction to the Conversion of the Slaves lies at the door of their Covetous, Atheistical, and Ungodly Masters."[115] It was this passage that first prompted Robertson to write a defense of West Indian planters and a "Short Essay Concerning the Conversion of Negro-Slaves in our Sugar-Colonies," which he printed alongside his Letter to the Lord Bishop. "Our Countrymen at Home," he wrote, "must not think to shake off the stupendous Load of Guilt that is contracted by this Affair, and throw it upon the White People of these Colonies; we have, all of us, more than enough to answer for otherwise."[116]

Robertson's publications help to illuminate several consequences of the Anglican approach to slave conversion. While the initial vision of the

Society included enslaved Africans only tangentially, colonial missionaries and catechists like Elias Neau and Francis Le Jau helped to bring increased focus to the plight of slaves. Yet as the Society became more involved in slave evangelization, they encountered new obstacles and challenges. The Society blamed their failures primarily on planter obstructionism. While this was undoubtedly a problem, the Society's focus on anticonversion sentiment prevented them from grasping many of the subtleties within the missionary encounters that were reported to them. The letters from Le Jau and Neau had hinted at a complex set of reasons that enslaved people were drawn to Christianity. Chief among these was the allure of books and literacy. Le Jau and Neau were both delighted by and distrustful of this dynamic. Le Jau, in particular, was suspicious of black "scholars" and concluded that the teaching of reading should be restricted. Elias Neau, meanwhile, feared that several of his catechumens came "only for the books." Rather than acknowledging and addressing these potentially subversive aspects of Christian instruction, the Society argued that that Christian slaves were more docile and obedient than non-Christian slaves. They ignored all evidence to the contrary, such as Robin's involvement in the 1712 insurrection. Instead, they blamed planters for impeding the spread of the gospel. As Robertson's writings indicate, this conclusion led planters to further resent missionary intrusion in their lives.

The focus on planter obstructionism was indicative of a broader problem with the SPG's approach: it was completely master-centered. As a result, the SPG spent decades attempting to pass a parliamentary law that would confirm the legality of baptizing slaves, trying to prove that Christianity and slavery were compatible. While such a bill was never passed, Travis Glasson has shown that the SPG's ongoing efforts to encourage legislation supporting slave baptism culminated with the influential Yorke-Talbot Opinion of 1729. The Yorke-Talbot Opinion, which was issued by Attorney General Philip Yorke and Solicitor General Charles Talbot, stated that a slave traveling to Britain would "not become free" and that baptism "doth not bestow Freedom upon him, nor make any alteration in his temporal Condition in these Kingdoms."[117] This legal advocacy was intended to convince planters that Christianity was not a threat to slavery but as Robertson's writings suggest, this was not actually the planters' concern. Robertson suggested, instead, that education, which was closely connected to Christian baptism, was the real threat, and that slave owners did not want to provide their slaves with tools—like literacy—that could help them advocate for their own rights. The consequence of the SPG's legal advocacy, then, was not a decrease in planter obstructionism but rather the codification of race as the legal foundation of enslavement.

The results of the Society's master-centered approach can be seen in their ownership of the Codrington estate. An underlying problem at Codrington was the failure of the Society—and its missionaries—to understand the enslaved population they were seeking to convert. Furthermore, the Society chose to use its mastery to coerce enslaved people into attending catechism classes and church, undermining their appeal to slaves. Within this context, resistance to slavery became resistance to Christianity, and the enslaved men and women on Codrington rejected the Anglican message. The Society's missionaries, who were unable to blame other slave owners for their failure to convert their own slaves, increasingly blamed the enslaved for their unwillingness to convert. Arthur Holt, for one, became increasingly pessimistic about the prospect of slave conversion over time. In the 1720s, when he was installed as minister of St. Joseph's parish, he responded to the query from Edmund Gibson, the Lord Bishop of London, regarding the "infidels" in his parish by stating that while "Free Negroes are commonly Baptized," as are "some natives, which are capable of Instruction . . . Transported Slaves are Stupidly ignorant."[118] His comments suggest that while he did not actively prevent slave conversion, he did little to support it. Perhaps more importantly, Holt's sentiments regarding slave conversion implied that he blamed his own failure as a missionary on the "stupid[ity]" of African slaves, rather than himself. Holt's changing perspective—and his increasingly racialized language—reflects a larger pattern. As missionaries faced difficulties converting slaves to Christianity, they blamed their enslaved congregants, rather than themselves.[119]

By 1730, the most powerful members of the Anglican establishment, including the bishop of London and the archbishop of Canterbury, were intimately acquainted with the practice of buying and selling enslaved people, and were in regular touch with other planters, merchants and politicians regarding the Codrington estate. Sugar cultivation and profitability remained the Society's priority while their slave conversion program flagged. As a result, Codrington never became the model for Christian slavery that was envisioned by Bishop Fleetwood in 1711. Instead, it was the Society that had molded itself to the demands of plantation slavery, not the other way around.

The master-centered outreach of the Anglicans, however, would contrast sharply with the arrival of a new wave of missionaries—Pietist Moravians who were part of the revivalist movement known as the Great
Awakening. The Moravians, a small Protestant denomination founded in
eastern Germany, built on the networks created by Anglican missionary
organizations throughout the Atlantic world. But while they were indebted
to Anglican connections, they transformed the missionary enterprise in the
plantation colonies with new evangelical strategies. Moravian missionaries
feuded with black Christians who were members of the established
churches, and introduced a new and radical form of Christianity to the
sugar colonies.

Chapter 7

Inner Slavery and Spiritual Freedom

On October 6, 1731, Anton Ulrich, an Afro-Caribbean man living in Copen-hagen, wrote a letter to Count Nikolaus Ludwig von Zinzendorf, the leader of the Moravian Church. Ulrich thanked the Count for inviting him to Herrnhut, the village on the Count's estate that served as headquarters for the Moravians.[1] Ulrich had just returned from a two-month visit to Herrnhut where he worshipped among the Moravian brethren. There, he had described life in St. Thomas, the island in the Danish West Indies where Ulrich had been born as a slave. Ulrich "spoke plaintively about his sister and the other blacks in St. Thomas" and urged the brethren to come to the aid of the enslaved men and women who, he insisted, desperately "wanted to learn about God and become Christians."[2] The response to Ulrich's appeal was recorded directly on a copy of his letter: "This is the letter from the Black, Anton Ulrich. . . . He created the opportunity for the St. Thomas [mission]."[3]

Anton Ulrich went down in Moravian history as the "doorway to the heathen," the man who initiated the Moravian missions to enslaved Afri-cans. His place in the church's history was not incidental: he was entered consciously into the Moravian archive by, among others, the Moravian scribe who not only recopied Ulrich's letter, but also added a short intro-duction to explain his significance (see Figure 8). Ulrich's status as a former slave allowed the Moravians to claim that they had received a direct invita-tion to evangelize, providing them with legitimacy they did not receive from slave owners. Even two decades later, when the Moravians began to plan a new slave mission on Jamaica, they remembered "the negro Anton," who "gave us the opportunity to begin our mission in St. Thomas," com-paring him to a black visitor from Jamaica who, like Anton, asked the brethren to preach the gospel to his family in the Caribbean.[4]

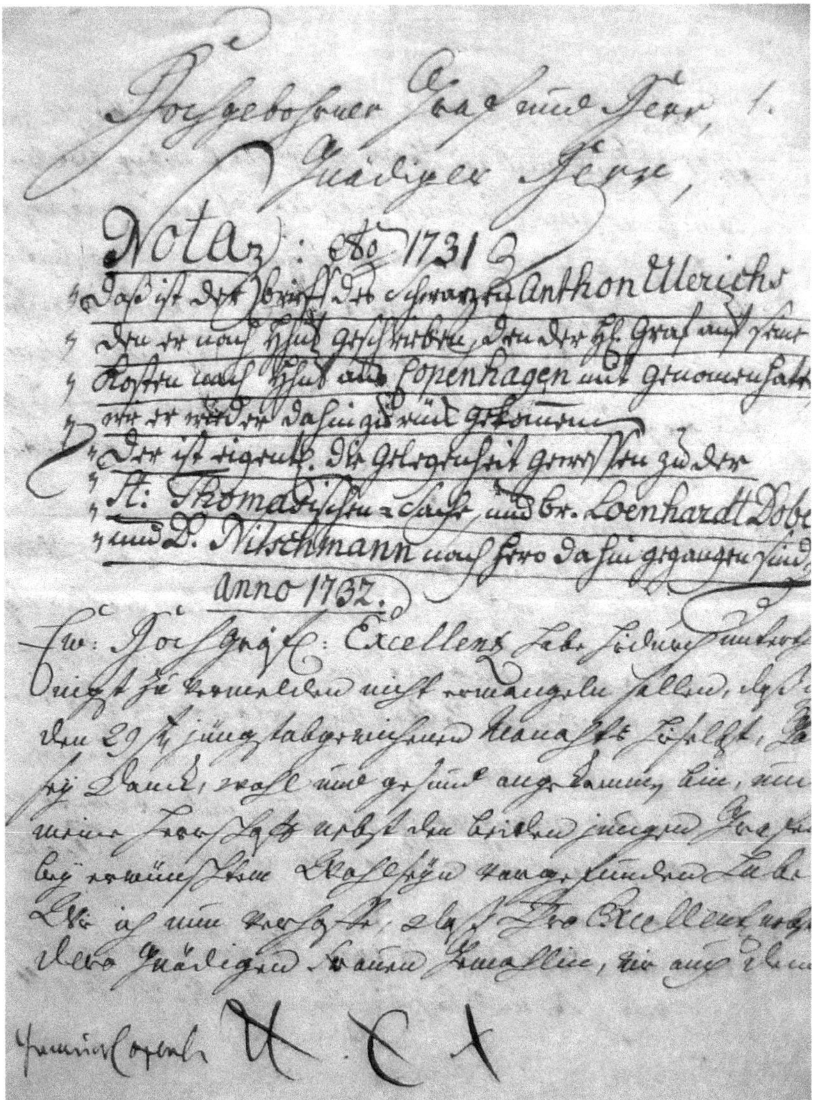

Figure 8. Copy of a letter from Anton Ulrich to Count Zinzendorf, October 6, 1731. The scribe who copied the letter credited Ulrich with providing the "opportunity for the St. Thomas [mission]" (UA R.15.Ba.3.1). Courtesy of the Moravian Archives, Herrnhut, Germany.

The Moravians were at the vanguard of a new transoceanic evangelical awakening and they were the first Protestant group to attract a large number of enslaved converts.[5] By the end of the eighteenth century, Moravian global missions had become a major force not only in the Americas, but also in Africa, and they provided an evangelical model for conversion that was copied by other Protestant groups, such as the Methodists and Baptists.[6] As a result, historians have usually examined the Moravian missions either in isolation or in conjunction with the later transatlantic evangelical awakening associated with the preaching of George Whitefield and the emergence of Methodism in the 1740s. The Moravians have rarely been tied to the previous Protestant missionary endeavors instigated by the SPG or its sister organization, the SPCK.[7] A careful examination of the origins of the Moravian missions, however, suggests that these groups were, in fact, connected in important ways. The Pietist reform movement in Germany, which aimed to reinvigorate the Lutheran Church, laid much of the groundwork for the later Moravian missions. German Pietists based in Halle developed close connections with members of the SPG and SPCK in London and made inroads with the royal family in Copenhagen. While Zinzendorf and the Moravians feuded bitterly with Halle Pietists, they still benefited from their decades of work cultivating relationships with Anglican voluntary societies like the SPG and the SPCK, as well as individuals in the Danish court. They used these communication channels and travel networks to gain access to the British and Danish colonies in the Americas. The Moravian evangelical strategies to enslaved people in the Caribbean, meanwhile, were modeled on previous missionary efforts. It was the Pietist mission to Tranquebar, India, a joint effort between the Danish Crown, the SPCK, and Halle Pietists, which inspired Count Zinzendorf and the Moravian Church to articulate a vision of a global church.

Once they arrived in the Danish West Indies in 1732, the Moravians clashed with slave owners and, more surprisingly, with black Christians who had been baptized in the Dutch Reformed Church. Their experience highlights a tension in the emergence of black Protestantism that is often overlooked: the conflict between black Christians who had been baptized in the established churches of the colonies, such as the Dutch Reformed or Anglican, and the Pietist and evangelical missionaries such as the Moravians, who embraced both slavery and spiritual equality. While a number of scholars have shown how the evangelical Protestant denominations, including the Moravians, Methodists, and Baptists, brought enslaved and free blacks into their fold with their ideas of salvation and their affective worship practices, we know less about the difficulties that these same missionaries had when they met blacks who had already converted to one of the established churches.[8]

As I showed in earlier chapters, slave conversion in the Protestant colonies was largely left in the hands of slave owners who tended to view conversion as a destabilizing and unpredictable force; yet at the same time, some slave owners chose to introduce favored slaves to Christianity, teaching them to read and allowing them to be baptized in the established church. As a result, Protestantism was reserved for the most "elite" slaves, some of whom were eventually freed by their masters. When a new wave of radical Pietists and evangelical Christians arrived in the colonies hoping to bring the gospel to enslaved Africans in the 1730s and later, their vision of conversion was at odds not only with white colonists in the established churches, but also with the black Christians they met. The conflict between these two radically different visions of Protestantism represents not only an important factor in the history of black Christianity, but also a major shift in the relationship between Protestantism and slavery in the Atlantic world.

Pietism and Pan-Protestant Reform

One of the most significant developments in European Protestantism during the late seventeenth and early eighteenth centuries was the emergence of Pietism, a reform movement within the Lutheran Church.[9] The term *pietismus* entered the German lexicon around 1674 when it was used to refer to the *collegia pietatis* of Philipp Jakob Spener, widely regarded as the father of Pietism. The *collegia pietatis* were small meetings that emphasized Bible study, devotional exercises, and the expression of personal piety. Envisioned to reform what was seen as an overly theological Lutheran Church, the *collegia pietatis* inspired religious revivals throughout Germany.[10]

One of the most important figures in the Pietist movement was August Hermann Francke, a Lutheran pastor and professor at the University of Halle in Saxony. In Halle, Francke founded several charitable and educational institutions, such as a school for poor children, an orphanage, and a *Collegium Orientale*. He also created several small businesses including a bookstore, a printing press, and a medical dispensary. These businesses served the interests of his charitable institutions and provided important streams of revenue. The Francke Foundations, as they were called, were closely tied to Francke's theology of conversion. Francke himself had experienced a dramatic conversion experience, which he described as a breakthrough (*Durchbruch*) preceded by a period of intense, penitential struggle (*Busskampf*). Francke believed that anyone could be guided to conversion and true godliness through Christian education, and his Foundations were intended to be the vanguard of a new, global religious renewal.[11]

By the turn of the eighteenth century, Halle had become the epicenter of Pietist activities in Europe. It was in Halle that several key Pietist leaders, including Bartholomäus Ziegenbalg, a missionary to Tranquebar, and Count Ludwig von Zinzendorf, the Moravian leader, gained their experience and connections. Pietist reformers quickly made connections with other Protestants who sought to reinvigorate or reform their national churches. In England, the first person to initiate Anglican-Pietist contact was Heinrich Ludolf, the former secretary to Prince George of Denmark and consort to Princess (later Queen) Anne of England. Ludolf made connections with Archbishop Tenison and Humfrey Wanley, the secretary of the SPCK, among others, and helped to spread news about the Halle orphanage and other charity institutions.[12] Around 1700, William III gave permission to Prince George of Denmark to found a Royal German Lutheran Chapel, which soon became the center for Pietism in London. Prince George appointed the Halle Pietist Anthony William Boehm as court preacher, a position that Boehm held until his death in 1722. With their connections to Prince George, Boehm and other German Pietists gained a respectable profile and were favorably received by the SPG and SPCK. Boehm and his successor, Frederick Michael Ziegenhagen, became critical conduits between Halle and the Anglican voluntary societies. Boehm, in particular, was largely responsible for introducing key Pietist texts and ideas into London, such as Francke's *Pietas Hallensis.* In the preface, Boehm emphasized that Pietism was not a separatist movement but a "new Reformation" within the Lutheran Church that "sought to revive the practice of Christianity through inward and personal spiritual renewal."[13]

As a result of these efforts, members of the SPG and SPCK did not view Pietists as "dissenters" but rather as foreign Protestants engaged in a common cause of moral reformation. Like the SPG and SPCK, Halle Pietists developed charitable programs emphasizing Christian education and they distributed devotional literature to the poor.[14] Archbishop Thomas Tenison "highly approved" of Francke's *Pietas Hallensis* and Josiah

Woodward advised the SPCK to distribute it. The Society sent multiple copies of the text to each of their correspondents and new versions were printed and distributed in 1707, 1710, and 1716.[15] After the English publication of *Pietas Hallensis*, Francke's *Waisenhaus* received large numbers of donations from prominent members of the Anglican Church. The publication also spawned similar institutions throughout Britain, Ireland, and America, and was an inspiration to later evangelists like George Whitefield and John Wesley.

Throughout the first three decades of the eighteenth century, both Boehm and Ziegenhagen used their position to support German Lutherans and Pietists in London and America. They helped to organize aid for Protestant refugees, joining together with Thomas Bray, the SPG, and the SPCK in these charitable endeavors.[16] Over time, Boehm and Ziegenhagen became the de facto organizers of German Lutheran immigration to the Americas, providing the ministers with widespread influence.[17]

Mission to Tranquebar

One of the most significant, and unlikely, collaborations between the SPCK and Halle Pietists was their involvement in a Protestant mission to Tranquebar sponsored by the Danish Crown.[18] Tranquebar, a small coastal town near Tanjore in southern India, had been a Danish trading colony since about 1620.[19] While the colony did not host any missionaries during the seventeenth century, the newly crowned Danish King Frederick IV felt that Protestants, like Catholics, should maintain both civil and religious responsibility for their colonial lands, so he formed the Royal Danish Mission in 1704. The SPG's missions in America may also have been a source of inspiration. In the Proceedings of the Annual Society for 1712, the SPG announced that the Danish missions to the East Indies "was one of the Fruits and Effects" of the Society's mission in the "Western-Indies."[20] Unlike the missions of the SPG, however, Frederick IV's proposal for a mission was aimed primarily at Tamil natives, rather than European settlers.

Once Frederick IV had established the Royal Danish Mission, he enlisted his court preacher, Franz Julius Lütkens, to identify potential missionaries. Since the leaders of the Danish Lutheran Church were opposed to sending missionaries outside the geographical borders of Denmark, Lütkens wrote to his contacts in Berlin for recommendations.[21] He eventually chose two

Halle-educated Pietists, Bartholomäus Ziegenbalg (1682–1719) and Henry Plütschau (1677–1746), as the first missionaries to Tranquebar. After their ordination in Copenhagen, the two men departed for India, where they arrived in July 1706. In Tranquebar, Ziegenbalg and Plütschau developed an evangelical strategy based on language learning and cultural observation. They studied Tamil, translated the Bible into the vernacular, and took care to act in accordance with local customs.[22] The missionaries adapted Francke's pedagogical principles developed at Halle for their mission. The Bible was always at the center of their lessons, though the missionaries also taught literacy, rhetoric, medicine, geography, and several other subjects.

In Germany, letters from Ziegenbalg and Plütschau were first published in 1708 under the title *Merkwürdige Nachrict* (Notable News). Then, in 1710, Francke began publishing the letters from Ziegenbalg and Plütschau in what would become the first German Lutheran missionary magazine, *Halle Reports*.[23] While the Tranquebar mission was initially unknown in England, Boehm began to publicize it in 1709 by publishing a translation of *Merkwürdige Nachricht* under the title *Propagation of the Gospel in the East*, which he dedicated to the SPG and Archbishop Thomas Tenison.[24] The SPG ordered copies of the text, and distributed them throughout England and the Americas. By 1718, *Propagation of the Gospel in the East* had gone through three editions. While the SPG, whose charter limited its involvement to missions in the "English Plantations in America," could not finance the Tranquebar mission, several of their members submitted personal contributions. The SPCK, however, took a more active role, sending books, funds, a printing press, and paper to India. They also hosted Bartholomäus Ziegenbalg when he visited London in 1716, where he met with Boehm and members of the SPCK. And Ziegenhagen, Boehm's successor, was a key figure in organizing the first SPCK mission to Madras, India in 1728.

Zinzendorf and the Renewed Unitas Fratrum

Halle Pietism and the Tranquebar mission had a formative effect on the young Nikolaus Ludwig von Zinzendorf (1700–1760). Zinzendorf, whose godfather was the "father" of Pietism himself, Philip Jakob Spener, was sent to Halle to be educated between the ages of ten and sixteen. There, Zinzendorf met not only the missionaries Ziegenbalg and Plütschau, but also a Tamil convert named Timotheus who had traveled to Germany with the missionaries. Years later, in 1753, Zinzendorf acknowledged the importance of the *Halle Reports* and the Tranquebar mission on the Moravian missionary enterprise.[25] The Tranquebar mission provided the inspiration for the Moravian missions in multiple ways: first, publications from Tranquebar, including the *Merkwürdige Nachrict* and the *Halle Reports*, were deeply influential in molding the Moravian approach to evangelization. They emphasized the importance of learning non-European languages and teaching literacy. Their approach to conversion was based on "heart religion"—the belief that anyone, regardless of their cultural or linguistic background, could become a true Christian by experiencing heartfelt devotion. On a more organizational level, the Tranquebar mission helped to solidify the wide-reaching pan-Protestant communication network centered in London, Halle, and Copenhagen.

After leaving Halle, Zinzendorf went to Wittenberg and then embarked on a Grand Tour. Then, beginning in 1722, Zinzendorf began to host a variety of persecuted Protestants, mostly from Bohemia and Moravia, on his estate in eastern Saxony.[26] Zinzendorf was intrigued by the beliefs and practices of the refugees and he allowed them to establish a settlement just up the hill from his own castle. The settlement was named Herrnhut, or "under the care of the Lord." Many of the Herrnhutters, as they were sometimes called, were members of the Unitas Fratrum, a persecuted group that claimed descent from the fourteenth-century martyr Jan Hus, a Czech reformer who anticipated several of Luther's later critiques of the Catholic Church.[27] In 1727, after a period of discord and struggle, the community went through a religious transformation that marked the founding of the Renewed Unitas Fratrum, also known as the Moravian Church.[28] The renewal was preceded by a community reorganization initiated by Zinzendorf: men and women were split into separate "choirs" based on their age, gender, and marital status and twelve elders were chosen to have spiritual oversight over the settlement. The Herrnhut community also introduced the use of the lot to make decisions, a method that was intended to allow the Brethren to determine God's will.

The Moravians took inspiration from Matthew 28:19: "Therefore go and make disciples of all nations, baptizing them in the name of the Father and of the Son and of the Holy Spirit." Almost immediately after their renewal, members of the Moravian Church began to travel around Europe to spread word of their revival. Seeking to "establish bonds of fellowship with the 'children of God' in other cities, lands, and churches," Moravian emissaries traveled to England, Denmark, and throughout Germany, building on the pan-Protestant networks established by Halle Pietists, Anglican voluntary societies, and individuals in the Danish court.[29]

The Moravians' far-flung connections proved to be of utmost importance as they became increasingly unpopular in Saxony. As the influence of the Herrnhuters and their revival spread, local clergy lodged complaints that their parishioners were being tempted away from the established churches. In 1732, Augustus the Strong, King of Poland and elector of Saxony, banished Zinzendorf and required him to sell his property. When Augustus the Strong died the following year, his successor, Stanislaw I, granted clemency, but by then, the Moravians' precarious position in Europe had worsened with their public clash with Halle Pietists.[30] These episodes encouraged the Moravians to embrace a new identity as a global missionary church.

While the Moravians' increasingly precarious political position in Saxony was a major factor in the development of their missions, they still relied on previously established Pietist networks connecting Halle, Copenhagen, and London. As they developed evangelical methods, they looked to Tranquebar as a model. The direction of Moravian outreach, meanwhile, was determined by a chance meeting at the coronation of the King of Denmark in 1731. It was there that Anton Ulrich met David Nitschmann, a Moravian carpenter traveling with Count Zinzendorf.

Anton Ulrich and the Caribbean Connection

Anton Ulrich was born a slave in St. Thomas, where he lived until traveling to Copenhagen with his master, the Danish Count Laurwig. In Denmark, Ulrich was baptized and manumitted. Ulrich's conversion to Christianity represented a model of slave conversion that embraced both spiritual and earthly salvation. He was singled out by his master as a "favored" slave and granted both attention and some education. When he returned to St. Thomas in 1734, he was a free man.[31]

In 1731, Ulrich met David Nitschmann, a Moravian carpenter who had accompanied Count Zinzendorf to Copenhagen to attend the king's coronation. Ulrich told Nitschmann that his interest in Christianity had been fostered on St. Thomas, but he criticized the unchristian behavior of most whites on the island, explaining that the so-called Christians said one thing and did another. This type of criticism appealed to Nitschmann, who agreed that many European Christians were similarly insincere. As the two men confided in one another, Ulrich told Nitschmann more about Caribbean slavery and the "miserable position of the blacks in St. Thomas." He mentioned that his own sister remained in St. Thomas and desperately wanted to know God. Nitschmann relayed this news to Zinzendorf, who saw the potential for a missionary venture to the small island. The Count convinced Ulrich's master, Count Laurwig, to allow his servant to visit the Brethren in Herrnhut. After making arrangements, Zinzendorf returned to Herrnhut ahead of Ulrich and Nitschmann, where he reported what Ulrich had told him about the slaves in St. Thomas and their desire to become Christians.[32]

Ulrich and Nitschmann arrived in Herrnhut on July 29, 1731, eight days after Count Zinzendorf. After being introduced to the congregation, Ulrich repeated his description of St. Thomas. He told the Brethren about the misery of the slaves and their ignorance of Christianity. Not only did the enslaved have very little time "for learning and instruction," but their masters were "openly against it." One of the brothers in the audience was Leonhard Dober, who "couldn't stop thinking" about the slaves in St. Thomas. Despite resistance from other brethren, who felt that his plan was poorly conceived, Dober insisted that he was called to work among the slaves in St. Thomas. He concluded that if he could find another Brother to accompany him, he would "give [him]self as a slave and tell [the slaves on St. Thomas] what [he] knew about our Lord."[33]

Dober's willingness to become a slave in order to carry the gospel to St. Thomas revealed a conception of slavery that was not based solely on racial difference. He and Nitschmann, who was also willing to become a slave, conceived of slavery as a malleable category that could be entered into by choice or by force. The missionaries' ignorance can be attributed to their lack of familiarity with Atlantic slavery, but it also reveals a general disregard for earthly standing. Nitschmann and Dober seemed to relish the idea of becoming slaves in order to spread the gospel. Their eagerness to toil among the unfree was an early indication of their belief that true freedom was spiritual. It is also important to note that Dober and Nitschmann did not conceive of the idea to become slaves on their own: it was Anton Ulrich who warned the brethren that the slave owners were so hostile to Christian missions that they "would have a very difficult time talking with or teaching the slaves, and if someone really wanted to do that, he would have to live among them and become a slave like them, so that he would be able to be among them and have the opportunity to instruct them."[34]

Ulrich's suggestion that the Moravian missionaries would need to become slaves perplexed the Moravian historian C. G. A. Oldendorp. Writing thirty years after Ulrich's visit to Herrnhut, Oldendorp commented: "The thought that they would have to become slaves was terrifying but also false and unnecessary. . . . It was well known to this Negro [Anton] that no whites could be made or taken as slaves and even if he wanted to become one, he wouldn't be allowed." Oldendorp was sure that Ulrich would have known that only blacks could be slaves, and he was left to ponder what he could have meant: maybe he was "trying to show just how difficult it would be to spend time with [the slaves]"; or "perhaps he thought that they should become a foreman or an overseer . . . and that this wasn't correctly understood."[35]

Oldendorp's horrified reaction to the idea that white Christians might become slaves is an indication of how the conceptions of race and slavery would change within the Moravian Church. Oldendorp's own experiences in the Danish West Indies in the 1760s gave him a thoroughly racial understanding of slavery. Using the Dutch creole term for whites, *blancken*, which was ubiquitous on St. Thomas, he denied that whites could ever be "made or taken as slaves," even if they desired it. In 1731, by contrast, neither Nitschmann nor Dober had seen a Caribbean slave society firsthand, and their only window into that world was Anton Ulrich.

Ulrich returned to Copenhagen after two months in Herrnhut. Dober and Nitschmann followed him the following year, arriving on September 15, 1732. After a year of anticipation and planning, they were eager to reunite with the man who had inspired their mission. Given these expectations, they were surely shocked to learn that Anton Ulrich no longer wanted them to travel to St. Thomas. While Ulrich and his new wife initially welcomed the missionaries on the day after their arrival, it later became clear that neither Ulrich nor his master, Count Laurwig, supported their missionary venture. In a letter to Herrnhut written on September 23, 1732, Dober and Nitschmann reported that Count Laurwig "has created a lot of difficulties for us; told us our plan would never work and he said that he would have nothing to do with it."[36] Ulrich later begged the brothers not to go through with their plan, and the Senior Chamberlain von Plessen, one of the directors of the Danish West India Company, asked them how they planned to support themselves on St. Thomas.[37] When Nitschmann replied that they "wanted to work among the Negroes," von Plessen informed him that they "don't let white people do that!" Nitschmann then suggested that he could work as a carpenter and that Dober could be his assistant. Despite this, von Plessen and Count Laurwig refused the brothers passage on the Danish West India Company's ships and they were forced to find transportation elsewhere.[38]

Dober and Nitschmann's negative reception in Copenhagen can be interpreted in a number of ways. Ulrich, von Plessen, and Laurwig may have been sincere in their attempt to dissuade the missionaries from going through with their mission. For in reality, Dober and Nitschmann's plan to carry the gospel to the slaves in St. Thomas *was* both dangerous and badly planned. With very little money and a dubious plan for earning a living, it was reasonable to suggest that their mission would never succeed.[39] The brothers' assertion that they could become slaves, an idea that had been suggested by Ulrich, made them seem ridiculous to the directors of the Danish West India Company. Yet Dober and Nitschmann's problems in Copenhagen cannot just be ascribed to their bad planning. The Danish West India Company was in a period of crisis and Count Laurwig had stepped down as the President of the Company on September 12, 1732, just days before Dober and Nitschmann's arrival in Copenhagen. The Senior Chamberlain von Plessen was in the process of lobbying for the purchase of St. Croix from the French, an acquisition he hoped would turn the Danish West India Company into a stronger and more profitable enterprise.[40] Nitschmann and Dober, with their aspiration of becoming white slaves, were probably seen as liabilities who could cause instability in the Danish islands.

While Laurwig and von Plessen had political and economic reasons for discouraging the missionaries, this does not explain why Anton Ulrich turned away from the Moravians. According to Oldendorp, Ulrich was "taken in by false Brothers and religious people who had clashed with Herrnhut, who were all against the Moravian congregation." Their influence, Oldendorp suggested, caused Ulrich to "take back what he had said and to convince the Brothers not to go through with their plan."[41] Oldendorp may have based this conclusion on Leonard Dober's *Mitteilung an eine Gräfin zu Stölberg-Wernigerode*, written in 1740, eight years after Dober's initial visit to Copenhagen. In his *Report*, Dober wrote, "the Moor was very changed when we arrived, and it was because of this that the Count Laurwig concluded that it was impractical to go [to St. Thomas]."[42] Yet the original diaries and letters from 1732 paint a slightly different picture. Nitschmann and Dober suggested that Ulrich had been mistreated by other servants in Copenhagen and that he was more subdued than usual. In their first letter to Zinzendorf, they wrote that Anton "was very serious and has been persecuted by the servants."[43] Dober did not mention if these servants were anti-Moravian, nor did he suggest that Ulrich had joined a separate anti-Moravian group. Moreover, Dober and Nitschmann continued meeting with Ulrich throughout their stay in Copenhagen, a fact that suggests that Ulrich did not reject the missionaries outright.

Another possibility is that Ulrich felt a variety of pressures—from peers as well as his master—that led him to grow more cautious in his dealings with the Moravians. He was mostly likely aware that Count Laurwig and von Plessen had refused to support the Moravians' venture, and it is clear from Dober and Nitschmann's letter that Ulrich was also feeling resentment from his peers. In all likelihood, Ulrich's break with the Moravians occurred slowly and gradually, and it was not due merely to the influence of anti-Moravian factions. The missionaries themselves may have contributed to the growing distance between themselves and the source of their inspiration. Nitschmann and Dober were often critical of their acquaintances in Copenhagen. In their first meeting with Ulrich and his new wife on September 16, 1732, Dober and Nitschmann commented that Ulrich's wife "had a good mind . . . but she was lacking the correct direction."[44] In another letter, they wrote that they had met "various brothers, one of whom had been awakened for twenty years, but he lacked a true knowledge of Christ."[45] The missionaries' judgmental mindset may also have been an important factor in their deteriorating relationship with Anton Ulrich. Still, the brethren maintained contact with Ulrich throughout their stay in Copenhagen, praying with him before boarding their ship. Ulrich also gave the missionaries a letter intended for his sister, Anna, a slave on St. Thomas.[46]

Anton Ulrich's relationship with the Moravian brethren worsened over time. In 1734, after Dober had been in St. Thomas for two years (Nitschmann returned after 16 weeks), Ulrich returned to the island of his birth. He was a free man, and he set to work as an overseer (*Meisterknecht*) before purchasing a small plantation and a slave of his own. In St. Thomas, he continued to drift from the Brethren. Dober considered Ulrich to be "too weak in order to stand up to the violence of his sins and stay true to what he knew," though this is clearly a one-sided judgment.[47] What is clear is that Anton Ulrich decided to pursue his own path in St. Thomas as a small-time landowner and slave owner, and that the Moravian brethren were no longer compatible with his convictions or aspirations.

The missionaries' failure to sustain their relationship with Ulrich was an early indicator of the problems they would have attracting educated black Christians into their fold. For Ulrich, like most other black Christians in St. Thomas, being a Christian was very much connected to rising social status and manumission. From Ulrich's point of view, the Moravians had initially provided an opportunity for travel and companionship. He also hoped that they would aid the members of his family who were still enslaved. But the Moravians' increasingly radical and marginalized reputation, combined with their condemnation of most Christians as "unawakened" and their embrace of earthly slavery, created a wedge between the missionaries and the man who inspired their mission.

Free Blacks and Christian Slaves

When Leonhard Dober and David Nitschmann arrived on the Caribbean island of St. Thomas, they found themselves on an island that was Danish in name only (see Map 3). St. Thomas and St. John, a neighboring island, were the property of the Danish West India and Guinea Company, a joint-stock company that was governed by a small number of directors and a group of stockholders. As a major stockholder, the King of Denmark had some stake in the West Indian venture, but he was only one voice among many.[48] While most of the Danish West Indian ruling class, including the Directors of the Company, were Danes, St. Thomas and St. John were also heavily influenced by Dutch culture. The lingua franca of the Danish West Indies was Dutch—not Danish—and the slaves on the island spoke Dutch Creole. Aside from the Danes and the Dutch, the islands included significant populations of English, Jews, Spaniards, and Frenchmen.

Regardless of their ethnic background, the white inhabitants of the Danish West Indies aimed to make a profit. To this end, they purchased thousands of enslaved people and developed scores of plantations. From 1691 to 1755, the white population remained relatively constant (389 in 1691; 325 in 1755) while the population of enslaved Africans jumped from 547 to nearly 4,000.[49] The increase in the slave population was largely due to the demands of sugar production, the crop that had proved to be so profitable in the English islands of Barbados and Jamaica. In 1696, there were seven sugar mills on St. Thomas. In 1715, less than twenty years later, this number had jumped to thirty-two.

As a result of these economic and demographic changes, the white planter class grew increasingly fearful for its safety and developed a caste system to control the slave majority. Individuals were stratified not only by their status as black, white or mulatto, but also by their adherence to Christianity. Religion was particularly important for free blacks. According to Johan Lorenz Carstens, a white Creole planter who was born on St. Thomas and would become one of the few advocates for the Moravians, free blacks were divided into two groups: free men and free slaves. Free men were blacks who had converted to Christianity. Once baptized and freed, the free blacks "bec[a]me citizens and enjoy[ed] privileges . . . just as white Christians." These privileges included the ability to build homes in the city, practice "respectable" trades, and wear a limited amount of fine clothing, including "a short vest and long narrow pants, along with stockings and shoes."[50]

Unconverted free blacks were referred to as "free slaves" and while they were technically free (that is, they were in possession of *fribrev* or free papers), they could not obtain full civic rights without baptism. Most "free slaves" were "mulattos," and Carstens believed that the majority were freed "upon the death of their master or mistress . . . because the surviving spouse cannot stand them since they are the offspring of the dead spouse's mixing and miscegenation with strangers." Others purchased their freedom. Regardless of their path to freedom, however, "none of the free slaves [could] enter any civilian trade, except those which the Christians do not wish to bother themselves with."[51] Free slaves were also limited in their dress and in their choice of living space.

Carstens estimated that the number of free men and free slaves, both male and female, was about 500 in the 1730s. By then, however, the status of baptized blacks had become increasingly tenuous. In the seventeenth century, masters were often expected to grant slaves their freedom immediately after baptism, a standard that was quickly eroded in the first decades of the eighteenth century. When Carstens wrote in the 1740s, he noted that slave owners had become very resistant to granting free papers to their baptized slaves and that while "a Christian, either male or female, cannot be a slave or a servant," masters "do not accept" this. "Even though many of their slaves are accepted and baptized in the Christian congregation," he wrote, "they keep them as serfs for their own purposes . . . until they eventually can acquire their *fribrev* ["free letter" or "free paper"] either by monetary purchase or with an action of one kind of another."[52]

Carstens' comments reveal a slave society in transition. As sugar cultivation took hold in the Danish West Indies and the number of enslaved

Africans increased, planters embraced the ideology of Protestant Supremacy and made Christian status attainable only for the most "elite" slaves. Over time, planters would increasingly define slavery in racial—rather than religious—terms, and Christianity was no longer a definite signifier of freedom. Yet even as White Supremacy replaced Protestant Supremacy, slave owners continued to restrict their slaves' access to Christianity. By the 1730s, a small number of enslaved and free blacks were granted access to the established churches, but most were not. As in the English Caribbean, Protestant missions to slaves were treated as a threat to the island's security.

When Dober and Nitschmann arrived on St. Thomas in 1732, they met a small number of free black Christians and slave converts who had followed a path similar to that of Anton Ulrich: often favored by their masters, they were able to receive some education, which led to baptism and, sometimes, freedom. While the missionaries showed interest in these individuals, they questioned whether they were "true Christians." Just as they had thrown doubt on the religious state of their acquaintances in Copenhagen, Dober and Nitschmann maintained a rigid standard for true Christianity among the black converts in St. Thomas. A few weeks after their arrival, they visited "a Moor who had lived in Berlin for 18 years." They noted that he "immediately began to speak to us out of the Bible" and that "he had a lot of knowledge," but they concluded that he was "completely drowned in the lusts of the flesh." Nitschmann told him that not all of those who were baptized could be considered true Christians. He read him the First Epistle of John, after which "[the moor] became uneasy and annoyed."[53]

A few days later, Dober and Nitschmann met another black man whom they described as a "well-known Moor." They "read the 3rd chapter of John to him and told him that the New Birth was the grandest, and without it, one could not see the Lord." Again, Dober and Nitschmann criticized this black Christian, telling him "he had to give more of an effort than just learning everything by heart." In an intriguing comparison, they added: "[The black Christians] place as much importance on learning as the Lutherans do on going to church and communion."[54] By connecting the black Christian interest in learning to the Lutheran emphasis on "church and communion," Dober and Nitschmann applied a Pietist critique of religion to the state of Christianity among blacks in St. Thomas. They implied that the desire to learn, like the Lutheran emphasis on church and communion, placed too much emphasis on form and too little on the heart. This analysis is confirmed by Dober and Nitschmann's message to the "well-known Moor." By referring to the "New Birth," which they considered necessary for being able to "see the Lord," the missionaries revealed their strong Pietist beliefs that led them to condemn Christians, both black and white, for excessive formalism and inadequate emotion.

During another encounter, Dober and Nitschmann visited a blacksmith named Alexander who had just been baptized. The missionaries dismissed Alexander's conversion as illegitimate, claiming "that he had never heard of true, living Christianity." The missionaries told Alexander that "true faith purifies the heart, and makes us into new men," adding that "the moors seem very eager to listen and learn how to read and write."[55] As these meetings suggest, nearly all the black Christians that Dober and Nitschmann mentioned in their journal showed a profound interest in learning. Whether male or female, Dober and Nitschmann noted that enslaved and free blacks often approached them so that they could learn how to read the Bible. While the missionaries were happy with the attention, they were extremely wary about "learning"—so much so that they often alienated themselves from potential converts and allies.

Dober and Nitschmann's critique of the black Christians on St. Thomas can be seen as an extension of the Pietist critique of the confessional churches in Europe. Most of the black Christians on St. Thomas had been educated and baptized within an established church, often the Dutch Reformed. This was reflected in the type of Christianity that these black Christians practiced. More important, however, is the fact that the missionaries did not connect Christianity to manumission. While many black Christians earned their freedom after receiving Christian education and baptism, Dober and Nitschmann defined true slavery as spiritual. They believed that anyone who engaged in non-Christian behavior was a "slave of the devil," regardless of whether that person was a master or a slave. For the missionaries, true freedom meant conversion, not manumission, a position that was most likely resented by blacks who either hoped to, or had, earned their freedom after conversion.

Instead of promising freedom, Dober and Nitschmann emphasized the danger of inner slavery to the small number of converts who showed an interest in them. When Anton Ulrich's sister Anna visited them on January 17, 1733, for example, she "complained that the overseer treated her too harshly." The missionaries refused to comfort her or take any action on her part, telling her that "this could be a great opportunity to truly call on God, so that she could be freed from her inner slavery, since her outward slavery was of little consequence."[56]

The missionaries' definition of true freedom had both behavioral and spiritual elements. Aside from experiencing a New Birth, truly "free" Christians were expected to maintain monogamous marriages and refrain from bodily sins. As the missionaries explained to a group of potential converts who hoped to learn how to read, "true conversion is absolutely necessary and when one converts, this person has to refrain from the sins of the body."[57] The missionaries' strict stance on behavior, coupled with their high standards for conversion, won them few friends on the island. Like most other whites, the missionaries considered the type of dancing practiced by most enslaved people to be "truly heathenish." But they also condemned the common practice of taking multiple partners or having more than one wife, a position that was seen by both blacks and whites as unreasonable.[58] Nonmonogamous family structures were common and accepted among most enslaved Africans, while white masters often took advantage of their power to coerce enslaved people into sexual relationships.

In their conversations with Alexander, the missionaries tried to convince the blacksmith that he should take only one wife. Reading from Paul, they classed polygamy with "whoring" [Hurerey] and warned him to stay true to one woman.[59] During another conversation, they argued that all those who had more than one partner were "slaves of the devil."[60] Alexander, clearly incredulous, explained that "all the citizens and masters who are called Christians engage in such behavior." The missionaries insisted that "these men did not belong to Christ, but to the Devil."[61] Dober and Nitschmann's standards grated on Alexander. After several months of regular meetings, the blacksmith lost his temper with the missionaries, calling them "papists" and telling them that "nobody could live up to their expectations."[62]

By maintaining specific standards for Christian behavior and conversion, the missionaries won few friends. Yet their rigid expectations also subverted the social hierarchy of the island. They condemned both white and black Christians as "slaves of the devil" while assuring black converts that they could ascend to Christ if they reformed their ways and experienced a true heart conversion. By placing so much emphasis on inner freedom, the missionaries created an alternative hierarchy that placed true Christians, black or white, over all others, black or white. Thus the missionaries could assure the enslaved that they were, in fact, better than their masters.

Dober and Nitschmann's expectations made "conversion" difficult to sustain. This was particularly true for Anna, Anton Ulrich's sister and the missionaries' prized first convert. Immediately after their arrival in 1732, the missionaries were pleased to see Anna's interest in Christian prayer and they learned that she used her reading lessons to memorize passages of scripture. She told the missionaries that "she was always praying in her heart, and that's why she couldn't sleep at night and she had a great desire to get to know the Savior." The missionaries also noted that Anna was greatly influenced by their reading of 1 Corinthians 6, which warned that sexual immorality would prevent anyone from inheriting the kingdom of God. Upon hearing this, Anna replied that "she didn't do that anymore," and the Brethren reiterated that such behavior was a sin. Two months later, she returned to the Brethren with her husband and complained "that [her husband] had allowed the negroes to dance in their house and this was a great burden for her."[63]

Anna was initially convinced that she needed to change her ways and she even went so far as to bring her husband to the Brethren so that he, too, could be reformed. Yet such shifts—if they happened at all—were rarely final. Within a few months, the Brethren noted that Anna, along with her brother and husband, occasionally "returned to their old accustomed ways." When the missionaries "spoke harshly with them and punished them earnestly," they "recognized [the problem] and promised to improve."[64] But by October, "things with the three awakened blacks on the company plantation were bad. Their unity was disrupted by various suspicions and misunderstandings."[65] In 1734, Anna returned to the Brethren, proclaiming that "she sought only to become truer to the Savior." Dober offered his forgiveness, thus initiating what would become a long process of disobedience and forgiveness in Anna's relationship with the Moravians. But Anna drifted again after she complained to the missionaries that her slavery was "hard." She was most likely displeased with their response that "the love of Christ makes such difficulties easy, and one just has to stay near his heart in all situations and make sure not to do anything to the Savior's dislike."[66]

While their rigid theology and fixed standards of morality often undermined their appeal to slaves, the missionaries also had much to offer their first converts. First of all, Anna and her brother Abraham were eager to gain access to the written word. In a place where literacy and books were carefully guarded by the master class, the missionaries introduced their pupils to scripture and taught them how to read. In later years, the Moravians' willingness to teach slaves how to read would earn them the wrath of white masters, but in the first few years it went largely unnoticed. Apart from the promise of literacy, Dober and Nitschmann could be seen as potential advocates. While they refused to defend the slaves against the wrath of their masters, they provided some support to slaves in their relationships with other enslaved people. When Anna complained that her husband Gerd was holding "heathen dances" in their home, for example, she sought to use the missionaries' influence to bolster her own power within her domestic relationship. While Dober and Oldendorp interpreted her actions as a sign of her conversion, her intentions were likely more complex than they realized. By persuading the missionaries to lobby on her behalf, she gained influence over her husband and convinced the missionaries of her religious sincerity. Finally, the missionaries were unique in their treatment of slaves as spiritual equals and they provided a religious community unlike any other available on the island.

Still, Dober and Nitschmann did not attract a wide following among either blacks or whites on St. Thomas. While a number of blacks approached them and requested lessons in reading and writing, others mocked them. In a journal entry from February 26, 1733, Nitschmann recorded that they "spoke a lot to the negroes that we work with and told them that they would be miserable beings as long as they lived without God, but they made fun of us."[67] Similarly, most whites on the island mocked the missionaries. During a visit to a white man who had offered to give the missionaries work, Dober and Nitschmann wrote that "his offer was fake, and he just ridiculed us."[68]

As Count Laurwig and von Plessen had predicted, the missionaries had trouble supporting themselves on the island despite the aid of a small number of sympathetic whites. Upon their arrival, they were approached by Gerhard Lorenzen, a planter on the island who had heard of the missionaries' plan from a friend in Copenhagen. Lorenzen offered the missionaries room and board until they were able to get their own footing. After some weeks working for Lorenzen, the missionaries met Johann Lorenz Carstens, the planter who would later write the *General Description of all the Danish, American or West Indian Islands.* Carstens hired Nitschmann, a trained carpenter, to build a house for him. Dober had more difficulty as a potter. After his attempt to make roof tiles failed, he hoped to become an overseer and live in a slave hut. Neither this plan nor his aspiration to become a fisherman was successful.

In April of 1733, Nitschmann returned to Europe as planned, leaving Dober to fend for himself. The lone missionary received permission from Lorenzen to live on his plantation among the slaves, but he soon found himself desperate for more funds. In May, after months of underemployment, Philip Gardelin, the recently appointed governor of St. Thomas, offered Dober work as his head house servant [*Hofmeister*]. Dober accepted the position, and Governor Gardelin provided him with new clothes and told him he would just need "to fear God and be true."[69]

The job at the governor's plantation appeared to be ideal for the young missionary. The governor urged Dober to maintain his religious discipline and he allowed him to leave his home in order to visit the slaves. But regardless of these benefits, Dober remained unhappy. "I was so ashamed," he wrote in 1740, "that I was not following my first plan, which was to be a slave on St. Thomas." He also felt that "the entire way of life was unfamiliar and excessive."[70] Dober's discomfort with the "way of life" at the governor's home, which was likely one of the more luxurious houses on the island, suggests that he did not want to indulge in opulence or engage with the wealthy. Indeed, his persistent unhappiness about not becoming a slave suggests that Dober felt invigorated by the idea of religious sacrifice and perhaps even martyrdom.

Dober's discomfort, however, was not due solely to the opulence of the environment or the fact that he was not a slave. Dober's tenure at the governor's home coincided with one of the most brutal years in Danish West Indian history. After a terrible drought during the spring, the island was hit by a hurricane in July 1733. Dober recorded "earthquakes and thunder and lightning," and noted that "several houses were destroyed."[71] In September, with tensions rising between masters and slaves, Governor Gardelin issued a mandate intended to regulate slave behavior more tightly. The "terrible severity" of Gardelin's Code of 1733 reflected "the prevailing tension between master and slave" in the Danish West Indies during the early 1730s.[72] That tension exploded two months later, when a group of recently arrived West African slaves rebelled against their masters and took control of St. John, a neighboring island in the Danish West Indies (see Map 3). Dober recorded the news of the rebellion in his diary: "a great alarm was sounded on the 23rd [of November]," he wrote, "and everyone was completely frightened to hear that the slaves had taken the fortress on St. John and . . . murdered all the whites [*Blancken*] on ¾ of the land."[73] While Dober did not go into detail about the effects of the rebellion, it had major effects—both materially and psychologically—on the inhabitants of St. Thomas.

By the end of December 1734, the slave rebels still controlled St. John but Dober was faced with a more personal crisis: he was sick and "close to death."[74] On January 1, 1734, Dober reported that he was finally able to get out of bed. Ten days later, he wrote to the governor and pleaded to be dismissed. The governor did not respond well. He refused to speak to Dober for eight days before concluding that "if [Dober] didn't want to stay with him, then he didn't want to keep him."[75] A week after leaving his position at the governor's home, Dober ran into Lorenzen, the man who had first taken pity on the missionaries. "He was surprised that I had left my master, and he asked whether I would go back home [to Europe]," Dober wrote. Lorenzen urged him to return to Germany and told him that he would be able to travel for very little money. Yet Dober was determined to continue spreading the gospel to the slaves, so he started working as a night watchman to support himself.[76] He lived in a small rented room in Tappus until April of 1734, when he was offered another job, this time as an overseer for Adrian Beverhout's plantation, "Brock."[77] He remained there until the following summer, when he was called back to Herrnhut to replace the deceased Martin Linner as an Elder in the Moravian Church.

Earthly Slavery, Spiritual Freedom

When Dober and Nitschmann returned to Germany, they brought with them new convictions that helped to shape the aims and policies of future Moravian missions. When Nitschmann arrived in Europe after sixteen weeks in St. Thomas, he revealed a surprising—and important—commitment to the institution of slavery that was informed by his experience on St. Thomas. In Copenhagen, Nitschmann met with Princess Hedwig and the Senior Chamberlain von Plessen, who told him that they would grant freedom to any slaves who converted, a gesture they considered to be both moral and efficacious. To their surprise, Nitschmann replied, "Such an idea would just make them hypocrites! The Apostle said: whoever was called to be a servant should not seek to be rid of his place, but rather remain a menial labourer and serve his master according to his desires. That way, the Masters will also be convinced and they will rejoice when lots of their negroes convert."[78]

Nitschmann's insistence that slaves should *not* be manumitted upon baptism was an important theological adaptation to West Indian slave society. Noting that "the Negroes [had] the ability to take on the appearance of being Christian quite easily without any true transformation of the heart,"

Nitschmann revealed both his commitment to Pietist reform and his recognition that blacks could take advantage of religious opportunities to improve their own standing. Thus, after just four months in St. Thomas, Nitschmann had come to the conclusion that Christianity needed to be divorced from manumission in order to prevent both opportunistic conversions and planter wrath.

As in previous transatlantic debates about slave conversion, Protestant missionaries, with their strong desire to promote slave conversion, developed and supported the argument that slaves should remain slaves even after baptism. Dober and Nitschmann—like the Quaker and Anglican missionaries that preceded them—had the strongest incentive to argue that slavery was compatible with true Christian conversion. Their vision of Christian Slavery was intended to appease planters, but the missionaries also believed that it prevented disingenuous slave conversion.

Aside from their theological commitment to slavery, Dober and Nitschmann returned to Europe with slaves of their own. Nitschmann arrived in Copenhagen with Jupiter while Dober brought back Oly-Carmel, both of them young boys. While Jupiter lived longer in Europe, it was the young Carmel who made the greater impression on the Moravian records. After arriving in Herrnhut in February 1735, Dober reported with pride that "the young Moor" had traveled "1400 miles from Guinea to St. Thomas and 1500 from there [to Herrnhut]."[79] Carmel, who was identified as Loango, was born in Africa but had lost both his parents during a war before being captured, sold into slavery, and taken to the Danish West Indies. In St. Thomas, Carmel was purchased by the Moravian brethren and the small boy was brought back to Europe with Dober, landing in Copenhagen on November 27, 1734.

In Herrnhut, Carmel quickly became beloved and was seen as "a sign of grace."[80] Zinzendorf wrote that the young boy "had a burning love for the Savior, even though he knows very little German."[81] Despite the objections of some, who considered Carmel to be too young and uneducated, the brethren concluded that he should be baptized as soon as possible.[82] On August 22, 1735, just over four years after David Nitschmann's chance meeting with Anton Ulrich in Copenhagen, the seven-year-old Carmel was baptized in Ebersdorf. Among those present were Dober, the Count Reuss-Ebersdorf, Philipp Friedrich Rentz, the court chaplain [Hofprediger] Steinhofer and Friedrich Martin, who was en route to St. Thomas to bring new life to the mission there (see Figure 9). Rentz later wrote that the baptism was a "fresh testimonial" and that the "young moor's spirit had been planted in the tree of Life."[83]

Figure 9. Johann Valentin Haidt, *Portrait of Friedrich Martin and Oly Carmel (Josua)*, oil on canvas. Courtesy of the Moravian Archives, Herrnhut, Germany, UA GS 343.

Carmel, who was baptized Josua, returned to Herrnhut, where he died the following March at the age of eight. Yet despite—or perhaps in part because of—the shortness of his life, Carmel became a poignant symbol of Moravian missionary pride. Unlike Anton Ulrich, who had drifted from the brethren and complicated their mission, Carmel could be forever remembered as the "first fruit," the embodiment of the Moravians' global

Figure 10. Johann Valentin Haidt, *The First Fruits*, depicting twenty-six Moravian converts from different nations standing around Jesus in heaven, 1747. Oly-Carmel and Jupiter are the two boys shown in the center of the painting. Photography by Fred Manschot / Mel Boas. Courtesy of the Stichting Museum "Het Hernhutter Huis."

reach. Oldendorp viewed Carmel's baptism as a "prelude" to the work the Moravians would do to carry the gospel to all the heathen, and Carmel himself was immortalized in Johann Valentin Haidt's painting of "The First Fruits" [*Erstlingsbild*], completed in 1747, and in the first Moravian plantation in Jamaica, which was named after the young boy, the first black person baptized in the Moravian Church.[84]

Carmel's revered place in Moravian history is an indicator of the changes that the Moravians would make to their global missions in the future. While Ulrich remained the "doorway to the heathen," he was not memorialized in Moravian paintings of the "first fruits" because he not only drifted from the Moravian Church but also criticized the Brethren and their approach to slave conversion. Carmel, whose short life did not provide an opportunity to question the missionary enterprise, was an easier figure to idealize.

As the Moravian missions developed, church leaders made several critical changes to their evangelical approach. While the first missionaries emphasized the importance of reading the Bible, later missionaries forbade reading and writing lessons. They also changed their stance on marriage, eventually permitting men with multiple wives to join the church. These policy changes demonstrate how the Moravians changed the meaning of "true" conversion in response to pressure from both planters and enslaved people.

Defining True Conversion

In 1788, August Gottlieb Spangenberg, the former head of the Moravian Church in the Americas, published *An Account of the Manner in which the Protestant Church of the Unitas Fratrum, or United Brethren, Preach the Gospel, and carry on their Missions among the Heathen.*[1] The 127-page pamphlet, translated from the German by Benjamin LaTrobe, described the conversion strategies the Moravians had developed since the establishment of their first mission in 1732. As one of the first Protestant groups to evangelize to slaves in the Atlantic world, Moravians had a significant influence on the development of later Protestant missions and the growth of black Christianity.[2] Still, the Moravians' approach was never fixed: they struggled to find an appropriate balance between appealing to enslaved Africans, appeasing their masters, and articulating an authentic yet easily translatable vision of Christian belief.

Spangenberg had overseen much of the process: after joining the Moravian Church in the early 1730s, he led the failed Moravian settlement in Georgia in 1735, visited the first Caribbean mission on St. Thomas in 1736, and helped to establish the successful settlement of Bethlehem, Pennsylvania in the 1740s. During his work as Bishop of the Unitas Fratrum in the Americas, Spangenberg pioneered the missionary use of creole languages and oversaw the missions in Pennsylvania, New York, Ohio, and the Caribbean. He communicated regularly with his brethren in Europe and the West Indies, advising missionaries on how best to develop and maintain their mission stations. Spangenberg's *Account* thus came at the culmination of a long and successful career as missionary strategist and developer. Spangenberg had firsthand experience of the initial frustrations of mission work, as well as its halting successes.

Spangenberg's fifty-year tenure as a leader of the church had led him to firm conclusions about the "dos and don'ts" of missionary work. Primary on the list of "don'ts" were lessons in reading and writing: according to Spangenberg, the teaching of literacy was an invention that "gradually arose in the church" and it led the "heathen" astray with its focus on knowledge as opposed to true heart religion. This was particularly true in the West Indies, where "the circumstances of the negroes, and their hard slavery" made it impossible to teach both literacy and true religion. Spangenberg advised missionaries to be wary of those who "merely wanted to know a good deal." For "to fill [their] head only with knowledge, and at the same time [to] have an empty and unfeeling heart" was a dangerous thing. Spangenberg warned that baptizing a learned "heathen" who had not yet received "a work of grace in his heart" would do "much hurt."[3]

As evidence for argument against literacy, Spangenberg cited the case of "a very aged negro woman" on St. Thomas whom he met during his visit to the island in 1736. This woman "attended meetings assiduously, and heard the gospel of Christ with eagerness, exhorting her people also to thank God." Yet when Spangenberg inquired as to whether she desired baptism, she exclaimed, "O Lord! I can never be baptized! How should I now learn to read, and get so much by rote?" Realizing that this faithful old woman was being held back from the holy sacrament by a misunderstanding, Spangenberg convinced her "that all that was not necessary." Instead, he "told her of the love of Jesus to her." The story ended well: "She was afterwards baptized, and obtained so much understanding in the gospel, as to become useful among the other negro women."[4]

What Spangenberg did not mention in his 1788 *Account* is that he had actively supported the teaching of literacy when he visited St. Thomas in 1736.[5] Also missing from Spangenberg's 1788 *Account* was the name of the "aged negro," Marotta, a free African woman who identified herself as a member of the Papaa nation.[6] Three years after Spangenberg's visit to St. Thomas, Marrotta—who was by then known by her Christian name Magdalena—either wrote or, more likely, dictated a petition to the Queen of Denmark on behalf of "the negro women of St. Thomas" whose masters would not allow them to "serve the Lord Jesus." Written in her native West African language and translated into Dutch Creole, Marrotta's petition was a stunning example of the use of the written word to appeal to powerful Europeans who could influence the St. Thomas master class (see Figure 11). Composed in 1739, the appeal was accompanied by another letter written in

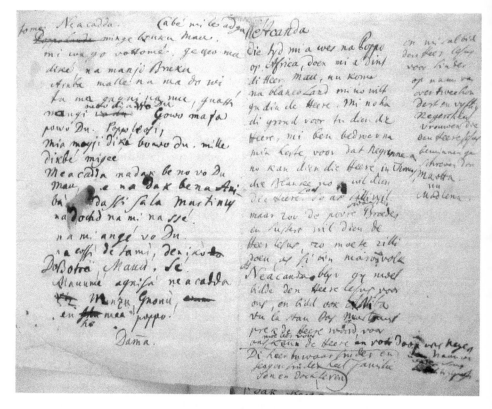

Figure 11. Draft of a letter from Marotta/Magdalena to the Queen of Denmark (UA R.15.Ba.3.61). Courtesy of the Moravian Archives, Herrnhut, Germany.

Dutch Creole and also signed by several other leading converts on St. Thomas. This letter went into more detail about the problems facing Christian slaves in the Caribbean: the white planters "beat and injure us when the *Baas* teaches us about the Savior," they wrote. "[They] burn our books, call our baptism the baptism of dogs, and call the Brethren beasts."[7] These two petitions, written or dictated by enslaved and free Christians, offer a glimpse into a very different type of mission strategy than the one described by Spangenberg in 1788. While the older Spangenberg insisted that teaching literacy placed too much emphasis on education, the younger Spangengberg had taught enslaved converts to read, write and use the written word.

Why did the Moravians redefine "true" conversion to exclude reading the Bible? As Spangenberg knew, many enslaved and free blacks joined the church to gain access to reading lessons and books. As Moravian popularity grew among the black population, however, white planters viewed the missionaries as a threat to island security. While Moravians never questioned the legitimacy of slavery as an institution—on the contrary, the missionaries purchased slaves and a plantation in 1736—their intimate relationships with blacks and their literacy classes fostered resentment among both planters and pastors on the island. Planters resented literacy education because it offered new opportunities for enslaved and free people of color. They also attacked the missionaries for providing blacks with leadership positions within the Church and performing an interracial marriage. The Dutch Reformed ministry, by contrast, felt that the Moravian missionaries had not properly prepared their converts for baptism, and they questioned black knowledge of Protestant theology.

In order to quell discontent among island whites, the Moravian missionaries emphasized their support of slavery and the beneficial consequences of slave conversion. Like earlier Protestant missionaries, they articulated a vision of Christian Slavery, arguing that Christian slaves would be more loyal and hardworking than their non-Christian counterparts. Black Moravians took a different approach by appealing to the authority of the Danish monarchs and criticizing white planters for their barbaric, unchristian behavior.

While planters feared the subversive potential of reading and writing, literacy lessons also proved troublesome for missionaries. As Afro-Caribbeans learned to read the Bible, they developed alternative interpretations of scripture that challenged the church's stance on polygamy, among other things. These twin challenges—of planter resistance and Afro-Caribbean interpretation—forced the Moravians to rethink their approach to mission work. After a number of conferences, the brethren decided to stop teaching literacy and to focus, instead, on the "essential" Christian teaching of Christ's crucifixion. Suspending reading instruction would rid the missionaries of "many unpromising students" and allow them to "dedicate themselves to those eager for salvation."[8] The Moravians also decided to lessen the severity of church discipline. The policy shifts produced mixed results. The missionaries had, in effect, offered concessions to both planters and slaves. Planters were pleased with the move away from literacy, while enslaved and free blacks were permitted to engage in some "non-Christian" practices such as polygyny.

These shifts show how Christianity was constantly being adjusted and redefined in response to plantation slavery and Afro-Caribbean culture.

They are indicative of wider changes taking place not only within the Moravian Church, but also in the emergent culture of Atlantic Protestantism. As evangelical revivals spread throughout the Atlantic World in the 1730s and 1740s, the role of literacy and knowledge was redefined and the definition of "true" conversion shifted.

The Spectacle of the Word

The mystique of the written word and the promise of literacy helped Moravians appeal to enslaved and free blacks during the first decade of their Caribbean mission. When Friedrich Martin, the newly appointed leader of the St. Thomas mission, arrived in 1736 to revive the dormant mission station, he found that "some Negroes could read, and others had a great desire to learn how to read." Within a month of his arrival, he was approached by one enslaved African who begged him to teach him how to write and spell. When Martin promised to give him lessons, the man "fell on his knees, thanked him and wanted to kiss his hands."[9] Such a display was not uncommon. As the Moravian historian Oldendorp wrote, "Among the blacks, there was an earnestness and eagerness to learn, to hear the Word of Life and to experience its immense power. They came often after work, late in the night, so as not to miss a lesson. Some of them travelled barefoot two or three miles through the stony mountains and returned home to begin work at sunrise."[10] During their lessons, Martin divided his pupils into groups. Some learned reading, while the more advanced students were taught spelling and writing. Within months, nearly two hundred slaves and free blacks were trekking through tough terrain to attend the Moravian meetings.

When August Gottlieb Spangenberg visited St. Thomas in September of 1736, just six months after Martin's arrival, he too was struck by the intense demand for lessons in reading and writing. On his fourth day on the island, Spangenberg spoke with an Afro-Caribbean man who "wanted nothing more than to learn how to read himself, and to be a Christian."[11] Three days later, "a few negro women came to us and implored us to give them a lesson. We had already turned them away many times to test them: but they desperately wanted to learn and refused to give up."[12] Both Spangenberg and Martin were pleased and gratified by the popularity of their reading lessons. Like other European Protestants, they believed that literacy was

Figure 12. Prosternatio, depicting a Moravian worship service in St. Thomas. The caption reads: "Baptized negroes after the prostration, or worship, are helped up and kissed by members of their Nation." Engraving in [David Cranz], *Kurze, zuverlässige Nachricht von der Unitas Fratrum* [1757]. Courtesy of the Moravian Archives, Bethlehem, Pennsylvania.

central to Christian piety and that an intimate engagement with scripture could create the "change of heart" that was necessary for true conversion.

Yet what did the practice of reading—and the accessibility of books—mean to enslaved and free Africans and Creoles on St. Thomas? And how much did the practice of reading overlap with the practice of Christianity? Spangenberg's 1736 journal provides insight into these questions. His observations suggest that books were not just a source of religious inspiration. They were also seen as physical objects that had spiritual, economic, and talismanic power. In a practical sense, it was through text-inscribed paper that Africans could prove their freedom or their status as Christians. Spangenberg strengthened the connection between text, freedom and Christianity by providing newly baptized Afro-Caribbeans with baptismal certificates and telling the converts that the paper would protect them against reenslavement by the Spanish. "If [you] don't have this proof," he explained, "[you] will be made into slaves again. But if [you] have a certificate of baptism, [you] will be set free."[13]

Afro-Caribbeans viewed instructional books as powerful objects. During the first years of the mission, Friedrich Martin gave many of his students spelling books, which quickly became highly prized possessions: "Everyone wanted to have a textbook," wrote Oldendorp. "Whoever was lucky enough to obtain one carried it with him everywhere and devoted every free moment to studying it." By May of 1737, Martin had given away over 133 spelling books in just two months, and he still had dozens of pupils eagerly waiting.[14] One Afro-Caribbean man, who had fought against the rebel slaves on St. John in 1732, recounted a story of how he was shot during the expedition. He said he owed his life to the Lord and that his book, which he carried around everywhere, had been with him when he was shot.[15]

The loss of books could be devastating. When Abraham, one of the first baptized blacks, learned that his house had burned down in early 1737, "he only lamented that his paper and his New Testament had burned, so he couldn't practice writing or remind himself about the word of God by reading." Martin comforted him by giving him new writing material and Abraham later received a New Testament from a friend in Amsterdam.[16] Another young man "had his book in his bag, and it was stolen from him in the night." He told Spangenberg that he hoped the person who stole his book would "learn so much from it that he becomes a true Christian."[17]

Afro-Caribbeans may have viewed both the act of reading and the possession of material texts as sources of European power that could be adopted and utilized. Robert Robertson, the Anglican clergyman on Nevis, wrote that newly arrived blacks referred to reading as "mak[ing] paper speak," suggesting that literacy was seen as an impressive, if not spiritual, skill.[18] This observation is important, particularly when viewed in the context of Moravian lessons. A typical Moravian meeting included the recitation of a chosen part of scripture. By organizing their meetings around scriptural readings, the missionaries reinforced their status as readers who had power to "make paper speak." As the audience, Afro-Caribbeans participated in this performance by both listening and interpreting. Spangenberg recorded a number of instances in which Afro-Caribbeans challenged or questioned the missionaries' interpretation of scripture. On one afternoon, the missionaries "read Christ's Sermon on the Mount in Matthew 5,

6 and 7," in which Jesus advocates turning the other cheek. This reading led into a discussion of "how one could accept being hit." At least one Afro-Caribbean man objected to this line of interpretation. Immanuel, an enslaved Creole, answered that he could never turn the other cheek because "it would cost him his honor if he didn't defend himself." The missionaries "explained to him that the Lord wanted it that way, and that he shouldn't believe in his own honor, but in the honor of the Lord." Immanuel responded with a compromise: "He decided that he would ask God to spare him from the possibility of getting in a fight. . . . Instead, he would prefer to stay home and learn."[19]

Immanuel's interactions with the missionaries provide insight into the negotiation over Christian practice and the construction of enslaved Christian masculinity. Immanuel was not willing to accept the idea that "turning the other cheek" meant submitting to abuse without complaint. Instead, he reinterpreted the passage to accommodate both his sense of honor and his desire to bolster his education. He affirmed the missionaries' desire for him to place God's honor over his own by asking God to "spare him from the possibility of getting in a fight." At the same time, his preference to "stay home and learn" suggested the existence of an alternate source of male honor: by becoming a learned man who had could read and "make paper speak," Immanuel could redefine Christian practice and create a literacy-based Christian identity that would imbue him with a different type of power.

Immanuel's approach gained him both respect and status within the Moravian congregation. Just fourteen days after the discussion of the Sermon on the Mount, he was one of the first three individuals baptized by Spangenberg. Immanuel, who was baptized Andreas, went on to become a leading male elder on the island. Later, he traveled to Pennsylvania and Europe, where he died in 1744. In 1747, he was commemorated as "the first believing Negro" in Johann Valentin Haidt's painting, *The First Fruits* (see Figure 13).[20]

Anti-Moravian Crusade: Books, Baptism, and Marriage

Like Protestant slave owners throughout the Caribbean, planters on St. Thomas reacted harshly to their slaves' interest in Christianity. Some feared that Christianity was synonymous with freedom and that converted slaves

Figure 13. Detail of Johann Valentin Haidt, *The First Fruits*. Immanuel/Andreas is standing behind the two boys, Oly-Carmel and Jupiter. Photography by Fred Manschot / Mel Boas. Courtesy of the Stichting Museum "Het Hernhutter Huis."

would be eligible for manumission. Others worried that Christian slaves would be more rebellious than others. Spangenberg observed that there were economic and political elements to planter resistance as well. If becoming a Christian meant that one had to observe the Sabbath, he noted, conversion threatened to diminish planter profits by allowing the enslaved a "day of rest." Also, whites were threatened by the idea that Christian slaves would be able to give testimony in court.[21]

Underlying these fears was the fact that Protestant Supremacy remained an important foundation of the slave society in the Danish West Indies. While whiteness had become central to the island hierarchy, Protestantism was still closely aligned with freedom and status. As a result, slave conversion was still perceived as a threat. As "a certain gentleman" explained to Spangenberg, "if the negros were told that all men were the same before God, it would weaken their respect for the whites. And our lives would not be safe."[22] These fears were not unique to St. Thomas: Protestant slave owners throughout the Atlantic world resisted the work of missionaries well into the eighteenth century. But on St. Thomas, planters developed a distinctive form of antimissionary resistance. In Barbados, slave owners fined and persecuted Quaker missionaries. In New York, they prevented enslaved people from walking to services at night without a lantern. In St. Thomas, they burned books. They also attacked Moravians for consecrating an interracial marriage and claimed that black Moravians were not true Christians.

Both male and female masters played a role in the attack on books, with white women often leading the charge. As Oldendorp wrote, "At the end of March there was another emergency because white women kept taking textbooks away from children and negro women. They ripped them up and burned them, making things even more difficult for Martin who already had a shortage."[23] White men also played a part, sometimes assaulting enslaved and free blacks on their way to meetings. During these encounters, Afro-Caribbeans were systematically stripped of their reading materials. In 1736, soon after Spangenberg's departure, Oldendorp reported that "the instructional books were taken away" and black converts "were beat up." Black women were especially targeted. Some enslaved blacks saw their mistreatment as validation of their decision to come to Moravian meetings and one black man reported that his persecution only intensified his desire to be a Christian.[24] Indeed, books were such powerful currency in the planter's war of terror that the Moravians sometimes called their attackers simply "bookburners."[25]

Friedrich Martin fought against book burning by appealing to his brethren in Europe. Within months of his arrival, he had already sent word to Amsterdam that he desperately needed more reading materials. Yet by May of the following year, he was still waiting. When he heard that two loads of books had been sent on separate ships—both of which were captured by pirates—he purchased books that had arrived from New York and further increased his supply by buying texts from Dutch people on the island. Martin even went so far as to "give his last Shillings out to provide books for those who desperately wanted to read, though it often happened that the book he bought for a negro woman one day would be taken away by her mistress the next."[26]

While Martin was sacrificing his depleted funds to provide texts for his students, literacy was becoming a central issue in the governmental response to the Moravian presence. As early as 1736, the governor of St. Thomas stated that he "did not hinder the conversion of blacks." But he did "forbid Martin to teach them how to write and threatened that if he continued to do so, the government would also forbid the learning of reading." He explained that fully literate slaves could ignite a rebellion and "reported that a few slaves had plotted a rebellion through writing on an English island."[27]

The governor's statement is a reminder that the brethren's decision to teach both reading *and* writing was strikingly radical. In the eighteenth century, it was common for individuals to be taught how to read without being taught how to write. Writing was a powerful skill—particularly for enslaved people. As the governor was well aware, the ability to write could facilitate communication among enslaved peoples across distant regions and provide blacks with the ability to forge documents. The missionaries did not seem to consider these aspects of writing, at least in the first years of their mission. Instead, their decision to teach writing was a response to overwhelming pressure from black men and women. As Oldendorp acknowledged, "Reading and learning to spell were not the main goal. But the [missionaries] did it gladly because the blacks wanted to learn."[28] The missionaries also discovered that they could use the lure of writing to convince Afro-Caribbeans to refrain from activities that the missionaries considered to be unchristian, such as partaking in African rituals or singing.[29]

Apart from teaching literacy, the Moravians clashed with the plantocracy and the Reformed ministry about black church leadership, baptism, and the meaning of marriage.[30] On November 30, 1737, Andreas and Petrus were the first two Afro-Caribbeans to take part in communion.[31] It was rare for blacks to become fully confirmed members of Christian churches, and the Moravians' decision to include blacks in the most exclusive Protestant rite was radical. Then, in February 1738, the missionaries appointed five

Figure 14. Moravian Meeting House, Friedensthal, St. Croix. Original image created by C. G. A. Oldendorp, ca. 1767. Engraving by G. P. Nussbiegel [1777]. Courtesy of the John Carter Brown Library, Brown University.

"Helpers" to take on leadership roles in the congregation. The chosen five were all baptized blacks—Andreas, Johannes, Petrus, Christoph, and Anna Maria. While all five had been active leaders before their appointment, the move confirmed the importance of black leadership within the Moravian Church. The Helpers led "bands," or small groups of congregants, in discussion, prayer, and worship. Bands could be organized by African ethnicity, language, or plantation, and they provided the opportunity for congregants to deepen bonds outside of the purview of white missionaries.[32]

The meaning of marriage was another point of conflict between missionaries and planters. Just a month after their appointment as Helpers, Andreas and Johannes—both of whom were married—were sold and sent to St. John, a neighboring island, to a man named Mr. Fries. Andreas, Johannes, and the missionaries were all devastated. Among other things, both Andreas and Johannes had wives who remained in St. Thomas, and the missionaries were shocked that white planters had so little respect for the marriages of enslaved men and women. "The worst thing," Oldendorp wrote, "was that they were both separated from their wives who stayed back in St. Thomas."[33] The missionaries tried to convince Johann Lorentz Carstens, one of the few white planters to support the brethren, to purchase the two men before they were forced to depart, but they were unsuccessful.[34]

In the months following Andreas and Johannes' departure, the Moravians made two controversial decisions. In May 1738, while Martin was still mourning the departure of Andreas and Johannes, he performed his first marriage ceremony, joining Rebecca, a mixed-race member of the church, to Matthias Freundlich, a white missionary. The union made perfect sense to the Moravians: by 1738, Rebecca was twenty years old, a free woman, and one of the leaders of the church. Martin believed that both she and Freundlich would be more effective as a married couple and that marriage would remove any indications of impropriety regarding Rebecca's relationship with the missionaries. While Rebecca initially resisted the arrangement, she and Freundlich were married on May 4 in the presence of the congregation.[35]

Then, two months after Rebecca and Matthias's marriage, the brethren purchased their own plantation, including nine slaves.[36] The decision affirmed the Moravians' acceptance of slavery as an institution, but it was nonetheless threatening to planters, who felt that they could no longer oversee Moravian actions. By purchasing slaves and a plantation, the missionaries also hoped to gain ownership over their church members, thereby preventing further marital separations. They were delighted that two black Helpers, Christoph and Anna Maria, were among the nine slaves purchased along with Salomon estate on the northern side of the island.[37] As long as their congregants were enslaved to masters who respected marriage and Christian practice, then slavery could be in harmony with Protestantism.

On August 27, 1738, just two weeks after the Moravians had moved to their new plantation, "Posaunenberg," the Dutch Reformed pastor Johannes Borm filed a petition accusing Friedrich Martin of performing a marriage ceremony without a valid ordination. In his petition, Borm singled out the Moravians' educational work, arguing that the brethren had bestowed baptism without properly preparing their congregants.[38] More charges followed, including a bizarre accusation of theft, and Martin was eventually imprisoned alongside Rebecca and Matthias.[39] As these charges signaled, both planters and pastors on the island saw the Moravians as a threat to their way of life. In just a few years, the missionaries had taught enslaved people to read and write, endorsed an interracial marriage, conducted their own baptismal ceremonies, included blacks in the celebration of the Lord's Supper, and purchased their own space for worship. The idea that dozens of blacks would be congregating outside of the purview of "trustworthy" whites was intolerable.

As the multiplicity of attacks against the brethren indicates, the Moravians incited resentment from different groups on the island. The vast majority of whites resented the Moravians' decision to teach reading and writing, as well as their willingness to place blacks in positions of leadership. Friedrich Martin's performance of an interracial marriage was also a lighting rod for resentment. Representatives of the Reformed Church, meanwhile, had somewhat different grievances. Johannes Borm, the Reformed minister, initially supported the missionaries and had even sent one of his own slaves to the brethren for lessons.[40] Borm's antipathy toward the missionaries was prompted by Martin's decision to baptize and confirm several blacks over the course of late 1737 and 1738.[41] While most whites feared that literacy and education would give the enslaved too much power, Rev. Borm argued that the baptized blacks knew nothing of "true" Christianity and had not been properly prepared for baptism. He also accused Friedrich Martin of conducting baptismal ceremonies and communion without proper ordination.

In order to prove his claims, Borm, along with a handful of other church and governmental officials, organized an examination of the baptized blacks. His stated intention was to test whether the black Moravians were worthy of Christian baptism, though the missionaries saw his actions as an attempt to banish them from the island. On January 25, several representatives of the Reformed Church, all of the officials of the lower court, and a number of planters and other whites congregated to observe the proceedings. Pastor Borm led the examination alongside the Fiscal and the bailiff. The interrogation initially focused on the sacraments and basic Christian theology. Questions included:

"In what were you baptized?" ("In Christianity"); "In any other name? ("Yes, in the name of the Father, son, and Holy Ghost, the triune God."); "What is baptism?" ("The washing away of sins by means of not just water, but also the Holy Ghost."); "What is sin?" ("We have inherited sin from our first parents, Adam and Eve; but in the new life, the spirit of God prevails."); "What has the Lord done, to become the Lord?" ("He died for us."); "Will He come again?" ("Yes, he would judge the living and the dead."; and "What is the Lord's Supper?" ("Wine and bread, and if one believes, then one receives the body and blood of Christ.")[42]

Eventually, the questions became more aggressive. Borm and the other examiners asked the black Moravians if God existed in Africa and whether they believed that they would return to Africa when they died.[43] They asked probing questions about how the sacraments had been performed. The examiners wanted to know if they had been baptized in God's name or in the name of Friedrich Martin and whether there had been blood under the water at their baptism. They also inquired about the difference between Martin's Diary and the Bible. Several questions focused on Martin himself. The examiners wanted to know whether Martin had represented his beliefs and teachings as better than the Lutheran or Reformed, or if he had presented himself as an Apostle of God. Most revealingly, they asked the baptized whether blacks would rule over whites after the resurrection and whether Martin had taught such things.[44]

Borm's interrogation exhibited many of the fears underlying anti-Moravian sentiment on the island. While the Moravians never questioned the legitimacy of slavery as an institution, their teachings challenged the racial and religious hierarchies that undergirded the Protestant slave society. Moravians recognized blacks as religious and spiritual leaders, taught them to read and write, and prioritized marriage over property rights. The Moravians' radical theology and their willingness to rely on black leadership threatened the emerging ideology of White Supremacy, which was built on Protestant Supremacy.

Count Zinzendorf and Proslavery Theology

After a full day of interrogation, Borm and the other examiners scheduled a second investigation eight days later. It is likely that Martin and the other missionaries would have been banished from the island if not for the unexpected arrival of Count Zinzendorf, the Moravians' charismatic leader. Zinzendorf landed on St. Thomas on January 29, 1739, just four days after Borm's examination. Using his high standing and influence, Zinzendorf was able to secure the release of Rebecca and Matthias from prison and put an end to the interrogation of the baptized blacks. He then purchased

Andreas and Johannes from Mr. Fries, so that the two men were able to return to their wives and the brethren.[45]

Zinzendorf was less successful in his efforts to convince white planters that the Moravian mission was not a threat to slavery. During his two weeks on the island, Zinzendorf met with several political and religious leaders. While the governor was sympathetic to the Moravians, most others were enraged by the Count's presence. On February 11, more than thirty white inhabitants met to draw up a petition against the Moravian mission. They wrote that the brethren should be forbidden from continuing Christian instruction. They argued that slave owners should control the education of their slaves and that the Moravian's presence was unnecessary and unwanted.[46] The court bailiff, who had presided over the examination of the baptized blacks, summarized the continued resentment toward the Moravians in a letter to the governor: "A man so dangerous as Martin should not be free," he wrote. Not only were the missionaries "careless with the sacraments," but they also allowed blacks to congregate at night, sometimes under the leadership of other blacks.[47] It was not only the content of their instruction, but also the form of the meetings that inflamed fears among whites. The Moravian services were too large and it was impossible to know whether they were being used for praising God or plotting revolt. The fear of slave rebellion, which had rocked the nearby island of St. John just five years before, was ever-present in the complaints about the brethren.[48]

In the face of continued white resistance, Zinzendorf made one final attempt to align the Moravian mission with the institution of slavery. At the request of the governor, Zinzendorf gave a farewell address to several hundred Afro-Caribbean men and women in Tappus. The speech, which was written in Dutch and translated into Creole by Mingo, one of the black Helpers, emphasized the compatibility of slavery and salvation. Zinzendorf praised the whites who guided their slaves "out of slavery to the devil to the freedom of Christ." To the enslaved and free blacks, he stressed that long working hours did not conflict with Christian practice. Rather, those who were "genuinely concerned about [their] salvation" would find that "Jesus will bless the little time that you have at your disposal." He urged them to "remain faithful to your masters and mistresses, your overseers" and asked them to "perform all your work with as much love and diligence as if you were working for yourselves."[49]

Zinzendorf reiterated that Christian baptism was in no way connected to manumission. "A heathen must have no other reason for conversion than to believe in Jesus," he asserted. For Zinzendorf, earthly stations were fixed and ordained by God: "The Lord has made everything Himself— kings, masters, servants, and slaves. And as long as we live in this world, everyone must gladly endure the state into which God has placed him and be content with God's wise counsel." Not only had God ordained earthly stations, but he had also created race-based slavery: "God punished the first Negroes with slavery," Zinzendorf stated. "The blessed state of your souls does not make your bodies accordingly free, but it does remove all evil thoughts, deceit, laziness, faithlessness, and everything that makes your condition of slavery burdensome."

The inclusion of a raced-based justification for slavery within Zinzend- orf's speech marked an important trend. As missionaries and their support- ers sought to appease the fears of white planters, they turned increasingly to the language of race to demonstrate the stability of slavery and its com- patibility with conversion. The same progression could be seen in the laws that Elias Neau advocated in New York. Faced with violent anticonversion sentiment, evangelizing Protestants tried to reframe the debate about Chris- tianity and slavery by arguing that race, rather than religion, was the defin- ing feature of mastery. Zinzendorf's articulation of these points was not new, but they were part of a growing chorus reverberating throughout the Atlantic World.

The Power of the Written Word

Despite Zinzendorf's efforts to assuage the fears of white planters and artic- ulate a vision of Christian Slavery, persecution reached a peak on the eve of the Count's departure. After his speech advocating for obedience and race-based slavery, a number of blacks accompanied the Count to town where "they were attacked on the public road by several Whites carrying sticks and bared swords." The assailants included the Fiscal, who had pre- sided over the examination, as well as other officials.[50] These men then rode to the Brethren's plantation where they "attacked the Negroes who had remained there, beat them, and injured them, forcing them to take flight . . . [and w]hen there were no more Negroes to beat up, they vented their wrath on chairs, glasses, dishes, and any other household utensils."[51] Despite the terrorizing violence toward the Brethren, Oldendorp reported that the individuals who had been assaulted "didn't complain about the beatings they received, but only about the loss of their books."[52]

The same evening, eight black leaders of the church took a bold step by writing directly to the King and Queen of Denmark to defend their missionaries and their right to become Christians. This was a "tactic of unprecedented daring," as Jon Sensbach has written, demonstrating an acute awareness of the powerful potential of the written word.[53] The first letter, dated February 15, 1739, was signed by Pieter, Mingo, Andreas, Magdalena, Rebecca, and Anna Maria in the name of 650 black men and women.[54] Addressed to the "Merciful King," the authors described the terrorizing violence that had plagued their congregation: "We are steadfast in our determination . . . despite all the oppression by those who have come to beat and injure us when the Baas [Martin] teaches us about the Savior, by those who burn our books, call our baptism the baptism of dogs, and call the brethren beasts, declaring that Negroes must not be saved and that a baptized Negro is no more than kindling wood for the flames of hell." As the authors indicated, the Moravians continued to be plagued by the "book terror" that had characterized the first years of the mission. On top of that, their antagonists now mocked their baptism and rejected the idea that blacks could be saved. Yet even this suffering, they asserted, could bring them closer to God: "We would gladly place our heads under the axe in defense of our congregation and for the sake of Lord Jesus."[55]

The second letter, addressed to the Queen of Denmark, was written by Magdalena, the woman who had caught Spangenberg's attention with her intense devotion. It appeared both in Magdalena's native African language and in Dutch Creole.[56] In it, Magdalena described her own spiritual journey from "Papaa, in Africa," where she "served the Lord Masu." Now she was in the "land of the Whites," but she was "not allowed to serve the Lord Jesus." In an intriguing statement, she wrote that "when the poor black brethren and sisters want to serve the Lord Jesus, they are looked upon as maroons." Her comparison suggests that whites believed that Christian slaves—like maroons—would be unwilling to labor on plantations and that they would demand a greater degree of freedom and mobility. Magdalena asked the Queen to "intercede with the King" and encourage him to "allow Baas Martin to preach the Lord's word" (see Figure 11).[57]

When Count Zinzendorf departed St. Thomas on February 16, 1739, he took with him his farewell speech and the two petitions written and signed by the Afro-Caribbean converts. Two years later, he printed them side by side in the *Büdingische Sammlung*, a collection of Moravian letters, diaries, and other documents related to the church. While the three documents had the same purpose—to save the Moravian mission on the island of St. Thomas—they displayed a tension between black and white strategies for defeating Protestant Supremacy. In his farewell speech, Zinzendorf emphasized the harmony between slavery and Christianity, capitalizing on the emerging language of race and arguing that Christian slaves would be more faithful workers. The petitions written by the enslaved and free blacks, by contrast, lingered on the injustice of white planters, their abuse of enslaved people, and their radical dedication to Christ. While Zinzendorf allayed white fears, black Moravians asserted their willingness—even eagerness—to "place [their] heads under the axe" for the sake of their "congregation" and for "Lord Jesus."

After the Count's departure, the governor reiterated and expanded his concerns about the mission. While he probably did not know about the petitions that the black Moravians had written to the Danish monarchs, he remained concerned about the Moravian practice of teaching enslaved and free blacks how to write. In addition to putting severe restrictions on when and where Moravian converts could meet, the governor proclaimed that Moravians "should not teach slaves how to write or educate them that they become free when they are Christian, or allow them to become as good as their masters or other gentlemen, nor should they think that they will not be required to do as much work or that they will be free from punishment, but rather the opposite, that as Christians they should be truer to their masters and turn in everything to the Word of God."[58]

Despite Zinzendorf's express declarations that the Moravians did not encourage manumission, and that they urged their enslaved congregants to be obedient to their masters, the perceived linkage between Christian education and freedom was hard to break. The governor's comments should not be read as a response to Moravian intentions, but rather as a lens into white perceptions of black literacy and black Christianity in the eighteenth-century Caribbean. The governor worried that learning how to write and converting to Christianity would make slaves believe that they were free, break down the social hierarchy, and destroy the work schedule.

Marriage and Literacy

Within a year of the governor's proclamation, the brethren met to confer about how to go forward. After a number of conferences, they made three changes in their approach to the mission: they decided to suspend reading and writing instruction "altogether," to focus their teachings on Christ on the cross, and to lesson the severity of church discipline.[59] Together, these new policies helped to end the "book terror" that had plagued them during the first years of the mission.

While the governor's pressure, paired with the violent attacks of planters, was influential in hastening the Moravians' turn away from literacy, the missionaries' perception of "backsliding" represented another important reason to reject reading and writing. Even at the beginning of the mission, the Moravian missionaries were probably aware that not all of their pupils came to lessons with the desire to convert to Christianity. Initially, missionaries believed that instruction in literacy could attract otherwise disinterested pupils. As Oldendorp wrote, "In addition to the fact that [the slaves'] newly acquired reading skills enabled the Negroes to read the Bible, it also induced many of those who had come to the meetings with the sole purpose of learning to read to partake of the desire to get to know Christ and to share in his doctrine."[60] Sometimes this method worked. In 1737, Friedrich Martin made some progress with a couple on Hans Clas's plantation when "they showed a desire to learn." Martin sent the couple a spelling book, and "the negro woman began to go to school . . . until she was awakened, and she converted and longed for the holy Baptism." Yet despite the missionaries' hopes, many of their students remained unseduced by the gospel. The husband of the convert from Hans Clas's plantation, for example, initially "liked the letters" in the book from Martin, but eventually decided "he didn't have a reason to convert." Martin wrote that "he knew why he stayed away, namely so that he could play his fiddle at festivals."[61]

Martin's belief that playing the "fiddle at festivals" was incompatible with conversion is indicative of a larger tension within the mission. Converts were not only expected to express their *belief* in Christian doctrine; they were also asked to engage in specific social practices that the missionaries defined as "Christian." Activities such as singing, for example, were acceptable only within approved cultural settings, such as a Moravian meeting. Content was also significant: singing was condoned when songs focused on Christian topics, but was otherwise condemned. As Spangenberg commented, "it's well known that both truths and falsehoods can be spread through songs, so it's important to distinguish the songs from one another."[62]

As time went on, the missionaries grew increasingly frustrated that some pupils learned to read and write but did not reform their behavior.

They characterized the problem using the "head" and "heart" dichotomy, a central trope of Pietists who sought to reform the church and excise "dead" theology. They described pupils "who only wanted to keep something in their heads" as "always dead in the heart." They "learned enough, but they didn't get to know their hearts."[63] Real converts, by contrast, had experienced a true "change of heart."

One of the sites of greatest tension between missionaries and converts revolved around the construction of the family and the meaning of marriage. While the missionaries defined marriage as a lifelong, monogamous union of one man and one woman, familial customs among most enslaved and free blacks did not conform to these ideas.[64] The majority of Afro-Caribbeans who attended Moravian meetings were either born in Africa or born to African parents, and many maintained African-based familial structures, such as polygynous households.[65] During his visit in 1736, Spangenberg recognized that these polygynous families posed a tricky problem for the mission. "What should we do about marriage among the negros?" he wondered. "Some have many wives, so which ones should they divorce?" Spangenberg assumed that divorce was the only way for an individual in a polygynous household to become a true Christian. But he also realized that divorce could pose other types of problems. He feared, for example, that if a man divorced a "true" wife who then went on to marry someone else, that woman would be committing adultery.[66]

Spangenberg was unable to come up with a workable solution to the "marriage problem" in 1736 and polygyny reemerged as a central topic of debate during the 1740 conferences. By this time, however, a number of enslaved and free converts had read the Bible themselves and could challenge European ideas about true Christian practice. During one of the meetings, "some [black Christians] searched in the Old Testament, pointing out parts that seemed to justify their polygamous practices and other disorderly things."[67] The congregants may have been referring to any number of Old Testament passages that condone polygyny. Exodus 21:10 (KJV) states, "if he take him another wife, her food, her raiment, and her duty of marriage shall he not diminish," and 2 Samuel 5:13 and 1 Chronicles 3:1–9 refer to King David's six wives and numerous concubines.[68] While the missionaries had accepted a degree of debate on other scriptural passages, such as the Sermon on the Mount, they resented the challenge regarding polygyny. They concluded not to "waste their precious time with such people anymore, so they largely stopped teaching reading."[69] As this disagreement shows, the decision to halt reading lessons was about more than just planter pressure. When a number of enslaved and free blacks used their reading ability to challenge the relationship between Christianity and social practice, the missionaries decided that the school "took too much time" and they did not want to deal with "such people any longer."

While the missionaries discontinued literacy lessons, literate black converts continued to teach reading and writing. The missionaries were aware that "there were some among the old and the new [congregants] who could read and they taught others."[70] Many of these black teachers held positions of power within the church as elders or Helpers who mentored new pupils and spread word of the gospel within the slave population.[71] Missionaries had relied heavily on helpers for years, integrating them into the structure of the church and holding separate conferences with them to discuss the state of the congregation, disciplinary measures for "backsliders," and questions about how to best translate the gospel into Dutch Creole and various African languages. A second consequence of the 1740 conferences was the decision to have more patience with "backsliders" who continued to partake in "non-Christian" practices. The missionaries couched their new policy in terms of love: "With love, [the sinners] were to be shown the cause of their fall, as well as the means to their salvation."[72] What this meant was that "non-Christian" practice was to be unofficially tolerated and converts would not necessarily be thrown out of meeting if their transgressions were discovered.

The missionaries' tenuous compromise of 1740 did not mark the end of their struggle with polygyny. When the missionary Christian Rauch visited the island in 1745, the Brethren tried to reach a new consensus on how to respond to the practice.[73] "We had a conference at [the] Prayer Day," Rauch wrote, where many "weighty Matters were spoken of especially ab[ou]t Polligamy some of ye Negroe men having 2 wifes." Again, black Moravians played a central role in the conversation. After the meeting, the white missionaries "spoke w[i]th Abraham & Peter [about] how they should deal with those men who have 2 wi[v]es." As Elders in the Moravian congregation, Abraham and Peter played a vital role in mediating the message of the church to the black congregants and communicating doctrine. After a discussion with these two men, the missionaries came to the conclusion that they should ignore the existence of polygyny in their congregation: "they should not unseasonably speak ab[ou]t it in publick or private Meetings," wrote Rauch, "but let our Sav[ior] . . . convince them in their hearts [that] it's not right."[74]

In 1749, during another set of conferences led by Bishop Johannes von Wattewille, the brethren tried again to "come to a decision about the practice that had previously caused uncertainty and disorder among the blacks."[75] They finally concluded that men with more than one wife would be allowed to join the congregation, but they forbid converts from taking any additional spouses after their baptism.[76] Based on a reading of 1 Timothy 3:2, they also forbade men with multiple wives from holding office within the church.[77] Finally, the missionaries accounted for the possibility that a couple could be broken up against their will: "When a master separates a married couple and sells one to another land," Wattewille wrote, "the other partner should wait at least a year and a day to see if anything can be done about it. But if they remain apart, and there is no hope left that they will be brought together, it's better to consider each partner to be divorced and allow them to take another man or women rather than to see them resort to whoring [*Hurerey*]."[78] As Wattewille's comments reveal, the Moravian missionaries became increasingly flexible in their dealings with polygyny, as well as other "non-Christian" practices, in the decade after they halted their reading lessons. This policy shift represented an important adaptation to slavery: influenced by their conversations with black congregants and their recognition that slave masters could separate families at will, the missionaries redefined marriage to accommodate the circumstances of slave life.

By the time Wattewille approved polygyny in 1749, only a few remnants remained of the Moravians' previous focus on literacy. Most poignantly, the word "school" had been adapted into the local Dutch Creole to signify "meeting house." The linguistic development intrigued Wattewille, who noted in his journal that "the word 'school' is an expression unique to St. Thomas and St. Croix. In other congregations, we would use the word 'Meeting' or '[bible] hour.'" Wattewille was well aware of the significance of this linguistic relic: "When our brethren first began their work among the negros," he explained, "they had a school where they taught reading, so now all of the Meetings are referred to as school." The word was used frequently. "One says, for example: 'where is school being held?' . . . or 'Today there is school on the north side,' etc."[79] Thus while the word "school" survived in the Danish West Indies, reading and writing lessons did not. Instead, "school" was redefined to fit a West Indian context, just as Moravian Christianity was reenvisioned to include, at least marginally, cultural practices such as polygyny.

The debates about literacy, marriage, and conversion on St. Thomas demonstrated the tensions inherent in adapting Protestantism to Atlantic slavery. As Moravian missionaries discovered, teaching enslaved and free blacks how to read and write was problematic: although it helped them recruit hundreds of baptismal candidates, it fostered resentment from white planters and the government who feared that literacy would allow slaves to incite rebellion or run away. It also created tension within the Moravian congregation, as black converts read the Bible and proposed competing definitions of "true" Christian practice. In the end, the Moravians decided it would be easier to excise literacy from their evangelical strategy and to be more flexible in their approach to "non-Christian" practices such as polygyny.

The Moravian's innovations were important both in and outside the West Indies. When Spangenberg published his *Account* in 1788, he wrote for both English- and German-speaking audiences who showed increasing interest in evangelizing to slaves. As other denominations became more invested in missionary activities during the late eighteenth and nineteenth centuries, Moravian publications were an important source of information for new missionaries.[80] Thus Moravian policies—including their position that literacy was not essential for true "heart" conversion—were read and discussed throughout the Atlantic world as Methodists, Baptists and other Protestant groups increased their proselytizing efforts.

As they publicized their missionary methods, the Moravians' rejection of reading represented an important adaptation to African slavery. European Protestants—including the Moravians—generally viewed the reading of scripture as a central feature of Protestant piety and embraced the concept of *sola scriptura,* the idea that the Bible was the supreme source of authority. But the pressures from both slaves and masters forced missionaries to redefine Christian practice. Moravian missionaries responded to Protestant Supremacy and black Christian resistance by replacing reading lessons with a stripped-down gospel teaching that provided a sympathetic ear to men and women whose daily lives were filled with brutality and pain. In the following decades, Protestants elsewhere in the Atlantic world would come to similar conclusions and literacy came to be viewed as a dangerous skill.[81]

Despite the missionaries' shifting stance on reading, black Christians continued to view literacy as an important practice. Literate black leaders taught others how to read and write, thereby creating an alternate hierarchy within the Moravian Church. The divergence between missionaries and black converts on literacy signaled a wider divide between white and black Protestant thought. While white Moravians tended to argue that conversion would make slaves more loyal and hardworking, black Christians insisted that they had a right to practice Christianity and they highlighted the injustice of their masters for refusing to let them learn about the gospel. By the late eighteenth century, missionary Protestantism had helped to form the foundation of proslavery thought, while black Christians developed a theology focused on liberation.

Proslavery Theology and Black Christianity

In 1740, the celebrity evangelist George Whitefield published "A Letter to the Inhabitants of Maryland, Virginia, North and South Carolina." In it, he criticized the ideology of Protestant Supremacy and chastised slave owners for keeping their slaves "ignorant of Christianity." Specifically, he contested the widespread belief that "Christianity would make [slaves] proud, and consequently unwilling to submit to Slavery." Whitefield appealed to the "hearts" of slave owners and argued that Christian slaves would be more faithful after their true conversion. "If teaching Slaves Christianity has such a bad Influence upon their Lives," he asked, "why are you generally desirous of having your Children taught?"[1]

Whitefield's letter has been described the first formal defense of slavery in the Atlantic world.[2] But it was part of a broader defense of Christian slavery that was forged through the encounters between missionaries, enslaved people, and slave owners. Whitefield elaborated upon several themes, such as the loyalty of Christian slaves and the necessity of Christianizing slavery, that had been circulating in the Atlantic world since at least the 1670s with the publication of George Fox's *Gospel Family-Order* and Morgan Godwyn's *Negro's and Indians Advocate*. Godwyn and Fox, like Whitefield, shared the heartfelt belief that blacks should have access to the Christian knowledge that they held so dear.

Whitefield himself had been in contact with both Anglican and Moravian missionaries in the years before and after the publication of his letter. In 1738, he traveled to the new colony of Georgia, which was organized by a philanthropic group closely connected to the SPG and SPCK. In Georgia, he met a group of Moravians and founded an orphanage modeled after Francke's *Waisenhaus* in Halle. Then, in 1740, he collaborated with

Moravians to found a school for orphaned slaves in Nazareth, Pennsylvania. The school never came into being, but the influence of Moravian and Anglican missionary networks and the ideology of Christian slavery was evident in Whitefield's developing convictions about religion and slavery.[3]

Whitefield's letter can be seen as a transitional document between the ideology of Christian slavery espoused by Quaker, Anglican and Moravian missionaries, and the formation of a new proslavery ideology. Proslavery thought emerged, in part, out of the efforts of missionaries and other concerned Protestants to Christianize slavery.[4] It gained new urgency with the introduction of antislavery policies and the rise of the abolitionist movement. In Georgia, the first colony to be founded without slavery, Whitefield sided with proslavery colonists to convince the Trustees of Georgia to change their antislavery policy.[5] As antislavery voices became more pronounced, ministers and planters built on the rhetoric of Christian Slavery to articulate more vehement proslavery positions. Still, it was not until the nineteenth century that the majority of white planters embraced the idea of a paternalistic vision of slavery that united bondage with Christian duty and evangelization.[6]

*   *   *

Twenty years after Whitefield published his letter, the Moravian missionary Christian Heinrich Rauch recorded a conversation with Mathew, an enslaved slave driver on the Mesopotamia estate in Westmoreland, Jamaica. Mathew was concerned about how his obligations as a slave driver were affecting his spiritual state. Mathew reported to Rauch that "his work as a driver was distressing him." He believed that if it were not for his brutal occupation, "he would have been able to convert already." Rauch disagreed and told Mathew that it was possible to do both.[7] In fact, Mathew's status as a driver was important to the missionaries. They made him one of their Helpers and noted that "he maintains a nice order among the people."[8] As their comments suggest, Mathew was not just a recipient of the Moravians' message. The missionaries were beneficiaries of Mathew's generosity and gifts.

Mathew's relationship with the missionaries strained his relationship with other enslaved people. In August of 1760, the missionaries noted that

"Mathew went to his grounds with his wife to avoid the devilishness" of other slaves, who had gathered for a celebration. He then "spent the afternoon" with the missionaries.[9] Since the missionaries encouraged their baptismal candidates to reject what they considered to be "heathen" behavior, their policies split the slave population and isolated "converts" from much of the social life on the plantation. In light of these complex factors, it is important to ask what Mathew wanted out of his relationship with the missionaries, particularly since the Moravians did not offer instruction in reading and writing at that point. There were certainly some material benefits, but it is clear that he became more isolated from sections of the slave community.

While kinship ties and socioeconomic factors helped to bring enslaved Africans like Mathew into Protestant communities, theology cannot be overlooked. Evidence of Mathew's curiosity on this front is not difficult to find. He peppered the missionaries with questions about the details of their worship so much that their daily diaries are filled with the content of their conversations. Mathew told the missionary Christian Rauch that he "had believed in God since he was a child" and had "been distressed about his [spiritual state] for 5 years." He revealed that he had "often eavesdropped around white people," as he was curious about their beliefs and rituals, but that they had "rejected him harshly."[10] Perhaps this experience of rejection was one of the reasons that Mathew was so eager to approach the missionaries and learn about Christian practice and belief. His questions ranged from the details of worship to the nature of God. On January 10, he asked "why [the missionaries] didn't say the Lord's prayer both before and after the sermon?"[11] On another occasion, he inquired about the missionaries' dress, asking why they "didn't bring any priests' clothing?" Regarding God, he wanted to know whether "the Father created himself as the Savior?" If so, "how could he be called a Savior and also have created himself?"[12] Mathew was particularly interested in "sin," a concept that was central to Christianity but absent from most African religious traditions. He asked "whether a person had to have sinned if he wanted to be saved?"[13] The question suggested that Mathew was both intrigued and perplexed by the meaning of "sin." Why would it be a prerequisite for salvation?[14]

Mathew's questions cut to the heart of debates within Protestant communities about the proper preparations for baptism and the meaning of true Christianity. On several occasions, Mathew questioned why the missionaries withheld certain rites from slaves. At one point, he wondered whether the missionaries would ever "have the Lord's supper with the blacks who believed in God." When Rauch said yes, Mathew went "back home full of joy." Over time, however, Mathew grew impatient that the missionaries were so hesitant to baptize even eager candidates. As a result, Mathew and other enslaved men and women grew increasingly irritated with the missionaries. He told them that he "really wanted to be baptized," and several months later, broached the topic again, asking why they had not yet baptized any of the blacks.[15]

Why did Mathew want to be baptized? The answers are many, but they cannot be reduced to social or material advancement. Mathew was theologically engaged with Christianity, and his conversations with the missionaries challenged both parties to reinterpret scripture and Christian practice. On August 24, 1760 Mathew visited the missionary Brother Gandrup and they discussed the story of Philip and the Ethiopian. This story, from Acts 8:26–40, recounts Philip's journey into Ethiopia, where he met and baptized an Ethiopian eunuch. The missionaries were fond of the story of Philip and the Ethiopian, whom they called "the moor," because it showed that the gospel should be spread to Africans as well as Europeans. Mathew, however, had a different interpretation of the story. After hearing it, he approached the missionaries to make a case for his own baptism. Why did the missionaries withhold from him what Philip had granted to the Ethiopian? Why did he not deserve the same treatment? Reenacting the role of the Ethiopian, Mathew declared that he "believed that [his] creator is the Lord who redeemed [him] with his blood," and requested immediate baptism.[16]

Despite Mathew's convincing arguments, the missionaries refused, and it would be three more years before Mathew was officially initiated into the Moravian community. Yet this passage shows that Mathew participated in theological discussions with the missionaries, including debates about the proper time and procedure for baptism. While Mathew did not win this discussion immediately, his argument challenged missionary perceptions about what it meant to be a true Christian. Mathew was not a "convert" in the sense that he exchanged one set of beliefs for another. Instead, his engagement with Christianity should be understood as a process in which Protestantism itself evolved as a lived practice.

*   *   *

Whitefield's "Letter to the Inhabitants of Maryland, Virginia, North and South Carolina" and Mathew's efforts to attain baptism in rural Jamaica may seem disconnected. But it is only by examining these conversations "on the ground" in conjunction with the transatlantic debates about Christian slavery that it is possible to understand the changes taking place within Atlantic Protestantism. As white evangelicals increasingly turned to the ideology of Christian slavery to articulate their embrace of both slavery and evangelization, black Christians continued to challenge white interpretations of the Bible and Christian practice to emphasize suffering, resistance, and liberation. While some black Christians, like Mathew, eventually fought their way into European Protestant denominations, others rejected Euro-American institutions in favor of separate churches—the "invisible institution."[17]

Protestant practice was never static, but the institution of African slavery and the conversion of enslaved Africans to Christianity challenged Europeans to reconsider what it meant to be Christian in new, important, and difficult ways. The first Protestant planters to settle in the Caribbean redefined Christianity as an exclusive ethnic category reserved for the master class. Juxtaposing "Christians" and "negros," they held up their religious identities as evidence of their superiority. Over the course of the seventeenth century, these planters created an ideology of Protestant Supremacy by founding religious and political institutions that were united in their support for the plantocracy and in their characterization of Afro-Caribbeans as "hereditary heathens."[18]

When enslaved and free blacks sought out and won baptism for themselves and their children, they forced planters to reconsider the relationship between freedom and Protestantism. Could slaves become Christians? Should all Christians be free? And could free black Christians become voters who had the same rights and liberties as European colonists? Protestant planters answered these questions by highlighting whiteness, rather than Christian status, as the primary indicator of mastery and freedom. In Barbados, planters introduced whiteness into their law books just as a population of free black Christians began to emerge. In 1697, they redefined freeholder status to exclude all nonwhites and in 1709, they further specified that no one "whose original Extract shall be proved to have been from a Negro" could be "admitted as a Freeholder."[19] These developments were part of a broader embrace of racial categories—rather than religious categories—to define the social and political hierarchies of the Protestant American colonies. Yet even as religious identifiers such as "Christian" were dropped from law books, whiteness still functioned in ways that recalled Protestant Supremacy. Planters continued to bar all but their most favored slaves from Christian rituals and they resisted the work of missionaries throughout the eighteenth century. The persistence of religious undertones within the meaning and function of whiteness needs to be acknowledged in broader histories of race.

While enslaved and free black Christians forced planters to redefine the connection between religion and freedom, missionaries offered a new vision for Christian slavery that included both masters and slaves. In the missionary vision, Protestantism was a stabilizing force that would help to maintain, support, and reform slavery. Beginning with the Quakers, these evangelizing Protestants tried to convince planters to embrace a more inclusive and paternalistic form of Christianity. They also advocated for legislation that would affirm that baptism would never lead to freedom. While they did not succeed in passing a parliamentary bill, members of the SPG were instrumental in creating colonial laws, such as the 1706 act in New York, that clarified that baptized slaves would not be freed. These laws were intended to perform a humanitarian function by encouraging conversion, but in reality they strengthened and solidified racial slavery.

Aside from legislative efforts, Protestant missionaries developed and circulated ideas that would help to form a foundation for the proslavery ideology of the late eighteenth and nineteenth centuries. They argued that Christian slaves would be more obedient and hardworking than others and that a slave system built on Christian paternalism would be more productive and humane. Quakers like George Fox were the first to articulate this vision for Christian slavery and their activism incited Anglican missionary efforts. Moravians tapped into networks of the SPG and SPCK, as well as Pietist circles in Copenhagen. Later missions continued to build on these and other contacts.

Publications were an important source of missionary influence. Morgan Godwyn began his *Negro's and Indians Advocate* with an anecdote about reading George Fox's polemic *To the Ministers*, which excoriated the Anglican clergy in Barbados for their failure to convert slaves. Godwyn's publications were read and discussed by members of the SPG, who in turn created their own publications that they distributed throughout Protestant circles in Europe. The Moravians also prioritized printing, particularly in the late eighteenth century as they tried to improve their image among non-Moravians. Beginning in the 1760s, they published a series of mission histories in German, Dutch, French, and English, touting their mission strategies in the Caribbean and elsewhere. These publications emerged just as other denominations were developing their own global missions, enhancing their significance and effect. They helped to spread and circulate the ideology of Christian slavery by explaining how Protestantism and slavery could support and reinforce each other.

While most scholars have focused on the failure of early Protestant missionaries to garner large numbers of converts, the more significant problem was imperial. When Quakers, Anglicans, and Moravians founded missions to Christianize the American colonies, they were responding to the failure of Protestant nations to fully "transplant" their churches in the Americas. Without strong state churches or robust religious orders like the Jesuits, Dominicans, or Franciscans, Protestant empires placed their colonial institutions in the hands of colonists. In the Americas, planters *did* replicate many of the institutions of their homeland, such as the Anglican and Dutch Reformed Churches, but in doing so, they changed the meaning of those institutions. Rather than serving all inhabitants of a region, these colonial churches were restricted to Euro-Americans and a small number of favored slaves. By the late seventeenth century, Protestant planters had succeeded in creating churches that promoted an ideology of mastery by associating Protestantism with freedom and superiority.

Missionaries did their best to combat the exclusive version of Protestantism that was cultivated in the plantation colonies, but their presence often exacerbated conflicts between the pro-conversion sentiment of the "metropole" and the anticonversion rhetoric of Protestant planters. When Quakers brought slaves into their meetings and agitated for Anglicans to do the same, their controversial tactics led to the condemnation of slave conversion as a threat to island security. This trope became an easy way to attack missionary efforts and it was integrated into the litany of arguments that planters used to combat intrusive missionaries and colonial authorities who supported slave conversion. Anticonversion sentiment was just one of many ways that Protestant planters resisted the authority of the metropole. Claiming their "rights" as Protestant citizens, these planters argued that slave conversion, like increased oversight in governmental affairs, represented an infringement on their "liberties."

Over time, the ideology of Protestant Supremacy made the Protestant plantation colonies vulnerable to moral criticism. By the late eighteenth century, it was easy for abolitionists to claim that the sugar islands were islands of depravity and to evoke the deep well of criticism focusing on the planters' refusal to convert their slaves. Planters' failure to even pay lip service to the missionary movement enraged abolitionists in Europe who made strong and successful arguments against the slave trade on moral and religious grounds. Yet while planter hostility to slave conversion fueled abolitionist fire in Europe, the legacy of the early Protestant missions lay in the ideology of Christian slavery as well as antislavery thought. The irony is dark and yet unambiguous: the most self-sacrificing, faithful, and zealous missionaries in the Atlantic world formulated and theorized a powerful and lasting religious ideology for a brutal system of plantation labor. In the words of the Anglican missionary Morgan Godwyn, it was Christianity that "presseth *absolute* and entire *Obedience* to *Rulers* and *Superiours* . . . [and] establisheth the *Authority of Masters*, over their Servants and Slaves."[20]

Notes

Introduction

1. Though there is no mention of his owner, it is unlikely that Lazarus was free. The first recorded free black baptism did not take place until 1677, and there were few, if any, free blacks living on the island in 1651. See Jerome S. Handler and John T. Pohlmann, "Slave Manumissions and Freedmen in Seventeenth-Century Barbados," *William and Mary Quarterly* 41, no. 3 (July 1984): 390–408.

2. Carl Bridenbaugh and Roberta Bridenbaugh, *No Peace Beyond the Line: The English in the Caribbean, 1624–1690* (New York: Oxford University Press, 1972); Richard S. Dunn, *Sugar and Slaves: The Rise of the Planter Class in the English West Indies, 1624–1713*, reprinted (Chapel Hill: University of North Carolina Press, 2000); Michael Craton, *Sinews of Empire: A Short History of British Slavery* (Garden City, NY: Anchor Press, 1974); Gary A. Puckrein, *Little England: Plantation Society and Anglo-Barbadian Politics, 1627–1700* (New York: New York University Press, 1984). Recently, some historians have begun to revise this narrative. See Nicholas M. Beasley, *Christian Ritual and the Creation of British Slave Societies, 1650–1780* (Athens: University of Georgia Press, 2010); Kristen Block, *Ordinary Lives in the Early Caribbean: Religion, Colonial Competition, and the Politics of Profit* (Athens: University of Georgia Press, 2012); Larry Gragg, "The Pious and the Profane: The Religious Life of Early Barbados Planters," *Historian* 62, no. 2 (January 2000): 264–83; Larry Gragg, *Englishmen Transplanted: The English Colonization of Barbados 1627–1660* (Oxford: Oxford University Press, 2003); Jenny Shaw, *Everyday Life in the Early English Caribbean: Irish, Africans, and the Construction of Difference* (Athens: University of Georgia Press, 2013).

3. CSP, vol. 5 (1661–1668), no. 24, 6–7; P. F. Campbell, *The Church in Barbados in the Seventeenth Century* (St. Michael, Barbados: Barbados Museum and Historical Society, 1982), 82–83.

4. CO, 391/3, 206–7.

5. See, for example, David Brion Davis, *The Problem of Slavery in Western Culture* (Oxford: Oxford University Press, 1988); Christopher Leslie Brown, *Moral Capital: Foundations of British Abolitionism* (Chapel Hill: University of North Carolina Press, 2006).

6. Two important exceptions include Block, *Ordinary Lives*, pt. 4; Geoffrey Plank, "Discipline and Divinity: Colonial Quakerism, Christianity, and "Heathenism" in the Seventeenth Century," *Church History* (2016) 85, no. 3, 502–28.

7. Even scholars who acknowledge that Fox's views cannot be deemed "antislavery" have placed his comments within the context of Quaker antislavery thought. See J. William Frost,

"George Fox's Ambiguous Anti-Slavery Legacy," in *New Light on George Fox, 1624–1691*, ed. Michael Mullett (York, England: Ebor Press, 1994), 69–88; Brycchan Carey, "'The Power That Giveth Liberty and Freedom': The Barbadian Origins of Quaker Antislavery Rhetoric, 1657–76," *Ariel* 38, no. 1 (2007): 27–47.

8. On the Society for the Propagation of the Gospel, see Frank Joseph Klingberg, *Codrington Chronicle: An Experiment in Anglican Altruism on a Barbados Plantation, 1710–1834* (Berkeley: University of California Press, 1949); Samuel Clyde McCulloch, *British Humanitarianism: Essays Honoring Frank J. Klingberg* (Philadelphia: Church Historical Society, 1950). See also Travis Glasson's helpful discussion of the Anglican historiography in Travis Glasson, "Missionaries, Slavery, and Race: The Society for the Propagation of the Gospel in Foreign Parts in the Eighteenth-Century British Atlantic World" (Ph.D. diss., Columbia University, 2005), 11–12. For the Moravians, see J. H. Buchner, *The Moravians in Jamaica: History of the Mission of the United Brethren's Church to the Negroes in the Island of Jamaica from the Year 1754 to 1854* (London: Longman, Brown, 1854), 18; John Taylor Hamilton, *A History of the Missions of the Moravian Church, During the Eighteenth and Nineteenth Centuries* (Bethlehem, PA: Times Publishing Company, 1901), 36.

9. Jon Sensbach has emphasized the Moravians' acceptance of slavery in their early mission, while Claus Füllberg-Stolberg and Jan Hüsgen have argued that late eighteenth- and nineteenth-century Moravian missions in the Caribbean were not "islands of humanity." Jon F. Sensbach, *Rebecca's Revival: Creating Black Christianity in the Atlantic World* (Cambridge, MA: Harvard University Press, 2006); Claus Füllberg-Stolberg, "The Moravian Mission and the Emancipation of Slaves in the Caribbean," in *The End of Slavery in Africia and the Americas: A Comparative Approach*, ed. Ulrike Schmieder, Michael Zeuske, and Katja Füllberg-Stolberg (Münster: LIT Verlag, 2011), 81–102; Jan Hüsgen, *Mission und Sklaverei: Die Herrnhuter Brüdergemeine und die Sklavenemanzipation in Britisch- und Dänisch-Westindien* (Stuttgart: Franz Steiner Verlag, 2016).

10. Travis Glasson, "'Baptism Doth Not Bestow Freedom': Missionary Anglicanism, Slavery, and the Yorke-Talbot Opinion, 1701–30," *William and Mary Quarterly* 67, no. 2 (April 2010): 279–318; Travis Glasson, *Mastering Christianity: Missionary Anglicanism and Slavery in the Atlantic World* (New York: Oxford University Press, 2011).

11. Colin Podmore, *The Moravian Church in England, 1728–1760* (Oxford: Oxford University Press, 1998).

12. Only a handful of Anglophone studies have capitalized on these sources. For studies using German Script that are related to the Caribbean, see Richard Price, *Alabi's World* (Baltimore: Johns Hopkins University Press, 1990); Aaron Spencer Fogleman, *Two Troubled Souls: An Eighteenth-Century Couple's Spiritual Journey in the Atlantic World* (Chapel Hill: University of North Carolina Press, 2013); Sensbach, *Rebecca's Revival*.

13. For more on this approach, see Katharine Gerbner, "'They Call Me Obea': German Moravian Missionaries and Afro-Caribbean Religion in Jamaica, 1754–1760," *Atlantic Studies* 12, no. 2 (2015): 160–78.

14. I elaborate on this issue in Katharine Gerbner, "Theorizing Conversion: Christianity, Colonization, and Consciousness in the Early Modern Atlantic World," *History Compass* 13, no. 3 (2015): 134–47. Parts of this section have been republished from that article, courtesy of *History Compass*.

15. Jean Comaroff and John L. Comaroff, *Of Revelation and Revolution: Christianity, Colonialism, and Consciousness in South Africa*, vol. 1 (Chicago: University of Chicago Press, 1991), 251.

16. Kenneth Mills and Anthony Grafton, eds., *Conversion: Old Worlds and New* (Rochester, NY: University of Rochester Press, 2003), x.

17. D. Bruce Hindmarsh, *The Evangelical Conversion Narrative: Spiritual Autobiography in Early Modern England* (Oxford: Oxford University Press, 2005), 21, 31. For a more in-depth analysis of the different meanings of "conversion" in early Christian and medieval European contexts, see the essays in James Muldoon, ed., *Varieties of Religious Conversion in the Middle Ages* (Gainesville: University Press of Florida, 1997); Kenneth Mills and Anthony Grafton, eds., *Conversion in Late Antiquity and the Early Middle Ages: Seeing and Believing* (Rochester, NY: University of Rochester Press, 2003).

18. Hindmarsh, *Evangelical Conversion Narrative*.

19. Edmund S. Morgan, *Visible Saints: The History of a Puritan Idea* (Ithaca, NY: Cornell University Press, 1965); E. Brooks Holifield, *The Covenant Sealed: The Development of Puritan Sacramental Theology in Old and New England, 1570–1720* (New Haven, CT: Yale University Press, 1974); Charles E. Hambrick-Stowe, *The Practice of Piety: Puritan Devotional Disciplines in Seventeenth-Century New England* (Chapel Hill: University of North Carolina Press, 1982); Anne Brown and David D. Hall, "Family Strategies and Religious Practice," in *Lived Religion in America: Toward a History of Practice*, ed. David D. Hall, (Princeton, NJ: Princeton University Press, 1997), 41–68; Carter Lindberg, ed., *The Pietist Theologians: An Introduction to Theology in the Seventeenth and Eighteenth Centuries* (Malden, MA: Wiley-Blackwell, 2004).

20. While Rufus Jones located Quakerism within Christian mysticism, Geoffrey Nuttall argued that it is best understood as an offshoot of English Puritanism. Rufus M. Jones, *The Life and Message of George Fox 1624 to 1924* (New York: Macmillan, 1924); Geoffrey F. Nuttall, *The Holy Spirit in Puritan Faith and Experience* (Chicago: University of Chicago Press, 1946).

21. For scholarly interpretations of seventeenth-century Quaker religious experience, see Leopold Damrosch, *The Sorrows of the Quaker Jesus: James Nayler and the Puritan Crackdown on the Free Spirit* (Cambridge, MA: Harvard University Press, 1996); Phyllis Mack, *Visionary Women: Ecstatic Prophecy in 17th-Century England* (Berkeley: University of California Press, 1992); Rosemary Anne Moore, *The Light of their Consciences: The Early Quakers in Britain, 1646–1666* (University Park: Pennsylvania State University, 2000).

22. Nuttall, *Holy Spirit in Puritan Faith*, 157.

23. See William C. Braithwaite, *The Beginnings of Quakerism* (London: Macmillan,1912); and William C. Braithwaite, *The Second Period of Quakerism* (London: Macmillan, 1919).

24. For an overview of how baptismal practices remained central in early modern England even as they were contested, see David Cressy, *Birth, Marriage, and Death: Ritual, Religion, and the Life Cycle in Tudor and Stuart England* (Oxford: Oxford University Press, 1999), pt. 2. For a broader history of the Protestant Reformation and its effect on Christian rituals such as baptism, see John Bossy, *Christianity in the West 1400–1700* (Oxford: Oxford University Press, 1985).

25. See, for example, Thomas Bray, *A Course of Lectures upon the Church Catechism in Four Volumes* (Oxford: Printed by Leonard Litchfield, 1696); Thomas Bray, *A Short Discourse upon the Doctrine of Our Baptismal Covenant Being an Exposition upon the Preliminary Questions and Answers of Our Church-Catechism: Proper to Be Read by All Young Persons in Order to Their Understanding the Whole Frame and Tenor of the Christian Religion, and to Their Being Duly Prepared for Confirmation: With Devotions Preparatory to That Apostolick and Useful Ordinance* (London: Printed by E. Holt for R. Clavel, 1697).

26. Anglican missionaries used the word "civility" to indicate the adoption of European cultural practices. For a useful overview of the SPG's changing strategies to convert non-Europeans, see Glasson, "Missionaries, Slavery, and Race," 96–120.

27. Rosalind Beiler has shown how Quaker missionaries used dissenting Protestant networks in continental Europe to spread their message, while Ernest Stoeffler has argued that the Pietist movement in Germany was closely connected to English Puritanism. Rosalind J Beiler, "Dissenting Religious Communication Networks and Migration, 1660–1710," in *Soundings in Atlantic History: Latent Structures and Intellectual Currents, 1500–1830*, ed. Bernard Bailyn and Patricia L. Denault (Cambridge, MA: Harvard University Press, 2009), 210–36; F. Ernest Stoeffler, *The Rise of Evangelical Pietism* (Leiden: Brill, 1965). On the connection between Anglican voluntary organizations and Pietist/Puritan networks in Europe and America, see Daniel L. Brunner, *Halle Pietists in England: Anthony William Boehm and the Society for Promoting Christian Knowledge* (Göttingen: Vandenhoeck & Ruprecht, 1993); Brijraj Singh, " 'One Soul, Tho' Not One Soyl'? International Protestantism and Ecumenism at the Beginning of the Eighteenth Century," *Studies in Eighteenth Century Culture* 31 (January 2002): 61–84. These networks were essential to the spread of evangelical revivals in the eighteenth century. See W. R. Ward, *The Protestant Evangelical Awakening* (Cambridge University Press, 1992).

28. For a helpful overview of Pietism research, see Jonathan Strom, "Problems and Promises of Pietism Research," *Church History* 71, no. 3 (September 2002): 536–54. For a broader, transatlantic perspective on Puritan and Pietist networks, see F. Ernest Stoeffler, ed., *Continental Pietism and Early American Christianity* (Grand Rapids, MI: Eerdmans, 1976); Jonathan Strom, Hartmut Lehmann, and James Van Horn Melton, *Pietism in Germany and North America 1680–1820* (Farnham, England: Ashgate, 2009).

29. Markus Matthias, "August Hermann Francke," in *The Pietist Theologians: An Introduction to Theology in the Seventeenth and Eighteenth Centuries*, ed. Carter Lindberg (Malden, MA: Wiley-Blackwell, 2004), 100–114; Richard F. Lovelace, *The American Pietism of Cotton Mather: Origins of American Evangelicalism* (Grand Rapids, MI: Christian University Press, 1979).

30. Hindmarsh, *Evangelical Conversion Narrative*, 162. See also Gisela Mettele, "Constructions of the Religious Self: Moravian Conversion and Transatlantic Communication," *Journal of Moravian History*, no. 2 (2007): 7–35. On the radical gendered dimensions of early Moravian theology, see Aaron Spencer Fogleman, *Jesus Is Female: Moravians and Radical Religion in Early America* (Philadelphia: University of Pennsylvania Press, 2008). For Moravian piety in colonial Bethlehem, see Craig D. Atwood, *Community of the Cross: Moravian Piety in Colonial Bethlehem* (University Park: Pennsylvania State University Press, 2012).

31. Erika Geiger, "Zinzendorf Stellung Zum Halleschen Busskampf Und Zum Bekehrungserlebnis," *Unitas Fratrum: Zeitschrift Für Geschichte Und Gegenwartsfragen Der Brudergemeine*, no. 49/50 (January 2002): 12–22. For more details on Zinzendorf and his theology, see Peter Vogt, "Nicholas Ludwig von Zinzendorf," in *The Pietist Theologians: An Introduction to Theology in the Seventeenth and Eighteenth Centuries*, ed. Carter Lindberg (Malden, MA: Wiley-Blackwell, 2004), 207–23; Martin Brecht and Paul Peucker, eds., *Neue Aspekte Der Zinzendorf-Forschung* (Göttingen: Vandenhoeck & Ruprecht, 2006). The Atlantic dimensions of the feud between Halle Pietists and Moravians is addressed in Fogleman, *Jesus Is Female*, pt. 3. For the Moravians in the Atlantic world more broadly, see Michele Gillespie and Robert

Beachy, eds., *Pious Pursuits: German Moravians in the Atlantic World* (New York: Berghahn Books, 2007).

32. John Thornton, *Africa and Africans in the Making of the Atlantic World, 1400–1800*, 2nd ed. (Cambridge: Cambridge University Press, 1998); John K. Thornton, "On the Trail of Voodoo: African Christianity in Africa and the Americas," *Americas* 44, no. 3 (January 1988): 261–78. See also John Thornton, *The Kongolese Saint Anthony: Dona Beatriz Kimpa Vita and the Antonian Movement, 1684–1706* (Cambridge: Cambridge University Press, 1998); Linda M. Heywood and John K. Thornton, *Central Africans, Atlantic Creoles, and the Foundation of the Americas, 1585–1660* (Cambridge: Cambridge University Press, 2007); Cécile Fromont, *The Art of Conversion: Christian Visual Culture in the Kingdom of Kongo* (Chapel Hill: University of North Carolina Press, 2014).

33. Michael A. Gomez, *Exchanging Our Country Marks: The Transformation of African Identities in the Colonial and Antebellum South* (Chapel Hill: University of North Carolina Press, 1998); Sylviane A. Diouf, *Servants of Allah: African Muslims Enslaved in the Americas, 15th Anniversary Edition* (New York: New York University Press, 2013).

34. C. G. A. Oldendorp, *Historie Der Caribischen Inseln Sanct Thomas, Sanct Crux Und Sanct Jan: Insbesondere Der Dasigen Neger Und Der Mission Der Evangelischen Brüder Unter Denselben*, ed. Gudrun Meier et al., vol. 1 (Berlin: VWB, Verlag für Wissenschaft und Bildung, 2000), 460.

35. While this book focuses on the conversion of enslaved and free people of African descent, my approach has been influenced by scholarship on native Christianity in the Americas. See, in particular, Tracy Leavelle, *The Catholic Calumet: Colonial Conversions in French and Indian North America* (Philadelphia: University of Pennsylvania Press, 2011); Emma Anderson, *The Betrayal of Faith: The Tragic Journey of a Colonial Native Convert* (Cambridge, MA: Harvard University Press, 2007); David J. Silverman, *Faith and Boundaries: Colonists, Christianity, and Community Among the Wampanoag Indians of Martha's Vineyard, 1600–1871* (New York: Cambridge University Press, 2005); David J. Silverman, "Indians, Missionaries, and Religious Translation: Creating Wampanoag Christianity in Seventeenth-Century Martha's Vineyard," *William and Mary Quarterly* 62, no. 2 (April 2005): 141–74; Linford Fisher, *The Indian Great Awakening: Religion and the Shaping of Native Cultures in Early America* (New York: Oxford University Press, 2012); Linford Fisher, "Native Americans, Conversion, and Christian Practice in Colonial New England, 1640–1730," *Harvard Theological Review* 102, no. 1 (2009): 101–24; Rachel Wheeler, *To Live upon Hope: Mohicans and Missionaries in the Eighteenth-Century Northeast* (Ithaca, NY: Cornell University Press, 2008); Kenneth M. Morrison, *The Solidarity of Kin: Ethnohistory, Religious Studies, and the Algonkian-French Religious Encounter* (Albany: State University of New York Press, 2002); Allan Greer, "Conversion and Identity: Iroquois Christianity in Seventeenth-Century New France," in *Conversion: Old Worlds and New*, ed. Kenneth Mills and Grafton Anthony, 175–98 (Rochester, NY: University Rochester Press, 2003); Allan Greer, *Mohawk Saint: Catherine Tekakwitha and the Jesuits* (New York: Oxford University Press, 2004). On the role of native and African-descended missionaries in the Atlantic world, see Edward E. Andrews, *Native Apostles: Black and Indian Missionaries in the British Atlantic World* (Cambridge, MA: Harvard University Press, 2013).

36. There is a vast quantity of literature on these terms. On "syncretism," see Charles Stewart and Rosalind Shaw, eds., *Syncretism/anti-syncretism: The Politics of Religious Synthesis* (London: Routledge, 1994). On "hybridity," see Peter Burke, *Cultural Hybridity* (Cambridge:

Polity Press, 2009). My approach takes inspiration from the concept of "lived religion" and the analysis of translation practices in missionary encounters. On lived religion, see David D. Hall, ed., *Lived Religion in America: Toward a History of Practice* (Princeton, NJ: Princeton University Press, 1997). For scholarship that uses translation as a central mode of analysis, see Louise M. Burkhart, *The Slippery Earth: Nahua-Christian Moral Dialogue in Sixteenth-Century Mexico* (Tucson: University of Arizona Press, 1989); William F. Hanks, *Converting Words: Maya in the Age of the Cross* (Berkeley: University of California Press, 2010).

37. While Sylvia Frey and Paul Lovejoy have used the term "revisionist," I have replaced it with the term "Africanization" because it is more descriptive of the Africa-centered dimension of this approach. Paul Lovejoy, "The African Diaspora: Revisionist Interpretations of Ethnicity, Culture and Religion under Slavery," *Studies in the World History of Slavery, Abolition and Emancipation* 2, no. 1 (1997): 1–23; Sylvia R. Frey, "The Visible Church: Historiography of African American Religion since Raboteau," *Slavery & Abolition* 29, no. 1 (January 2008): 83–110.

38. The origins of this debate can be traced to the earlier dispute about African cultural "retentions." In the 1940s, Melville Herskovits argued that African Americans had not "lost" their culture in their forced migration across the Atlantic. E. Franklin Frazier challenged his position by insisting that Herskovits had not fully accounted for the destructive impact of slavery. In the 1970s, the anthropologists Sidney Mintz and Richard Price introduced the "creolization" thesis, which revised Herskovits's argument. Mintz and Price critiqued Herskovits's static conception of culture and argued that while African institutions were destroyed, Africans in the Americas drew on their cultural histories to create new institutions. A classic study translating the "creolization" model to the study of conversion is Michel Sobel's *Trabelin' On*, while a more recent formulation can be found in the work of the anthropologist Stephan Palmié. Melville J. Herskovits, *The Myth of the Negro Past* (New York: Harper & Bros., 1941); Melville J. Herskovits, "The Negro in Bahia, Brazil: A Problem in Method," *American Sociological Review* 8, no. 4 (August 1943): 394–404; E. Franklin Frazier, "The Negro Family in Bahia, Brazil," *American Sociological Review* 7, no. 4 (August 1942): 465–78; E. Franklin Frazier, *The Negro Church in America* (New York: Schocken, 1974); Mechal Sobel, *Trabelin' on: The Slave Journey to an Afro-Baptist Faith* (Princeton, NJ: Princeton University Press, 1988); Sidney W. Mintz and Richard Price, *The Birth of African-American Culture: An Anthropological Perspective* (Boston: Beacon Press, 1992); Stephan Palmié, ed., *Africas of the Americas: Beyond the Search for Origins in the Study of Afro-Atlantic Religions* (Leiden: Brill, 2008).

39. Mark M. Smith, *Stono: Documenting and Interpreting a Southern Slave Revolt* (Columbia: University of South Carolina Press, 2005); Jason R. Young, *Rituals of Resistance: African Atlantic Religion in Kongo and the Lowcountry South in the Era of Slavery* (Baton Rouge: Louisiana State University Press, 2011), 184.

40. The two classic texts on early Afro-Protestantism are Albert J. Raboteau, *Slave Religion: The "Invisible Institution" in the Antebellum South* (New York: Oxford University Press, 1978); Sylvia R. Frey and Betty Wood, *Come Shouting to Zion: African American Protestantism in the American South and British Caribbean to 1830* (Chapel Hill: University of North Carolina Press, 1998). Other influential studies include Margaret Washington Creel, *A Peculiar People: Slave Religion and Community-culture among the Gullahs* (New York: New York University Press, 1988); Jon Butler, "Africans' Religions in British America, 1650–1840," *Church History* 68, no. 1 (1999): 118–27; Sensbach, *Rebecca's Revival*.

41. While I have identified an important link between whiteness and Christianity in the Protestant Caribbean, the development of race was also deeply dependent on local factors. See, for example, Winthrop D. Jordan, *White Over Black: American Attitudes Toward the Negro, 1550–1812*, 2nd ed. (Chapel Hill: University of North Carolina Press, 2012); Edmund S. Morgan, *American Slavery, American Freedom: The Ordeal of Colonial Virginia* (New York: W. W. Norton, 2003); Colin Kidd, *The Forging of Races: Race and Scripture in the Protestant Atlantic World, 1600–2000* (Cambridge: Cambridge University Press, 2006); Peter Silver, *Our Savage Neighbors: How Indian War Transformed Early America* (New York: W. W. Norton, 2009); Rebecca Anne Goetz, *The Baptism of Early Virginia: How Christianity Created Race* (Baltimore: Johns Hopkins University Press, 2012).

Chapter 1

1. Richard Ligon, *A True and Exact History of the Island of Barbados*, ed. Karen Ordahl Kupperman (Indianapolis: Hackett, 2011), 100–101.

2. For Christian slaves in Mexico City, see Herman L. Bennett, *Africans in Colonial Mexico: Absolutism, Christianity, and Afro-Creole Consciousness, 1570–1640* (Bloomington: Indiana University Press, 2005). For scholarship on European slavery and captivity in North Africa, see Linda Colley, *Captives: Britain, Empire, and the World, 1600–1850*, reprint ed. (New York: Anchor, 2004); Robert C. Davis, *Christian Slaves, Muslim Masters: White Slavery in the Mediterranean, The Barbary Coast, and Italy, 1500–1800* (Basingstoke: Palgrave Macmillan, 2003); Michael Guasco, *Slaves and Englishmen: Human Bondage in the Early Modern Atlantic World* (Philadelphia: University of Pennsylvania Press, 2014), chap. 4; Nabil Matar, "English Accounts of Captivity in North Africa and the Middle East: 1577–1625," *Renaissance Quarterly* 54, no. 2 (July 2001): 553–72; Nabil Matar, *British Captives from the Mediterranean to the Atlantic, 1563–1760* (Leiden: Brill, 2014).

3. Enslaving Native American Christians was illegal in most cases, but still occurred in practice. On the possibility that Native Christians were enslaved in New England and shipped to Barbados, see Linford D. Fisher, "'Dangerous Designes': The 1676 Barbados Act to Prohibit New England Indian Slave Importation," *William and Mary Quarterly* 71, no. 1 (2014): 116–17. I am grateful to Linford Fisher for sharing his thoughts on this issue with me.

While the topic of Native enslavement and conversion is outside of the scope of this book, the scholarship on Native American slavery, particularly in North America and the Caribbean, has undergone a transformation in the past fifteen years. Scholars have demonstrated that the enslavement of Native Americans was far more widespread than previously understood. Furthermore, it is likely that Native slaves were sometimes subsumed under the category of "Negro." See James F. Brooks, *Captives and Cousins: Slavery, Kinship, and Community in the Southwest Borderlands* (Chapel Hill: University of North Carolina Press, 2002); Alan Gallay, *The Indian Slave Trade: The Rise of the English Empire in the American South, 1670–1717* (New Haven, CT: Yale University Press, 2002); Christina Snyder, *Slavery in Indian Country: The Changing Face of Captivity in Early America* (Cambridge, MA: Harvard University Press, 2010); Brett Rushforth, *Bonds of Alliance: Indigenous and Atlantic Slaveries in New France* (Chapel Hill: University of North Carolina Press, 2012); Margaret Ellen Newell, *Brethren by Nature: New England Indians, Colonists, and the Origins of American Slavery* (Ithaca, NY: Cornell University Press, 2016); Andrés Reséndez, *The Other Slavery: The Uncovered Story of Indian Enslavement in America* (Boston: Houghton Mifflin Harcourt, 2016). For a helpful overview of recent scholarship, see Arne Bialuschewski and Linford D. Fisher, "Guest Editor's

Introduction: New Directions in the History of Native American Slavery Studies," *Ethnohistory* 64, no. 1 (January 2017): 1–17.

4. In 1946, Frank Tannenbaum used this observation to draw broad conclusions about the differences between British and Latin American slavery. In Latin America, he argued, the Spanish could draw on a well-established slave tradition that came through the Justinian code and *Las Siete Partidas* and was deeply influenced by Catholicism. In northwestern Europe, by contrast, the lack of a well-known legal tradition regarding slavery led Anglo-Americans to "identify the Negro with the slave," and legal obstacles were quickly placed in the way of manumission. The role of the church further differentiated slave life in the British and Spanish empires, as slaves in British colonies "were almost completely denied the privileges of Christianity." Tannenbaum's *Slave and Citizen* has generated a passionate and extensive historiographic debate about slavery, race, law, and religion over the past several decades. Tannenbaum has been rightly criticized for evaluating the relative "humanity" of different forms of slavery and for underestimating English and Dutch familiarity with slavery and Roman law. But recently, Alejandro de la Fuente has suggested that despite its flaws, Tannenbaum's thesis has remained relevant because a number of his observations regarding the legal and religious differences among colonial empires require explanation. While Tannenbaum emphasized that the law granted slaves a "moral personality" in the abstract, de la Fuente follows more recent scholarship in showing that enslaved people learned how to use the law to their advantage. Furthermore, instead of making large generalizations about the nature of slavery in a colonial empire, de la Fuente has suggested that research should be firmly grounded in local cultures. Following de la Fuente, recent scholarship on Catholicism in Latin America has shown that enslaved blacks exhibited "legal activism" and capitalized on legal opportunities. In *Africans in Colonial Mexico*, Herman Bennett showed how enslaved and free blacks used the institutional structures of Catholicism, such as church support for conjugal rights, to navigate daily life. As this scholarship shows, enslaved Africans in colonial Latin America sometimes sought out the Catholic Church and the Spanish legal system to sue for their freedom or to prevent the separation of their families. Catholic priests and missionaries sometimes played an important role as advocates for enslaved men and women. Frank Tannenbaum, *Slave and Citizen: The Negro in the Americas* (New York: Vintage Books, 1946), 65, 82; Alan Watson, *Slave Law in the Americas* (Athens: University of Georgia Press, 1989); Gwendolyn Midlo Hall, *Social Control in Slave Plantation Societies: A Comparison of St. Domingue and Cuba* (Baton Rouge: Louisiana State University Press, 1996); Alejandro de la Fuente, "Slave Law and Claims-Making in Cuba: The Tannenbaum Debate Revisited," *Law and History Review* 22, no. 2 (July 2004): 339–69; Alejandro de la Fuente and Ariela Gross, "Comparative Studies of Law, Slavery, and Race in the Americas," *Annual Review of Law and Social Science* 6, no. 1 (2010): 469–85; Sally E. Hadden, "The Fragmented Laws of Slavery in the Colonial and Revolutionary Eras," in *The Cambridge History of Law in America*, ed. Michael Grossberg and Christopher Tomlins (Cambridge: Cambridge University Press, 2008), 253–87; Sue Peabody, "Slavery, Freedom, and the Law in the Atlantic World, 1420–1807," in *The Cambridge World History of Slavery*, ed. David Eltis and Stanley L. Engerman (Cambridge: Cambridge University Press, 2011), 594–630. For recent scholarship emphasizing the "legal activism" of enslaved and free blacks, see Bennett, *Africans in Colonial Mexico*; Michelle McKinley, "Fractional Freedoms: Slavery, Legal Activism, and Ecclesiastical Courts in Colonial Lima, 1593–1689," *Law and History Review* 28, no. 3 (August 2010): 749–90; Michelle

McKinley, *Fractional Freedoms: Slavery, Intimacy, and Legal Mobilization in Colonial Lima, 1600–1700* (New York: Cambridge University Press, 2016); Block, *Ordinary Lives*, pt. 1.

5. Robin Blackburn, *The Making of New World Slavery: From the Baroque to the Modern, 1492–1800* (London: Verso, 2010), 36. See also Jennifer A. Glancy, *Slavery in Early Christianity* (Oxford: Oxford University Press, 2002).

6. William D. Phillips, *Slavery from Roman Times to the Early Transatlantic Trade* (Minneapolis: University of Minnesota Press, 1985), 35.

7. See Davis, *Problem of Slavery in Western Culture*, 78–83.

8. Phillips, *Slavery from Roman Times*, 35.

9. Davis, *Problem of Slavery in Western Culture*, 86.

10. Phillips, *Slavery from Roman Times*, 60; Michael McCormick, *Origins of the European Economy: Communications and Commerce AD 300–900* (Cambridge: Cambridge University Press, 2002), 740, 751–54. The classic work on medieval slavery is Charles Verlinden, *L'esclavage dans l'Europe medieval*, 2 vols. (Brugge, Belgium: De Tempel, 1955 and 1977). For Verlinden's scholarship in English, see Charles Verlinden, *The Beginnings of Modern Colonization* (Ithaca, NY: Cornell, University Press, 1970).

11. Watson, *Slave Law in the Americas*, 34.

12. Seymour Drescher and Stanley L. Engerman, eds., *A Historical Guide to World Slavery* (New York: Oxford University Press, 1998), 365.

13. Blackburn, *Making of New World Slavery*, 43.

14. McCormick, *Origins of the European Economy*, 733–77; Blackburn, *Making of New World Slavery*, 43.

15. Blackburn, *Making of New World Slavery*, 38; McCormick, *Origins of the European Economy*, 740.

16. In 1335, for example, the King of Sweden freed all children of Christian slaves. Ruth Karras has argued, "Christian attitude did not amount to a campaign for abolition but combined with economic and social factors to bring about the end of slavery." Ruth Mazo Karras, *Slavery and Society in Medieval Scandinavia* (New Haven: Yale University Press, 1988), 138–142; see also Phillips, *Slavery from Roman Times to the Early Transatlantic Trade*, 58.

17. Phillips, *Slavery from Roman Times*, 43–65; Blackburn, *Making of New World Slavery*, 38. Even as the enslavement of Christians became taboo, the practice sometimes continued. In her study of fifteenth-century Valencia, Debra Blumenthal has written that while "certain Christians clearly had misgivings about enslaving other Christians, ultimately it is difficult to maintain the contention that the enslavement of Eastern Orthodox Christians was regarded dramatically differently from that of other slaves in fifteenth-century Valencia." Debra Blumenthal, *Enemies and Familiars: Slavery and Mastery in Fifteenth-Century Valencia* (Ithaca, NY: Cornell University Press, 2009), 40.

18. Blackburn, *Making of New World Slavery*, 50.

19. Phillips, *Slavery from Roman Times*, 91–101; Blackburn, *Making of New World Slavery*, 50.

20. Phillips, *Slavery from Roman Times*, 91–101; Blackburn, *Making of New World Slavery*, 50. They also colonized the Canary Islands, which raised new questions about the conversion and enslavement of native Canarians. See Eduardo Aznar Vallejo, "Conquests of the Canary Islands," in *Implicit Understandings: Observing, Reporting and Reflecting on the Encounters Between Europeans and Other Peoples in the Early Modern Era*, ed. Stuart B. Schwartz (Cambridge University Press, 1994).

21. Blackburn, *Making of New World Slavery*, 100–103.

22. Cited in John Francis Maxwell, *Slavery and the Catholic Church: The History of Catholic Teaching Concerning the Moral Legitimacy of the Institution of Slavery* (Chichester: Barry Rose Publishers, 1975), 53.

23. John Maxwell has argued that these Popes "had been led by the Portuguese to believe that the military situation in West Africa was an extension of the military conditions already existing in the Mediterranean," and therefore a Holy War. Ibid., 55.

24. Charles R. Boxer, *The Church Militant and Iberian Expansion, 1440–1770* (Baltimore: Johns Hopkins University Press, 1978), 78; Isabel Dos Guimarães Sá, "Ecclesiastical Structures and Religious Action" in Francisco Bethencourt and Diogo Ramada Curto, eds., *Portuguese Oceanic Expansion, 1400–1800* (Cambridge: Cambridge University Press, 2007), 256–57.

25. Maxwell, *Slavery and the Catholic Church*, 54–55; Blackburn, *Making of New World Slavery*, 103–6.

26. Cited in Blackburn, *Making of New World Slavery*, 118. For the development of Kongo Christianity, see Cécile Fromont, *The Art of Conversion: Christian Visual Culture in the Kingdom of Kongo* (Chapel Hill: University of North Carolina Press, 2014); John K. Thornton and Linda M. Heywood, *Central Africans, Atlantic Creoles, and the Foundation of the Americas, 1585–1660* (Cambridge: Cambridge University Press, 2007), chap. 2; John K. Thornton, "The Development of an African Catholic Church in the Kingdom of Kongo, 1491–1750," *The Journal of African History* 25, no. 2 (1984), 147–67.

27. Blackburn, *Making of New World Slavery*, 117. For a description of baptisms in São Tomé and other Atlantic islands, see Alonso de Sandoval, *Treatise on Slavery: Selections from De Instauranda Aethiopum Salute*, trans. Nicole von Germeten (Indianapolis: Hackett Publishing Company, Inc., 2008), 111–12, 116.

28. Enslaved Africans in Iberia, who were usually employed in households, government offices, hospitals or workshops, usually learned Portuguese and often participated in Catholic rituals and lay organizations. Some formed Catholic brotherhoods, while a small number were ordained within the Church. In Iberian society, black slaves were preferred to Muslims or *Moriscos*, who were viewed with suspicion and distrust. For African slaves in Iberia, see A. C. de C. M. Saunders, *A Social History of Black Slaves and Freedmen in Portugal, 1441–1555* (New York: Cambridge University Press, 1982). Enslaved Africans who arrived in the Atlantic islands encountered a different type of society. The introduction of sugar cultivation on São Tomé and other Atlantic islands set a new precedent for enslavement and conversion in the Atlantic world. Beginning in 1446, Henry the Navigator sponsored sugar production in Madeira and by the early fifteenth century, sugar cultivation had been introduced to the Canaries, São Tomé, and other Atlantic islands. Initially, the labor on sugar plantations was varied, consisting of a mix of free workers, natives, European immigrants, and slaves. But by the mid-sixteenth century, São Tomé relied almost exclusively on the labor of African slaves to plant, cut, and process the cane grown on the island. Enslaved Africans worked under brutal conditions on large plantations owned by Europeans. Mortality rates were high and little effort was made for cultural integration or religious conversion. While African slaves were regularly baptized and branded with a cross upon arrival, this was often their only "instruction" in the Christian religion. The plantation complex in São Tomé would provide the model for Brazilian plantations in the sixteenth century and, later, sugar cultivation in the English and French Caribbean. For overviews of the movement of sugar cane from the

Mediterranean across the Atlantic, see Philip D. Curtin, *The Rise and Fall of the Plantation Complex: Essays in Atlantic History*, 2nd ed. (Cambridge: Cambridge University Press, 1998); David Eltis, *The Rise of African Slavery in the Americas* (Cambridge: Cambridge University Press, 1999); Stuart B. Schwartz, ed., *Tropical Babylons: Sugar and the Making of the Atlantic World, 1450–1680* (Chapel Hill: University of North Carolina Press, 2004).

29. Boxer, *Church Militant and Iberian Expansion*, 78–79; Rachel Sarah O'Toole, "(Un)Making Christianity: The African Diaspora in Slavery and Freedom," in *The Oxford Handbook of Christianity in Latin America*, ed. Susan Fitzpatrick-Behrens, David Orique, and Manuel Vasquez (New York: Oxford University Press, forthcoming). I am grateful to Rachel O'Toole for sharing her forthcoming article with me.

30. The Spanish monarchs initially permitted only Christianized blacks to be transported to the Americas, apparently because they wanted to limit Indian exposure to African idolatry. They also feared that some Africans were Muslim. Throughout the sixteenth century, Spaniards were instructed to avoid transporting African slaves from Islamic regions, as these slaves were perceived to be more rebellious and less trustworthy. This meant that only *ladinos*, blacks who had resided in Iberia and converted to Christianity, were legally permitted in the Americas. By 1517, however, it was clear that this requirement was impossible to implement, and the Crown authorized the forced migration of four thousand enslaved Africans directly to America, "provided they be Christian." The Spanish Crown still sought tight control over the slave trade, requiring traders to pay a license fee to transport any slaves to the Americas. Spanish officials viewed the conversion of slaves as a method of control and security. F. P. Bowser, *The African Slave in Colonial Peru, 1524–1650* (Stanford, CA: Stanford University Press, 1974), 3, 27–28, 360n7, 368n6; Bennett, *Africans in Colonial Mexico*, cited 41.

31. Bowser, *African Slave in Colonial Peru*, 222–23; Jane Landers, *Black Society in Spanish Florida* (Urbana: University of Illinois Press, 1999), 108.

32. James H. Sweet, *Domingos Alvares, African Healing, and the Intellectual History of the Atlantic World* (Chapel Hill: University of North Carolina Press, 2011), 200–201. On Jesuit slaveholding and evangelizing practices, see Alonso de Sandoval, *Treatise on Slavery: Selections from De Instauranda Aethiopum Salute*, trans. Nicole von Germeten (Indianapolis: Hackett, 2008); Nicholas P. Cushner, *Lords of the Land: Sugar, Wine, and Jesuit Estates of Coastal Peru, 1600–1767* (Albany: State University of New York Press, 1980); O'Toole, "(Un)Making Christianity."

33. Bowser, *African Slave in Colonial Peru*, 237.

34. Ibid., 79.

35. Ibid., 233.

36. The penalty for those slave owners who failed to comply with these instructions was one-third of the assessed value of the slave. Ibid., 234.

37. Cited in ibid.

38. McKinley, "Fractional Freedoms."

39. Sweet, *Domingos Alvares*, 47.

40. Bennett, *Africans in Colonial Mexico*. For a discussion of slave marriage in Peru, see Bowser, *African Slave in Colonial Peru*, 255–67. In Brazil, marriage was uncommon among rural slaves, and only a minority of urban slaves partook in the sacrament. According to the 1872 census, only 10 percent of slaves in Brazil were married. Watson, *Slave Law in the Americas*, 158n22; Katia M. De Queiros Mattoso, *To Be A Slave in Brazil: 1550–1888*, trans. Arthur Goldhammer (New Brunswick, NJ: Rutgers University Press, 1987), 110.

41. Over time, the legal implications of marriage were altered. According to *Las Siete Partidas*, a slave who married a free person would become free, as long as he or she received consent from the owner. In Spanish America, Queen Juana altered this provision in 1538 so that slaves would remain slaves regardless of the status of their spouse. Carlos II reaffirmed the point in 1680 in his *Recopilación*, which stated that slaves would not be freed through marriage. Watson, *Slave Law in the Americas*, 48.

42. Bennett, *Africans in Colonial Mexico*, 81–90, 127; Watson, *Slave Law in the Americas*, 98; McKinley, "Fractional Freedoms." O'Toole emphasizes that while some enslaved Africans were able to "claim limited protections" through marriage and baptism, many Africans, particularly those who were newly arrived and those in rural areas, "were unaware of these colonial laws." Rachel Sarah O'Toole, *Bound Lives: Africans, Indians, and the Making of Race in Colonial Peru* (Pittsburgh: University of Pittsburgh Press, 2012), 35.

43. O'Toole, "(Un)Making Christianity"; Patricia A. Mulvey, "Black Brothers and Sisters: Membership in the Black Lay Brotherhoods of Colonial Brazil," *Luso-Brazilian Review* 17, no. 2 (December 1980): 253–79; Patricia A. Mulvey, "Slave Confraternities in Brazil: Their Role in Colonial Society," *Americas* 39, no. 1 (July 1982): 39–68; Bowser, "Africans in Spanish American Colonial Society," in *The Cambridge History of Latin America*, ed. Leslie Bethell, vol. 2 (Cambridge: Cambridge University Press, 1984), 372.

44. The African *cofradías* in Spain, whose practices included singing and dancing, became known as *cabildos*, a term that also crossed the Atlantic. Landers, *Black Society in Spanish Florida*, 9.

45. James H. Sweet, *Recreating Africa: Culture, Kinship, and Religion in the African-Portuguese World, 1441–1770* (Chapel Hill: University of North Carolina Press, 2003), 206.

46. Mulvey, "Black Brothers and Sisters," 254; Sweet, *Recreating Africa*, 206.

47. Mulvey, "Slave Confraternities in Brazil," 41.

48. Mulvey, "Black Brothers and Sisters," 254.

49. Jane Landers, *Atlantic Creoles in the Age of Revolutions* (Cambridge, MA: Harvard University Press, 2010), 108.

50. Sweet, *Recreating Africa*, 207.

51. Jane Landers writes that the *cabildos* "blended" African traditions and Catholicism. Landers, *Atlantic Creoles*, 109. James Sweet argues that Brazilian confraternities "provided Africans with the opportunity to forge their own social spaces within the repressive slave society." Sweet, *Recreating Africa*, 207. See also O'Toole, "(Un)Making Christianity."

52. Mulvey, "Black Brothers and Sisters," 255.

53. Guasco, *Slaves and Englishmen*, 127. See also Nabil Matar, *Turks, Moors, and English-men in the Age of Discovery* (New York: Columbia University Press, 2000), 71–82; Matar, "English Accounts of Captivity"; Linda Colley, *Captives: Britain, Empire, and the World, 1600–1850*, reprint ed. (New York: Anchor, 2004).

54. Cited in Christopher Tomlins, *Freedom Bound: Law, Labor, and Civic Identity in Colonizing English America, 1580–1865* (Cambridge: Cambridge University Press, 2010), 421.

55. Ibid., 423.

56. Hadden, "Fragmented Laws," 257.

57. Davis, *Problem of Slavery in Western Culture*, 46; Blackburn, *Making of New World Slavery*, 61. While many historians have assumed a general principle of "free air" in English towns, Stephen Alsford has argued that the principle was neither universal nor particularly

beneficial to those hoping to escape servitude. Stephen Alsford, "Urban Safe Havens for the Unfree in Medieval England: A Reconsideration," *Slavery & Abolition* 32, no. 3 (September 2011): 363–75.

58. Sue Peabody, "An Alternative Genealogy of the Origins of French Free Soil: Medieval Toulouse," *Slavery & Abolition* 32, no. 3 (September 2011): 341–62; Robin Blackburn, *The American Crucible: Slavery, Emancipation And Human Rights* (London: Verso, 2013), 89; Davis, *Problem of Slavery in Western Culture*, 46.

59. Davis, *Problem of Slavery in Western Culture*, 46.

60. Peabody, "Alternative Genealogy"; Aurelia Martín Casares and Margarita García Barranco, "Legislation on Free Soil in Nineteenth-Century Spain: The Case of the Slave Rufino and Its Consequences (1858–1879)," *Slavery & Abolition* 32, no. 3 (September 2011): 461–76. While "free soil" is most commonly associated with the English legal tradition, Peabody and Grinberg have argued that its "historical trajectory . . . was neither consistent nor always uniformly progressive in its effects." Sue Peabody and Keila Grinberg, "Free Soil: The Generation and Circulation of an Atlantic Legal Principle," *Slavery & Abolition* 32, no. 3 (September 2011): 331–39.

61. The slave in this case was Russian, not African. Helen Tunnicliff Catterall, *Judicial Cases Concerning American Slavery and the Negro* (Washington, D.C.: Carnegie Institute of Washington, 1926), 9.

62. George van Cleve, " 'Somerset's Case' and Its Antecedents in Imperial Perspective," *Law and History Review* 24, no. 3 (2006): 614.

63. Dienke Hondius, "Access to the Netherlands of Enslaved and Free Black Africans: Exploring Legal and Social Historical Practices in the Sixteenth–Nineteenth Centuries," *Slavery & Abolition* 32, no. 3 (September 2011): 380.

64. van Cleve, " 'Somerset's Case,' " 615–17. Holly Brewer has suggested that *Butts v. Penny* was a lightly veiled attempt by Charles II to solidify legal support for slavery. Thomas Butts was a naval officer and employee of the Royal Africa Company, which was headed by James of York, the brother of Charles II and the future James II. After the case, Charles II rewarded Butts for his "services." Holly Brewer, "Creating a Common Law of Slavery for England and its Empire," unpublished chapter draft presented at the Yale Legal History Forum, October 14, 2014. I am grateful to Holly Brewer for sharing this and other chapter drafts of her forthcoming book, *Inheritable Blood*.

65. Blackburn, *Making of New World Slavery*, 64, 87–88n78, 188–90. Quotation is originally printed in Robert Carl-Heinz Shell, *Children of Bondage: A Social History of the Slave Society at the Cape of Good Hope, 1652–1838* (Hanover, NH: University Press of New England, 1994), 335.

66. Patricia U. Bonomi, " 'Swarms of Negroes Comeing about My Door': Black Christianity in Early Dutch and English North America," *Journal of American History* (June 2016), 38.

67. Davis, *Problem of Slavery in Western Culture*, 200.

68. Cited in Davis, *Problem of Slavery in Western Culture*, 199.

69. Ibid., 201–4.

70. Morgan Godwyn, *The Negro's [and] Indians Advocate, Suing for Their Admission into the Church: Or A Persuasive to the Instructing and Baptizing of the Negro's and Indians in Our Plantations. Shewing, That as the Compliance Therewith Can Prejudice No Mans Just Interest;*

so the Wilful Neglecting and Opposing of It, Is No Less than a Manifest Apostacy from the Christian Faith. To Which Is Added, a Brief Account of Religion in Virginia (London: Printed by J[ohn] D[arby], 1680).

71. Cotton Mather, *The Negro Christianized: An Essay to Excite and Assist the Good Work, The Instruction of Negro-Servants in Christianity* (Boston: Printed by B. Green, 1706).

72. Chapter 4 elaborates on the relationship between French and English approaches to slave conversion. For debates in the French empire about the relationship between Catholicism and slavery leading to the *Code Noir*, see Guillaume Aubert, " 'To Establish One Law and Definite Rules': Race, Religion, and the Transatlantic Origins of the Louisiana Code Noir," in *Louisiana: Crossroads of the Atlantic World*, ed. Cécile Vidal (Philadelphia: University of Pennsylvania Press, 2013), 21–43. Aubert shows that there were many similarities between French and English discourses surrounding slavery, baptism, and freedom.

73. In the seventeenth century, the Danish West Indies were governed by the Danske Lov (1683), which did not mention slavery. Following a slave rebellion in 1733, Gardelin's Code was introduced as the first law to regulate slavery in the Danish West Indies, though it did not apply outside the Danish Caribbean. In the English Atlantic, Barbados passed a slave code in 1661 that became the model for later slave codes in Jamaica, South Carolina, and elsewhere (see Chapter 2). There was, however, no imperial slave code. Holly Brewer has argued that while Charles II promoted slavery, he was unable to pass empire-wide legislation. Similarly, Alan Watson has written that the Dutch "had no slave law." Watson, *Slave Law in the Americas*, 103; Hadden, "Fragmented Laws"; van Cleve, " 'Somerset's Case' "; Holly Brewer, "Creating a Common Law of Slavery."

74. Jeroen Dewulf, "Emulating a Portuguese Model," *Journal of Early American History* 4, no. 1 (January 2014): 19–20.

75. Evan Haefeli, "Breaking the Christian Atlantic: The Legacy of Dutch Toleration," in *The Legacy of Dutch Brazil*, ed. Michiel van Groesen (Cambridge: Cambridge University Press, 2014), 125. For background on the development of Dutch toleration policies, see Evan Haefeli, *New Netherland and the Dutch Origins of American Religious Liberty* (Philadelphia: University of Pennsylvania Press, 2012), chap. 1.

76. Haefeli, "Breaking the Christian Atlantic," 128.

77. Dewulf, "Emulating a Portuguese Model"; Jonathan Irvine Israel and Stuart B. Schwartz, *The Expansion of Tolerance: Religion in Dutch Brazil (1624–1654)* (Amsterdam University Press, 2007), 13–31. Israel argues that the form of toleration practiced in Dutch Brazil was more radical that in other Dutch colonies, due to the WIC's weak position in the region.

78. Dewulf, "Emulating a Portuguese Model," 24–25; Haefeli, "Breaking the Christian Atlantic," 138.

79. Dewulf, "Emulating a Portuguese Model," 28.

80. Linda M. Rupert, *Creolization and Contraband: Curaçao in the Early Modern Atlantic World* (Athens: University of Georgia Press, 2012), 85–88, 140–41; Wim Klooster, "Subordinate but Proud: Curaçao's Free Blacks and Mulattoes in the Eighteenth Century," *New West Indian Guide/Nieuwe West-Indische Gids* 68, no. 3/4 (1994): 291–93. See also Armando Lampe, "Christianity and Slavery in the Dutch Caribbean," in *Christianity in the Caribbean: Essays on Church History*, ed. Armando Lampe (Kingston, Jamaica: University of the West Indies Press, 2001), 126–53.

81. Bonomi, " 'Swarms of Negroes,' " 2; Susanah Shaw Romney, *New Netherland Connections: Intimate Networks and Atlantic Ties in Seventeenth-Century America* (Chapel Hill: University of North Carolina Press, 2014).

82. Cited in Graham Russell Hodges, *Root and Branch: African Americans in New York and East Jersey, 1613–1863* (Chapel Hill: University of North Carolina Press, 1999), 22.

83. Haefeli, *New Netherland*, 129; John K. Thornton and Linda M. Heywood, "Intercultural Relations Between Europeans and Blacks in New Netherland," in *Four Centuries of Dutch-American Relations: 1609–2009*, ed. Hans Krabbendam, Cornelis A. van Minnen, and Giles Scott-Smith (Albany: State University of New York Press, 2009), 192–203; Dewulf, "Emulating a Portuguese Model," 32–33; Hodges, *Root and Branch*, 22.

84. Dewulf, "Emulating a Portuguese Model," 29.

85. James Bell, *The Imperial Origins of the King's Church in Early America: 1607–1783* (New York: Palgrave Macmillan, 2004), 3–4; J. H. Elliot, "Religions on the Move," in *Religious Transformations in the Early Modern Americas*, ed. Stephanie Kirk and Sarah Rivett (Philadelphia: University of Pennsylvania Press, 2014), 25–45.

86. Bell, *Imperial Origins*; Elliot, "Religions on the Move."

87. On the partial transplantation of the Church of England in English America, see Patricia U. Bonomi, *Under the Cope of Heaven: Religion, Society, and Politics in Colonial America.* (New York: Oxford University Press, 1986); Jon Butler, *Awash in a Sea of Faith: Christianizing the American People* (Cambridge, MA: Harvard University Press, 1990).

88. Arthur Charles Dayfoot, *The Shaping of the West Indian Church, 1492–1962* (Gainesville: University Press of Florida, 1999), 71–72. For more on the role of the governor and colonial legislatures, see Jack P. Greene, "Liberty and Slavery: The Transfer of British Liberty to the West Indies, 1627–1865," in *Exclusionary Empire: English Liberty Overseas, 1600–1900*, ed. Jack P. Greene (Cambridge: Cambridge University Press, 2009), 50–76.

89. In 1649, the Rump Parliament approved the founding of the Society for the Propagation of the Gospel in New England, but it "depended for its activities on the voluntary contributions of the faithful." Elliot, "Religions on the Move," 36.

90. Heather Miyano Kopelson, *Faithful Bodies: Performing Religion and Race in the Puritan Atlantic* (New York: New York University Press, 2014), 125. On efforts to convert Native Americans in New England, see Richard W. Cogley, *John Eliot's Mission to the Indians Before King Philip's War* (Cambridge, MA: Harvard University Press, 1999); David J. Silverman, *Faith and Boundaries: Colonists, Christianity, and Community Among the Wampanoag Indians of Martha's Vineyard, 1600–1871* (New York: Cambridge University Press, 2005); Linford D. Fisher, "Native Americans, Conversion, and Christian Practice in Colonial New England, 1640–1730," *Harvard Theological Review* 102, no. 1 (2009): 101–24; Linford D. Fisher, *The Indian Great Awakening: Religion and the Shaping of Native Cultures in Early America* (New York: Oxford University Press, 2012).

91. Goetz, *Baptism of Early Virginia*.

92. Ligon, *A True and Exact History*, 1.

Chapter 2

1. *An Act for the better ordering and governing of Negroes*, clause 23, CO 30/2, 16–26.

2. David Barry Gaspar, "With a Rod of Iron: Barbados Slave Laws As a Model for Jamaica, South Carolina, and Antigua, 1661–1697," in *Crossing Boundaries: Comparative History of Black People in Diaspora*, ed. Darlene Clark Hine and Jacqueline McLeod (Bloomington: Indiana University Press, 1999), 343–66; Susan Dwyer Amussen, *Caribbean Exchanges: Slavery and the Transformation of English Society, 1640–1700* (Chapel Hill: University of North Carolina Press, 2007), 130–44; Edward B. Rugemer, "The Development of Mastery and Race

in the Comprehensive Slave Codes of the Greater Caribbean During the Seventeenth Century," *William and Mary Quarterly* 70, no. 3 (July 2013): 429–58.

3. *An Act for the better ordering and governing of Negroes*, CO 30/2, 16–26.

4. This taxonomy was evident elsewhere in the Protestant Atlantic, though it seems to have been more common in plantation colonies with larger populations of enslaved people. See Goetz, *Baptism of Early Virginia*; Kopelson, *Faithful Bodies*.

5. Dunn, *Sugar and Slaves*, 103; Michael Craton, *Sinews of Empire: A Short History of British Slavery* (Garden City, NY: Anchor Press, 1974), 205–6. Cited in Gragg, "Pious and the Profane," 266.

6. For the argument that the English West Indian colonies were islands of depravity, see Dunn, *Sugar and Slaves*; Bridenbaugh and Bridenbaugh, *No Peace Beyond the Line*; Puckrein, *Little England*; Craton, *Sinews of Empire*. Larry Gragg and Nicholas Beasley have recently contested this characterization. See Gragg, "Pious and the Profane"; Gragg, *Englishmen Transplanted*; Beasley, *Christian Ritual*.

7. Keith Hunte, "Protestantism and Slavery in the British Caribbean," in *Christianity in the Caribbean: Essays on Church History*, ed. Armando Lampe (Mona, Jamaica: University of the West Indies Press, 2000), 86.

8. Campbell, *Church in Barbados*, 29–42.

9. Hunte, "Protestantism and Slavery," 87.

10. Beasley, *Christian Ritual*, 22.

11. In 1684, for example, they ordered that "the Women's pew under the Governor's pew be kept only for those for whom it was first ordered, and that a lock be put on the pew." "Records of the Vestry of St. Michael, Barbados," reprinted in *JBMHS* 17, no. 1 (1949), 59.

12. "Records of the Vestry of St. Michael, Barbados," reprinted in *JBMHS* 17, no. 4 (1950), 194.

13. Ibid., 198.

14. "Records of the Vestry of St. Michael, Barbados," reprinted in *JBMHS* 19, no. 1 (1952), 44.

15. Beasley, *Christian Ritual*, 32–33.

16. "Records of the Vestry of St. John," reprinted in *JBMHS* 33, no. 1 (1969), 38–39.

17. "Records of the Vestry of St. Michael, Barbados," *JBMHS* 16, no. 1 (1949), 62; "Records of the Vestry of St. Michael, Barbados," reprinted in *JBMHS* 19, no. 1 (1952), 34–45.

18. "Records of the Vestry of St. Michael, Barbados," reprinted in *JBMHS* 19, no. 1 (1952), 39.

19. Ibid., 44.

20. "Records of the Vestry of St. Michael, Barbados," reprinted in *JBMHS* 16, no. 1 (1949), 59; "Records of the Vestry of St. Michael, Barbados," reprinted in *JBMHS* 17, no. 2 (1950), 126.

21. "Records of the Vestry of St. Michael, Barbados," reprinted in *JBMHS* 17, no. 2 (1950), 138.

22. "Records of the Vestry of St. Michael, Barbados," reprinted in *JBMHS* 16, no. 1 (1949): 59.

23. Vere Langford Oliver, *Monumental Inscriptions: Tombstones of the Island of Barbados* (San Bernardino, CA: Borgo Press, 1995), 2, 9.

24. Ibid., 122.

25. Ibid., 141; Edward Littleton, *The Groans of the Plantations: or A True Account of their Grievous and Extreme Sufferings by the Heavy Impositions upon Sugar, And other Hardships.* (London: Printed by M. Clark, 1689).

26. Oliver, *Monumental Inscriptions,* 153. See Chapter 3 for a description of the attempted rebellion.

27. T[homas] Walduck to James Petiver, November 12, 1710. Reprinted in *JBMHS* 15, no. 1 (1947): 27–51; Beasley, *Christian Ritual,* 57.

28. In 1705, the Barbadian government passed an act requiring inhabitants to pay five shillings for church weddings and twenty shillings for weddings outside the home. Beasley, *Christian Ritual,* 57–60.

29. The ability to marry privately could be used to challenge parental controls. Preventing clandestine marriage was the incentive for a Barbadian law threatening ministers with a £100 fine if they performed a marriage without banns or license. See Beasley, *Christian Ritual,* 63.

30. Walduck to Petiver; Beasley, *Christian Ritual,* 66.

31. Cited in Beasley, *Christian Ritual,* 65.

32. Walduck to Petiver; Beasley, *Christian Ritual,* 67.

33. For more on this topic, see Chapter 4.

34. Richard Hall, *Acts, Passed in the Island of Barbados. From 1643, to 1762, Inclusive* (London: Printed for Richard Hall, 1764), 4–5, 63–64.

35. Hall, *Acts, Passed in the Island,* 24–25, 258.

36. *The Laws of Barbados, Collected in One Volume, by William Rawlin, of the Middle-Temple, London, Esquire. And Now Clerk of the Assembly of the Said Island* (London: Printed for William Rawlin, Esq, 1699), 203.

37. *Memorandum by the Bishop of London Concerning the Church in Barbadoes,* August 28, 1680, CO 1/45, no. 77.

38. Hall, *Acts, Passed in the Island,* 112–21.

39. Dayfoot, *Shaping,* 71.

40. Dayfoot, *Shaping,* 74.

41. Cited in Carla Gardina Pestana, *The English Atlantic in an Age of Revolution, 1640–1661* (Cambridge, MA: Harvard University Press, 2004), 125.

42. Ibid., chap. 4; Larry Gragg, *The Quaker Community on Barbados: Challenging the Culture of the Planter Class* (Columbia: University of Missouri Press, 2009).

43. Pestana, *English Atlantic,* chap. 5.

44. Carla Gardina Pestana, *Protestant Empire: Religion and the Making of the British Atlantic World* (Philadelphia: University of Pennsylvania Press, 2010); Pestana, *English Atlantic.*

45. CO 1/14, no. 59 i.

46. Bennett, J. H., "English Bishops and Imperial Jurisdiction, 1660–1725," *Historical Magazine of the Protestant Episcopal Church* 32 (1963): 177.

47. Bennett, "English Bishops," 178.

48. Dayfoot, *Shaping,* 104.

49. Cited in Dayfoot, *Shaping,* 105–6.

50. Hunte, "Protestantism and Slavery," 87–89. On the role of the bishop of London in the colonies, see Geoffrey Yeo, "A Case Without Parallel: The Bishops of London and the

Anglican Church Overseas, 1660–1748," *Journal of Ecclesiastical History* 44, no. 3 (1993): 450–75 and Bennett, "English Bishops," 175–88.

51. Cited in Dayfoot, *Shaping*, 87. See also C. S. S. Higham, "The Early Days of the Church in the West Indies," *Church Quarterly Reviews* 92 (1921): 113.

52. LPL Fulham Papers, vol. 15, 204.

53. LPL Fulham Papers, vol. 15, 205.

54. See, for example, Ligon, *A True and Exact History*; Godwyn, *Negro's and Indians Advocate*.

55. Hall, *Acts*, 4–5; Dayfoot, *Shaping*, 72.

56. Hall, *Acts*, 4–5.

57. On the sugar revolution in Barbados, see Dunn, *Sugar*; Richard B. Sheridan, *Sugar and Slavery: The Economic History of the British West Indies, 1623–1775* (Baltimore: Johns Hopkins University Press, 1974); B. W. Higman, "The Sugar Revolution," *Economic History Review* 53, no. 2 (2000), 213–36; Russell Menard, *Sweet Negotiations: Sugar, Slavery, and Plantation Agriculture in Early Barbados* (Charlottesville: University of Virginia Press, 2006).

58. Of the 159 families that constituted the planter elite in 1680, 62 already held property on the island in 1638. These planters sought to show off their newly acquired wealth by purchasing items of luxury, such as tables, silver, cushions, carpets, and four-poster beds. Dunn, *Sugar and Slaves*; Gragg, *Englishmen Transplanted*.

59. On Native Americans enslaved in New England and transported to Barbados, see Fischer, "Dangerous Designes"; Margaret Newell, *Brethren By Nature: New England Indians, Colonists, and the Origins of American Slavery* (Ithaca: Cornell University Press, 2015); Wendy Warren, *New England Bound: Slavery and Colonization in Early North America* (New York: W. W. Norton, 2016).

60. On the shift from indentured servitude to African slavery in Barbados, see Dunn, *Sugar*; Hilary Beckles, *White Servitude and Black Slavery in Barbados, 1627–1715* (Knoxville: University of Tennessee Press, 1989); Amussen, *Caribbean Exchanges*; Menard, *Sweet Negotiations*; Simon Newman, *A New World of Labor: The Development of Plantation Slavery in the British Atlantic* (Philadelphia: University of Pennsylvania Press, 2013); Jerome Handler and Matthew C. Reilly, "Contesting "White Slavery" in the Caribbean: Enslaved Africans and European Indentured Servants in Seventeenth-Century Barbados," *New West Indian Guide* 91 (2017) 30–55.

61. Shaw, *Everyday Life*, 17.

62. Marcellus Rivers and Oxenbridge Foyle, *Englands Slavery or Barbados Merchandize* (London, 1659), 4–6, 10.

63. Rivers and Foyle, *Englands Slavery*, 5. See also Shaw, *Everyday Life*, chap. 1.

64. Ligon, *A True and Exact History*, 75, 96.

65. Hall, *Acts*, 39.

66. "An Act for the better ordering and governing of Negroes," CO 30/2, 16–26.

67. Rugemer, "Development of Mastery," 438.

68. Ibid., 437–41.

69. Kristen Block and Jenny Shaw, "Subjects Without an Empire: The Irish in the Early Modern Caribbean," *Past & Present* 210, no. 1 (February 2011): 33–60.

70. Hall, *Acts, Passed in the Island*, 112–21. Cited in David Barry Gaspar, "With a Rod of Iron," 350.

71. Amussen, *Caribbean Exchanges*, 144.

72. Shaw, *Everyday Life*, 35.

73. Ibid., 37.

74. Godwyn, *Negro's and Indians Advocate*. Cited in Goetz, *Baptism of Early Virginia*, 1.

75. See Chapters 6 and 7.

76. Kopelson, *Faithful Bodies*, 125.

77. Ibid., 193, 200.

Chapter 3

1. George Fox, *Gospel Family-Order, Being a Short Discourse Concerning the Ordering of Families, Both of Whites, Blacks and Indians* (London, 1676).

2. Thomas Drake, *Quakers and Slavery in America* (New Haven, CT: Yale University Press, 1950), 4–6; Frost, "George Fox's Ambiguous Anti-Slavery Legacy"; Carey, " 'Power That Giveth Liberty.' "

3. Important exceptions are Geoffrey Plank, "Discipline and Divinity: Colonial Quakerism, Christianity, and 'Heathenism' in the Seventeenth Century," *Church History* (2016) 85, no. 3: 502–28; Kristen Block, "Cultivating Inner and Outer Plantations: Property, Industry, and Slavery in Early Quaker Migration to the New World," *Early American Studies* 8, no. 3 (2010): 515–48; Block, *Ordinary Lives*.

4. Reprinted in Hall, *Acts, Passed in the Island*, 97–98.

5. William Edmundson, *A Journal of the Life, Travels, Sufferings, and Labour of Love in the Work of the Ministry* (London, 1829), 78.

6. For more on the origins and growth of the Quaker community on Barbados, see Barbara Ritter Dailey, "The Early Quaker Mission and the Settlement of Meetings in Barbados, 1655–1700," *Journal of the Barbados Museum and Historical Society* 39 (1991): 24–46; Gragg, *Quaker Community on Barbados*.

7. See Braithwaite, *Beginnings of Quakerism*, chap. 1. On religious radicalism and the early Quaker movement in England, see Christopher Hill, *The World Turned Upside Down: Radical Ideas during the English Revolution* (New York: Viking, 1972); Barry Reay, *The Quakers and the English Revolution* (New York: St. Martin's, 1985); Moore, *The Light of their Consciences*.

8. Cited in Gragg, *Quaker Community on Barbados*, 15.

9. For a survey of early Quaker missions, see Braithwaite, *Beginnings of Quakerism*, chap. 16.

10. Dunn, *Sugar and Slaves*; Braithwaite, *Beginnings of Quakerism*.

11. Block, *Ordinary Lives*, 149.

12. Gragg, *Quaker Community on Barbados*, 124–25.

13. Henry Fell to Margaret Fell, November 3, 1656, FHL Swarthmore Mss., 1.66. I have updated the Quaker dating system to reflect modern usage. Early modern Quakers did not use the names of months or days and instead used the phrases "first day, second day, etc." and "first month, second month, etc." Before 1752, the first month of the year was March, so when seventeenth-century Quakers referred to the "ninth month," for example, they meant November, not September.

14. Henry Fell to Margaret Fell, November 3, 1656, FHL Swarthmore Mss., 1.66.

15. Gragg, *Quaker Community on Barbados*, 39. For a more in-depth biography of Col. Lewis Morris, see Block, *Ordinary Lives*, pt. 4; Kristen Block, "Faith and Fortune: Religious

Identity and the Politics of Profit in the Seventeenth-Century Caribbean" (Ph.D. diss, Rutgers University, 2007), 225; Block, "Cultivating."

16. In 1656, for example, Henry Fell wrote that he was "abused & beaten" on his way to see Col. Morris in his house. When he informed Morris of what had transpired, Morris "tould me he would have the men before the Governour & sayd that ye Governour he was sure would punish them & would not suffer any to abuse me if he knew of it." Henry Fell to Margaret Fell, December 19, 1656, FHL Swarthmore Mss, 1.67.

17. George Fox, "To Friends beyond the Sea, that have Blacks and Indian Slaves," in *Selections from the Epistles of George Fox*, ed. Samuel Tuke (York: W. Alexander and Son, 1825), 94–95.

18. George Fox, John Stubbs, and Benjamin Furly, *A Battle-Door for Teachers & Professors to Learn Singular & Plural You to Many, and Thou to One, Singular One, Thou, Plural Many, You* (London: Printed for Robert Wilson, 1660), 6.

19. Richard Pinder, *A Loving Invitation (to Repentance, and Amendment of Life) unto all the Inhabitants of the Island Barbados Before the Lords sore Judgements come upon them, which is seen to be Nigh, and which they cannot escape; except Fruits meet for Repentance, and Amendment of Life be brought forth. With Somthing more particularly to the Heads, and Owners, of the several Plantations* (London: Printed for Robert Wilson, 1660).

20. "Minutes of the Council of Barbadoes," June 26/27, 1660. CSP, vol. 1, no. 2646, 483.

21. Campbell, *Church in Barbados*, 73.

22. Dunn, *Sugar and Slaves*, 104; Joseph, *A Collection of the Sufferings of the People Called Quakers*, vol. 2 (London: Printed and sold by Luke Hinde, 1753).

23. Besse, *Collection of the Sufferings*, 289.

24. Ibid., 283.

25. Frederick Barnes Tolles, *Quakers and the Atlantic Culture* (New York: Octagon Books, 1980), chap. 2. Comparing the Quaker community to a body, Tolles identified the itinerant ministry as its "bloodstream" and the hierarchy of meetings as its "bony structure." Ibid., 29.

26. Braithwaite, *Second Period of Quakerism*, 267.

27. Fox, *Gospel Family-Order*.

28. Mary Fisher to George Fox, January 30, 1655[?], FHL Swarthmore Mss., 4.193.

29. Henry Fell to Margaret Fell, November 3, 1656. FHL Swarthmore Mss., 1.66.

30. Barry Levy, *Quakers and the American Family: British Settlement in the Delaware Valley* (New York: Oxford University Press, 1988), 68.

31. The centrality of the family within Quaker practice was similar to Puritanism, but Quakers tended to place more emphasis on the importance of marriage, while Puritans focused on purifying churches. Ibid., 71–72.

32. Fox, *Gospel Family-Order*. Fox also encouraged Friends to limit the terms of their slaves. While some have argued that this is evidence of nascent antislavery sentiment, it is better understood as an attempt to modify and reform the slave system. In the late seventeenth century, slavery was still in the process of becoming defined as lifelong, inheritable, and race-based. Seventeenth-century Quakers, a number of whom had been slaves as well, would have been particularly attuned to the malleable definition of slavery at the time.

33. John Stubbs to Margaret Fox, December 2, 1671, FHL Abraham Mss., 15.

34. Joan Vokins, *God's Mighty Power Magnified as Manifested and Revealed in His Faithful Handmaid Joan Vokins, Who Departed This Life the 22d of the 5th Month, 1690, Having Finished Her Course, and Kept the Faith: Also Some Account of Her Exercises, Works of Faith,*

Labour of Love, and Great Travels in the Work of the Ministry, for the Good of Souls (London: Printed for Thomas Northcott, 1691), 43. See also Hilary Hinds, "An Absent Presence: Quaker Narratives of Journeys to America and Barbados, 1671–81," *Quaker Studies* 10, no. 1 (September 2005): 14.

35. Quakers settled in Maryland as early as 1658. Like their coreligionists in Barbados, they were quickly persecuted for their refusal to take oaths and support the militia, but they were not persecuted for any attempts to convert their slaves. On Quakerism in Maryland, see Kenneth L. Carroll, "Maryland Quakers in the Seventeenth Century," *Maryland Historical Magazine* 100, no. 1 (2005): 81–96. On Quaker familial practices in North Carolina, particularly related to gender, see Kirsten Fischer, *Suspect Relations: Sex, Race, and Resistance in Colonial North Carolina* (Ithaca, NY: Cornell University Press, 2001), 42–54.

36. "Third Haven Monthly Meeting Minutes, 1676–1871," September 2, 1681, HQC HV film 73, SW box 132.

37. "Lower Virginia Monthly Meeting Minutes, 1673–1723," (carbon copy), October 11, 1699, HQC HV 1116, box HW-43.

38. "Lower Virginia Monthly Meeting Minutes, 1673–1723," (carbon copy), October 11, 1699. HQC HV 1116, box HW-43.

39. "Lower Virginia Monthly Meeting Minutes, 1673–1723," (carbon copy), October 9, 1707, HQC HV 1116, box HW-43.

40. Block, *Ordinary Lives*, 157.

41. George Fox, *To the Ministers, Teachers and Priests (So called and so Stileing your Selves) in Barbadoes* (London, 1672).

42. Godwyn, *Negro's [and] Indians Advocate*, 105.

43. Godwyn, *Negro's [and] Indians Advocate*, 4–7.

44. Though many of the bills are undated, Paley, Malcolmson, and Hunter date them to the period after Restoration and before 1688. Ruth Paley, Cristina Malcolmson, and Michael Hunter, "Parliament and Slavery, 1660–c. 1710," *Slavery & Abolition* 31, no. 2 (June 2010): 257–81.

45. The documents are reprinted in Paley, Malcolmson, and Hunter, "Parliament and Slavery." The authors tentatively link Godwyn to these bills (261–62).

46. Paley, Malcolmson, and Hunter, "Parliament and Slavery," 268–69.

47. Ibid., 269–71.

48. Ibid., 271.

49. Ibid., 271–72.

50. Francis Brokesby, *Some Proposals Towards Propagating of the Gospel in Our American Plantations. Humbly Offerr'd in a Letter to Mr. Nelson, a worthy Member of the Society for propagating the Gospel in foreign Parts* (London, 1708), 3; D. A. Brunton, "Brokesby, Francis (1637–1714)," in *Oxford Dictionary of National Biography* online ed., edited by David Cannadine (Oxford: Oxford University Press, 2004).

51. Paley, Malcolmson, and Hunter, "Parliament and Slavery," 275.

52. Travis Glasson makes a similar argument regarding the Yorke-Talbot Opinion of 1729. See Glasson, " 'Baptism Doth Not Bestow Freedom.' "

53. Cited in Campbell, *Church in Barbados*, 73.

54. Anonymous, *Great Newes from the Barbadoes. Or, A True and Faithful Account of the Grand Conspiracy of the Negroes against the English and the Happy Discovery of the Same with*

the *Number of Those That Were Burned Alive, Beheaded, and Otherwise Executed for Their Horrid Crimes: With a Short Discription of That Plantation* (London: Printed for L. Curtis, 1676), 9.

55. Ibid., 10; Jerome S. Handler, "The Barbados Slave Conspiracies of 1675 and 1692," *Journal of the Barbados Museum and Historical Society* 36, no. 4 (1982): 314.

56. Handler, "Barbados Slave Conspiracies," 315.

57. The house slave is referred to as Anna in *Great Newes from the Barbadoes*, but as Fortuna in the *Calendar of State Papers*. Anonymous, *Great Newes from the Barbadoes*, 10; "Minutes of the Assembly of Barbadoes," November 25, 1675, CSP, vol. 9, no. 712, 303. Handler writes, "As was not uncommon, she easily could have been known by both names." Handler, "Barbados Slave Conspiracies," 313.

58. Richard Waterhouse, *A New World Gentry: The Making of a Merchant and Planter Class in South Carolina 1670–1770* (Charleston, SC: History Press, 2005), 29–30.

59. Anonymous, *A Continuation of the State of New-England: Being a Farther Account of the Indian Warr, and of the Engagement Betwixt the Joynt Forces of the United English Collonies and the Indians, on the 19th. of December 1675. With the True Number of the Slain and Wounded, and the Transactions of the English Army since the Said Fight. With All Other Passages That Have There Hapned from the 10th. of November, 1675. to the 8th. of February 1675/6. Together with an Account of the Intended Rebellion of the Negroes in the Barbadoes* (London: Printed by T. M. for Dorman Newman, 1676), 9; Anonymous, *Great Newes from the Barbadoes*, 10.

60. Anonymous, *Great Newes from the Barbadoes*, 12; Handler, "Barbados Slave Conspiracies," 313.

61. "Minutes of the Assembly of Barbadoes," November 25, 1675, CSP, vol. 9, no. 712, 303.

62. Hilary Beckles, *Black Rebellion in Barbados: The Struggle against Slavery, 1627–1838* (Bridgetown, Barbados: Antilles Publications, 1984), 38.

63. CO 30/1, 94–100. The full text of the act is available in Harriet Frorer Durham, *Caribbean Quakers* (Hollywood, FL: Dukane Press, 1972), 22–23.

64. Besse, *Collection of the Sufferings*, vol. 2, 310–11.

65. Edmundson, *Journal of the Life*, 75–79.

66. CO 391/3, 206–7. A summary of these proceedings is printed in CSP vol. 10, 611–12.

67. CO 391/3, 207.

68. Hall, *Acts, Passed in the Island*, 102–4.

69. John Rous to George Fox, George Whitehead, and Alexander Parker, December 25, 1681, FHL A. R. Barclay Ms., 48.

70. Richard Hoskins to George Whitehead, January 19, 1695, FHL Epistles Received, 1.217.

71. Epistle from Barbados, March 24, 1707, FHL Epistles Received, 1.438.

72. Ibid.

73. Darold D. Wax, "Quaker Merchants and the Slave Trade in Colonial Pennsylvania," *Pennsylvania Magazine of History and Biography* 86, no. 2 (April 1962): 143–59; Darold D. Wax, "The Negro Slave Trade in Colonial Pennsylvania" (Ph.D. diss., University of Washington, 1962); Block, "Cultivating."

74. Block, "Cultivating," 519.

75. Over the past three centuries, scholars have disagreed about the ethnic, national, and religious identities of these original settlers. What must be taken into account is that these boundaries were not defined as they are today. It is clear, however, that nearly all of the Krefelders and Krisheimers were Quakers when they arrived in Pennsylvania and had practiced Quakerism in their native lands. The majority had been Mennonites before Quaker missionaries like William Ames and William Penn arrived in the Netherlands and Germany in the mid-seventeenth century. William Isaac Hull, *William Penn and the Dutch Quaker Migration to Pennsylvania* (Philadelphia: Patterson & White, 1935), 285, Appendix 4. For more information, see James M. Duffin, *Acta Germanopolis: Records of the Corporation of Germantown, Pennsylvania, 1691–1707* (Philadelphia: Colonial Society of Pennsylvania, 2008), 3–13.

76. The original Germantown Protest is housed at the Quaker & Special Collections Library at Haverford College, Haverford, PA. A digital version of the text is available online at http://triptych.brynmawr.edu/cdm/ref/collection/HC_QuakSlav/id/5837.

77. See, for example, Epistle No. 366, cited in Braithwaite, *Second Period of Quakerism*, 431; [Samuel Tuke], *Account of the Slavery of Friends in the Barbary States, towards the Close of the 17th Century* (London, 1848). For more on the fear of captivity by Islamic ships, see Bethany Wiggin, "Slavery in Translation: German Baroque Figurations of African Enslavement in the Americas" in *Opening Spaces: Constructions, Visions, and Depictions of Spaces and Boundaries in the Baroque*, ed. Karin Friedrich (Wiesbaden: Harrasowitz, 2014), 723–40.

78. "Germantown Protest of 1688."

79. Ibid.

80. Ibid.

81. "Minutes of the Philadelphia Yearly Meeting," 1688. Reprinted in J. William Frost, ed., *The Quaker Origins of Antislavery* (Norwood, PA: Norwood Editions, 1980), 74.

82. *An Exhortation & Caution to Friends Concerning buying or keeping of Negroes* (New York: Printed by William Bradford, 1693). Most historians have assumed that Keith was the author of the *Exhortation*. I have argued elsewhere that the ideas in the *Exhortation* were most likely promoted by Keith's supporters, including at least Germantown Quakers who were directly involved with the 1688 protest. For more on Keith and antislavery, see Katharine Gerbner, "Antislavery in Print: The Germantown Protest, the 'Exhortation,' and the Seventeenth-Century Quaker Debate on Slavery," *Early American Studies* 9, no. 3 (2011): 552–75.

83. One of them, written by the Welsh Quaker Cadwallader Morgan, questioned whether enslaved Africans could be fully integrated into their families and worried that black "strangers" would corrupt their households. Another, authored by Robert Piles, elaborated upon a dream that led him to question the legitimacy of slavery. Both texts are reprinted in Frost, *Quaker Origins of Antislavery*. A third text, which has recently been rediscovered, made a humanitarian argument against slavery. See Nicholas Wood and Jean Soderlund, " 'To Friends and All Whom It May Concerne': William Southeby's Rediscovered 1696 Antislavery Protest," *Pennsylvania Magazine of History and Biography* 141, no. 2 (2017): 177–98. I am grateful to Nicholas Wood for sharing the article with me. These texts led the Philadelphia Yearly Meeting to discourage the importation of slaves, though it had little effect. For scholarly interpretations of Robert Piles's antislavery statement, see Jean R. Soderlund, *Quakers and Slavery: A Divided Spirit* (Princeton, NJ: Princeton University Press, 1985), 19–20; Gary B. Nash and Jean R.

Soderlund, *Freedom by Degrees: Emancipation in Pennsylvania and Its Aftermath* (New York: Oxford University Press, 1991), 44–45; Mechal Sobel, *Teach Me Dreams: The Search for Self in the Revolutionary Era* (Princeton, NJ: Princeton University Press, 2002), 55–56; Carla Gerona, *Night Journeys: The Power of Dreams in Transatlantic Quaker Culture* (Charlottesville, VA: University of Virginia Press, 2004), 21–27; Brycchan Carey, *From Peace to Freedom: Quaker Rhetoric and the Birth of American Antislavery, 1657–1761* (New Haven, CT: Yale University Press, 2012), 99–103.

84. George Gray's paper is reprinted in Frost, "George Fox's Ambiguous Anti-Slavery Legacy," 82–84. Notably, while Fox referred to blacks and Indians in *Gospel Family-Order*, Gray referred only to "Nigro[s]," not to Indians.

85. Ibid.

86. While there are no exact figures on slave imports in late seventeenth-century Pennsylvania, Gary Nash has calculated that "about one in fifteen Philadelphia families owned slaves" between 1682 and 1705. Gary B. Nash, "Slaves and Slaveowners in Colonial Philadelphia," *William and Mary Quarterly* 30, no. 2 (April 1973): 226.

87. Frost, "George Fox's Ambiguous Anti-Slavery Legacy."

Chapter 4

1. *Laws of Barbados*, 203–4; emphasis added.

2. Jordan, *White Over Black*; Morgan, *American Slavery*; Goetz, *Baptism of Early Virginia*; Rugemer, "Development of Mastery." There have been a number of important studies examining the emergence of "whiteness" in the Atlantic world over the past two decades. Some of the most influential for the British Atlantic world include Roxann Wheeler, *The Complexion of Race: Categories of Difference in Eighteenth-Century British Culture* (Philadelphia: University of Pennsylvania Press), 2000; Peter Silver, *Our Savage Neighbors: How Indian War Transformed Early America* (New York: W. W. Norton, 2009). On the malleability of whiteness in the United States, see Matthew Frye Jacobson, *Whiteness of a Different Color: European Immigrants and the Alchemy of Race* (Cambridge: Harvard University Press, 1999). For broader histories of whiteness, see Nell Irvin Painter, *The History of White People* (New York: W. W. Norton, 2010); Theodore W. Allen, *The Invention of the White Race*. 2 vols. (London: Verso, 1994–1997.

3. Ann Laura Stoler, "Tense and Tender Ties: The Politics of Comparison in North American History and (Post) Colonial Studies," in *Haunted by Empire: Geographies of Intimacy in North American History*, ed. Ann Laura Stoler (Durham, NC: Duke University Press, 2006), 23. For other studies showing the connection between gender relations and the development of race see Kathleen M. Brown, *Good Wives, Nasty Wenches, and Anxious Patriarchs: Gender, Race, and Power in Colonial Virginia* (Chapel Hill: University of North Carolina Press, 1996); Kirsten Fischer, *Suspect Relations: Sex, Race, and Resistance in Colonial North Carolina* (Ithaca, NY: Cornell University Press, 2001).

4. For a list of ministers, see Campbell, *Church in Barbados*, Appendix 1. Richard Gray, who was minister until 1658, used the term "servant" rather than "slave" in three entries. See Sanders, *Barbados Records: Baptisms* or the original records, NAB RL1/17, 24–33. It was not uncommon to refer to African slaves as "servants" in the mid-seventeenth century, though it is unlikely that these "negro servant[s]" were actually indentured or under contract. As Winthrop Jordan writes, "*servant* was a more generic term than *slave*. Slaves could be

'servants'—as they were eventually and ironically to become in the antebellum South—but servants *should not* be 'slaves.'" Jordan, *White Over Black,* 53.

5. LPL Fulham Papers, vol. 15, 209.

6. The ministers did not always provide the age of the individuals they baptized. Of the eighty-seven male slaves baptized during this period, twenty-seven were adults, twenty-nine were children, and fifty-six cannot be identified by age.

7. Richard Dunn has found that "chief slaves" were usually the first to be baptized in the Moravian mission to Jamaica. Richard S. Dunn, *Moravian Missionaries at Work in a Jamaican Slave Community: 1754–1835* (Minneapolis: James Ford Bell Library, University of Minnesota, 1994); Richard S. Dunn, *A Tale of Two Plantations: Slave Life and Labor in Jamaica and Virginia* (Cambridge, MA: Harvard University Press, 2014).

8. Rhys Isaac, *Landon Carter's Uneasy Kingdom: Revolution and Rebellion on a Virginia Plantation* (Oxford: Oxford University Press, 2004), 318–19.

9. Philip D. Morgan, "Interracial Sex in the Chesapeake and the British Atlantic World, 1700–1820," in *Sally Hemings and Thomas Jefferson: History, Memory, and Civic Culture,* ed. Jan Lewis and Peter S. Onuf (Charlottesville: University Press of Virginia, 1999), 52–85; Richard Godbeer, *Sexual Revolution in Early America* (Baltimore: Johns Hopkins University Press, 2002).

10. Kirsten Fischer and Jennifer Morgan, "Sex, Race, and the Colonial Project," *William and Mary Quarterly* 60, no. 1 (January 2003): 197; Sharon Block, *Rape and Sexual Power in Early America* (Chapel Hill: University of North Carolina Press, 2006); Wendy Anne Warren, "'The Cause of Her Grief': The Rape of a Slave in Early New England," *Journal of American History* 93, no. 4 (March 2007): 1031–49. On the constraints of the archive on telling the stories of enslaved women, see Saidiya V. Hartman, "Venus in Two Acts," *Small Axe* 26 (2008): 1–14; Marisa J. Fuentes, *Dispossessed Lives: Enslaved Women, Violence, and the Archive* (Philadelphia: University of Pennsylvania Press, 2015); Marisa J. Fuentes, "Power and Historical Figuring: Rachael Pringle Polgreen's Troubled Archive," *Gender & History* 22, no. 3 (November 2010): 564–84. On the centrality of gender for understanding Atlantic slavery, see Jennifer Morgan, *Laboring women: reproduction and gender in New World slavery* (Philadelphia: University of Pennsylvania Press, 2004).

11. Block, *Rape and Sexual Power,* 68.

12. All of the cases that I have found that clearly acknowledge sustained relationships between white masters and enslaved women were in Christ Church Parish. This suggests that there are important differences in the recording styles of the various ministers on the island.

13. Sanders, *Barbados Records: Baptisms,* 91.

14. The only reference to Dorothy Spendlove in the baptismal record is on August 13, 1683: "Frances 6 yrs, Ann 4 yrs, John 2 ½ yrs, chn of John Peers begotten of Dorothy Spendlove." Ibid., 275. The fact that the minister records Susanna and Elizabeth alternately as "negro women slaves" and "mul[attos]" speaks to the somewhat haphazard usage of the two terms. Since "mulattos" were sometimes referred to as "negros," there is an underrepresentation of "mulattos" in the baptismal records.

15. For more on Susannah Mingo, see Jenny Shaw, "Writing a History of Susanna Mingo: Slavery, Community, and the Problem of the Archive in Early Modern Barbados" (paper presented at the Omohundro Institute for Early American History and Culture conference, "Africans in the Americas," Barbados, March 2013). I am grateful to Jenny Shaw for

sharing her research on John Peers with me. There are two slightly different versions of Peers's will. The one cited above is in ibid., 39. Another version, which is not fully intact, is published in "Extracts from Wills Recorded in England," *Journal of the Barbados Museum and Historical Society* 13 (1945): 83. The second will suggests that Peers may have provided apprenticeship opportunities for his children.

16. Sanders, *Barbados Records: Baptisms*, 599.

17. By the time of Cuffee's baptism in 1677, there had been at least forty-six nonwhite baptisms, but Cuffee was the first person who was listed as "free."

18. Joanne Mcree Sanders, *Barbados Records: Marriages, 1643–1800*, 2 vols. (Houston, TX: Sanders Historical Publications, 1982). Two of these marriages may have been interracial. The minister did not list Elizabeth Bullard or Izabella Robinson as "free negro" women, though he did list their husbands as "free negroes." These women may have still been enslaved, or they may have been white.

19. Data compiled from Sanders, *Barbados Records: Marriages*. Data are only available for four of the eleven parishes, so these figures most likely underestimate the actual number of free baptized blacks.

20. Handler and Pohlmann identified 133 slaves who were manumitted between 1650 and 1700: 123 from wills, and 10 from deeds. As they point out, however, only 44.7 percent of the wills stated that the enslaved person should be manumitted immediately. In the majority of the cases, "conditions in the wills could greatly extend the time before manumission," meaning that the number of slaves actually freed by these wills was probably much lower than 123. Furthermore, it is likely that the executors of estates did not always follow through with the intentions of the testator, meaning that not all manumitted slaves received their freedom. This may explain why, when the earliest estimates of the free black population were produced in 1748, just 107 individuals, or 0.2 percent of the population, were estimated to be free. While this latter number probably underestimated the number of free people of color, Handler has argued that the free black population never surpassed 5 percent of the total population until the 1830s. Before 1725, the number was much lower, probably between 100 and 400 individuals. During the same time period, 107 free blacks were baptized in four of the eleven parishes. While data is not available from the seven remaining parishes, it is reasonable to assume that there were free blacks baptized in those parishes as well. While exact figures remain obscure, it is likely that at least 25 percent and probably over 50 percent of the free black population chose to be baptized before 1725. Handler and Pohlmann, "Slave Manumissions and Freedmen"; Jerome S. Handler, *The Unappropriated People: Freedmen in the Slave Society of Barbados* (Baltimore: Johns Hopkins University Press, 1974), 16; Sanders, *Barbados Records: Baptisms*.

21. I did not find evidence of Native Americans baptized in the Anglican church in Barbados. It is possible that some people identified as "negro" were, in fact, indigenous Americans. Legally, English people tended to treat the enslavement of Africans and Native Americans differently. In the Leeward Islands, for example, the enslavement of an Indian boy named Warner was disputed because he claimed to be a Christian. In a file sent to the Lords of Trade and Plantations, two depositions cited his lack of baptism as evidence of his slave status. "Col. Stapleton, Governor of the Leeward Islands, to the Committee of Council for Plantations," December 20, 1675. CO 1/35, Nos. 63, 63 I.-IV; "Governor Stapleton to Lords of Trade and Plantations," April 26, 1676. CO 1/36, Nos. 52, 52 I.-XIII.

22. Hall, *Acts, Passed in the Island*, 242–43.

23. These calculations are based on an analysis of all Barbadian laws available in print as well as four manuscript laws relating to slave control. I am grateful to Jerome Handler for sharing his copies of the slave codes that exist only in manuscript form. Sources: "An Act for the Better Ordering and Governing of Negroes," September 27, 1661, CO 30/2, 16–26; "A Supplemental Act to a Former Act for the Better Ordering and Governing of Negroes," April 21, 1676, CO 30/2, 114–25; "An Act for the Continuance of An Act Entitled a Supplemental Act to a Former Act for the Better Ordering and Governing of Negroes," March 15, 1677, CO 30/2, 125–26; "An Act to Explain a Branch of a Former Act for Ordering and Governing of Negroes," December 13, 1677, CO 30/2, 126–27; acts printed in *Laws of Barbados*; Hall, *Acts, Passed in the Island.*.

24. "An Act for the Better Ordering and Governing of Negroes," September 27, 1661, CO 30/2, 16–26.

25. "A Supplemental Act to a Former Act for the Better Ordering and Governing of Negroes," April 21, 1676, CO 30/2, 114–25.

26. Hall, *Acts, Passed in the Island*, 112–21.

27. Acts reprinted in Hall, *Acts, Passed in the Island*.

28. *Laws of Barbados*, 203–4; emphasis added.

29. Hall, *Acts, Passed in the Island* 237–38.

30. Ibid.

31. William H. Browne, ed., *Archives of Maryland: Proceedings and Acts of the General Assembly of Maryland, January 1637/8–September 1664* (Baltimore: Maryland Historical Society, 1883), 526; John C. Van Horne, ed., *Religious Philanthropy and Colonial Slavery: The American Correspondence of the Associates of Dr. Bray, 1717–1777* (Urbana: University of Illinois Press, 1985), 26–27. Another important incentive was the clarification of the status of white women who married slaves. The final text of the act stated: "And forasmuch as divers freeborne English women forgettfull of their free Condicon and to the disgrace of our Nation doe intermarry with Negro Slaues by which alsoe diuers suites may arise touching the Issue of such woemen and a great damage doth befall the Masters of such Negros for preuention whereof for deterring such freeborne women from such shamefull Matches Bee itt further Enacted by the Authority advice and Consent aforesaid That whatsoever free borne woman shall inter marry with any slaue from and after the Last day of this present Assembly shall Serue the master of such slaue dureing the life of her husband And that all the Issue of such freeborne woemen soe marryed shall be Slaues as their fathers were And Bee itt further Enacted that all the Issues of English or other freeborne woemen that haue already marryed Negroes shall serve the Masters of their Parents till they be Thirty yeares of age and noe longer."

32. See also Charles II's instructions to lawmakers. CO 1/14, no. 59 i.

33. William H. Browne, ed., *Archives of Maryland: Proceedings and Acts of the General Assembly of Maryland, April 1666–June 1676* (Baltimore: Maryland Historical Society, 1884), 272; Van Horne, *Religious Philanthropy*, 27; Whittington B. Johnson, "The Origin and Nature of African Slavery in Seventeenth Century Maryland," *Maryland Historical Magazine* 73, no. 3 (Fall 1978): 236–45.

34. Cited in Van Horne, *Religious Philanthropy*, 27.

35. CO 1/21, no. 113, 228. See also Goetz, *Baptism of Early Virginia*. Goetz argues that the law actually discouraged slave baptism in Virginia.

36. Goetz, *Baptism of Early Virginia*, 101.

37. Cited in ibid., 102.

38. In this case, the statute was intended to determine "whither Indians taken in war by any other nation" would be "servants for life or terme of yeares." William Waller Hening, *The Statutes at Large; Being a Collection of all the Laws of Virginia from the First Session of the Legislature in the Year 1619*, vol. 2 (New York: Printed for the Author by R. & W. & G. Bartow, 1823), 283; Glasson, *Mastering Christianity*, 78. Debates about Indians played an important role in the development of racial terminology throughout the British colonies, and were particularly significant in Virginia. For more on the development of race in the Chesapeake, see Edmund Morgan, *American Slavery, American Freedom* (New York: W. W. Norton, 2003); Goetz, *Baptism of Virginia*.

39. Rugemer, "Development of Mastery," 451–52.

40. Rugemer, "Development of Mastery."

41. On the mobilization of White Supremacy in Barbados and the British Atlantic during the late eighteenth and early nineteenth centuries, see David Lambert, *White Creole Culture, Politics and Identity during the Age of Abolition* (Cambridge: Cambridge University Press, 2005). Lambert argues that white supremacism "developed with the entrenchment of plantation slavery in Barbados and was predicated upon the assertion of absolute racial otherness between a white, free, Christian 'master subject' and subhuman 'other' of African origin, which included both enslaved people and the free people of colour." This was the dominant view among poor whites, while more elite planters used "a less overtly racialised discourse." Lambert, *White Creole Culture*, 208–9.

Chapter 5

1. CO 153/6, 448–88; CSP, vol. 17 (1699), no. 766, 422–24.

2. CO 152/3, no. 23; CSP, vol. 17 (1699), no. 458, 252–53.

3. CO 152/3, no. 23; CSP, vol. 17 (1699), no. 458, 252–53.

4. The full text relating to the SPG reads as follows: "I give and Bequeath my two Plantations in the Island of Barbados to the Society for propagation of the Christian Religion in Forreighn parts, Erected and Established by my Late good master, King William the Third, and my desire is to have the Plantations Continued Intire and three hundred negros at Least Kept always thereon, and A Convenient number of Professors and Scholars Maintained there, all of them to be under the vows of Poverty Chastity and obedience, who shall be oblidged to Studdy and Practice Physick and Chyrurgery as well as divinity, that by the apparent usefulness of the former to all mankind, they may Both indear themselves to the People and have the better oppertunitys of doeing good To mens Souls whilst they are Takeing Care of their Bodys. But the Particulars of the Constitution I Leave to the Society Compos'd of good and wise men." Reprinted in Vincent Harlow, *Christopher Codrington, 1668–1710* (New York: St. Martin's Press, 1990), 218.

5. Sue Peabody has shown that the "free soil" tradition in France had multiple origins: (1) the long-held "pious tradition" of free slaves; (2) a 1314 ordinance by Louis X, which "equat[ed] the kingdom of France with the condition of freedom and authori[zed] the freeing of serfs by 'good and suitable conditions'"; (3) a sixteenth-century rivalry between France and Spain, during which Spanish slaves were publicly manumitted; and (4) a number of late medieval legal decisions proclaiming freedom within a particular city, the earliest of which was made in 1402 in Toulouse. Peabody, "Alternative Genealogy," 341.

6. Cited in Aubert, "'To Establish One Law and Definite Rules': Race, Religion, and the Transatlantic Origins of the Louisiana Code Noir," in *Louisiana: Crossroads of the Atlantic World*, ed. Cécile Vidal (Philadelphia: University of Pennsylvania Press, 2013), 25.

7. Cited in ibid.

8. Ibid., 25–26, 28–33; Sue Peabody, "'A Dangerous Zeal': Catholic Missions to Slaves in the French Antilles, 1635–1800," *French Historical Studies* 25, no. 1 (December 21, 2002): 69.

9. Cited in Aubert, "'To Establish One Law," 26.

10. Ibid., 25–26; Peabody, "'A Dangerous Zeal,'" 69.

11. Cited in Aubert, "'To Establish One Law," 26–27.

12. Cited in Peabody, "'A Dangerous Zeal,'" 60.

13. Ibid., 63.

14. Ibid., 68–69.

15. Aubert, "'To Establish One Law," 27–28.

16. Ibid., 28.

17. The edict was not known as the Code Noir until the eighteenth century. Brett Rushforth, *Bonds of Alliance: Indigenous and Atlantic Slaveries in New France* (Williamsburg, VA: University of North Carolina Press, 2012), 124. The origins of the code have been a subject of debate. For the view that the Code Noir was based largely on Roman law, see Watson, *Slave Law in the Americas*. Vernon Palmer has argued that the Code Noir was based on colonial precedent. Vernon Valentine Palmer, "The Origins and Authors of the Code Noir," *Louisiana Law Review* 56, no. 2 (1996): 363–408. Guillaume Aubert has suggested that the *Code Noir* was, in part, a response to the mounting efforts of the Capuchins and Propaganda Fide to censure Atlantic slavery. Aubert, "'To Establish One Law and Definite Rules': Race, Religion, and the Transatlantic Origins of the Louisiana Code Noir."

18. Aubert, "'To Establish One Law," 33.

19. Aubert, "'To Establish One Law"; Peabody, "'A Dangerous Zeal.'"

20. The demographic shifts also increased concerns about social order. Colonial officials responded by adding restrictions to manumissions and erecting a color barrier to citizenship which, unlike the Code Noir, restricted full citizenship to all free people. Officials also cracked down on all gatherings of slaves and free blacks. Within this new context, missionaries were sometimes seen as a threat and the Jesuits were accused of fomenting rebellion. Peabody, "'A Dangerous Zeal,'" 74–84.

21. On the significance of Protestant identity and anti-Catholicism in the Glorious Revolution, particularly in the American colonies, see Owen Stanwood, *The Empire Reformed: English America in the Age of the Glorious Revolution* (Philadelphia, PA: University of Pennsylvania Press, 2011).

22. Brent S. Sirota, *The Christian Monitors: The Church of England and the Age of Benevolence, 1680–1730* (New Haven, CT: Yale University Press, 2014).

23. Shelley Burtt, "The Societies for the Reformation of Manners: Between John Locke and the Devil in Augustan England," in *The Margins of Orthodoxy: Heterodox Writing and Cultural Response, 1660–1750*, ed. Roger D. Lund (Cambridge: Cambridge University Press, 1996), 149–69.

24. Bray, *Course of Lectures*, epistle dedicatory (unpaginated); cited in Craig Rose, "The Origins and Ideals of the SPCK 1699–1716," in *The Church of England c.1689–c.1833: From Toleration to Tractarianism*, ed. John Walsh, Colin Haydon, and Stephen Taylor (Cambridge: Cambridge University Press, 1993), 178.

25. Scott Mandelbrote, "The Vision of Christopher Codrington," in *All Souls under the Ancien Régime: Politics, Learning and the Arts, c. 1600–1850*, ed. S. J. D. Green and Peregrine Horden (Oxford: Oxford University Press, 2007), 159–60.

26. Harlow, *Christopher Codrington*, 6–37; Mandelbrote, "Vision of Christopher Codrington," 135–39.

27. Gragg, *Englishmen Transplanted*, 9. See also Natalie Zacek, *Settler Society in the English Leeward Islands, 1670–1776* (New York: Cambridge University Press, 2010). Codrington himself reserved the term "Creole" for people of African descent, preferring to claim a full English identity. James Dator, "Search for a New Land: Imperial Power and Afro-Creole Resistance in the British Leeward Islands 1624–1745," (Ph.D. diss., University of Michigan, 2011), 9.

28. Harlow, *Christopher Codrington*, 50.

29. Ibid., 64–67.

30. Matthew Prior served as the secretary to King William at the Hague in 1690 before being appointed secretary to the ambassadors at the Treaty of Ryswick. In 1700, he became one of the Lords Commissioners of Trade and Plantations. From this post, he would defend and support his friend Codrington during his tenure as governor-general of the Leeward Islands. Ibid., 86–87. See also Frances Mayhew Rippy, "Prior, Matthew (1664–1721)," *Oxford Dictionary of National Biography* (Oxford: Oxford University Press, 2004).

31. Harlow, *Christopher Codrington*, 73–85, 99–100.

32. CO 152/3, no. 23; CSP, vol. 17 (1699), no. 458, 252–53.

33. James Pritchard, *In Search of Empire: The French in the Americas, 1670–1730* (Cambridge: Cambridge University Press, 2004), 49.

34. CSP, vol. 17 (1699), no. 264, 147–48.

35. CSP, vol. 17 (1699), no. 282, 159–60.

36. CO 152/3, no. 15; CSP, vol. 17 (1699), no. 74, 39–46.

37. CO 152/3, no. 32; CSP, vol. 17 (1699), no. 628, 337–38. For more on French baptismal practices in the Caribbean, see Peabody, "'A Dangerous Zeal.'"

38. CO 152/3, no. 32; CSP, vol. 17 (1699), no. 628, 337–38.

39. CO 152/3, no. 30; CSP, vol. 17 (1699), no. 576, 308.

40. CO 152/3, no. 30; CSP, vol. 17 (1699), no. 576, 308. Codrington was not the only one to recognize that the proximity to Catholic colonies would entice slaves to run away for baptism. See, for example, 152/14, 260, viii, "Governor Hart's replies to Queries by the Board of Trade."

41. Bennett, *Africans in Colonial Mexico*; Block, *Ordinary Lives*, pt. 1. See also see Dator, "Search for a New Land," 167–81.

42. For more on the Huguenot diaspora in the Atlantic world, see Randy J. Sparks and Bertrand Van Ruymbeke, eds., *Memory and Identity: The Huguenots in France and the Atlantic Diaspora* (Columbia: University of South Carolina Press, 2008); Susanne Lachenicht, *Hugenotten in Europa und Nordamerika: Migration und Integration in der Frühen Neuzeit* (Frankfurt: Campus Verlag, 2010); Owen Stanwood, "Between Eden and Empire: Huguenot Refugees and the Promise of New Worlds," *American Historical Review* 118, no. 5 (2013): 1319–44.

43. S. Charles Bolton, "Le Jau, Francis," *American National Biography Online*, online ed., (Oxford University Press, 2000).

44. "The Abstract of Dr. L'Jaus Papers relating to the Condicon of the Clergy, and other material Things in the Leeward Caribbean islands, offered to the consideracon of the Society p. ppaganda fide." RHL SPG-J, appendix B, no. 67.

45. RHL SPG-J, appendix B, no. 67.

46. RHL SPG-J, appendix B, no. 67.

47. RHL SPG-J, appendix B, no. 67.

48. Jean-Baptiste Labat, *Nouveau voyage aux isles de l'Amerique: contenant l'histoire naturelle de ces pays, l'origine, les moeurs, la religion & le gouvernement des habitans anciens & modernes. Les guerres & les evenemens singuliers qui y sont arrivez pendant le séjour que l'auteur y a fait. Par le R.P. Labat, de l'ordre des freres prêcheurs.* 8 vols. (Paris, 1742).

49. Jean-Baptiste Labat, *The Memoirs of Père Labat, 1693–1705*, trans. John Eaden (London: F. Cass, 1970), xviii.

50. Jean-Baptiste Labat, "Father Labat's Visit to Barbados in 1700," trans. Neville Connell, *Journal of the Barbados Museum and Historical Society* 24, no. 4 (1957): 168–69.

51. Labat, *Memoirs of Père Labat*, 212.

52. Ibid., 212–15.

53. Ibid.

54. Harlow, *Christopher Codrington*, 147–56.

55. A number of scholars have assumed that Codrington's will was written in 1702, since Codrington dated it February 22, 1702. Scott Mandelbrote confirms, however, that the will was written in 1703. See Mandelbrote, "Vision of Christopher Codrington," 140.

56. Reprinted in Harlow, *Christopher Codrington*, 217–20.

57. RHL C/WI/COD/1, 3–6. For more on Codrington's friendship with Gordon, see Mandelbrote, "Vision of Christopher Codrington," 163–71.

58. William Gordon, *A Sermon Preach'd at the Funeral of the Honourable Colonel Christopher Codrington, Late Captain General and Governor in Chief of Her Majesty's Carribbee Islands; Who Departed This Life at His Seat in Barbadoes, on Good-Friday the 7th of April 1710 and Was Interr'd the Day Following in the Parish Church of St. Michael.* (London: Printed for G. Strahan, 1710), 20–21, 3–4.

59. Woodbridge and Ramsay to the Secretary, June 20, 1711, RHL A6/111.

60. Gordon, *Sermon Preach'd at the Funeral*, 4.

61. Samuel Clyde McCulloch and John A. Schutz, "Of the Noble and Generous Benefaction of General Christopher Codrington," in *Codrington Chronicle: An Experiment in Anglican Altruism on a Barbados Plantation, 1710–1834*, ed. Frank Joseph Klingberg (Berkeley: University of California Press, 1949), 23.

62. RHL C/WI/COD/1, 3–6.

63. Papers of the Barbados Committee, November 17, 1710. RHL SPG X-Series, vol. 1.

64. Cited in Harlow, *Christopher Codrington*, 213.

65. Archbishop Tenison to the Secretary, March 22, 1710/11, RHL A6/38.

Chapter 6

1. Gilbert Burnet, *Of the Propagation of the Gospel in Foreign Parts. A Sermon Preach'd at St. Mary-Le-Bow, Feb. 18. 1703/4* (London: Printed for D. Brown and R. Sympson, 1704), 20.

2. Elias Neau, *An Account of the Sufferings of the French Protestants, Slaves on Board the French Kings Galleys* (London: Printed for Richard Parker, 1699), 1.

3. Paula Wheeler Carlo, "Neau, Elias," *American National Biography Online* (online ed., Oxford University Press, 2000, accessed June 26, 2015); Elias Neau, *An Account of the Sufferings of the French Protestants, Slaves on Board the French Kings Galleys* (London: Printed for Richard Parker, 1699).

4. Neau, *An Account of the Sufferings.*

5. Travis Glasson has identified the Society's first Secretary, John Chamberlayne, Sir John Phillips, and Dr. Josiah Woodward as early supporters of Neau. Glasson, "Missionaries, Slavery, and Race," 149–50.

6. Glasson, *Mastering Christianity,* 76.

7. Elias Neau to Mr. Hodges, July 10, 1703, RHL SPG Letters, A1/106.

8. Elias Neau to SPG Secretary, July 4, 1703, RHL SPG Letters, A1/177.

9. Mr. Neau to Dr. Woodward, September 5, 1704, RHL SPG Letters, A2/48.

10. Elias Neau to Mr. Chamberlayne, October 3, 1705, RHL SPG Letters, A2/124; Elias Neau to Mr. Chamberlayne, July 24, 1707, RHL SPG Letters, A3/298–304.

11. Neau wrote that he translated the Lord's Prayer into "Indian in Cormantin & in Cymadingo." Mr. Neau to the Secretary, July 5, 1710, RHL SPG Letters, A5/134.

12. Elias Neau to Mr. Chamberlayne, July 22, 1707, RHL SPG Letters, A3/188–95.

13. Mr. Neau to the Secretary, February 27, 1708/9, RHL SPG Letters, A4/402–13.

14. Elias Neau to Mr. Chamberlayne, July 24, 1707, RHL A3/298–304.

15. Aside from his new methods, Neau's school also benefited from the endorsement of local ministers and the newly passed act of assembly, discussed later in this section. Elias Neau to Mr. Chamberlayne, July 22, 1707, RHL SPG Letters, A3/188–95.

16. Elias Neau to Mr. Chamberlayne, July 24, 1707, RHL SPG Letters, A3/298–304.

17. Mr. Neau to Dr. Woodward, September 5, 1704, RHL SPG Letters, A2/48.

18. Mr. Vesey to SPG Secretary, October 26, 1704, RHL SPG Letters, A2/26; Mr. Vesey to the Ld Bp of London, October 26, 1704, RHL SPG Letters, A2/40.

19. Mr. Neau to Dr. Woodward, September 5, 1704, RHL SPG Letters, A2/48.

20. Elias Neau to Mr. Chamberlayne, October 3, 1705, RHL SPG Letters, A2/124.

21. Elias Neau to Mr. Chamberlayne, March 1, 1705/6, RHL SPG Letters, A2/159.

22. Elias Neau to Mr. Chamberlayne, July 22, 1707, RHL SPG Letters, A3/188–95; Mr. Neau to the Secretary, July 5, 1710, RHL SPG Letters, A5/134.

23. Elias Neau to John Hodges, April 15, 1704, RHL SPG Letters, A1/178.

24. Elias Neau to John Hodges, April 15, 1704, RHL SPG Letters, A1/178; Elias Neau to SPG Secretary, July 4, 1704, RHL SPG Letters, A1/177.

25. Elias Neau to SPG Secretary, July 4, 1704, RHL SPG Letters, A1/177.

26. Elias Neau to John Hodges, July 10, 1703, RHL SPG Letters, A1/106.

27. Mr. Neau to Dr. Woodward, September 5, 1704, RHL SPG Letters, A2/48.

28. Elias Neau to John Hodges, April 15, 1704, RHL SPG Letters, A1/178.

29. Elias Neau to John Hodges, April 15, 1704, RHL SPG Letters, A1/178.

30. Nicholas Trott, *The Laws of the British Plantations in America, Relating to the Church and the Clergy, Religion and Learning: Collected in One Volume.* (London: Printed for B. Cowse, 1721), 272–73.

31. Elias Neau to Mr. Chamberlayne, July 22, 1707, RHL SPG Letters, A3/188–95.

32. Trott, *Laws of the British Plantations,* 272–73.

33. Glasson, *Mastering Christianity,* 81–82.

34. RHL SPG Journal, vol. 1/120–23, October 15, 1703.

35. Glasson, *Mastering Christianity,* 80; RHL SPG Journal, vol. 1/120–23, October 15, 1703.

36. RHL SPG Journal, vol. 1/123–27, November 19, 1703; RHL SPG Journal, vol. 1/128–20, December 17, 1703.

37. "A Draught of a Bill for Converting the Negros &c In the Plantation," LPL Gibson Papers 941/72.

38. LPL SPG Minutes, vol. 1/91, April 1, 1706; LPL SPG Minutes, vol. 1/92, April 8, 1706; LPL SPG Minutes, vol. 1/93–94; RHL SPG Journal, vol. 1/234–36, April 19, 1706; Glasson, *Mastering Christianity*, 81.

39. George Ashe, *A Sermon Preach'd before the Incorporated Society for the Propagation of the Gospel in Foreign Parts; at their Anniversary Meeting in the Parish-Church of St. Mary-le-Bow; On Friday the 18th of Befruary, 1714.* (London: Printed and sold by J. Downing, 1715).

40. John Sharpe to the Secretary, June 23, 1712, RHL SPG Letters, A7/216. For the African influence on the rebellion, see John Thornton, "The Coromantees: An African Cultural Group in Colonial North America and the Caribbean," *Journal of Caribbean History* 32, no. 1/2 (1998): 161–78. The most comprehensive analysis of the revolt is Kenneth Scott, "The Slave Insurrection in New York in 1712," *New York Historical Society Quarterly* 45 (1961): 43–74.

41. John Sharpe to the Secretary, June 23, 1712, RHL SPG Letters, A7/216.

42. Glasson, *Mastering Christianity*, 194.

43. Governor Hunter to the Lords of Trade, June 23, 1712. In E. B. O'Callaghan, ed., *Documents Relative to the Colonial History of the State of New-York: Procured in Holland, England, and France by John Romeyn Brodhead*, vol. 5 (Albany: Weed, Parsons, 1855), 341–42.

44. John Sharpe reported that "about 18 have suffered death," while Governor Hunter wrote that twenty-seven had been convicted and twenty-one had been executed. John Sharpe to the Secretary, June 23, 1712, RHL SPG Letters, A7/216.

45. Governor Hunter to the Lords of Trade, June 23, 1712. In O'Callaghan, *Documents*, 5:341–42.

46. John Sharpe to the Secretary, June 23, 1712, RHL SPG Letters, A7/216.

47. Mr. Neau to the Secretary, [December?] 15, 1712, RHL SPG Letters, A7/226.

48. Mr. Neau to the Secretary, [December?] 15, 1712, RHL SPG Letters, A7/226.

49. Mr. Neau to the Secretary [n.d.; 1710 or 1711?], trans. Amélie Allard, RHL SPG Letters, A6/87.

50. Mr. Neau to the Secretary, [December?] 15, 1712, RHL SPG Letters, A7/226. Even Reverend Vesey became less vocal in his support of Neau's mission, and for several years he refused to urge his congregants to send their slaves to be catechized. Thomas Barclay to the Secretary, May 31, 1712, RHL SPG Letters, A7/206.

51. John Sharpe to the Secretary, June 23, 1712, RHL SPG Letters, A7/216.

52. Scott, "Slave Insurrection in New York," 65–66; Glasson, *Mastering Christianity*, 83.

53. John Sharpe to the Secretary, June 23, 1712, RHL SPG Letters, A7/216.

54. Sharpe visited the two suspects in prison, where he said they "declared their innocency" and "behaved themselves as became Christians." John Sharpe to the Secretary, June 23, 1712, RHL SPG Letters, A7/216.

55. Scott, "Slave Insurrection in New York."

56. Mr. Neau to Mr. Chamberlayne, September 8, 1713, RHL SPG Letters, A8/173–74.

57. Mr. Neau to Mr. Chamberlayne, September 8, 1713, RHL SPG Letters, A8/173–74.

58. Elias Neau to Mr. Chamberlayne, July, 22, 1707, RHL SPG Letters, A3/188–95.

59. Mr. Neau to the Secretary, January 22, 1719/20, RHL SPG Letters, A14/110.

60. John Sharpe to the Secretary, June 23, 1712, RHL SPG Letters, A7/216.

61. John Moore, *A Sermon Preach'd before the Society for the Propagation of the Gospel in Foreign Parts, at their Anniversary Meeting, In the Parish-Church of St. Mary-le-Bow, February 20, 1712/13* (London: Printed and sold by Joseph Dowling, 1713), 48–49.

62. Undated abstract and other papers by Dr. Le Jau describing religious situation in Leeward and Caribbee Islands, LPL SPG XVII 286–92.

63. Undated abstract and other papers by Dr. Le Jau describing religious situation in Leeward and Caribbee Islands, LPL SPG XVII 286–92.

64. LPL SPG Minutes, vol. 1/71, November 12, 1705.

65. On Le Jau's mission, particularly to enslaved Africans, see also Annette Laing, " 'Heathens and Infidels'? African Christianization and Anglicanism in the South Carolina Low Country, 1700–1750," *Religion and American Culture* 12, no. 2 (2002): 197–228.

66. Le Jau to Secretary, April 15, 1707, RHL SPG Letters, A3/98. Le Jau's predecessor, Samuel Thomas, had targeted enslaved men and women in the region. He reported that about twenty blacks attended church services, that he had one black communicant, and that several could read. Frank Klingberg, ed., *The Carolina Chronicle of Dr. Francis Le Jau, 1706–1717* (Berkeley: University of California Press, 1956), 3.

67. Le Jau to Secretary, June 30, 1707, RHL SPG Letters, A3/326.

68. Le Jau to the Secretary, November 15, 1708, RHL SPG Letters, A4/91.

69. Le Jau to the Secretary, February 15, 1708/9, RHL SPG Letters, A4/96.

70. Le Jau to the Secretary, March 22, 1708/9, RHL SPG Letters, A4/142.

71. Le Jau to the Secretary, October 20, 1709, RHL SPG Letters, A5/49.

72. Le Jau to Mr. Stubs, April 15, 1707, RHL SPG Letters, A3/141.

73. Le Jau to the Secretary, February 1, 1709/10, RHL SPG Letters, A5/98. The full description reads:

> He had a Book wherein he read some description of the several judgmts that Chastise men because of their Sins in these that Chastise men because of their Sins in these latter days, that description made an Impression upon his Spirit, and he told his master abruptly there woud be a dismal time and the moon wou'd be turned into Blood and there wou'd be dearth of darkness and went away: When I heard of that I sent for the Negroe who ingeniously told me he had read so in a Book, I advised him and Charged him not to put his own Constructions upon his reading after that manner, and to be Cautious not to speak so, which he promised to me but yet wou'd never shew me the Book; but when he spoke those few words to his Master, some Negroe overheard a part, and it was publickly blazed abroad that an Angel came and spake to the Man, he had seen a hand that gave him a Book, he had heard Voices, seen fires &c.

74. Le Jau to the Secretary, February 19, 1710. Cited in Klingberg, *Carolina Chronicle,* 74.

75. Le Jau to the Secretary, February 1, 1709/10, RHL SPG Letters, A5/98.

76. Le Jau to the Secretary, June 13, 1710. Cited in Klingberg, *Carolina Chronicle,* 77.

77. In his annual sermon in 1704, Gilbert Burnet spent some time comparing English attempts to convert the "heathens" to those of Catholic Spain, but he referred primarily to Indians rather than slaves. See Burnet, *Of the Propagation of the Gospel.*

78. John Williams, *A Sermon Preached before the Society for the Propagation of the Gospel in Foreign Parts on February 15. 1705/6.* (London: Printed by John Downing, 1706), 21.

79. William Beveridge, *A Sermon Preach'd . . . February 21st, 1706–7* (London: Printed by Joseph Downing, 1707), 21. On Native and black missionaries, see Andrews, *Native Apostles*.

80. LPL SPG Minutes, vol. 1/137, December 16, 1706; LPL SPG Minutes, vol. 1/138–39, December 20, 1706. White Kennett preached the annual sermon in 1712, in which he built on Godwyn's texts to criticize impediments to slave and Indian conversion. White Kennett, *The Lets and Impediments in Planting and Propagating the Gospel of Christ. A Sermon Preach'd before the Society for the Propagation of the Gospel in Foreign Parts* (London: Printed and sold by Joseph Downing, 1712).

81. Beveridge, *A Sermon Preach'd . . . February 21st, 1706–7*, 21.

82. William Fleetwood, *A Sermon Preached before the Society for the Propagation of the Gospel in Foreign Parts, at the Parish Church of St. Mary-Le-Bow, on Friday the 16th of February, 1710/11* (London: Printed and sold by Joseph Downing, 1711), 18–28.

83. Ibid., 30–32.

84. Moore, *A Sermon Preach'd . . . February 20, 1712/13*, 49–50.

85. Mr. Holt to the Secretary, June 8, 1713, RHL SPG X/34, 33–36.

86. Mr. Holt to the Secretary, July 7, 1713, RHL SPG X/34, 36–38.

87. Mr. Holt to the Secretary, July 7, 1713, RHL SPG X/34, 36–38.

88. Mr. Holt to the Secretary, June 8, 1713, RHL SPG X/34, 33–36.

89. Mr. Holt to the Secretary, July 7, 1713, RHL SPG X/34, 36–38; Glasson, *Mastering Christianity*, 154–55.

90. J. H. Bennett, *Bondsmen and Bishops: Slavery and Apprenticeship on the Codrington Plantations of Barbados, 1710–1838* (Berkeley: University of California Press, 1958), 76.

91. The Society originally agreed to give the slaves Saturday afternoons free in 1713. See RHL SPG X/14, February 6, 1712/3. For the news that Smalridge had adjusted the Saturday schedule, see RHL SPG X/14, November 12, 1714. In 1725, the Society again received word that the enslaved were working six days per week. See Arthur Holt to Bishop Gibson, St. Michael's, April 30, 1725, LPL Fulham Papers XV, 215–16. When the Society wrote to Smalridge to repeat their demands, Smalridge suggested that the enslaved could have Saturday afternoons free "Except on Some Extrodinary Occasion in the Crop Time." See Bennett, *Bondsmen and Bishops*, 22–23.

92. Mr. Holt to the Secretary, June 8, 1713, RHL SPG X/34, 33–36.

93. Secretary to Mr. Ramsay, December 15, 1713, RHL SPG X/34, 222–24.

94. Holt was able to garner support from several individuals on the island to write testimonials on his behalf. Testimonials to Rev. Joseph Holt, 1714–1715, RHL C/WI/COD/62.

95. Even in 1745, the building of the college remained incomplete, and the school closed again in 1775 for financial reasons. Maud E. O'Neil, "Of the Buildings in Progress with Which to House the College," in Klingberg, *Codrington Chronicle*, 27–42.

96. Bennett, *Bondsmen and Bishops*, 78–79. The SPG had encountered political and legal obstructionism as early as 1710, when Christopher Codrington's cousin, Col. William Codrington, contested the terms of the will. McCulloch and Schutz, "Noble and Generous Benefaction," 23–24; Bennett, *Bondsmen and Bishops*, 45–46.

97. Glasson, *Mastering Christianity*, 155–57.

98. Thomas Wilkie to Bishop Gibson, March 7, 1726/7, LPL Fulham Papers XV 249–50.

99. Thomas Wilkie to Bishop Gibson, March 7, 1726/7, LPL Fulham Papers XV 249–50.

100. Thomas Wilkie to Bishop Gibson, March 7, 1726/7, LPL Fulham Papers XV 249–50.

101. RHL SPG X/14, 16 June 16, 1727. The full quotation reads: "A Letter from Mr Wilkie the Society's Society's catechist at Barbadoes directed to the Lord Bishop of London was read acquainting with the Endeavours he uses to instruct the Negroes and prepare them for Baptism. Agreed that Mr. Smalridge be writt to and put in mind of the former Orders of the Society concerning the Negroes, and that he take care to observe such Orders; and that he give all proper Encouragement to Mr. Wilkie in teaching the Negroes, and Instructing the Children of the Poor Whites; and when Mr. Wilkie shall acquaint him any Negroes are so far instructed that they may be edifyed by coming to Church, he should oblige them to come to church on Sunday."

102. RHL SPG X/14, December 18, 1730 and January 15, 1730/1.

103. For an in-depth discussion of this dynamic, see Glasson, *Mastering Christianity*, 154–62.

104. Arthur Holt to the Secretary, April 3, 1732, RHL A24/267; Bennett, *Bondsmen and Bishops*, 27.

105. Glasson, *Mastering Christianity*, 156.

106. Glasson, "Missionaries, Slavery, and Race," 238.

107. David Humphreys, *An Historical Account of the Incorporated Society for the Propagation of the Gospel in Foreign Parts: Containing Their Foundation, Proceedings, and the Success of Their Missionaries in the British Colonies, to the Year 1728* (London: Printed by Joseph Downing, 1730), vi–vii.

108. LPL Fulham Papers XV, 203–14.

109. Glasson, *Mastering Christianity*, 98.

110. Ibid.

111. [Robert Robertson], "Case of Negroes and Planters Stated," *Gentleman's Magazine* 11 (1741): 145.

112. [Robert Robertson], *A Letter To the Right Reverend the Lord Bishop of London from An Inhabitant of his Majesty's Leeward-Caribee Islands* (London: Printed by J. Wilford, 1730), 33–34.

113. Ibid., 45.

114. Ibid., 73.

115. Ibid., 5–6.

116. Ibid., 20.

117. Glasson, "'Baptism Doth Not Bestow Freedom,'" 279.

118. LPL Fulham Papers XV, 207.

119. Glasson, *Mastering Christianity*, 194.

Chapter 7

1. Anton Ulrich to Zinzendorf, October 6, 1731, UA R.15.Ba.3.1. All translations by the author, unless otherwise stated.

2. Oldendorp, *Historie der caribischen Inseln*, 18.

3. Anton Ulrich to Zinzendorf, October 6, 1731, UA R.15.Ba.3.1.

4. *Gemein Nachrichten*, vol 1 (1754): 378–80. UA GN.A.34.1754.1.

5. On the Great Awakening as a transatlantic phenomenon, see Susan O'Brien, "A Transatlantic Community of Saints: The Great Awakening and the First Evangelical Network, 1735–1755," *American Historical Review* 91, no. 4 (1986): 811–32; Ward, *Protestant Evangelical*

Awakening. On the role of the Moravians in creating Afro-Protestantism, see Frey and Wood, *Come Shouting to Zion*; Sensbach, *Rebecca's Revival.*

6. A. G. Roeber, "The Waters of Rebirth: The Eighteenth Century and Transoceanic Protestant Christianity," *Church History* 79.1 (March 2010): 40–76; Ward, *Protestant Evangelical Awakening*; Frey and Wood, *Come Shouting to Zion*; Sensbach, *Rebecca's Revival*; Frederick Dreyer, *The Genesis of Methodism* (Bethlehem, PA: Lehigh University Press, 1999).

7. A handful of studies have tied the Moravians to the Anglican voluntary societies, though they focus on connections in Europe or North America. See, for example, Ward, *Protestant Evangelical Awakening*; Brunner, *Halle Pietists in England*; Podmore, *Moravian Church in England.*

8. See, for example, Sensbach, *Rebecca's Revival*; Sparks, *On Jordan's Stormy Banks*; Frey and Wood, *Come Shouting to Zion.* Frey and Wood acknowledge the efforts of the SPG to convert slaves, but characterize their attempts as a failure. While this is mostly true, an overemphasis on missionary efforts obscures the conversion of "elite" slaves who were offered special privileges by their masters. See Chapter 4.

9. The most extensive survey of Pietism is the four-volume *Geschichte des Pietismus*: Martin Brecht, ed., *Geschichte des Pietismus*, vol. 1, *Der Pietismus vom siebzehnten bis zum frühen achtzehnten Jahrhundert* (Göttingen: Vandenhoeck & Ruprecht, 1993); Martin Brecht and Klaus Depperman, eds., *Geschichte des Pietismus*, vol. 2, *Der Pietismus im achtzehnten Jahrhundert* (Göttingen: Vandenhoeck & Ruprecht, 1995); Ulrich Gäbler, ed., *Geschichte des Pietismus*, vol. 3, *Der Pietismus im neunzehnten und zwanzigsten Jahrhundert* (Göttingen: Vandenhoeck & Ruprecht, 2000); Hartmut Lehmann, ed., *Geschichte des Pietismus*, vol. 4, *Glaubenswelt und Lebenswelten des Pietismus* (Göttingen: Vandenhoeck & Ruprecht, 2004). The yearbook *Pietismus und Neuzeit*, which has been published annually since 1974, is another important source of German scholarship on Pietism. Ernest Stoeffler has written three surveys of Pietism in English: Stoeffler, *Rise of Evangelical Pietism*; F. Ernest Stoeffler, *German Pietism During the Eighteenth Century* (Leiden: Brill, 1973); Stoeffler, *Continental Pietism.* In the past fifteen years, there have been several important studies emphasizing the connections between Pietism in Europe and North America. See, for example, Strom, Lehmann, and Melton, eds., *Pietism in Germany and North America.* For a helpful overview of Pietism research, see Strom, "Problems and Promises."

10. Johannes Wallmann, "Was Ist Pietismus?," in *Pietismus und Neuzeit: Ein Jahrbuch zur Geschichte des neueren Protestantismus*, 20 (1994): 11–27.

11. Matthias, "August Hermann Francke"; Douglas H. Shantz, *An Introduction to German Pietism: Protestant Renewal at the Dawn of Modern Europe* (Baltimore: Johns Hopkins University Press, 2013), 117–46.

12. As early as 1699, just two months after the founding of the SPCK, members of the Society were writing to Francke to learn more about his charitable institutions. Both Francke and Ludolf became corresponding members of the SPCK, as did several other Pietist leaders. Aside from providing advice, they translated SPCK documents into German. Brunner, *Halle Pietists in England*, 43–45.

13. Ibid., 34; August Hermann Francke, *Pietas Hallensis: Or a Publick Demonstration of the Foot-Steps of a Divine Being yet in the World: In an Historical Narration of the Orphan-House, And Other Charitable Institutions, at Glaucha near Hall in Saxony.*, trans. Anthony William Boehm (London: Printed by Joseph Downing, 1705).

14. Brunner, *Halle Pietists in England*, 46–49.

15. Ibid., 85.

16. Ibid., 60–61.

17. Ibid., 67–69.

18. On the Tranquebar mission and the Protestant International, see Edward E. Andrews, "Tranquebar: Charting the Protestant International in the British Atlantic and Beyond," *William and Mary Quarterly* 74, no. 1 (2017), 3–34.

19. In return for a tribute, the Danes were permitted to "build a fort, establish a trading station, have an army, administer justice, and follow their own religious customs." Brijraj Singh, *The First Protestant Missionary to India: Bartholomaeus Ziegenbalg, 1683–1719* (New Dehli: Oxford University Press, 1999), 40.

20. Kennett, *Lets and Impediments*, 47. Other influences were John Eliot's mission to Indians in New England and Thomas Bray's work with the SPCK. Daniel Jeyaraj, *Bartholomaus Ziegenbalg: The Father of the Modern Protestant Mission* (New Delhi: Indian Society for the Promoting Christian Knowledge, 2006), 30–31; Ernst Benz, "The Pietist and Puritan Sources of Early Protestant World Missions (Cotton Mather and A H Francke)," *Church History* 20, no. 2 (June 1951): 28–55; Andrews, *Tranquebar*.

21. While Pietist Lutherans were in favor of evangelism, the aftermath of the Thirty Years War made many orthodox Lutherans hesitant to send ministers outside of national geographic boundaries unless there had been a specific request for the missionary from the native population. Jeyaraj, *Bartholomaus Ziegenbalg*, 33–37.

22. Daniel Jeyaraj, "Mission Reports from South India and Their Impact on the Western Mind: The Tranquebar Mission of the Eighteenth Century," in *Converting Colonialism: Visions and Realities in Mission History, 1706–1914*, ed. Dana L. Robert (Grand Rapids, MI: Eerdmans, 2008), 23–25.

23. Ibid., 26.

24. Bartholomaeus Ziegenbalg, *Propagation of the Gospel in the East: Being an Account of the Success of Two Danish Missionaries, Lately Sent to the East-Indies, for the Conversion of the Heathens in Malabar*, trans. Anthony William Boehm (London: Printed by Joseph Downing, 1709).

25. Thomas Ruhland, "'Ein paar Jahr muß Tranquebar und Coromandel wol Serieus das Object seyn'—Südasien als pietistisches Konkurrenzfeld," in Udo Sträter et. al, eds., *Pietismus und Neuzeit*, 39 (Göttingen: Vendenhoeck & Ruprecht, 2013), 92–93.

26. Sensbach notes that the first refugees were "not Czech, but the descendants of German Waldensians who had migrated to Moravia and joined the Unity in 1480. They thus constituted the historical link between the old Unitas Fratrum and what would soon become, under Zinzendorf's patronage, the Renewed Unity of the Brethren." Jon F. Sensbach, *A Separate Canaan: The Making of an Afro-Moravian World in North Carolina, 1763–1840* (Chapel Hill: University of North Carolina Press, 1998), 24.

27. On the medieval roots of the Unitas Fratrum, see Craig D. Atwood, *The Theology of the Czech Brethren from Hus to Comenius* (University Park, PA: Pennsylvania State University Press, 2009).

28. For details on the social and religious conflicts leading up to the Renewal, see W. R. Ward, "The Renewed Unity of the Brethren: Ancient Church, New Sect or Interconfessional Movement?" *Bulletin of the John Rylands University Library of Manchester* 70, no. 3 (October 1988): 77–92.

29. Podmore, *Moravian Church in England*, 8.

30. A number of factors led to the clash, but the most important was the death of August Hermann Francke in 1727. When Francke's son, Gotthilf, succeeded his father, he did so with less imagination and more legalism. Another factor was the conflict surrounding August Spangenberg, who would later become a Bishop of the Moravian Church. Appointed to Halle in 1731, Spangenberg was ejected two years later, leading to another sensational controversy that reverberated through the Protestant world and led to Zinzendorf's fall from favor in Denmark in 1734. Ward, *Protestant Evangelical Awakening*, chap. 4.

31. Sensbach, *Rebecca's Revival*, 36–37.

32. Oldendorp, *Historie der caribischen Inseln*, 2:17. Nitschmann recounted the meeting himself in a report about his travels with Dober, though he did not go into as much detail as Oldendorp. "Bericht David Nitschmanns über seine Reise mit Dober," reprinted in Rüdiger Kröger, ed., *Johann Leonhard Dober und der Beginn der Herrnhuter Mission* (Herrnhut: Comenius-Buchhandlung, 2006), 62–63.

33. Leonard Dober, "Mitteilung Dobers an die Gemeine Herrnhut über seine Bereitschaft nach St. Thomas zu gehen. Herrnhut, 16. Juni 1731," reprinted in Kröger, *Johann Leonhard Dober*, 28.

34. Oldendorp, *Historie der caribischen Inseln*, 2:18. I have not found Oldendorp's source for this description. It may be based on oral interviews he conducted.

35. Ibid., 2:19. In Bossart's edition, which has been translated into English, most of this section is deleted. Christian Georg Andreas Oldendorp, *A Caribbean Mission*, ed. Johann Jakob Bossart, trans. Arnold R. Highfield and Vladimir Barac (Ann Arbor: Karoma, 1987).

36. "Brief Dobers Und Nitschmanns [an die Gemeine Herrnhut?]. Kopenhagen, 23. September 1732," reprinted in Kröger, *Johann Leonhard Dober*, 37–39; Oldendorp, *Historie der caribischen Inseln*, 2:29–30.

37. Oddly, Nitschmann and Dober's original diary does not mention's Ulrich's part in this. It is only later, in a report to the Countess of Stölberg-Wernigerode, that Dober wrote: "The Moor was also very changed when we arrived, and it was because of this that the Count Laurwig concluded that it was impractical to go there." "Mittelung an eine Gräfin zu Stölberg-Wernigerode über die Missionsarbeit in Westindien. Anfang 1740," reprinted in Kröger, *Johann Leonhard Dober*, 85–90.

38. "Bericht David Nitschmanns über seine Reise mit Dober," reprinted in Kröger, *Johann Leonhard Dober*, 62–63.

39. Dober and Nitschmann departed Herrnhut with just three thaler and two ducats. J. Taylor Hamilton and Kenneth G. Hamilton, *History of the Moravian Church: The Renewed Unitas Fratrum 1722–1757*. (Bethlehem, PA: Interprovincial Board of Christian Education, Moravian Church in America, 1967), 46.

40. Waldemar Westergaard, *The Danish West Indies Under Company Rule* (New York: Macmillan, 1917), 202–3.

41. Oldendorp, *Historie der caribischen Inseln*, 2:29–30.

42. "Mittelung an eine Gräfin zu Stölberg-Wernigerode über die Missionsarbeit in Westindien," reprinted in Kröger, *Johann Leonhard Dober*, 85–90.

43. "Brief Dobers Und Nitschmanns [an die Gemeine Herrnhut?]. Kopenhagen, 23. September 1732," reprinted in Kröger, *Johann Leonhard Dober*, 37–39.

44. Ibid., 37–39.

45. "Brief Dobers und Nitschmanns an Zinzendorf. Kopenhagen, 6. Oktober 1732," reprinted in Kröger, *Johann Leonhard Dober*, 40–42.

46. "Diarium David Nitschmanns und Leonhard Dobers von der Reise und dem Aufenthalt in St. Thomas. 5 Oktober 1732 bis 17. April 1733," reprinted in Kröger, *Johann Leonhard Dober*, 43–60.

47. Oldendorp, *Historie der caribischen Inseln*, 2:114.

48. The King's shares notwithstanding, the Company's powers were "almost as absolute within their West Indian sphere as were the powers of the Danish king within his European dominions." Westergaard, *Danish West Indies*, 179.

49. Hall, *Slave Society*, 5.

50. Johann Lorentz Carstens, "A General Description of All the Danish, American or West Indian Islands," in *The Kamina Folk: Slavery and Slave Life in the Danish West Indies*, ed. George F. Tyson and Arnold R. Highfield, trans. Arnold R. Highfield (U.S. Virgin Islands: Virgin Islands Humanities Council, 1994), 2–3.

51. Ibid., 2.

52. Ibid.

53. "Diarium David Nitschmanns und Leonhard Dobers von der Reise und dem Aufenthalt in St. Thomas. 5 Oktober 1732 bis 17. April 1733," entry for December 25, 1732, reprinted in Kröger, *Johann Leonhard Dober*, 47–48.

54. Dober and Nitschmann do not record whether this individual is free or Christian, though it is likely that he was Christian, since they refer to his knowledge of Christian doctrine. If he was not a free black, then he was probably an elite slave, considering that he was "very well-known."

55. "Diarium David Nitschmanns und Leonhard Dobers von der Reise und dem Aufenthalt in St. Thomas. 5 Oktober 1732 bis 17. April 1733," entry for December 31, 1732, reprinted in Kröger, *Johann Leonhard Dober*, 48.

56. Dober and Nitschmann, "Diarium," in Kröger, *Johann Leonhard Dober*, 50.

57. Ibid., 52.

58. Ibid., 48.

59. Ibid., 51–52.

60. Ibid., 53.

61. Ibid., 48–49.

62. It was not uncommon for the Moravians to be called Catholics or papists. On March 23, 1733, Nitschmann wrote that a black man "said we were just like the Catholics who forbid everything." Ibid., 58.

63. Ibid., 51–52, 59. Oldendorp combines these two events. See Oldendorp, *Historie der caribischen Inseln*, 2:53..

64. Oldendorp, *Historie der caribischen Inseln*, 2:64–65. This is Oldendorp's summary. Dober's diary mentions a few different moments of "backsliding" among the converts. See "Diarium Leonhard Dobers von seinem Aufenthalt in St. Thomas. 16 April 1733 bis 6. Februar 1734," reprinted in Kröger, *Johann Leonhard Dober*, 66.

65. Oldendorp, *Historie der caribischen Inseln*, 2:68. Oldendorp is summarizing Dober's diary. See Kröger, *Johann Leonhard Dober*, 69.

66. Oldendorp, *Historie der caribischen Inseln*, 2:108.

67. Dober and Nitschmann, "Diarium," in Kröger, *Johann Leonhard Dober*, 55.

68. Dober and Nitschmann, "Diarium" in Kröger, *Johann Leonhard Dober*, 47.

69. Dober, "Diarium," in Kröger, *Johann Leonhard Dober*, 65–66.

70. Dober, "Mittelung an eine Gräfin zu Stölberg-Wernigerode" in Kröger, *Johann Leonhard Dober*, 85–90. Oldendorp recounts Dober's feelings in Oldendorp, *Historie der caribischen Inseln*, 2:64.

71. Dober, "Diarium," in Kröger, *Johann Leonhard Dober*, 68.

72. Westergaard, *Danish West Indies*, 166–67.

73. Dober, "Diarium," in Kröger, *Johann Leonhard Dober*, 69.

74. Dober, "Diarium," in Kröger, *Johann Leonhard Dober*.

75. Dober, "Diarium," in Kröger, *Johann Leonhard Dober*, 69–70.

76. Dober, "Diarium," in Kröger, *Johann Leonhard Dober*, 70.

77. Oldendorp, *Historie der caribischen Inseln*, 2:91. Beverhout had eighteen slaves who planted cotton and raised cattle.

78. "Bericht David Nitschmanns über seine Reise mit Dober," reprinted in Kröger, *Johann Leonhard Dober*, 62–63.

79. "Nachrichten über den Aufenthalt des Sklavenjungen Oly-Carmel in Herrnhut. Herrnhut, 1735," in Kröger, *Johann Leonhard Dober*, 99–102.

80. "Nachrichten über den Aufenthalt des Sklavenjungen Oly-Carmel in Herrnhut" in Kröger, *Johann Leonhard Dober*, 99.

81. "Gemälde der Erstlinge" in Kröger, *Johann Leonhard Dober*, 106–110. Oldendorp, *Historie der caribischen Inseln*, 2:111.

82. Oldendorp, *Historie der caribischen Inseln*, 2:111.

83. "Brief Philipp Friedrich Rentz an die Gemeine Herrnhut. Ebersdorf, 23. August 1735," in Kröger, *Johann Leonhard Dober*, 103–4.

84. Oldendorp, *Historie der caribischen Inseln*, 2:140–41. See also UA R.15.C.b.1 (1), entry for June 30, 1758.

Chapter 8

1. August Gottlieb Spangenberg, *An Account of the Manner in which the Protestant Church of the Unitas Fratrum, or United Brethren, Preach the Gospel, and Carry on Their Missions among the Heathen.* (London: Printed and sold by H. Trapp, 1788).

2. Sensbach, *Rebecca's Revival*; Ward, *Protestant Evangelical Awakening*; Frey and Wood, *Come Shouting to Zion*; Jeffrey Cox, *The British Missionary Enterprise since 1700* (New York: Routledge, 2008); Andrew Porter, *Religion Versus Empire? British Protestant Missionaries and Overseas Expansion, 1700–1914* (Manchester, UK: Manchester University Press, 2004); J. C. S. Mason, *The Moravian Church and the Missionary Awakening in England, 1760–1800* (Woodbridge, UK: Boydell, 2001).

3. Spangenberg, *Account*, 74–76.

4. Ibid., 75.

5. On September 14, 1736, he noted, "the brethren make a huge effort to teach the negros how to read." He found this to be "very useful" for a number of reasons. First, it allowed enslaved and free Afro-Caribbeans to distinguish "true" Christianity from the "so-called" Christianity of their "terrible" masters. Second, reading allowed Afro-Caribbeans to learn about Christianity even outside of missionary supervision; they could then "teach others about the Lord." Spangenberg bemoaned the lack of textual material: "If only we had more books so that we could teach them how to write—but they're so expensive!" August Gottlieb

Spangenberg, "Nachricht von einigen in St. Thomas erweckten Neger und von dem Segen des Herrn unter ihnen," September 14, 1736, UA R.15.Ba.17.9. All German sources have been translated by the author unless otherwise stated.

6. Spangenberg, "Nachricht," September 15 and October 11, 1736, UA R.15.Ba.17.9. Spangenberg does not identify the "aged negro woman" by name in the entry from September 15, but he is most likely referring to Marotta. He mentions Marotta by name for the first time on October 11. She, like the woman in the September 15 entry, is referred to as an "aged negro woman" who discusses her religious experiences in Africa and the influence of her parents in teaching her how to pray and sacrifice.

7. "Letters to the Danish King," MAB St. Thomas Letters, 1734–1766. Jon Sensbach reproduced a printed copy of Marrotta's appeal in Sensbach, *Rebecca's Revival*, 147.

8. Oldendorp, *Caribbean Mission*, 385–86.

9. Oldendorp, *Historie der caribischen Inseln*, 2:158.

10. Ibid., 2:185.

11. Spangenberg, "Nachricht," September 13, 1736, UA R.15.Ba.17.9.

12. Spangenberg, "Nachricht," September 17, 1736, UA R.15.Ba.17.9.

13. Spangenberg, "Nachricht," October 1, 1736, UA R.15.Ba.17.9.

14. Oldendorp, *Historie der caribischen Inseln*, 2:210.

15. Spangenberg, "Nachricht," October 10, 1736, UA R.15.Ba.17.9.

16. Oldendorp, *Historie der caribischen Inseln*, 2:225.

17. Spangenberg, "Nachricht," October 14, 1736, UA R.15.Ba.17.9.

18. [Robertson], *Letter*, 32.

19. Spangenberg, "Nachricht," September 16, 1736, UA R.15.Ba.17.9. For more on Immanuel, also known as Emanuel or Bartel, see Paul Peucker, "Aus allen Nationen: Nichteuropäer in den deutschen Brüdergemeinen des 18. Jahrhunderts," *Unitas Fratrum: Zeitschrift für Geschichte und Gegenwartsfragen der Brüdergemeine* 59/60 (2007): 1–35.

20. "Gemälde der Erstlinge," reprinted in Kröger, *Johann Leonhard Dober*, 106–10.

21. Spangenberg, "Nachricht," September 18, 1736, UA R.15.Ba.17.9.

22. Spangenberg, "Nachricht," October 17, 1736, UA R.15.Ba.17.9.

23. Oldendorp, *Historie der caribischen Inseln*, 2:253, 210.

24. Oldendorp, *Historie der caribischen Inseln*, 2:200.

25. See Oldendorp, *Caribbean Mission*, 370.

26. Oldendorp, *Historie der caribischen Inseln*, 2:210.

27. Ibid., 2:200–1.

28. Ibid., 2:187.

29. Ibid., 2:231–32.

30. As radical Protestants who traced their lineage to the Hussite movement of the fifteenth century, Moravians claimed to be an ancient episcopal church with their own bishops, separate from the Lutheran or Dutch Reformed Churches. Spangenberg had come to St. Thomas, in part, to baptize several of the new converts. When Spangenberg departed in September 1736, Martin was ordained from afar by David Nitschmann, one of the original St. Thomas missionaries. Nitschmann had been appointed bishop after his arrival in Europe and he sent Martin's ordination notice by mail in 1737. When the ordination, which specified that Martin could baptize "Blancke oder Neger" (whites or negroes), arrived in St. Thomas, Martin began to baptize black congregants. The ordination is printed in Nicolaus Ludwig Zinzendorf, ed., *Büdingische Sammlung*, vol. 1 (Hildesheim: G. Olms, 1965), 165–67.

31. Oldendorp, *Caribbean Mission*, 332.

32. Sensbach, *Rebecca's Revival*, 96.

33. Oldendorp, *Historie der caribischen Inseln*, 2:249.

34. Moravians believed that marriage was not just fundamental, but also sacramental. This stance was both radical and controversial, and gained them enemies on both sides of the Atlantic. Zinzendorf called marriage *eine selige Gemeinschaft* (a holy union) and developed the concept of *Streiter ehe* (militant marriage)—the idea that a marital union would further the religious and communal goals of the Church. He viewed sexual intercourse as a spiritual act, symbolizing Christ's union with the Church, a stance that had been one of the precipitating factors in the Moravians' break with Halle Pietists. A. G. Roeber, *Hopes for Better Spouses: Protestant Marriage and Church Renewal in Early Modern Europe, India, and North America* (Grand Rapids, MI: Eerdmans, 2013), 148–51. Zinzendorf's stance on marriage can be found in Peter Vogt, "Zinzendorf's 'Seventeen Points of Matrimony': A Fundamental Document on the Moravian Understanding of Marriage and Sexuality," *Journal of Moravian History*, no. 10 (Spring 2011): 39–67. For more on the Moravians' views on marriage, see Peter Vogt, " 'Ehereligion': The Moravian Theory and Practice of Marriage as Point of Contention in the Conflict Between Ephrata and Bethlehem," *Communal Societies* 21 (2001): 37–48. For Moravian views on marriage during the "Sifting Time," see Paul Peucker, *A Time of Sifting: Mystical Marriage and the Crisis of Moravian Piety in the Eighteenth Century* (University Park: Pennsylvania State University Press, 2015).

35. Oldendorp, *Historie der caribischen Inseln*, 2:258–59; Sensbach, *Rebecca's Revival*, 101–6.

36. The decision to purchase land was largely the result of persecution. In Tappus, the town where the missionaries rented a meeting space, enslaved and free congregants were often abused on their way to and from meetings. The meetings themselves were frequently disrupted by drunken whites who clamored at the doors and windows of their space. By purchasing their own plantation, the missionaries and their congregants hoped to avoid these unpleasant encounters. The decision to purchase more slaves, meanwhile, was at least partially a response to the Moravians' experience with Johannes and Andreas.

37. Friedrich Martin, "Wie die Brüder zu Plantagen mit Sklaven gekommen, nebst einigen Anmerkungen über den ökonomischen Stand der Mission" July 10, 1738 (recopied in 1755), UA R.15.Ba.3.31; Oldendorp, *Historie der caribischen Inseln*, 2:265–67.

38. Friedrich Martin vehemently contested this statement. He argued that only one baptized person (Nathanael) had gone to Pastor Borm for further instruction, and that he had been excluded from the Moravian congregation. As a result of Borm's petition, Martin was forbidden from performing any sacraments until the King of Denmark had confirmed the legality of his ordination. Ibid., 2:275–77. A copy of Borm's petition, written in Dutch, can be found at UA R.15.Ba.3.32.

39. Timotheus Fiedler, a disaffected Moravian, was accused of stealing valuables from a plantation in St. Croix where he had previously worked. The manager of the St. Croix estate accused Martin, Rebecca, and Matthias of being accomplices in the theft, though it is likely that the entire case was fabricated. All four appeared in court and Fiedler testified that he had not stolen anything. When Martin and Matthias took the stand, however, they refused to take an oath. Like other radical Protestants, they believed that oath taking was ungodly. As a result, they were all imprisoned, though Martin was eventually released due to illness. For a full analysis of this case, see Sensbach, *Rebecca's Revival*, 110–23.

40. Oldendorp, *Historie der caribischen Inseln*, 2:257.

41. Borm may also have been motivated by the Moravians' increasingly marginalized position in Europe. Friedrich Martin certainly exacerbated the conflict with the pastor by accusing him of drunkenness. Ibid., 2:272.

42. Oldendorp, *Historie der caribischen Inseln*, 2:320–21.

43. The belief that one returned to Africa after death was widespread among Afro-Caribbeans. See Vincent Brown, *The Reaper's Garden: Death and Power in the World of Atlantic Slavery* (Cambridge, MA: Harvard University Press, 2008).

44. "Attestat des Herrn Carstens von der Arbeit der Brüder under den Negern," February 14, 1739, UA R.15.Ba.3.58; Oldendorp, *Historie der caribischen Inseln*, 2:319–22.

45. Ibid., 2:336–37.

46. Zinzendorf, *Büdingische Sammlung*, 3:211; Oldendorp, *Historie der caribischen Inseln*, 2:344–45.

47. Cited in Sensbach, *Rebecca's Revival*, 136–37.

48. The 1730s were a particularly turbulent time in the British and Danish colonies in the greater Caribbean. David Barry Gaspar, "A Dangerous Spirit of Liberty: Slave Rebellion in the West Indies in the 1730s," in *Origins of the Black Atlantic*, ed. Laurent Dubois and Julius S. Scott (New York: Routledge, 2013), 11–25.

49. Zinzendorf's *Abschiedsschreiben* can be found in manuscript form in the Unitätsarchiv R.15.Ba.1.II.6. In 1742, it was printed in Dutch Creole in Zinzendorf, *Büdingische Sammlung*, 1:453–57. It was translated into German in Oldendorp, *Historie der caribischen Inseln*, 2:349–52. An English translation is available in Oldendorp, *A Caribbean Mission*, 361–63. I have slightly amended the English translation based on a comparison of the Dutch Creole and German versions.

50. Oldendorp, *Historie der caribischen Inseln*, 2:352.

51. Oldendorp, *A Caribbean Mission*, 363–64.

52. Oldendorp, *Historie der caribischen Inseln*, 2:370.

53. Sensbach, *Rebecca's Revival*, 143.

54. A manuscript copy of the letter, written in Dutch Creole, can be found in the Unitätsarchiv R.15.Ba.3.60, and a printed version (also in Dutch Creole) can be found in Zinzendorf, *Büdingische Sammlung*, 1:483–85, though there are some mistakes and missing words. It is translated into German in Oldendorp, *Historie der caribischen Inseln*, 2:356–57. An English translation is available in Oldendorp, *A Caribbean Mission*, 365. It is likely that the letter was written in the hand of one of the black leaders. Mingo and Rebecca had good handwriting and could write in excellent Dutch, while Petrus and Abraham had already written letters to brethren in Europe. Oldendorp, *Historie der caribischen Inseln*, 2:211.

55. Oldendorp, *A Caribbean Mission*, 365–66.

56. Based on an exchange with Bernard Gadagbui, Jon Sensbach speculates that the African language was Fon, "a colloquial branch of Ewe still spoken in parts of modern Benin." Sensbach, *Rebecca's Revival*, 273n20.

57. Oldendorp, *A Caribbean Mission*, 365. See also Ray Kea, "From Catholicism to Moravian Pietism: The World of Marotta/Magdalena, Woman of Popo and St. Thomas" in Elizabeth Mancke and Carole Shammas, eds., *The Creation of the British Atlantic World* (Baltimore: Johns Hopkins University Press, 2005), 115–36.

58. Oldendorp, *Historie der caribischen Inseln*, 2:339.

59. Gottlieb Israel, "Diarium von St. Thomas, 1740," UA R.15.Bb.2.2; Oldendorp, *A Caribbean Mission*, 386. While the missionaries suspended reading lessons, they did specify that literate black converts could potentially perform teaching duties on their own. They also made provisions for those who were truly interested in conversion to learn to read.

60. Oldendorp, *A Caribbean Mission*, 318.

61. Oldendorp, *Historie der caribischen Inseln*, 2:231–32.

62. Spangenberg, "Nachricht," September 13, 1736, UA R.15.Ba.17.9.

63. Oldendorp, *Historie der caribischen Inseln*, 2.1:397.

64. Within a Protestant European context, the Moravians had radical ideas about marriage, though they continued to support monogamous marriages. See Fogleman, *Jesus Is Female*, 91.

65. Only eighteen of the sixty-nine individuals baptized between 1736 and 1740 were identified as Creoles. For more on Afro-Caribbean familial structures, see Jean Besson, "The Creolization of African-American Slave Kinship in Jamaican Free Village and Maroon Communities," in *Slave Cultures and the Cultures of Slavery*, ed. Stephan Palmié (Knoxville: University of Tennessee Press, 1995), 189–90.

66. Spangenberg, "Nachricht," September 17, 1736, UA R.15.Ba.17.9.

67. Oldendorp, *Historie der caribischen Inseln*, 2:432–33.

68. See also 1 Kings 11:3, 2; Chronicles 11:21; and Deuteronomy 21:15.

69. Oldendorp, *Historie der caribischen Inseln*, 2:433.

70. Ibid., 2:432–33.

71. For more on the role of national helpers within the Moravian congregation, see Sensbach, *Rebecca's Revival*, 92–100.

72. Oldendorp, *A Caribbean Mission*, 386.

73. Oldendorp, *Historie der caribischen Inseln*, 2:631.

74. Christian Heinrich Rauch, "Journal to St. Thomas," August 3, 1745, MAB Journals box JD V 1.

75. Oldendorp, *Historie der caribischen Inseln*, 2:758.

76. Ibid., 2:769.

77. 1 Timothy 3:2 (KJV) states: "A bishop then must be blameless, the husband of one wife, vigilant, sober, of good behaviour, given to hospitality, apt to teach." See ibid., 2:758.

78. Johannes von Watteville, "Reise Diarium von Bethlehem nach St. Thomas und wieder zurück," June 6, 1749, MAB Journals box JF IV 2.

79. Wattewille, "Reise Diarium," May 7, 1749, MAB Journals box JF IV 2.

80. Mason, *Moravian Church*.

81. Several slave colonies passed antiliteracy laws, beginning with South Carolina in 1740. Peter Wallenstein, "Antiliteracy Laws," in *The Historical Encyclopedia of World Slavery*, ed. Junius P. Rodriguez (Santa Barbara, CA: ABC-CLIO, 1997), 42.

Epilogue

1. George Whitefield, "A Letter from the Rev. George Whitefield to the Inhabitants of Maryland, Virginia, North and South Carolina," *Pennsylvania Gazette*, February 1740. For more on Whitefield's views on slavery, see Thomas S. Kidd, *George Whitefield: America's Spiritual Founding Father* (New Haven: Yale University Press, 2014); Philippa Koch, "Slavery, Mission, and the Perils of Providence in Eighteenth-Century Christianity: The Writings of Whitefield and the Halle Pietists," *Church History* 84, no. 2 (2015): 369–93; Jessica M. Parr,

Inventing George Whitefield: Race, Revivalism, and the Making of a Religious Icon (Jackson, MI: University Press of Mississippi, 2015); Stephen J. Stein, "George Whitefield on Slavery: Some New Evidence," *Church History* 42, no. 2 (1973): 243–56.

2. Whitefield's letter is the oldest document reprinted in Jeffrey Young's anthology of proslavery thought. Jeffrey Robert Young, *Proslavery and Sectional Thought in the Early South, 1740–1829: An Anthology* (Columbia: University of South Carolina Press, 2006). Earlier scholarship on proslavery thought focused on the antebellum South in the United States. This limited chronological and geographical view was critiqued by Larry Tise. Larry E. Tise, *Proslavery: A History of the Defense of Slavery in America, 1701–1840* (Athens: University of Georgia Press, 1987). Recently, more scholars have looked beyond the southern antebellum colonies to understand proslavery thought. For a helpful review of scholarship on proslavery thought, see Young, *Proslavery and Sectional Thought*, 1–11.

3. On the theological foundations of Whitefield's acceptance of slavery, as well as his connections to Pietists, see Koch, "Slavery, Mission, and the Perils of Providence."

4. Whitefield famously feuded with the Anglican commissary in the Carolinas, Alexander Garden. After Whitefield published his "Letter to the Inhabitants," Garden published a rebuke under the title "Six Letters to the Rev. George Whitefield." Garden wrote that Whitefield's characterization of white planters was unfounded, but the two men shared the conviction that slavery should be Christianized. Their shared belief in Christian slavery demonstrates how ubiquitous the ideology had become among ministers, regardless of theological and denominational differences. Young, *Proslavery and Sectional Thought*, 27, 68–78.

5. The vision for the Georgia colony was largely inspired by Thomas Bray, the founder of the SPCK and SPG, and led by James Oglethorpe. The trustees governed the colony from London and forbade slavery for pragmatic reasons. They hoped that Georgia would become a haven for poor Europeans and they wanted to create a buffer zone between South Carolina and Spanish Florida. Betty Wood, *Slavery in Colonial Georgia, 1730–1775* (Athens: University of Georgia Press, 1984).

6. Young, *Proslavery and Sectional Thought*, 21.

7. Rauch, "Diarium," May 23, 1760, UA R.15.C.b.1 (3).

8. Rauch, "Diarium," December 9, 1759, UA R.15.C.b.1 (3).

9. Rauch, "Diarium," August 10, 1760, UA R.15.C.b.1 (3).

10. Rauch, "Diarium," December 11, 1759, UA R.15.C.b.1 (3).

11. Rauch, "Diarium," January 10, 1760, UA R.15.C.b.1 (3).

12. Rauch, "Diarium," December 15, 1759, UA R.15.C.b.1 (3).

13. Rauch, "Diarium," March 28, 1760, UA R.15.C.b.1 (3).

14. Rauch, "Diarium," March 28, 1760, UA R.15.C.b.1 (3).

15. Rauch, "Diarium," May 18, 1760, UA R.15.C.b.1 (3).

16. Rauch, "Diarium," August 24, 1760, UA R.15.C.b.1 (3).

17. Raboteau, *Slave Religion*.

18. Goetz, *Baptism of Early Virginia*.

19. *Acts of Assembly*, 237–38.

20. Godwyn, *Negro's [and] Indians Advocate*, 112.

Bibliography

Archival Sources and Abbreviations

CO   Colonial Office, National Archives (Kew), London, England
CSP   Calendar of State Papers, Colonial Series
FHL   Friends House Library, London, England
HQC   Haverford College Quaker & Special Collections, Haverford, Pennsylvania
JBMHS   Journal of the Barbados Museum and Historical Society
LPL   Lambeth Palace Library, London, England
MAB   Moravian Archives, Bethlehem, Pennsylvania
NAB   National Archives, Barbados
RHL   Rhodes House Library, Oxford, England
UA   Unitätsarchiv der Evangelischen Brüder-Unität, Herrnhut, Germany

Published Primary Sources

Acts of Assembly, Passed in the Island of Barbadoes, From 1648, to 1718. London: Printed by John Baskett, 1732.

An Exhortation & Caution to Friends Concerning buying or keeping of Negroes. New York: Printed by William Bradford, 1693.

A Continuation of the State of New-England: Being a Farther Account of the Indian Warr, and of the Engagement Betwixt the Joynt Forces of the United English Collonies and the Indians, on the 19th of December 1675. With the True Number of the Slain and Wounded, and the Transactions of the English Army since the Said Fight. With All Other Passages That Have There Hapned from the 10th. of November, 1675. to the 8th. of February 1675/6. Together with an Account of the Intended Rebellion of the Negroes in the Barbadoes. London: Printed by T. M. for Dorman Newman, 1676.

Ashe, George. *A Sermon Preach'd before the Incorporated Society for the Propagation of the Gospel in Foreign Parts; at their Anniversary Meeting in the Parish-Church of St. Mary-le-Bow; On Friday the 18th of February, 1714.* London: Printed and Sold by J. Downing, 1715.

Besse, Joseph. *A Collection of the Sufferings of the People Called Quakers.* 2 vols. London: Printed and sold by Luke Hinde, 1753.

Beveridge, William. *A Sermon Preach'd Before the Society for the Propagation of the Gospel in Foreign Parts, at the Parish Church of St. Mary Le Bow, February 21st, 1706–7.* London: Printed by Joseph Downing, 1707.

Bray, Thomas. *A Course of Lectures upon the Church Catechism in Four Volumes.* Oxford: Printed by Leonard Litchfield, 1696.

————. *A Short Discourse upon the Doctrine of Our Baptismal Covenant Being an Exposition upon the Preliminary Questions and Answers of Our Church-Catechism: Proper to Be Read by All Young Persons in Order to Their Understanding the Whole Frame and Tenor of the Christian Religion, and to Their Being Duly Prepared for Confirmation: With Devotions Preparatory to That Apostolick and Useful Ordinance.* London: Printed by E. Holt for R. Clavel, 1697.

Brokesby, Francis. *Some Proposals Towards Propagating of the Gospel in Our American Plantations. Humbly Offerr'd in a Letter to Mr. Nelson, a worthy Member of the Society for propagating the Gospel in foreign Parts.* London, 1708.

Browne, William H., ed. *Archives of Maryland: Proceedings and Acts of the General Assembly of Maryland, January 1637/8-September 1664.* Baltimore: Maryland Historical Society, 1883.

————. *Archives of Maryland: Proceedings and Acts of the General Assembly of Maryland, April 1666–June 1676.* Baltimore: Maryland Historical Society, 1884.

Burnet, Gilbert. *Of the Propagation of the Gospel in Foreign Parts. A Sermon Preach'd at St. Mary-Le-Bow, Feb. 18. 1703/4.* London: Printed for D. Brown and R. Sympson, 1704.

Carstens, Johann Lorentz. "A General Description of All the Danish, American or West Indian Islands." In *The Kamina Folk: Slavery and Slave Life in the Danish West Indies,* edited by George F. Tyson and Arnold R. Highfield, translated by Arnold R. Highfield, 1–17. U.S. Virgin Islands: Virgin Islands Humanities Council, 1994.

Cranz, David. *Kurze, zuverlässige Nachricht von der Unitas Fratrum.* [Halle, 1757]

Edmundson, William. *A Journal of the Life, Travels, Sufferings, and Labour of Love in the Work of the Ministry.* London, 1829.

Fleetwood, William. *A Sermon Preached before the Society for the Propagation of the Gospel in Foreign Parts, at the Parish Church of St. Mary-Le-Bow, on Friday the 16th of February, 1710/11.* London: Printed and sold by Joseph Downing, 1711.

Fox, George. *Gospel Family-Order, Being a Short Discourse Concerning the Ordering of Families, Both of Whites, Blacks and Indians.* London, 1676.

————. "To Friends beyond the Sea, that have Blacks and Indian Slaves." In *Selections from the Epistles of George Fox.* Edited by Samuel Tuke, 94–95. York: W. Alexander and Son, 1825.

————. *To the Ministers, Teachers and Priests (So called and so Stileing your Selves) in Barbadoes.* London, 1672.

Fox, George, John Stubbs, and Benjamin Furly. *A Battle-Door for Teachers & Professors to Learn Singular & Plural You to Many, and Thou to One, Singular One, Thou, Plural Many, You.* London: Printed for Robert Wilson, 1660.

Francke, August Hermann. *Pietas Hallensis: Or a Publick Demonstration of the Foot-Steps of a Divine Being yet in the World: In an Historical Narration of the Orphan-House, And Other Charitable Institutions, at Glaucha near Hall in Saxony.* Trans. Anthony William Boehm. London: Printed by Joseph Downing, 1705.

Godwyn, Morgan. *The Negro's [and] Indians Advocate, Suing for Their Admission into the Church: Or A Persuasive to the Instructing and Baptizing of the Negro's and Indians in Our Plantations. Shewing, That as the Compliance Therewith Can Prejudice No Mans Just Interest; so the Wilful Neglecting and Opposing of It, Is No Less than a Manifest Apostacy from* the Christian Faith. To Which Is Added, a Brief Account of Religion in Virginia. London: Printed by J[ohn] D[arby], 1680.

———. A Supplement to The Negro's [and] Indian's Advocate: Or, Some Further Considerations and Proposals for the Effectual and Speedy Carrying on of the Negro's Christianity in Our Plantations (notwithstanding the Late Pretended Impossibilities) without Any Prejudice to Their Owners. London: Printed by J[ohn] D[arby], 1681.

———. Trade Preferr'd before Religion, and Christ Made to Give Place to Mammon: Represented in a Sermon Relating to the Plantations. London: Printed for B. Took, 1685.

Gordon, William. A Sermon Preach'd at the Funeral of the Honourable Colonel Christopher Codrington, Late Captain General and Governor in Chief of Her Majesty's Carribbee Islands; Who Departed This Life at His Seat in Barbadoes, on Good-Friday the 7th of April 1710 and Was Interr'd the Day Following in the Parish Church of St. Michael. London: Printed for G. Strahan, 1710.

Great Newes from the Barbadoes. Or, A True and Faithful Account of the Grand Conspiracy of the Negroes against the English and the Happy Discovery of the Same with the Number of Those That Were Burned Alive, Beheaded, and Otherwise Executed for Their Horrid Crimes: With a Short Discription of That Plantation. London: Printed for L. Curtis, 1676.

Hall, Richard. Acts, Passed in the Island of Barbados. From 1643, to 1762, Inclusive. London: Printed for Richard Hall, 1764.

Hening, William Waller. The Statutes at Large; Being a Collection of all the Laws of Virginia from the First Session of the Legislature in the Year 1619. Vol. 2. New York: Printed for the Author by R. & W. & G. Bartow, 1823.

Humphreys, David. An Historical Account of the Incorporated Society for the Propagation of the Gospel in Foreign Parts: Containing Their Foundation, Proceedings, and the Success of Their Missionaries in the British Colonies, to the Year 1728. London: Printed by Joseph Downing, 1730.

Kennett, White. The Lets and Impediments in Planting and Propagating the Gospel of Christ. A Sermon Preach'd before the Society for the Propagation of the Gospel in Foreign Parts. London: Printed and sold by Joseph Downing, 1712.

Kröger, Rüdiger, ed. Johann Leonhard Dober und der Beginn der Herrnhuter Mission. Herrnhut: Comenius-Buchhandlung, 2006.

Labat, Jean-Baptiste. "Father Labat's Visit to Barbados in 1700." Translated by Neville Connell. JBMHS 24, no. 4 (1957): 160–73.

———. The Memoirs of Père Labat, 1693–1705. Translated by John Eaden. London: F. Cass, 1970.

———. Nouveau voyage aux isles de l'Amerique: contenant l'histoire naturelle de ces pays, l'origine, les moeurs, la religion & le gouvernement des habitans anciens & modernes. Les guerres & les evenemens singuliers qui y sont arrivez pendant le séjour que l'auteur y a fait. Par le R.P. Labat, de l'ordre des freres prêcheurs. 8 vols. Paris: Delespine, 1742.

Littleton, Edward. The Groans of the Plantations: or A True Account of their Grievous and Extreme Sufferings by the Heavy Impositions upon Sugar, And other Hardships. London: Printed by M. Clark, 1689.

Mather, Cotton. The Negro Christianized: An Essay to Excite and Assist the Good Work, The Instruction of Negro-Servants in Christianity. Boston: Printed by B. Green, 1706.

Moore, John. A Sermon Preach'd before the Society for the Propagation of the Gospel in Foreign Parts, at their Anniversary Meeting, In the Parish-Church of St. Mary-le-Bow, February 20, 1712/13. London: Printed by Joseph Dowling, 1713.

Neau, Elias. *An Account of the Sufferings of the French Protestants, Slaves on Board the French Kings Galleys.* London: Printed for Richard Parker, 1699.

[Robertson, Robert]. *A Letter To the Right Reverend the Lord Bishop of London from An Inhabitant of his Majesty's Leeward-Caribee Islands.* London: Printed by J. Wilford, 1730.

———. "Case of Negroes and Planters Stated." *Gentleman's Magazine* 11 (1741): 145–47, 186–88.

O'Callaghan, E. B., ed. *Documents Relative to the Colonial History of the State of New-York: Procured in Holland, England, and France by John Romeyn Brodhead.* Vol. 5. Albany: Weed, Parsons, 1855.

Oldendorp, C[hristian] G[eorg] A[ndreas]. *A Caribbean Mission.* Edited by Johann Jakob Bossart. Translated by Arnold R. Highfield and Vladimir Barac. Ann Arbor: Karoma, 1987.

———. *Historie der caribischen Inseln Sanct Thomas, Sanct Crux und Sanct Jan, insbesondere der dasigen Neger und der Mission der evangelischen Brüder unter denselben.* Edited by Gudrun Meier, Hartmut Beck, Stephan Palmié, Aart H. van Soest, Peter Stein, and Horst Ulbricht. 2 vols. Berlin: VWB, Verlag für Wissenschaft und Bildung, 2000.

Pinder, Richard. *A Loving Invitation (to Repentance, and Amendment of Life) unto all the Inhabitants of the Island Barbados Before the Lords sore Judgements come upon them, which is seen to be Nigh, and which they cannot escape; except Fruits meet for Repentance, and Amendment of Life be brought forth. With Somthing more particularly to the Heads, and Owners, of the several Plantations.* London: Printed for Robert Wilson, 1660.

Rivers, Marcellus, and Oxenbridge Foyle. *Englands Slavery, or Barbados Merchandize; Represented in a Petition to the High Court of Parliament, by Marcellus Rivers and Oxenbridge Foyle Gentlemen, on Behalf of Themselves and Three-Score and Ten More Free-Born Englishmen Sold (uncondemned) into Slavery: Together With Letters Written to Some Honourable Members of Parliament.* London, 1659.

Rous, John. *A Warning to the Inhabitants of Barbadoes.* [London?], 1656.

Sanders, Joanne Mcree. *Barbados Records: Baptisms, 1637–1800.* Baltimore: Genealogical Publishing, 1984.

———. *Barbados Records: Marriages, 1643–1800.* 2 vols. Houston, TX: Sanders Historical Publications, 1982.

———. *Barbados Records: Wills and Administrations.* 2 vols. Houston, TX: Sanders Historical Publications, 1979.

Sandoval, Alonso de. *Treatise on Slavery: Selections from De Instauranda Aethiopum Salute.* Translated by Nicole von Germeten. Indianapolis: Hackett, 2008.

Spangenberg, August Gottlieb. *An Account of the Manner in which the Protestant Church of the Unitas Fratrum, or United Brethren, Preach the Gospel, and carry on their Missions among the Heathen.* London: Printed and sold by H. Trapp, 1788.

The Laws of Barbados, Collected in One Volume, by William Rawlin, of the Middle-Temple, London, Esquire. And Now Clerk of the Assembly of the Said Island. London: Printed for William Rawlin, 1699.

Trimnell, Charles. *A Sermon Preached before the Society for Propagation of the Gospel in Foreign Parts, at the Parish-Church of St. Mary-Le-Bow, on Friday the 17th of February, 1709/10.* London: Printed and sold by Joseph Downing, 1710.

Trott, Nicholas. *The Laws of the British Plantations in America, Relating to the Church and the Clergy, Religion and Learning: Collected in One Volume.* London: Printed for B. Cowse, 1721.

[Tuke, Samuel.] *Account of the Slavery of Friends in the Barbary States, towards the Close of the 17th Century.* London, 1848.

Vokins, Joan. *God's Mighty Power Magnified as Manifested and Revealed in His Faithful Handmaid Joan Vokins, Who Departed This Life the 22d of the 5th Month, 1690, Having Finished Her Course, and Kept the Faith: Also Some Account of Her Exercises, Works of Faith, Labour of Love, and Great Travels in the Work of the Ministry, for the Good of Souls.* London: Printed for Thomas Northcott, 1691.

Whitefield, George. "A Letter from the Rev. George Whitefield to the Inhabitants of Maryland, Virginia, North and South Carolina." *Pennsylvania Gazette*, February 1740.

Williams, John. *A Sermon Preached before the Society for the Propagation of the Gospel in Foreign Parts on February 15, 1705/6.* London: Printed by John Downing, 1706.

Ziegenbalg, Bartholomaeus. *Propagation of the Gospel in the East: Being an Account of the Success of Two Danish Missionaries, Lately Sent to the East-Indies, for the Conversion of the Heathens in Malabar.* Translated by Anthony William Boehm. London: Printed by Joseph Downing, 1709.

Zinzendorf, Nikolaus Ludwig, ed. *Büdingische Sammlung.* 3 vols. Hildesheim: G. Olms, 1965.

Selected Secondary Sources

Allen, Theodore W. *The Invention of the White Race.* 2 vols. London: Verso, 1994–1997.

Alsford, Stephen. "Urban Safe Havens for the Unfree in Medieval England: A Reconsideration." *Slavery & Abolition* 32, no. 3 (2011): 363–75.

Amussen, Susan Dwyer. *Caribbean Exchanges: Slavery and the Transformation of English Society, 1640–1700.* Chapel Hill: University of North Carolina Press, 2007.

Anderson, Emma. *The Betrayal of Faith: The Tragic Journey of a Colonial Native Convert.* Cambridge, MA: Harvard University Press, 2007.

Andrews, Edward E. *Native Apostles: Black and Indian Missionaries in the British Atlantic World.* Cambridge, MA: Harvard University Press, 2013.

———. "Tranquebar: Charting the Protestant International in the British Atlantic and Beyond." *William and Mary Quarterly* 74, no. 1 (2017), 3–34.

Anesko, Michael. "So Discreet a Zeal: Slavery and the Anglican Church in Virginia, 1680–1730." *Virginia Magazine of History and Biography* 93, no. 3 (July 1985): 247–78.

Asad, Talal. "Comments on Conversion." In *Conversion to Modernities*, edited by Peter van der Veer, 263–74. New York: Routledge, 1995.

Atwood, Craig D. *Community of the Cross: Moravian Piety in Colonial Bethlehem.* University Park: Pennsylvania State University Press, 2012.

———. *The Theology of the Czech Brethren from Hus to Comenius.* University Park: Pennsylvania State University Press, 2009.

Aubert, Guillaume. "'To Establish One Law and Definite Rules': Race, Religion, and the Transatlantic Origins of the Louisiana Code Noir. In *Louisiana: Crossroads of the Atlantic world*, edited by Cécile Vidal, 21–43. Philadelphia: University of Pennsylvania Press, 2013.

Beahrs, Andrew. "'Ours Alone Must Needs Be Christians': The Production of Enslaved Souls on the Codrington Estates." *Plantation Society in the Americas* 4, no. 2/3 (April 1997): 279–310.

Beasley, Nicholas M. *Christian Ritual and the Creation of British Slave Societies, 1650–1780.* Athens: University of Georgia Press, 2010.

Beckles, Hilary. *Black Rebellion in Barbados: The Struggle against Slavery, 1627–1838.* Bridgetown, Barbados: Antilles Publications, 1984.

———. *White Servitude and Black Slavery in Barbados, 1627–1715.* Knoxville: University of Tennessee Press, 1989.

Beiler, Rosalind J. "Dissenting Religious Communication Networks and Migration, 1660–1710." In *Soundings in Atlantic History: Latent Structures and Intellectual Currents, 1500–1830,* edited by Bernard Bailyn and Patricia L. Denault, 210–36. Cambridge, MA: Harvard University Press, 2009.

Bell, James. *The Imperial Origins of the King's Church in Early America: 1607–1783.* New York: Palgrave Macmillan, 2004.

Bennett, Herman L. *Africans in Colonial Mexico: Absolutism, Christianity, and Afro-Creole Consciousness, 1570–1640.* Bloomington: Indiana University Press, 2005.

Bennett, J. H. *Bondsmen and Bishops: Slavery and Apprenticeship on the Codrington Plantations of Barbados, 1710–1838.* Berkeley: University of California Press, 1958.

———. "English Bishops and Imperial Jurisdiction 1660–1725." *Historical Magazine of the Protestant Episcopal Church* 32, no. 3 (September 1964): 175–88.

Benz, Ernst. "The Pietist and Puritan Sources of Early Protestant World Missions (Cotton Mather and A H Francke)." *Church History* 20, no. 2 (June 1951): 28–55.

Besson, Jean. "The Creolization of African-American Slave Kinship in Jamaican Free Village and Maroon Communities." In *Slave Cultures and the Cultures of Slavery,* edited by Stephan Palmié. Knoxville: University of Tennessee Press, 1995.

Bialuschewski, Arne and Linford D. Fisher. "Guest Editor's Introduction: New Directions in the History of Native American Slavery Studies." *Ethnohistory* 64, no. 1 (January 2017): 1–17.

Blackburn, Robin. *The American Crucible: Slavery, Emancipation And Human Rights.* London: Verso, 2013.

———. *The Making of New World Slavery: From the Baroque to the Modern, 1492–1800.* London: Verso, 2010.

———. "The Old World Background to European Colonial Slavery." *William and Mary Quarterly* 54, no. 1 (January 1997): 65–102.

Block, Kristen. "Cultivating Inner and Outer Plantations: Property, Industry, and Slavery in Early Quaker Migration to the New World." *Early American Studies* 8, no. 3 (2010): 515–48.

———. "Faith and Fortune: Religious Identity and the Politics of Profit in the Seventeenth-Century Caribbean." Ph.D. diss., Rutgers University, 2007.

———. *Ordinary Lives in the Early Caribbean: Religion, Colonial Competition, and the Politics of Profit.* Athens: University of Georgia Press, 2012.

Block, Kristen and Jenny Shaw. "Subjects Without an Empire: The Irish in the Early Modern Caribbean." *Past & Present* 210, no. 1 (February 2011): 33–60.

Block, Sharon. *Rape and Sexual Power in Early America.* Chapel Hill: University of North Carolina Press, 2006.

Blumenthal, Debra. *Enemies and Familiars: Slavery and Mastery in Fifteenth-Century Valencia.* Ithaca, NY: Cornell University Press, 2009.

Bolton, S. Charles. "Le Jau, Francis," *American National Biography Online,* online ed., Oxford University Press, 2000.

Bonomi, Patricia U. *Under the Cope of Heaven: Religion, Society, and Politics in Colonial America.* New York: Oxford University Press, 1986.

———. "'Swarms of Negroes Comeing about My Door': Black Christianity in Early Dutch and English North America." *Journal of American History* (June 2016): 34–58.

Bosher, J. F. "Huguenot Merchants and the Protestant International in the Seventeenth Century." *William and Mary Quarterly* 52, no. 1 (January 1995): 77–102.

Bossy, John. *Christianity in the West, 1400–1700.* Oxford: Oxford University Press, 1985.

Bowser, Frederick P. "Africans in Spanish American Colonial Society." In *The Cambridge History of Latin America: Economic and Social Structures: Spanish America*, Vol. 2, edited by Leslie Bethell, 357–80. Cambridge: Cambridge University Press, 1984.

———. *The African Slave in Colonial Peru, 1524–1650.* Stanford, CA: Stanford University Press, 1974.

Boxer, Charles R. *The Church Militant and Iberian Expansion, 1440–1770.* Baltimore: Johns Hopkins University Press, 1978.

Braithwaite, William C. *The Beginnings of Quakerism.* London: Macmillan, 1912.

———. *The Second Period of Quakerism.* London: Macmillan, 1919.

Brecht, Martin, ed. *Geschichte des Pietismus.* Vol. 1, *Der Pietismus vom siebzehnten bis zum frühen achtzehnten Jahrhundert.* Göttingen: Vandenhoeck & Ruprecht, 1993.

Brecht, Martin, and Klaus Depperman, eds. *Geschichte des Pietismus.* Vol. 2. *Der Pietismus im achtzehnten Jahrhundert.* Göttingen: Vandenhoeck & Ruprecht, 1995.

Brecht, Martin, and Paul Peucker, eds. *Neue Aspekte Der Zinzendorf-Forschung.* Göttingen: Vandenhoeck & Ruprecht, 2006.

Brewer, Holly. "Creating a Common Law of Slavery for England and its Empire." Unpublished chapter draft presented at the Yale Legal History Forum, New Haven, CT, October 14, 2014.

Bridenbaugh, Carl, and Roberta Bridenbaugh. *No Peace Beyond the Line: The English in the Caribbean, 1624–1690.* New York: Oxford University Press, 1972.

Brooks, James F. *Captives and Cousins: Slavery, Kinship, and Community in the Southwest Borderlands.* Chapel Hill: University of North Carolina Press, 2002.

Brown, Anne, and David D. Hall. "Family Strategies and Religious Practice." In *Lived Religion in America: Toward a History of Practice*, edited by David D. Hall, 41–68. Princeton, NJ: Princeton University Press, 1997.

Brown, Christopher Leslie. *Moral Capital: Foundations of British Abolitionism.* Chapel Hill: University of North Carolina Press, 2006.

Brown, Vincent. *The Reaper's Garden: Death and Power in the World of Atlantic Slavery.* Cambridge, MA: Harvard University Press, 2008.

———. "Social Death and Political Life in the Study of Slavery." *American Historical Review* 114, no. 5 (December 2009): 1231–49.

Brunner, Daniel L. "Collaboration and Conflict in Europe around the Early Tranquebar Mission." *Covenant Quarterly* 65, no. 2 (May 2007): 3–15.

———. *Halle Pietists in England: Anthony William Boehm and the Society for Promoting Christian Knowledge.* Göttingen: Vandenhoeck & Ruprecht, 1993.

Brunton, D. A. "Brokesby, Francis (1637–1714)." In *Oxford Dictionary of National Biography*, edited by David Cannadine. Oxford: Oxford University Press, 2004.

Buchner, J. H. *The Moravians in Jamaica: History of the Mission of the United Brethren's Church to the Negroes in the Island of Jamaica from the Year 1754 to 1854.* London: Longman, Brown, 1854.

Burke, Peter. *Cultural Hybridity*. Cambridge: Polity Press, 2009.

Burkhart, Louise M. *The Slippery Earth: Nahua-Christian Moral Dialogue in Sixteenth-Century Mexico*. Tucson: University of Arizona Press, 1989.

Burtt, Shelley. "The Societies for the Reformation of Manners: Between John Locke and the Devil in Augustan England." In *The Margins of Orthodoxy: Heterodox Writing and Cultural Response, 1660–1750*, edited by Roger D. Lund, 149–69. Cambridge: Cambridge University Press, 1996.

Butler, Jon. "Africans' Religions in British America, 1650–1840." *Church History* 68, no. 1 (1999): 118–27.

———. *Awash in a Sea of Faith: Christianizing the American People*. Cambridge, MA: Harvard University Press, 1990.

Campbell, P. F. *The Church in Barbados in the Seventeenth Century*. St. Michael, Barbados: Barbados Museum and Historical Society, 1982.

Carey, Brycchan. *From Peace to Freedom: Quaker Rhetoric and the Birth of American Antislavery, 1657–1761*. New Haven, CT: Yale University Press, 2012.

———. "'The Power That Giveth Liberty and Freedom': The Barbadian Origins of Quaker Antislavery Rhetoric, 1657–76." *Ariel* 38, no. 1 (2007): 27–47.

Carlo, Paula Wheeler. "Neau, Elias." *American National Biography Online*. Oxford: Oxford University Press, 2000.

Carroll, Kenneth L. "George Fox and Slavery." *Quaker History* 86, no. 2 (1997): 16–25.

———. "Maryland Quakers in the Seventeenth Century." *Maryland Historical Magazine* 100, no. 1 (2005): 81–96.

Casares, Aurelia Martín, and Margarita García Barranco. "Legislation on Free Soil in Nineteenth-Century Spain: The Case of the Slave Rufino and Its Consequences (1858–1879)." *Slavery & Abolition* 32, no. 3 (September 2011): 461–76.

Catterall, Helen Tunnicliff. *Judicial Cases Concerning American Slavery and the Negro*. Washington, D.C.: Carnegie Institute of Washington, 1926.

Catron, John W. *Embracing Protestantism: Black Identites in the Atlantic World*. Gainesville: University Press of Florida, 2016.

Clossey, Luke. *Salvation and Globalization in the Early Jesuit Missions*. Cambridge: Cambridge University Press, 2008.

Cogley, Richard W. *John Eliot's Mission to the Indians Before King Philip's War*. Cambridge, MA: Harvard University Press, 1999.

Colley, Linda. *Captives: Britain, Empire, and the World, 1600–1850*. Reprint ed. New York: Anchor, 2004.

Comaroff, Jean, and John L. Comaroff. *Of Revelation and Revolution: Christianity, Colonialism, and Consciousness in South Africa*. Vol. 1. Chicago: University of Chicago Press, 1991.

Cox, Jeffrey. *The British Missionary Enterprise Since 1700*. New York: Routledge, 2008.

Craton, Michael. *Sinews of Empire: A Short History of British Slavery*. Garden City, NY: Anchor Press, 1974.

Creel, Margaret Washington. *A Peculiar People: Slave Religion and Community-culture among the Gullahs*. New York: New York University Press, 1988.

Cressy, David. *Birth, Marriage, and Death: Ritual, Religion, and the Life Cycle in Tudor and Stuart England*. Oxford: Oxford University Press, 1999.

Curtin, Philip D. *The Rise and Fall of the Plantation Complex: Essays in Atlantic History*. 2nd ed. Cambridge: Cambridge University Press, 1998.

Cushner, Nicholas P. *Lords of the Land: Sugar, Wine, and Jesuit Estates of Coastal Peru, 1600–1767*. Albany: State University of New York Press, 1980.

Dailey, Barbara Ritter. "The Early Quaker Mission and the Settlement of Meetings in Barbados, 1655–1700." *Journal of the Barbados Museum and Historical Society* 39 (1991): 24–46.

Damrosch, Leopold. *The Sorrows of the Quaker Jesus: James Nayler and the Puritan Crackdown on the Free Spirit*. Cambridge, MA: Harvard University Press, 1996.

Dator, James. "Search for a New Land: Imperial Power and Afro-Creole Resistance in the British Leeward Islands 1624–1745." Ph.D. diss., University of Michigan, 2011.

Davis, David Brion. *The Problem of Slavery in Western Culture*. Reprint Ed. Oxford: Oxford University Press, 1988.

Davis, Robert C. *Christian Slaves, Muslim Masters: White Slavery in the Mediterranean, The Barbary Coast, and Italy, 1500–1800*. Basingstoke: Palgrave Macmillan, 2003.

Dayfoot, Arthur Charles. *The Shaping of the West Indian Church, 1492–1962*. Gainesville: University Press of Florida, 1999.

de la Fuente, Alejandro. "Slave Law and Claims-Making in Cuba: The Tannenbaum Debate Revisited." *Law and History Review* 22, no. 2 (July 2004): 339–69.

de la Fuente, Alejandro, and Ariela Gross. "Comparative Studies of Law, Slavery, and Race in the Americas." *Annual Review of Law and Social Science* 6, no. 1 (2010): 469–85.

Dewulf, Jeroen. "Emulating a Portuguese Model." *Journal of Early American History* 4, no. 1 (January 2014): 3–36.

Diouf, Sylviane A. *Servants of Allah: African Muslims Enslaved in the Americas, 15th Anniversary Edition*. New York: New York University Press, 2013.

Dos Guimarães Sá, Isabel. "Ecclesiastical Structures and Religious Action." In *Portuguese Oceanic Expansion, 1400–1800*, edited by Francisco Bethencourt and Diogo Ramada Curto, 255–82. Cambridge: Cambridge University Press, 2007.

Drake, Thomas. *Quakers and Slavery in America*. New Haven, CT: Yale University Press, 1950.

Drescher, Seymour, and Stanley L. Engerman, eds. *A Historical Guide to World Slavery*. New York: Oxford University Press, 1998.

Dreyer, Frederick. *The Genesis of Methodism*. Bethlehem, PA: Lehigh University Press, 1999.

Duffin, James M. *Acta Germanopolis: Records of the Corporation of Germantown, Pennsylvania, 1691–1707*. Philadelphia: Colonial Society of Pennsylvania, 2008.

Dunn, Richard S. *Moravian Missionaries at Work in a Jamaican Slave Community: 1754–1835*. Minneapolis: James Ford Bell Library, University of Minnesota, 1994.

———. *Sugar and Slaves: The Rise of the Planter Class in the English West Indies, 1624–1713*. Chapel Hill: University of North Carolina Press, 2000.

———. *A Tale of Two Plantations: Slave Life and Labor in Jamaica and Virginia*. Cambridge, MA: Harvard University Press, 2014.

Durham, Harriet Frorer. *Caribbean Quakers*. Hollywood, FL: Dukane Press, 1972.

Elliot, John H. "Religions on the Move." In *Religious Transformations in the Early Modern Americas*, edited by Stephanie Kirk and Sarah Rivett, 25–45. Philadelphia: University of Pennsylvania Press, 2014.

Eltis, David. *The Rise of African Slavery in the Americas*. Cambridge: Cambridge University Press, 1999.

Fischer, Kirsten. *Suspect Relations: Sex, Race, and Resistance in Colonial North Carolina*. Ithaca, NY: Cornell University Press, 2001.

Fischer, Kirsten, and Jennifer Morgan. "Sex, Race, and the Colonial Project." *William and Mary Quarterly* 60, no. 1 (January 2003): 197–98.

Fisher, Linford D. " 'Dangerous Designes': The 1676 Barbados Act to Prohibit New England Indian Slave Importation." *William and Mary Quarterly* 71, no. 1 (2014): 99–124.

———. *The Indian Great Awakening: Religion and the Shaping of Native Cultures in Early America.* New York: Oxford University Press, 2012.

———. "Native Americans, Conversion, and Christian Practice in Colonial New England, 1640–1730." *Harvard Theological Review* 102, no. 1 (2009): 101–24.

Fogleman, Aaron Spencer. *Jesus Is Female: Moravians and Radical Religion in Early America.* Philadelphia: University of Pennsylvania Press, 2008.

———. *Two Troubled Souls: An Eighteenth-Century Couple's Spiritual Journey in the Atlantic World.* Chapel Hill: University of North Carolina Press, 2013.

Frazier, E. Franklin. *The Negro Church in America.* New York: Schocken, 1974.

———. "The Negro Family in Bahia, Brazil." *American Sociological Review* 7, no. 4 (August 1942): 465–78.

Frey, Sylvia R. "The Visible Church: Historiography of African American Religion Since Raboteau." *Slavery & Abolition* 29, no. 1 (January 2008): 83–110.

Frey, Sylvia R., and Betty Wood. *Come Shouting to Zion: African American Protestantism in the American South and British Caribbean to 1830.* Chapel Hill: University of North Carolina Press, 1998.

Fromont, Cécile, *The Art of Conversion: Christian Visual Culture in the Kingdom of Kongo.* Chapel Hill: University of North Carolina Press, 2014.

Frost, J. William. "George Fox's Ambiguous Anti-Slavery Legacy." In *New Light on George Fox, 1624–1691,* edited by Michael Mullett, 69–88. York, England: Ebor Press, 1994.

———, ed. *The Quaker Origins of Antislavery.* Norwood, PA: Norwood Editions, 1980.

Fuentes, Marisa J. *Dispossessed Lives: Enslaved Women, Violence, and the Archive.* Philadelphia: University of Pennsylvania Press, 2015.

———. "Power and Historical Figuring: Rachael Pringle Polgreen's Troubled Archive." *Gender & History* 22, no. 3 (November 2010): 564–84.

Füllberg-Stolberg, Claus. "The Moravian Mission and the Emancipation of Slaves in the Caribbean." In *The End of Slavery in Africia and the Americas: A Comparative Approach,* edited by Ulrike Schmieder, Michael Zeuske, and Katja Füllberg-Stolberg, 81–102. Münster, Germany: LIT Verlag, 2011.

Gäbler, Ulrich, ed. *Geschichte des Pietismus.* Vol. 4. *Der Pietismus im neunzehnten und zwanzigsten Jahrhundert.* Göttingen: Vandenhoeck & Ruprecht, 2000.

Gallay, Alan. *The Indian Slave Trade: The Rise of the English Empire in the American South, 1670–1717.* New Haven, CT: Yale University Press, 2002.

Games, Alison. *The Web of Empire: English Cosmopolitans in an Age of Expansion, 1560–1660.* Oxford: Oxford University Press, 2008.

Gaspar, David Barry. "A Dangerous Spirit of Liberty: Slave Rebellion in the West Indies in the 1730s." In *Origins of the Black Atlantic,* edited by Laurent Dubois and Julius S. Scott, 11–25. New York: Routledge, 2013.

———. "With a Rod of Iron: Barbados Slave Laws As a Model for Jamaica, South Carolina, and Antigua, 1661–1697." In *Crossing Boundaries: Comparative History of Black People in Diaspora,* edited by Darlene Clark Hine and Jacqueline McLeod, 343–66. Bloomington: Indiana University Press, 1999.

Geiger, Erika. "Zinzendorf Stellung Zum Halleschen Busskampf Und Zum Bekehrungserleb-nis." *Unitas Fratrum: Zeitschrift Für Geschichte Und Gegenwartsfragen Der Brudergemeine*, no. 49/50 (January 2002): 12–22.

Gerbner, Katharine. "Antislavery in Print: The Germantown Protest, the 'Exhortation,' and the Seventeenth-Century Quaker Debate on Slavery." *Early American Studies* 9, no. 3 (2011): 552–75.

———. "The Ultimate Sin: Christianising Slaves in Barbados in the Seventeenth Century." *Slavery & Abolition* 31, no. 1 (March 2010): 57–73.

———. "Theorizing Conversion: Christianity, Colonization, and Consciousness in the Early Modern Atlantic World," *History Compass* 13, no. 3 (2015): 134–47.

———. " 'They Call Me Obea': German Moravian Missionaries and Afro-Caribbean Religion in Jamaica, 1754–1760." *Atlantic Studies* 12, no. 2 (2015): 160–78.

———. " 'We Are Against the Traffik of Men-Body': The Germantown Quaker Protest of 1688 and the Origins of American Abolitionism." *Pennsylvania History* 74, no. 2 (2007): 149–72.

Gerona, Carla. *Night Journeys: The Power of Dreams in Transatlantic Quaker Culture.* Charlottesville: University of Virginia Press, 2004.

Gillespie, Michele, and Robert Beachy, eds. *Pious Pursuits: German Moravians in the Atlantic World.* New York: Berghahn Books, 2007.

Glancy, Jennifer A. *Slavery in Early Christianity.* Oxford: Oxford University Press, 2002.

Glasson, Travis. " 'Baptism Doth Not Bestow Freedom': Missionary Anglicanism, Slavery, and the Yorke-Talbot Opinion, 1701–30." *William and Mary Quarterly* 67, no. 2 (April 2010): 279–318.

———. *Mastering Christianity: Missionary Anglicanism and Slavery in the Atlantic World.* New York: Oxford University Press, 2011.

———. "Missionaries, Slavery, and Race: The Society for the Propagation of the Gospel in Foreign Parts in the Eighteenth-Century British Atlantic World." Ph.D. diss., Columbia University, 2005.

Godbeer, Richard. *Sexual Revolution in Early America.* Baltimore: Johns Hopkins University Press, 2002.

Goetz, Rebecca Anne. *The Baptism of Early Virginia: How Christianity Created Race.* Baltimore: Johns Hopkins University Press, 2012.

Gomez, Michael A. *Exchanging Our Country Marks: The Transformation of African Identities in the Colonial and Antebellum South.* Chapel Hill: University of North Carolina Press, 1998.

Gordon, Sarah Barringer. "The African Supplement: Religion, Race, and Corporate Law in Early National America." *William and Mary Quarterly* 72, no. 3 (July 2015): 385–422.

Gragg, Larry. *Englishmen Transplanted: The English Colonization of Barbados 1627–1660.* Oxford: Oxford University Press, 2003.

———. "The Pious and the Profane: The Religious Life of Early Barbados Planters." *Historian* 62, no. 2 (January 2000): 264–83.

———. *The Quaker Community on Barbados: Challenging the Culture of the Planter Class.* Columbia: University of Missouri Press, 2009.

Gray, Richard. *Black Christians and White Missionaries.* New Haven, CT: Yale University Press, 1959.

———. "The Papacy and the Atlantic Slave Trade: Lourenço Da Silva, the Capuchins and the Decisions of the Holy Office." *Past & Present*, no. 115 (May 1987): 52–68.

Greene, Jack P. "Liberty and Slavery: The Transfer of British Liberty to the West Indies, 1627–1865." In *Exclusionary Empire: English Liberty Overseas, 1600–1900*, edited by Jack P. Greene, 50–76. Cambridge: Cambridge University Press, 2009.

Greer, Allan. "Conversion and Identity: Iroquois Christianity in Seventeenth-Century New France." In *Conversion: Old Worlds and New*, edited by Kenneth Mills and Grafton Anthony, 175–98. Rochester, NY: University Rochester Press, 2003.

———. *Mohawk Saint: Catherine Tekakwitha and the Jesuits*. New York: Oxford University Press, 2004.

Gregerson, Linda, and Susan Juster, eds. *Empires of God: Religious Encounters in the Early Modern Atlantic*. Philadelphia: University of Pennsylvania Press, 2013.

Guasco, Michael. *Slaves and Englishmen: Human Bondage in the Early Modern Atlantic World*. Philadelphia: University of Pennsylvania Press, 2014.

Hadden, Sally E. "The Fragmented Laws of Slavery in the Colonial and Revolutionary Eras." In *The Cambridge History of Law in America*, edited by Michael Grossberg and Christopher Tomlins, 253–87. Cambridge: Cambridge University Press, 2008.

Haefeli, Evan. "Breaking the Christian Atlantic: The Legacy of Dutch Toleration." In *The Legacy of Dutch Brazil*, edited by Michiel van Groesen, 124–45. Cambridge: Cambridge University Press, 2014.

———. *New Netherland and the Dutch Origins of American Religious Liberty*. Philadelphia: University of Pennsylvania Press, 2012.

Hall, David D., ed. *Lived Religion in America: Toward a History of Practice*. Princeton, NJ: Princeton University Press, 1997.

Hall, Gwendolyn Midlo. *Social Control in Slave Plantation Societies: A Comparison of St. Domingue and Cuba*. Baton Rouge: Louisiana State University Press, 1996.

Hall, Neville A. T. *Slave Society in the Danish West Indies: St. Thomas, St. John and St Croix*. Edited by B. W. Higman. Mona, Jamaica: University of the West Indies Press, 1992.

Hambrick-Stowe, Charles E. *The Practice of Piety: Puritan Devotional Disciplines in Seventeenth-Century New England*. Chapel Hill: University of North Carolina Press, 1982.

Hamilton, J. Taylor. *A History of the Missions of the Moravian Church, During the Eighteenth and Nineteenth Centuries*. Bethlehem, PA: Times Publishing Company, 1901.

Hamilton, J. Taylor, and Kenneth G. Hamilton. *History of the Moravian Church: The Renewed Unitas Fratrum 1722–1757*. Bethlehem, PA: Interprovincial Board of Christian Education, Moravian Church in America, 1967.

Handler, Jerome S. *A Guide to Source Materials for the Study of Barbados History, 1627–1834*. Carbondale: The Southern Illinois University Press, 1971.

———. "The Barbados Slave Conspiracies of 1675 and 1692." *Journal of the Barbados Museum and Historical Society* 36, no. 4 (1982): 312–33.

———. *Supplement to A Guide to Source Materials for the Study of Barbados History, 1627–1834*. Brown University: John Carter Brown Library, 1991.

———. *The Unappropriated People: Freedmen in the Slave Society of Barbados*. Baltimore: Johns Hopkins University Press, 1974.

Handler, Jerome S., and John T. Pohlmann. "Slave Manumissions and Freedmen in Seventeenth-Century Barbados." *William and Mary Quarterly* 41, no. 3 (July 1984): 390–408.

Handler Jerome S. and Matthew C. Reilly. "Contesting "White Slavery" in the Caribbean: Enslaved Africans and European Indentured Servants in Seventeenth-Century Barbados." *New West Indian Guide* 91 (2017): 30–55.

Hanks, William F. *Converting Words: Maya in the Age of the Cross.* Berkeley: University of California Press, 2010.

Hannaford, Ivan. *Race: The History of an Idea in the West.* Baltimore: Johns Hopkins University Press, 1996.

Harlow, Vincent. *Christopher Codrington, 1668–1710.* New York: St. Martin's Press, 1990.

Hartman, Saidiya V. "Venus in Two Acts." *Small Axe* 26 (2008): 1–14.

Herskovits, Melville J. *The Myth of the Negro Past.* New York: Harper & Bros., 1941.

———. "The Negro in Bahia, Brazil: A Problem in Method." *American Sociological Review* 8, no. 4 (August 1943): 394–404.

Heyrman, Christine Leigh. *Southern Cross: The Beginnings of the Bible Belt.* New York: Knopf, 1997.

Heywood, Linda M., and John K. Thornton. *Central Africans, Atlantic Creoles, and the Foundation of the Americas, 1585–1660.* Cambridge: Cambridge University Press, 2007.

Higham, C. S. S. "The Early Days of the Church in the West Indies." *Church Quarterly Reviews* 92 (1921): 106–30.

Highfield, Arnold R. "Patterns of Accommodation and Resistance: The Moravian Witness to Slavery in the Danish West Indies." *Journal of Caribbean History* 28, no. 2 (December 1994): 138–64.

Higman, B. W. "The Sugar Revolution." *Economic History Review* 53, no. 2 (2000): 213–36.

Hill, Christopher. *The World Turned Upside Down: Radical Ideas during the English Revolution.* New York: Viking, 1972.

Hindmarsh, D. Bruce. *The Evangelical Conversion Narrative: Spiritual Autobiography in Early Modern England.* Oxford: Oxford University Press, 2005.

Hinds, Hilary. "An Absent Presence: Quaker Narratives of Journeys to America and Barbados, 1671–81." *Quaker Studies* 10, no. 1 (September 2005): 6–30.

Hodges, Graham Russell. *Root and Branch: African Americans in New York and East Jersey, 1613–1863.* Chapel Hill: University of North Carolina Press, 1999.

Holifield, E. Brooks. *The Covenant Sealed: The Development of Puritan Sacramental Theology in Old and New England, 1570–1720.* New Haven, CT: Yale University Press, 1974.

Hondius, Dienke. "Access to the Netherlands of Enslaved and Free Black Africans: Exploring Legal and Social Historical Practices in the Sixteenth–Nineteenth Centuries." *Slavery & Abolition* 32, no. 3 (September 2011): 377–95.

Hull, William Isaac. *William Penn and the Dutch Quaker Migration to Pennsylvania.* Philadelphia: Patterson & White, 1935.

Hunte, Keith. "Protestantism and Slavery in the British Caribbean." In *Christianity in the Caribbean: Essays on Church History,* edited by Armando Lampe, 86–125. Mona, Jamaica: University of the West Indies Press, 2000.

Hüsgen, Jan. *Mission und Sklaverei: Die Herrnhuter Brüdergemeine und die Sklavenemanzipation in Britisch- und Dänisch-Westindien.* Stuttgart: Franz Steiner Verlag, 2016.

Ingersoll, Thomas N. "'Releese Us out of This Cruell Bondegg': An Appeal from Virginia in 1723." *William and Mary Quarterly* 51, no. 4 (October 1994): 777.

Isaac, Rhys. *Landon Carter's Uneasy Kingdom: Revolution and Rebellion on a Virginia Plantation.* Oxford: Oxford University Press, 2004.

Israel, Jonathan Irvine, and Stuart B. Schwartz. *The Expansion of Tolerance: Religion in Dutch Brazil (1624–1654)*. Amsterdam: Amsterdam University Press, 2007.

Jacobson, Matthew Frye. *Whiteness of a Different Color: European Immigrants and the Alchemy of Race*. Cambridge: Harvard University Press, 1999.

Jernegan, Marcus W. "Slavery and Conversion in the American Colonies." *American Historical Review* 21, no. 3 (1916): 504–29.

Jeyaraj, Daniel. *Bartholomaus Ziegenbalg: The Father of the Modern Protestant Mission*. New Delhi: Indian Society for Promoting Christian Knowledge, 2006.

————. "Mission Reports from South India and Their Impact on the Western Mind: The Tranquebar Mission of the Eighteenth Century." In *Converting Colonialism: Visions and Realities in Mission History, 1706–1914*, edited by Dana L. Robert. Grand Rapids, MI: Eerdmans, 2008.

Johnson, Whittington B. "The Origin and Nature of African Slavery in Seventeenth Century Maryland." *Maryland Historical Magazine* 73, no. 3 (Fall 1978): 236–45.

Jones, Rufus M. *The Life and Message of George Fox 1624 to 1924*. New York: Macmillan, 1924.

Jordan, Winthrop D. *White Over Black: American Attitudes Toward the Negro, 1550–1812*. 2nd ed. Chapel Hill: University of North Carolina Press, 2012.

Karras, Ruth Mazo. *Slavery and Society in Medieval Scandinavia*. New Haven, CT: Yale University Press, 1988.

Kea, Ray. "From Catholicism to Moravian Pietism: The World of Marotta/Magdalena, Woman of Popo and St. Thomas." In *The Creation of the British Atlantic World*, edited by Elizabeth Mancke and Carole Shammas, 115–36. Baltimore: Johns Hopkins University Press, 2005.

Kidd, Colin. *The Forging of Races: Race and Scripture in the Protestant Atlantic World, 1600–2000*. Cambridge: Cambridge University Press, 2006.

Kidd, Thomas S. *George Whitefield: America's Spiritual Founding Father*. New Haven: Yale University Press, 2014.

Klingberg, Frank Joseph, ed. *The Carolina Chronicle of Dr. Francis Le Jau, 1706–1717*. Berkeley: University of California Press, 1956.

————. *Codrington Chronicle: An Experiment in Anglican Altruism on a Barbados Plantation, 1710–1834*. Berkeley: University of California Press, 1949.

Klooster, Wim. "Subordinate But Proud: Curaçao's Free Blacks and Mulattoes in the Eighteenth Century." *New West Indian Guide/Nieuwe West-Indische Gids* 68, no. 3/4 (1994): 283–300.

Koch, Philippa. "Slavery, Mission, and the Perils of Providence in Eighteenth-Century Christianity: The Writings of Whitefield and the Halle Pietists." *Church History* 84, no. 2 (2015): 369–93.

Kopelson, Heather Miyano. *Faithful Bodies: Performing Religion and Race in the Puritan Atlantic*. New York: New York University Press, 2014.

Lachenicht, Susanne. *Hugenotten in Europa und Nordamerika: Migration und Integration in der Frühen Neuzeit*. Frankfurt: Campus Verlag, 2010.

Laing, Annette. "'Heathens and Infidels'? African Christianization and Anglicanism in the South Carolina Low Country, 1700–1750." *Religion and American Culture* 12, no. 2 (July 2002): 197–228.

Lambert, David. *White Creole Culture, Politics and Identity during the Age of Abolition*. Cambridge: Cambridge University Press, 2005.

Lampe, Armando. "Christianity and Slavery in the Dutch Caribbean." In *Christianity in the Caribbean: Essays on Church History*, edited by Armando Lampe, 126–53. Kingston, Jamaica: University of the West Indies Press, 2001.

Landers, Jane. *Atlantic Creoles in the Age of Revolutions*. Cambridge, MA: Harvard University Press, 2010.

———. *Black Society in Spanish Florida*. Urbana: University of Illinois Press, 1999.

Leavelle, Tracy. *The Catholic Calumet: Colonial Conversions in French and Indian North America*. Philadelphia: University of Pennsylvania Press, 2011.

Lehmann, Hartmut, ed. *Geschichte des Pietismus*. Vol. 4. *Glaubenswelt und Lebenswelten des Pietismus*. Göttingen: Vandenhoeck & Ruprecht, 2004.

Levy, Barry. *Quakers and the American Family: British Settlement in the Delaware Valley*. New York: Oxford University Press, 1988.

Ligon, Richard. *A True and Exact History of the Island of Barbados*. Edited by Karen Ordahl Kupperman. Indianapolis: Hackett Publishing, 2011.

Lindberg, Carter, ed. *The Pietist Theologians: An Introduction to Theology in the Seventeenth and Eighteenth Centuries*. Malden, MA: Wiley-Blackwell, 2004.

Lovejoy, Paul. "The African Diaspora: Revisionist Interpretations of Ethnicity, Culture and Religion under Slavery." *Studies in the World History of Slavery, Abolition and Emancipation* 2, no. 1 (1997): 1–23.

Lovelace, Richard F. *The American Pietism of Cotton Mather: Origins of American Evangelicalism*. Grand Rapids, MI: Christian University Press, 1979.

Mack, Phyllis. *Visionary Women: Ecstatic Prophecy in 17th-Century England*. Berkeley: University of California Press, 1992.

Mandelbrote, Scott. "The Vision of Christopher Codrington." In *All Souls Under the Ancien Régime: Politics, Learning and the Arts, c. 1600–1850*, edited by S. J. D. Green and Peregrine Horden, 132–71. Oxford: Oxford University Press, 2007.

Mason, J. C. S. *The Moravian Church and the Missionary Awakening in England, 1760–1800*. Woodbridge, UK: Boydell, 2001.

Matar, Nabil. *British Captives from the Mediterranean to the Atlantic, 1563–1760*. Leiden: Brill, 2014.

———. "English Accounts of Captivity in North Africa and the Middle East: 1577–1625." *Renaissance Quarterly* 54, no. 2 (July 2001): 553–72.

———. *Turks, Moors, and Englishmen in the Age of Discovery*. New York: Columbia University Press, 2000.

Matthias, Markus. "August Hermann Francke." In *The Pietist Theologians: An Introduction to Theology in the Seventeenth and Eighteenth Centuries*, edited by Carter Lindberg, 100–114. Malden, MA: Wiley-Blackwell, 2004.

Mattoso, Katia M. De Queiros. *To Be A Slave in Brazil: 1550–1888*. Trans. Arthur Goldhammer. New Brunswick, NJ: Rutgers University Press, 1987.

Maxwell, John Francis. *Slavery and the Catholic Church: The History of Catholic Teaching Concerning the Moral Legitimacy of the Institution of Slavery*. Chichester, England: Barry Rose Publishers, 1975.

McCormick, Michael. *Origins of the European Economy: Communications and Commerce AD 300–900*. Cambridge: Cambridge University Press, 2002.

McCulloch, Samuel Clyde. *British Humanitarianism: Essays Honoring Frank J. Klingberg*. Philadelphia: Church Historical Society, 1950.

McCulloch, Samuel Clyde, and John A. Schutz. "Of the Noble and Generous Benefaction of General Christopher Codrington." In *Codrington Chronicle: An Experiment in Anglican Altruism on a Barbados Plantation, 1710–1834*, edited by Frank Joseph Klingberg. Berkeley: University of California Press, 1949.

McKinley, Michelle. *Fractional Freedoms: Slavery, Intimacy, and Legal Mobilization in Colonial Lima, 1600–1700*. New York: Cambridge University Press, 2016.

———. "Fractional Freedoms: Slavery, Legal Activism, and Ecclesiastical Courts in Colonial Lima, 1593–1689." *Law and History Review* 28, no. 3 (August 2010): 749–90.

Meier, Gudrun, Peter Stein, Stephan Palmié, and Horst Ulbricht, eds. *Christian Georg Andreas Oldendorp: Historie Der Caraibischen Inseln Sanct Thomas, Sanct Crux Und Sanct Jan: Kommentarband*. Herrnhut: Herrnhuter Verlag, 2010.

Menard, Russell. *Sweet Negotiations: Sugar, Slavery, and Plantation Agriculture in Early Barbados*. Charlottesville: University of Virginia Press, 2006.

Mettele, Gisela. "Constructions of the Religious Self: Moravian Conversion and Transatlantic Communication." *Journal of Moravian History*, no. 2 (2007): 7–35.

Mills, Kenneth, and Anthony Grafton, eds. *Conversion: Old Worlds and New*. Rochester, NY: University of Rochester Press, 2003.

———. *Conversion in Late Antiquity and the Early Middle Ages: Seeing and Believing*. Rochester, NY: University of Rochester Press, 2003.

Mintz, Sidney W., and Richard Price. *The Birth of African-American Culture: An Anthropological Perspective*. Boston: Beacon Press, 1992.

Moore, Rosemary Anne. *The Light of their Consciences: The Early Quakers in Britain, 1646–1666*. University Park: Pennsylvania State University, 2000.

Morgan, Edmund S. *American Slavery, American Freedom*. New York: W. W. Norton, 2003.

———. *Visible Saints: The History of a Puritan Idea*. Ithaca, NY: Cornell University Press, 1965.

Morgan, Jennifer. *Laboring Women: Reproduction and Gender in New World Slavery*. Philadelphia: University of Pennsylvania Press, 2004.

Morgan, Philip D. "Interracial Sex in the Chesapeake and the British Atlantic World, 1700–1820." In *Sally Hemings and Thomas Jefferson: History, Memory, and Civic Culture*, edited by Jan Lewis and Peter S. Onuf, 52–85. Charlottesville: University Press of Virginia, 1999.

Morrison, Kenneth M. *The Solidarity of Kin: Ethnohistory, Religious Studies, and the Algonkian-French Religious Encounter*. Albany: State University of New York Press, 2002.

Muldoon, James. *The Spiritual Conversion of the Americas*. Gainesville: University Press of Florida, 2004.

———, ed. *Varieties of Religious Conversion in the Middle Ages*. Gainesville: University Press of Florida, 1997.

Mulvey, Patricia A. "Black Brothers and Sisters: Membership in the Black Lay Brotherhoods of Colonial Brazil." *Luso-Brazilian Review* 17, no. 2 (December 1980): 253–79.

———. "Slave Confraternities in Brazil: Their Role in Colonial Society." *Americas* 39, no. 1 (July 1982): 39–68.

Nash, Gary B. "Slaves and Slaveowners in Colonial Philadelphia." *William and Mary Quarterly* 30, no. 2 (April 1973): 223–56.

Nash, Gary B., and Jean R. Soderlund. *Freedom by Degrees: Emancipation in Pennsylvania and Its Aftermath*. New York: Oxford University Press, 1991.

Newell, Margaret Ellen. *Brethren by Nature: New England Indians, Colonists, and the Origins of American Slavery*. Ithaca, NY: Cornell University Press, 2016.

Newman, Simon P. *A New World of Labor: The Development of Plantation Slavery in the British Atlantic*. Philadelphia: University of Pennsylvania Press, 2013.

Nuttall, Geoffrey F. *The Holy Spirit in Puritan Faith and Experience*. Chicago: University of Chicago Press, 1946.

Oliver, Vere Langford. *Monumental Inscriptions: Tombstones of the Island of Barbados*. San Bernardino, CA: Borgo Press, 1995.

Olwell, Robert. *Masters, Slaves, and Subjects: The Culture of Power in the South Carolina Low Country, 1740–1790*. Ithaca, NY: Cornell University Press, 1998.

O'Brien, Susan. "A Transatlantic Community of Saints: The Great Awakening and the First Evangelical Network, 1735–1755." *American Historical Review* 91, no. 4 (1986): 811–32.

O'Neil, Maud E. "Of the Buildings in Progress with Which to House the College." In Klingberg, *Codrington Chronicle: An Experiment in Anglican Altruism on a Barbados Plantation, 1710–1834*, edited by Frank Joseph Klingberg, 27–42. Berkeley: University of California Press, 1949.

O'Toole, Rachel Sarah. *Bound Lives: Africans, Indians, and the Making of Race in Colonial Peru*. Pittsburgh: University of Pittsburgh Press, 2012.

———. "(Un)Making Christianity: The African Diaspora in Slavery and Freedom." In *The Oxford Handbook of Christianity in Latin America*, edited by Susan Fitzpatrick-Behrens, David Orique, and Manuel Vasquez. New York: Oxford University Press, forthcoming.

Painter, Nell Irvin. *The History of White People*. New York: W. W. Norton, 2010.

Paley, Ruth, Cristina Malcolmson, and Michael Hunter. "Parliament and Slavery, 1660–c. 1710." *Slavery & Abolition* 31, no. 2 (June 2010): 257–81.

Palmer, Vernon Valentine. "The Origins and Authors of the Code Noir." *Louisiana Law Review* 56, no. 2 (1996): 363–408.

Palmié, Stephan. *Africas of the Americas: Beyond the Search for Origins in the Study of Afro-Atlantic Religions*. Leiden: Brill, 2008.

Parr, Jessica M. *Inventing George Whitefield: Race, Revivalism, and the Making of a Religious Icon*. Jackson, MI: University Press of Mississippi, 2015.

Peabody, Sue. "An Alternative Genealogy of the Origins of French Free Soil: Medieval Toulouse." *Slavery & Abolition* 32, no. 3 (September 2011): 341–62.

———. "'A Dangerous Zeal': Catholic Missions to Slaves in the French Antilles, 1635–1800." *French Historical Studies* 25, no. 1 (December 21, 2002): 53–90.

———. "'A Nation Born to Slavery': Missionaries and Racial Discourse in Seventeenth-Century French Antilles." *Journal of Social History* 38, no. 1 (October 2004): 113–26.

———. "Slavery, Freedom, and the Law in the Atlantic World, 1420–1807." In *The Cambridge World History of Slavery*, edited by David Eltis and Stanley L. Engerman, 594–630. Cambridge: Cambridge University Press, 2011.

———. *"There Are No Slaves in France": The Political Culture of Race and Slavery in the Ancien Régime*. New York: Oxford University Press, 2002.

Peabody, Sue, and Keila Grinberg. "Free Soil: The Generation and Circulation of an Atlantic Legal Principle." *Slavery & Abolition* 32, no. 3 (September 2011): 331–39.

Pestana, Carla Gardina. *The English Atlantic in an Age of Revolution, 1640–1661*. Cambridge, MA: Harvard University Press, 2004.

———. *Protestant Empire: Religion and the Making of the British Atlantic World*. Philadelphia: University of Pennsylvania Press, 2010.

Peucker, Paul. "Aus allen Nationen. Nichteuropäer in den deutschen Brüdergemeinen des 18. Jahrhunderts," *Unitas Fratrum. Zeitschrift für Geschichte und Gegenwartsfragen der Brüdergemeine* 59/60 (2007): 1–35.

———. *A Time of Sifting: Mystical Marriage and the Crisis of Moravian Piety in the Eighteenth Century*. University Park: Pennsylvania State University Press, 2015.

Phillips, William D. *Slavery from Roman Times to the Early Transatlantic Trade*. Minneapolis: University of Minnesota Press, 1985.

Plank, Geoffrey. "Discipline and Divinity: Colonial Quakerism, Christianity, and "Heathenism" in the Seventeenth Century." *Church History* 85, no. 3 (2016): 502–528.

Podmore, Colin. *The Moravian Church in England, 1728–1760*. Oxford: Oxford University Press, 1998.

Porter, Andrew. *Religion Versus Empire? British Protestant Missionaries and Overseas Expansion, 1700–1914*. Manchester, UK: Manchester University Press, 2004.

Price, Richard. *Alabi's World*. Baltimore: Johns Hopkins University Press, 1990.

Pritchard, James. *In Search of Empire: The French in the Americas, 1670–1730*. Cambridge: Cambridge University Press, 2004.

Puckrein, Gary A. *Little England: Plantation Society and Anglo-Barbadian Politics, 1627–1700*. New York: New York University Press, 1984.

Raboteau, Albert J. *Slave Religion: The "Invisible Institution" in the Antebellum South*. New York: Oxford University Press, 1978.

Reay, Barry. *The Quakers and the English Revolution*. New York: St. Martin's, 1985.

Reséndez, Andrés. *The Other Slavery: The Uncovered Story of Indian Enslavement in America*. Boston: Houghton Mifflin Harcourt, 2016.

Rippy, Frances Mayhew. "Prior, Matthew (1664–1721)." *Oxford Dictionary of National Biography*. Oxford: Oxford University Press, 2004.

Roeber, A. G. *Hopes for Better Spouses: Protestant Marriage and Church Renewal in Early Modern Europe, India, and North America*. Grand Rapids, MI: Eerdmans, 2013.

———. "The Waters of Rebirth: The Eighteenth Century and Transoceanic Protestant Christianity." *Church History* 79, no. 1 (March 2010): 40–76.

Romney, Susanah Shaw. *New Netherland Connections: Intimate Networks and Atlantic Ties in Seventeenth-Century America*. Chapel Hill: University of North Carolina Press, 2014.

Rose, Craig. "The Origins and Ideals of the SPCK 1699–1716." In *The Church of England c. 1689–c. 1833: From Toleration to Tractarianism*, edited by John Walsh, Colin Haydon, and Stephen Taylor. Cambridge: Cambridge University Press, 1993.

Rosenberg, Philippe. "Thomas Tryon and the Seventeenth-Century Dimensions of Antislavery." *William and Mary Quarterly* 61, no. 4 (October 2004): 609–42.

Rugemer, Edward B. "The Development of Mastery and Race in the Comprehensive Slave Codes of the Greater Caribbean During the Seventeenth Century." *William and Mary Quarterly* 70, no. 3 (July 2013): 429–58.

Ruhland, Thomas. " 'Ein paar Jahr muß Tranquebar und Coromandel wol Serieus das Object seyn'—Südasien als pietistisches Konkurrenzfeld." In *Pietismus und Neuzeit*, 39, edited by Udo Sträter et. al. Göttingen: Vendenhoeck & Ruprecht, 2013.

Rupert, Linda M. *Creolization and Contraband: Curaçao in the Early Modern Atlantic World*. Athens, GA: University of Georgia Press, 2012.

Rushforth, Brett. *Bonds of Alliance: Indigenous and Atlantic Slaveries in New France.* Williamsburg, VA: University of North Carolina Press, 2012.

Saunders, A. C. de C. M. *A Social History of Black Slaves and Freedmen in Portugal, 1441–1555.* New York: Cambridge University Press, 1982.

Schwartz, Stuart B., ed. *Tropical Babylons: Sugar and the Making of the Atlantic World, 1450–1680.* Chapel Hill: University of North Carolina Press, 2004.

Scott, Kenneth. "The Slave Insurrection in New York in 1712." *New York Historical Society Quarterly* 45 (1961): 43–74.

Seeman, Erik R. *Death in the New World: Cross-Cultural Encounters, 1492–1800.* Philadelphia: University of Pennsylvania Press, 2010.

———. " 'Justise Must Take Plase': Three African Americans Speak of Religion in Eighteenth-Century New England." *William and Mary Quarterly* 56, no. 2 (April 1999): 393–414.

Sensbach, Jon. F. " 'Don't Teach My Negroes to Be Pietists': Pietism and the Roots of the Black Protestant Church." In *Pietism in Germany and North America 1680–1820,* edited by Jonathan Strom, Hartmut Lehmann, and James Van Horn Melton, 183–98. Farnham, England: Ashgate, 2009.

———. "Race and the Early Moravian Church: A Comparative Perspective." *Transactions of the Moravian Historical Society* 31 (January 2000): 1–10.

———. *Rebecca's Revival: Creating Black Christianity in the Atlantic World.* Cambridge, MA: Harvard University Press, 2006.

———. "Religion and the Early South in an Age of Atlantic Empire." *Journal of Southern History* 73, no. 3 (August 2007): 631–42.

———. *A Separate Canaan: The Making of an Afro-Moravian World in North Carolina, 1763–1840.* Chapel Hill: University of North Carolina Press, 1998.

Shantz, Douglas H. *An Introduction to German Pietism: Protestant Renewal at the Dawn of Modern Europe.* Baltimore: Johns Hopkins University Press, 2013.

Shaw, Jenny. *Everyday Life in the Early English Caribbean: Irish, Africans, and the Construction of Difference.* Athens: University of Georgia Press, 2013.

———. "Writing a History of Susanna Mingo: Slavery, Community, and the Problem of the Archive in Early Modern Barbados." Paper presented at the Omohundro Institute for Early American History and Culture conference, "Africans in the Americas," Barbados, March 2013.

Shell, Robert Carl-Heinz. *Children of Bondage: A Social History of the Slave Society at the Cape of Good Hope, 1652–1838.* Hanover, NH: University Press of New England, 1994.

Sheridan, Richard B. *Sugar and Slavery: The Economic History of the British West Indies, 1623–1775.* Baltimore: Johns Hopkins University Press, 1974.

Silva, Cristina Nogueira Da, and Keila Grinberg. "Soil Free from Slaves: Slave Law in Late Eighteenth- and Early Nineteenth-Century Portugal." *Slavery & Abolition* 32, no. 3 (September 2011): 431–46.

Silver, Peter. *Our Savage Neighbors: How Indian War Transformed Early America.* New York: W. W. Norton, 2009.

Silverman, David J. *Faith and Boundaries: Colonists, Christianity, and Community Among the Wampanoag Indians of Martha's Vineyard, 1600–1871.* New York: Cambridge University Press, 2005.

———. "Indians, Missionaries, and Religious Translation: Creating Wampanoag Christianity in Seventeenth-Century Martha's Vineyard." *William and Mary Quarterly* 62, no. 2 (April 2005): 141–74.

Singh, Brijraj. *The First Protestant Missionary to India: Bartholomaeus Ziegenbalg, 1683–1719.* New Dehli: Oxford University Press, 1999.

———. " 'One Soul, Tho' Not One Soyl'? International Protestantism and Ecumenism at the Beginning of the Eighteenth Century." *Studies in Eighteenth-Century Culture* 31 (January 2002): 61–84.

Sirota, Brent S. *The Christian Monitors: The Church of England and the Age of Benevolence, 1680–1730.* New Haven, CT: Yale University Press, 2014.

Smallwood, Stephanie E. *Saltwater Slavery: A Middle Passage from Africa to American Diaspora.* Cambridge, MA: Harvard University Press, 2008.

Smith, Mark M. *Stono: Documenting and Interpreting a Southern Slave Revolt.* Columbia: University of South Carolina Press, 2005.

Snyder, Christina. *Slavery in Indian Country: The Changing Face of Captivity in Early America.* Cambridge, MA: Harvard University Press, 2010.

Sobel, Mechal. *Teach Me Dreams: The Search for Self in the Revolutionary Era.* Princeton, NJ: Princeton University Press, 2002.

———. *Trabelin' On: The Slave Journey to an Afro-Baptist Faith.* Princeton, NJ: Princeton University Press, 1988.

Soderlund, Jean R. *Quakers and Slavery: A Divided Spirit.* Princeton, NJ: Princeton University Press, 1985.

Stanwood, Owen. "Between Eden and Empire: Huguenot Refugees and the Promise of New Worlds." *American Historical Review* 118, no. 5 (2013): 1319–44.

———. *The Empire Reformed: English America in the Age of the Glorious Revolution.* Philadelphia, PA: University of Pennsylvania Press, 2011.

Stewart, Charles, and Rosalind Shaw, eds. *Syncretism/anti-syncretism: The politics of religious synthesis.* London: Routledge, 1994.

Sparks, Randy J. *On Jordan's Stormy Banks: Evangelicalism in Mississippi, 1773–1876.* Athens: University of Georgia Press, 1994.

Sparks Randy J. and Bertrand Van Ruymbeke, eds., *Memory and Identity: The Huguenots in France and the Atlantic Diaspora.* Columbia: University of South Carolina Press, 2008.

Stein, Stephen J. "George Whitefield on Slavery: Some New Evidence." *Church History* 42, no. 2 (1973): 243–56.

Stoeffler, F. Ernest, ed. *Continental Pietism and Early American Christianity.* Grand Rapids, MI: Eerdmans, 1976.

———. *German Pietism During the Eighteenth Century.* Leiden: Brill, 1973.

———. *The Rise of Evangelical Pietism.* Leiden: Brill, 1965.

Stoler, Ann Laura. "Tense and Tender Ties: The Politics of Comparison in North American History and (Post) Colonial Studies." In *Haunted by Empire: Geographies of Intimacy in North American History*, edited by Ann Laura Stoler. Durham, NC: Duke University Press, 2006.

Strom, Jonathan. "Problems and Promises of Pietism Research." *Church History* 71, no. 3 (September 2002): 536–54.

Strom, Jonathan, Hartmut Lehmann, and James Van Horn Melton, eds. *Pietism in Germany and North America 1680–1820.* Farnham, England: Ashgate, 2009.

Sweet, James H. *Domingos Alvares, African Healing, and the Intellectual History of the Atlantic World.* Chapel Hill: University of North Carolina Press, 2011.

——. *Recreating Africa: Culture, Kinship, and Religion in the African-Portuguese World, 1441–1770*. Chapel Hill: University of North Carolina Press, 2003.

Tannenbaum, Frank. *Slave and Citizen: The Negro in the Americas*. New York: Vintage Books, 1946.

Thornton, John K. *Africa and Africans in the Making of the Atlantic World, 1400–1800*. 2nd ed. Cambridge: Cambridge University Press, 1998.

——. "The Coromantees: An African Cultural Group in Colonial North America and the Caribbean." *Journal of Caribbean History* 32, no. 1/2 (1998): 161–78.

——. "The Development of an African Catholic Church in the Kingdom of Kongo, 1491–1750." *Journal of African History* 25, no. 2 (January 1984): 147–67.

——. *The Kongolese Saint Anthony: Dona Beatriz Kimpa Vita and the Antonian Movement, 1684–1706*. Cambridge: Cambridge University Press, 1998.

——. "On the Trail of Voodoo: African Christianity in Africa and the Americas." *Americas* 44, no. 3 (January 1988): 261–78.

Thornton, John K., and Linda M. Heywood. "Intercultural Relations Between Europeans and Blacks in New Netherland." In *Four Centuries of Dutch-American Relations: 1609–2009*, edited by Hans Krabbendam, Cornelis A. van Minnen, and Giles Scott-Smith, 192–203. Albany: State University of New York Press, 2009.

Thorp, Daniel B. "New Wine in Old Bottles: Cultural Persistence Among Non-White Converts to the Moravian Church." *Transactions of the Moravian Historical Society* 30 (January 1998): 1–8.

Tise, Larry E. *Proslavery: A History of the Defense of Slavery in America, 1701–1840*. Athens: University of Georgia Press, 1987.

Tolles, Frederick Barnes. *Quakers and the Atlantic Culture*. New York: Octagon Books, 1980.

Tomlins, Christopher. *Freedom Bound: Law, Labor, and Civic Identity in Colonizing English America, 1580–1865*. Cambridge: Cambridge University Press, 2010.

Vallejo, Eduardo Aznar. "Conquests of the Canary Islands." In *Implicit Understandings: Observing, Reporting and Reflecting on the Encounters Between Europeans and Other Peoples in the Early Modern Era*, edited by Stuart B. Schwartz, 134–56. Cambridge: Cambridge University Press, 1994.

van Cleve, George. "'Somerset's Case' and Its Antecedents in Imperial Perspective." *Law and History Review* 24, no. 3 (2006): 601–45.

Van Horne, John C., ed. *Religious Philanthropy and Colonial Slavery: The American Correspondence of the Associates of Dr. Bray, 1717–1777*. Urbana: University of Illinois Press, 1985.

Verlinden, Charles. *L'esclavage dans l'Europe medieval*. 2 Vols. Brugge, Belgium: De Tempel, 1955 & 1977.

——. *The Beginnings of Modern Colonization*. Ithaca, NY: Cornell, University Press, 1970.

Vogt, Peter. "'Ehereligion': The Moravian Theory and Practice of Marriage as Point of Contention in the Conflict Between Ephrata and Bethlehem." *Communal Societies* 21 (2001): 37–48.

——. "Nicholas Ludwig von Zinzendorf." In *The Pietist Theologians: An Introduction to Theology in the Seventeenth and Eighteenth Centuries*, edited by Carter Lindberg, 207–23. Malden, MA: Wiley-Blackwell, 2004.

——. "Zinzendorf's 'Seventeen Points of Matrimony': A Fundamental Document on the Moravian Understanding of Marriage and Sexuality." *Journal of Moravian History*, no. 10 (Spring 2011): 39–67.

Wallenstein, Peter. "Antiliteracy Laws." In *The Historical Encyclopedia of World Slavery*, edited by Junius P. Rodriguez, 42. Santa Barbara, CA: ABC-CLIO, 1997.

Wallmann, Johannes. "Was Ist Pietismus?" In *Pietismus und Neuzeit: Ein Jahrbuch zur Geschichte des neueren Protestantismus*, 20 (1994): 11–27.

Ward, W. R. *The Protestant Evangelical Awakening*. Cambridge: Cambridge University Press, 1992.

———. "The Renewed Unity of the Brethren: Ancient Church, New Sect or Interconfessional Movement?" *Bulletin of the John Rylands University Library of Manchester* 70, no. 3 (October 1988): 77–92.

Warren, Wendy. " 'The Cause of Her Grief': The Rape of a Slave in Early New England." *Journal of American History* 93, no. 4 (March 2007): 1031–49.

———. *New England Bound: Slavery and Colonization in Early North America*. New York: W. W. Norton, 2016.

Waterhouse, Richard. *A New World Gentry: The Making of a Merchant and Planter Class in South Carolina 1670–1770*. Charleston, SC: History Press, 2005.

Watson, Alan. *Slave Law in the Americas*. Athens: University of Georgia Press, 1989.

Wax, Darold D. "The Negro Slave Trade in Colonial Pennsylvania." Ph.D. diss., University of Washington, 1962.

———. "Quaker Merchants and the Slave Trade in Colonial Pennsylvania." *Pennsylvania Magazine of History and Biography* 86, no. 2 (April 1962): 143–59.

Westergaard, Waldemar. *The Danish West Indies Under Company Rule*. New York: Macmillan, 1917.

Wheeler, Rachel. *To Live upon Hope: Mohicans and Missionaries in the Eighteenth-Century Northeast*. Ithaca, NY: Cornell University Press, 2008.

Wheeler, Roxann. *The Complexion of Race: Categories of Difference in Eighteenth-Century British Culture*. Philadelphia: University of Pennsylvania Press, 2000.

Wiggin, Bethany. "Slavery in Translation: German Baroque Figurations of African Enslavement in the Americas." In *Opening Spaces: Constructions, Visions, and Depictions of Spaces and Boundaries in the Baroque*, edited by Karin Friedrich, 723–40. Wiesbaden: Harrasowitz, 2014.

Wolf, Stephanie Grauman. *Urban Village: Population, Community, and Family Structure in Germantown, Pennsylvania, 1683–1800*. Princeton, NJ: Princeton University Press, 1980.

Wood, Betty. *Slavery in Colonial Georgia, 1730–1775*. Athens: University of Georgia Press, 1984.

Wood, Nicholas and Jean Soderlund. " 'To Friends and All Whom It May Concerne': William Southeby's Rediscovered 1696 Antislavery Protest." *Pennsylvania Magazine of History and Biography* 141, no. 2 (2017): 177–98.

Yeo, Geoffrey. "A Case Without Parallel: The Bishops of London and the Anglican Church Overseas, 1660–1748." *Journal of Ecclesiastical History* 44, no. 3 (July 1993): 450–75.

Young, Jason R. *Rituals of Resistance: African Atlantic Religion in Kongo and the Lowcountry South in the Era of Slavery*. Baton Rouge: Louisiana State University Press, 2011.

Young, Jeffrey Robert. *Proslavery and Sectional Thought in the Early South, 1740–1829: An Anthology*. Columbia: University of South Carolina Press, 2006.

Zacek, Natalie. *Settler Society in the English Leeward Islands, 1670–1776*. New York: Cambridge University Press, 2010.

Index

Note: Page numbers in italics refer to figures and accompanying captions.

Acknowledgments

This project began as a study of Quaker antislavery thought. With the help and encouragement of colleagues, mentors, family, and friends, it has become something much bigger. At Harvard, I benefited from the guidance of Vincent Brown and David D. Hall. Vincent Brown has an astonishing ability to help me coalesce my thoughts into cohesive, far-reaching, and incisive arguments, and he has helped to guide and inspire this project over the past decade. David D. Hall has been a steadfast supporter of my work, and he has taught me how to parse the religious dimensions of social life with careful analysis. He has also consistently encouraged me to study what I love, regardless of scholarly trends. David Hempton, Joyce Chaplin, James Kloppenberg, Laurel Ulrich, Jill Lepore, John Stauffer, and Joanne van der Woude all provided crucial comments at various stages of the research and writing process, and I thank them for their suggestions and advice. I presented numerous chapters of this book to the Early Americanist Workshop at Harvard and the North American Religions Colloquium at Harvard Divinity School. I am especially grateful to Ann Braude, Healan Gaston, Dan McKanan, Jon Roberts, Heather Curtis, Elizabeth Jemison, Kip Richardson, Brett Grainger, Hillary Kaell, Eva Payne, Max Mueller, Deirdre DeBruyn Rubio, Sara Georgini, Gloria Whiting, Liz Covart, Chris Allison, and the other members of NARC and EAW for their thoughtful comments.

In the Twin Cities and at the University Minnesota, I have found a vibrant intellectual home and a tremendous set of colleagues. David Chang, Kirsten Fischer, JB Shank, and Karin Vélez have all read multiple chapters of this book, and I am indebted to them for their insight and suggestions. Over the past five years, I have also found a rich intellectual community in the Early Modern Atlantic Workshop. I am grateful to my co-organizer, Joanne Jahnke-Wegner, and to the colleagues and graduate students who have made the Atlantic workshop an invigorating scholarly space. A residential fellowship at the Institute for Advanced Study at the University of

Minnesota allowed me to devote a semester to research and writing, and introduced me a wonderful interdisciplinary cohort of scholars. I would like to thank the other Fall 2015 fellows, IAS Director Jennifer Gunn, and the staff at the IAS for their support and feedback.

At the University of Minnesota, I have presented chapters of this book at the Atlantic Workshop, the Center for Early Modern History workshop, and the workshop on the Comparative History of Women, Gender and Sexuality. I am especially grateful to Jon Butler, Sarah Chambers, Michael Gaudio, Ruth Karras, Michael Lower, Austin Mason, Nabil Matar, Saje Mathieu, Lisa Norling, Linda Sturtz, MJ Maynes, Marguerite Ragnow, and Serena Zabin for their thoughtful suggestions in these and other venues. My colleagues in the History department have helped to make the University of Minnesota an exceptionally warm and exciting place to be. In addition to those listed above, I am grateful to Tracey Deutsch, Barbara Welke, Giancarlo Casale, and Elaine Tyler May for their guidance and support at critical points in my career.

Generous financial support from the University of Minnesota, Harvard University, the Deutsche Akademischer Austauch Dienst, the Library Company of Philadelphia, the John Carter Brown Library, the American Philosophical Society, the Colonial Dames, and the Quaker and Special Collections at Haverford College made this book possible. I am indebted to many archivists and librarians who helped me with this project. In particular, I would like to thank Paul Peucker and Lanie Graf at the Moravian Archives in Bethlehem, Pennsylvania; Jim Green and Connie King at the Library Company of Philadelphia; Lorraine Parsons at the Moravian Church House Library in London, England; Kim Nusco, Ken Ward, and Margot Nishimura at the John Carter Brown Library; Rüdiger Kröger and Olaf Nippe at the Universitätsarchiv der Evangelischen Brüder-Unität; Pat O'Donnell and Chris Densmore at the Swarthmore Friends Historical Library; and John Anderies and Diana Peterson at the Haverford Quaker and Special Collections. I would also like to thank my research assistants Adam Blackler, Amélie Allard, Emma Waldie, and Lia Von Huben.

A number of scholars have improved the quality of this book with their illuminating conversation and thoughtful advice. I would especially like to thank Kristen Block, Courtney Bender, Richard Dunn, Curtis Evans, Linford Fisher, Aaron Fogleman, Cécile Fromont, Glenda Goodman, Sarah Gronningsater, Evan Haefeli, Jerome Handler, Jan Hüsgen, John Mason, Dan Richter, Eric Slauter, Jon Sensbach, Michelle McKinley, Bob Pollack, Ted

Andrews, Brandon Bayne, Brycchan Carey, Holly Brewer, Trevor Burnard, Travis Glasson, Jane Landers, Jenny Shaw, Angela Sutton, and Bethany Wiggin. I am also grateful for the suggestions I received from participants at the WMQ-EMSI "Religion in the Early Americas" Workshop in Pasadena, California, especially Catherine Brekus, Josh Piker, Brett Rushforth, Owen Stanwood, Rachel Wheeler, Peter Mancall, and Adrian Weimer; the faculty and graduate students at the University of Chicago Divinity School, especially Curtis Evans; the Columbia University Seminar on Religion in America; the Quellen workshop at Leibniz Universität, Hanover; the John Carter Brown Seminar Series; the Summer Academy for Atlantic History in Galway, Ireland; the McNeil Center's Brown Bag Seminar Series; the Quakers & Slavery Conference in Philadelphia; and the Moravian History & Music Conference in Bethlehem.

I am indebted to Bob Lockhart, my editor at the University of Pennsylvania Press, whose thoughtful suggestions and careful reading have greatly improved the quality of this book. Dan Richter has read multiple versions of this manuscript and has helped me to define and articulate the concepts at the heart of this book. The two anonymous reviewers for Penn Press provided extremely helpful feedback, as well as much-appreciated encouragement for this project. I would also like to thank Lily Palladino for her careful editing and the rest of the Penn Press staff who have worked on various aspects of this book, from marketing to packaging. Portions of the Introduction appeared previously in *History Compass* under the title "Theorizing Conversion," while various parts of Chapter 3 appeared in *Early American Studies* under the title "Antislavery in Print" and *Slavery and Abolition* as "The Ultimate Sin: Christianising Slaves in Seventeenth Century Barbados." I am grateful to these journals for allowing me to reprint portions of my articles here.

A number of friends have helped me through the long process of researching and writing. Stephen Vider and Caitlin DeAngelis have read multiple chapter drafts over the years, and have helped me to sharpen my prose. Tom Wickman has read and annotated every page of this manuscript. Finally, I owe many thanks to Caitlin Rosenthal, who has read nearly everything I have written, and has been a great friend and excellent archival buddy over the past decade.

I come from a family of teachers. My grandparents, John Jarvis, Sally Jarvis, Ilona Gerbner, and George Gerbner, all encouraged me to continue my education and to engage critically in the study of history and culture.

My parents, John and Anne Gerbner, have read countless pages of my writing, and have given me both insight and inspiration. I am fortunate to have two fantastic sisters, Erzsi and Emily, and a wonderful set of cousins, aunts, uncles, and in-laws who have all, in their own ways, supported my research. My husband, Sean Blanchet, helps me to keep my work in perspective. He and our two daughters, Ilona and Clarissa, who have joined us in the past four years, remind me why the study of the past is important for the present and the future.